The Eisenstein Universe

The Eisenstein Universe

Edited by
Ian Christie and Julia Vassilieva

BLOOMSBURY ACADEMIC
LONDON • NEW YORK • OXFORD • NEW DELHI • SYDNEY

BLOOMSBURY ACADEMIC
Bloomsbury Publishing Plc
50 Bedford Square, London, WC1B 3DP, UK
1385 Broadway, New York, NY 10018, USA
29 Earlsfort Terrace, Dublin 2, Ireland

BLOOMSBURY, BLOOMSBURY ACADEMIC and the Diana logo
are trademarks of Bloomsbury Publishing Plc

First published in Great Britain 2021
Paperback edition published 2023

Copyright © Ian Christie, Julia Vassilieva and contributors, 2021, 2023

Ian Christie, Julia Vassilieva and contributors have asserted their right under the Copyright, Designs and Patents Act, 1988, to be identified as Authors of this work.

For legal purposes the Acknowledgements on p. xvi constitute
an extension of this copyright page.

Cover design by Charlotte Daniels
Cover images: Sergei Eisenstein © Archive PL / Alamy; *Battleship Potemkin* posters
© TCD / Prod DB / Alamy; *Que Viva Mexico* poster © Everett Collection / Alamy

All rights reserved. No part of this publication may be reproduced or transmitted in any form or by any means, electronic or mechanical, including photocopying, recording, or any information storage or retrieval system, without prior permission in writing from the publishers.

Bloomsbury Publishing Plc does not have any control over, or responsibility for, any third-party websites referred to or in this book. All internet addresses given in this book were correct at the time of going to press. The author and publisher regret any inconvenience caused if addresses have changed or sites have ceased to exist, but can accept no responsibility for any such changes.

A catalogue record for this book is available from the British Library.

Library of Congress Cataloging-in-Publication Data
Names: Vassilieva, Julia, editor. | Christie, Ian, 1945- editor.
Title: The Eisenstein universe / Julia Vassilieva and Ian Christie (eds.).
Description: London ; New York : Bloomsbury Academic, 2021. | Includes bibliographical references and index. | Summary: "In-depth, innovative study of the Soviet era film director, Sergei Eisenstein (1898-1948), which reassess his legacy in the twenty-first century using new research"– Provided by publisher.
Identifiers: LCCN 2020045899 (print) | LCCN 2020045900 (ebook) | ISBN 9781350142107 (hardback) | ISBN 9781350142091 (pdf) | ISBN 9781350142114 (epub)
Subjects: LCSH: Eisenstein, Sergei, 1898-1948–Criticism and interpretation.
| Motion picture producers and directors–Soviet
Union–Biography. | Motion pictures–Soviet Union–History.
Classification: LCC PN1998.3.E34 E37 2021 (print) | LCC PN1998.3.E34 (ebook) | DDC 792.02/30947092 [B]–dc23
LC record available at https://lccn.loc.gov/2020045899
LC ebook record available at https://lccn.loc.gov/2020045900

	ISBN:		
	HB:	978-1-3501-4210-7	
	PB:	978-1-3502-3961-6	
	ePDF:	978-1-3501-4209-1	
	eBook:	978-1-3501-4211-4	

Typeset by Integra Software Services Pvt Ltd.

To find out more about our authors and books visit www.bloomsbury.com
and sign up for our newsletters.

To the memory of Robert Bird

Contents

List of Illustrations	ix
Notes on Contributors	xi
Acknowledgements	xvi
Introduction: Eisenstein Unbound *Ian Christie and Julia Vassilieva*	1

Part One Creativity, Nature, Politics

1	Odd and Even: Eisenstein and Unfinished Work *Dustin Condren*	15
2	Eisenstein's Collectives: The Politics of Nature *Joan Neuberger*	26
3	The Politics of Nonindifference in Eisenstein's Dialectics of Nature *Robert Bird*	41

Part Two *Grundproblem*, Regress, Sensuality

4	*Regress–Progress* in Proust, Surrealism and Joyce *Ilaria Aletto*	61
5	'The Old IT': Eisenstein and D. H. Lawrence *Ian Christie*	73
6	Sokurov contra Eisenstein: The Balance of Gender *Evgenii Bershtein*	91

Part Three Pathos, Immersion, Affect

7	*Formula pafosa, Pathosformel*: Eisenstein and Warburg *Antonio Somaini*	109
8	Hypnosis, Psychotechnics and Magic of Art *Julia Vassilieva*	130
9	Eisenstein's Scream(s) *Ada Ackerman*	152

Part Four History, Representation, Montage

10	*October*: On the Cinematic Allegorizing of History *Håkan Lövgren*	173
11	Attraction and Subversion: 'Montage 1938' *Felix Lenz*	190
12	The Two-Headed Ecstasy: The Philosophical Roots of Late Eisenstein *Massimo Olivero*	209

13 *Ivan the Terrible* in the Context of Shakespearean Tragedy
   Nikita Lary   219

Part Five Space, Place, Legacy

14 From Moscow to Ferghana, or from the Avant-garde to National
   Form *Nariman Skakov*   231
15 March 1949, Melbourne: Eisenstein in Australia *Adrian Danks*   251
16 How to Curate Eisenstein? *Oksana Bulgakowa*   261

Index   284

Illustrations

5.1	D. H. Lawrence's *Studies in Classic American Literature*, first published in the United States in 1923	78
5.2	A drawing that illustrates Eisenstein's analysis of the early D. H. Lawrence Story 'The Prussian Officer', made in January 1944 when he was working on the Disney section of *Method*	83
6.1	Eisenstein's self-portrait, pasted into his diary (1932)	98
6.2	Eisenstein, 'Le Christ & Johnnie' (1932)	99
6.3	Alexander Sokurov's *Alexandra* (2007)	102
8.1	*Doctor Mabuse, The Gambler* (1922)	131
8.2	*The Strike* (1924)	131
9.1	Caravaggio, *Medusa*, 1597–8	154
9.2	'The Screaming Nurse'. Still from Sergei Eisenstein's *The Battleship Potemkin* (1925)	155
9.3	Vasily Surikov, *Boyaryna Morozova*, 1887	157
9.4	Nicolas Poussin, *The Massacre of the Innocents*, 1625	158
9.5a and b	Materials from Francis Bacon's studio, 'Screaming Nurse' stills from Eisenstein's *The Battleship Potemkin* (1925)	160–1
9.6	Francis Bacon, *Study for the Nurse in the film Battleship Potemkin by Eisenstein*, 1957	163
9.7	Valerio Adami, *The Battleship Potemkin*, 1971	165
14.1	Eisenstein, *The Uzbek Extends His Hand to the Tajik*	238
14.2	'Eastern' effects achieved by placing figures and objects on different 'podiums', either tilted or at various heights	244–5
14.3	Eisenstein in an Uzbek teahouse	246
16.1	Exhibition in Amsterdam, 1972	265
16.2	Exhibition in Tokyo, 1973	265
16.3	Exhibition in West Berlin, 1971	266
16.4	*Eisenstein: His Life and Work*, Museum of Modern Art, Oxford, 1988	269

16.5	*Unexpected Eisenstein*, GRAD, London, 2016	270
16.6	*L'Œil extatique: Sergueï Eisenstein, cinéaste à la croisée des arts*, Centre Pompidou-Metz, September 2019–February 2020	274
16.7	Eisenstein's apartment at the Film Museum in Moscow	278

Contributors

Ada Ackerman is a Permanent Researcher at THALIM/CNRS (French National Research Center). A former student of the Ecole Normale Supérieure (ENS), Ackerman is an art historian focusing on cultural exchange between the Soviet Union, Europe, and the United States. She is the author of *The Endless Library of Sergei Eisenstein* (2019) and co-editor, with Luka Arsenjuk, of *Reading with Eisenstein* (forthcoming). Ackerman collaborated on the exhibition *1917* at the Centre Pompidou-Metz (2012), curated the show *Golem! Avatars d'une légende d'argile* (Paris, 2017), and co-curated the exhibition *The Ecstatic Eye: Sergei Eisenstein at the Crossroads of Arts*, at the Centre Pompidou-Metz (September 2019–February 2020).

Ilaria Aletto is Assistant Professor of Russian Language and Literature at the universities of Pisa and Rome (Sapienza, Roma Tre). Aletto obtained her PhD in Comparative Cultures and Literatures from Roma Tre University, with a thesis on the influence of James Joyce's *Ulysses* on the aesthetics of Sergei Eisenstein. Her publications have investigated Eisenstein's thought in relation to the work of Viktor Shklovsky, the reception of Joyce's oeuvre in Russian literature, the autobiographical texts of Velimir Khlebnikov, the stage directions of Mikhail Lermontov's *Masquerade*, and Italian translations of the work of Ivan Turgenev. She has been on the editorial board of the journal *Russica Romana* (2015–18).

Evgenii Bershtein is Professor and Chair, Russian department, Reed College, Portland, Oregon. He graduated from Tartu University (Estonia), earned his PhD in Slavic Languages and Literatures at the University of California, Berkeley, and held research fellowships at Columbia University, Helsinki University and the University of Cambridge. Bershtein has published on the cultural and intellectual history of Russian symbolism, on Russian poetry, on Lotman and Tartu semiotics, and more recently on Eisenstein and Sokurov. His current book project is entitled *Eisenstein, Sexuality, and Decadence*. Bershtein has also edited the English edition of Yuri Lotman's *Non-Memoirs* (2014).

Robert Bird † **(1969–2020)** was Professor in the Departments of Slavic Languages and Literatures and Cinema and Media Studies at the University of Chicago. He published essays on a variety of topics and was the author of *Andrei Rublev [by Andrei Tarkovsky]* (2004), *The Russian Prospero: The Creative Universe of Viacheslav Ivanov* (2006), and *Andrei Tarkovsky: Elements of Cinema* (2008). He translated works by Viacheslav Ivanov, Boris Jakim and Pavel Florenskij. Recently he was co-editor, with Christina Kiaer and Zachary Cahill, of *Revolution Every Day: A Calendar* (2017), the catalogue to the exhibition *Revolution Every Day* at the Smart Museum of Art at the University of Chicago, on which he was co-curator. Robert sadly died while this book was in press, and the editors have dedicated it to the memory of his scholarly achievement.

Oksana Bulgakowa is Professor of Film Studies at the Johannes Gutenberg University in Mainz, having previously taught at the Humboldt University and Free University, Berlin; Stanford; UC Berkeley; and the International Film School in Cologne. She is the author of many books on Russian and German cinema including *Resonance-Space: The Voice and The Media* (2012) and *Voice as a Cultural Phenomenon* (2015). She has directed several films including *The Different Faces of Sergei Eisenstein* (1998). She curated the film section of the exhibition *Berlin Moscow/Moscow Berlin 1900–1950* (Berlin, Moscow, 2003–4) and *Eisenstein's Mexican Drawings* (Antwerp 2009*)*, and she has developed several multimedia projects.

Dustin Condren is Assistant Professor of Russian at the University of Oklahoma. His research focuses primarily on the literature and intellectual culture of the early Soviet period, and the visual and physical forms (cinema, photography, painting, performance) that often frame them. He is the English-language translator of two recent volumes of Eisenstein's writing published by Berlin's PotemkinPress: *Disney* (2013) and *The Primal Phenomenon: Art* (2017), as well as of Leo Tolstoy's *The Gospel in Brief* (2011).

Ian Christie is Professor of Film and Media History, Birkbeck College, London University, and a Fellow of the British Academy. He has been responsible for a number of conferences, exhibitions, broadcasts and publications on Eisenstein, starting with the 1988 UK exhibition, with David Elliott, *Eisenstein: His Life and Art* (Oxford, London, Manchester). Most recently, he co-curated *Unexpected Eisenstein* (GRAD, London, 2016) and introduced *Eisenstein on Paper* (Naum Kleiman, 2017). He was co-editor of the Routledge Soviet Cinema series with Richard Taylor. Other work has included curatorial contributions to the exhibitions *Modernism: Designing a New World* (V&A, 2008) and *Revolution: Russian Art 1917–32* (Royal Academy, 2017).

Adrian Danks is Deputy Dean in the School of Media and Communication, RMIT University, Australia. He is also co-curator of the Melbourne Cinémathèque and was an editor of *Senses of Cinema* (2002–14). He has published widely on film history, national cinemas and Australian cinema. He is the editor of *A Companion to Robert Altman* (2015) and is currently writing several books including a monograph devoted to *3-D Cinema* (forthcoming), a co-edited collection on the nexus between Australian and US cinema (forthcoming) and a volume examining 'international' feature film production in Australia during the post-war era with Con Verevis (forthcoming).

Nikita Lary is a retired professor of Humanities and Graduate English from York University, Toronto. He is the author of *Dostoevsky and Dickens* (1973; republished as Vol. 9 of *The Dickens Library* in 2009) and of *Dostoevsky and Soviet Film* (1986). He is also the co-compiler, co-editor and co-translator of *The Alexander Medvedkin Reader* (2016; recipient of the AATSEEL 1917 Prize for the Best Scholarly Translation). He is the author of various conference papers and essays on Eisenstein and on Shklovsky, including an essay contributed to *The Flying Carpet: Studies on Eisenstein and Russian Cinema in Honor of Naum Kleiman*.

Felix Lenz teaches film and literature in the Institute for Literature and Media at the University of Bamberg, Germany. His research interests include Eisenstein and the theory of montage, theories of screenwriting and adaptation, genre theory, the works of the brothers Taviani, Terrence Malick and Dominik Graf as well as Goethe's theory of colours, Hegel as theorist of media, and the emergence of media in the Enlightenment. Lenz has worked as a script consultant, has directed several short and experimental films, and is the author of *Sergej Eisenstein: Montagezeit. Rhythmus, Formdramaturgie, Pathos* (2008) and the editor of *Sergej Eisenstein: Jenseits der Einstellung. Schriften zur Filmtheorie* (2006).

Håkan Lövgren is an independent film scholar, translator and photographer based in Sweden and the United States. He has a BA in Art History and Comparative Literature from Indiana University, a MS in Film from Boston University and a PhD in Slavic Languages from Stockholm University. His research, writings and translations have focused primarily on Sergei Eisenstein, Andrei Tarkovsky and Aleksandr Sokurov. Translations include the script of Tarkovsky's last film, *Zhertvoprinoshenie* (Swedish and English), Tarkovsky's creative biography, *Zapechatlennoe vremia* (Swedish), and the director's diaries, *Martyrolog* (Swedish). He has also served as curator of the Ingmar Bergman Foundation Archives at the Swedish Film Institute in Stockholm.

Joan Neuberger is Professor of History at the University of Texas at Austin. She is the author of numerous works on the history and politics of the arts, including *Ivan the Terrible: The Film Companion* (2003), co-editor with Antonio Somaini of *The Flying Carpet: Essays on Eisenstein and Russian Cinema in Honor of Naum Kleiman* (2017) and *This Thing of Darkness: Eisenstein's Ivan the Terrible in Stalin's Russia* (2018). She is currently writing *Singing about the Dark Times: Eisenstein's Socialism in Stalin's Time and Ours*.

Massimo Olivero is Lecturer in History and Aesthetics of Cinema at Paul Valéry University, Montpellier. He holds a PhD in Cinema Studies from Sorbonne Nouvelle University (Paris), where he taught the history of classical Hollywood cinema and the aesthetics of Soviet avant-gardes for six years. He is the author of *Figures of Extasis: Eisenstein and the Aesthetics of Pathos in Cinema* (2017).

Nariman Skakov is Assistant Professor of Slavic Languages and Literatures at Stanford University. He holds an MPhil degree in European Literature and a DPhil degree in Modern and Medieval Languages from the University of Oxford. His teaching and research interests lie primarily in twentieth-century Russian, Soviet and post-Soviet literature and culture. His first monograph, *The Cinema of Tarkovsky: Labyrinths of Space and Time*, was published in 2012. His articles have appeared in *Slavic Review*, *Russian Review*, *Dostoevsky Studies*, *Studies in Russian and Soviet Cinema*, and *Новое литературное обозрение*.

Antonio Somaini is Professor in Film, Media, and Visual Culture Theory at the Université Sorbonne Nouvelle Paris 3. His publications include *Eisenstein: Cinema, Art History, Montage* (published in Italian in 2011, forthcoming in English) and, together with Naum Kleiman, the English edition of Eisenstein's *Notes for a General History of Cinema* (2016). He has edited works by Benjamin, Moholy-Nagy and Vertov, and anthologies on media and visual culture theory, both in Italian and French.

Julia Vassilieva is Australian Research Council Research Fellow and lecturer at Monash University, Australia. She is the author of *Narrative Psychology: Identity, Transformation and Ethics* (2016), and co-editor of two volumes: *Beyond the*

Essay Film (with Deane Williams, 2020) and *After Taste: Cultural Value and the Moving Image* (with Con Verevis, 2013). Her publications have also appeared in *Camera Obscura*, *Film-Philosophy*, *Continuum: Journal of Media & Cultural Studies*, *Screening the Past*, *Critical Arts*, *Kinovedcheskie Zapiski*, *Rouge*, *Lola*, *Senses of Cinema*, *History of Psychology* and a number of edited collections. She is the author of a monograph *Cinema and the Brain: Eisenstein, Vygotsky, Luria* (forthcoming).

Acknowledgements

This collection is based on new research presented at the symposium 'Eisenstein for the Twenty-First Century' conducted in Prato, Italy (June 2018), and supported by the Australian Research Council, the Arts Faculty and School of Media, Film and Journalism at Monash University. We would like to extend our gratitude to all the participants of the symposium in Prato, whose collegiality and enthusiasm made this book possible. We also want to thank the editorial team at Bloomsbury: Rebecca Barden, our editor, for her reassuring patience, Veidehi Hans, and the designer Charlotte Daniels. Finally, we are grateful to Belinda Glynn, our eagle-eyed copy editor.

The final stages of the preparation of this manuscript coincided with the onset of the Covid-19 pandemic around the world. The geographical distance between the co-editors, working in the UK and Australia, and our multilingual contributors, spread around the globe, became palpable, our connections occasionally fragile. We are grateful to everyone involved for staying on board, and staying sane during this trying time. Your resolute commitment was living proof that 'Eisenstein's Universe' is not only one of ideas but also a universe of people and minds.

Introduction: Eisenstein Unbound

Ian Christie and Julia Vassilieva

What can possibly remain to be said about Sergei Eisenstein? Has not this 'ruined filmmaker', as Peter Wollen described him, been comprehensively resurrected, at least since the 1990s? Wollen had played an important part in arguing for a new understanding of Eisenstein in the pioneering essay that formed part of his seminal book *Signs and Meaning in the Cinema*.[1] This came soon after Annette Michelson had lamented his ultimate 'defeat' in the face of Stalinist repression in an equally famous 1966 essay, while paying tribute to his 'energy, courage and intellectual passion'.[2]

And so the case of Eisenstein, one of Stalin's 'noblest' victims according to Michelson, remained largely settled, at least in the West, for much of the remainder of the century. Solzhenitsyn had provided a reminder of how he appeared to many Russians in his debut novel *One Day in the Life of Ivan Denisovich*, with the gulag prisoner X-123 describing *Ivan the Terrible* as 'an arse-licker obeying a vile dog's order' in what was to be his last film, *Ivan the Terrible*.[3] Yet it was only Khrushchev's cultural 'thaw' that had released both the second part of *Ivan*, banned by Stalin, and Eisenstein's hitherto unseen first film, *The Strike*, thus making possible the 'new Eisenstein' discovered by Michelson and Wollen. Few of their Western readers would have encountered an important revised verdict by one of Eisenstein's own contemporaries, Viktor Shklovsky, who confessed that he only came to understand what *October* had attempted in 1927 after he had travelled abroad – as Oksana Bulgakowa noted.[4] By the end of the 1990s, there was indeed an 'expanded' Eisenstein to contemplate, with the *Memoirs* widely available in new editions, and a growing awareness of the 'third text' that his drawings represented.[5]

In the early 2000s, Eisenstein's major theoretical writings, including a full version of his important study *Montage*, and uncensored versions of *Nonindifferent Nature* and his magnum opus, *Method* came to light.[6] This period also saw a wave of new translations into English including *Disney*, *Notes for a General History of Cinema* and several chapters of *Method* as *The Primal Phenomenon: Art*.[7]

Has the continuing publication and translation of his later writings substantially altered the earlier image of a filmmaker 'haunted by writing' (as the great French critic Serge Daney described him)? Have exhibitions, increasingly focused on drawings that would have scandalized his supporters a generation earlier, revealed an unrepentant rebel hiding beneath the conformist figure that Solzhenitsyn reviled in 1961?[8] The truth – as revealed by this collection – is much more complex. There are now many more Eisensteins to choose between, or to contemplate, as the scholars represented here demonstrate in contributions to the first of the series of recent international conferences, held in Prato in 2018.

Eisenstein has become, we suggest, a universe of possibilities – posing questions that still lack any definitive answer; while continuing to inspire researchers and artists in many fields. Certainly, much new material continues to emerge for biographers, for historians of modern Russian culture, as well as for students of the contradictions of Modernism. But rather than try to synthesize these into yet another 'new Eisenstein', we have chosen to let them point in different directions. And as will be clear from the following chapters, while some return to Eisenstein's own writings to offer new readings of major texts that have been neglected, others view him from the standpoint of highly contemporary concerns in art history and aesthetics, and in the cognitive sciences, which passionately engaged Eisenstein.

* * *

Part One, 'Creativity, Nature, Politics', opens up the reconsideration of Eisenstein's legacy from several new angles. Dustin Condren's chapter expands our view of Eisenstein's oeuvre by placing his unrealized projects alongside his completed works – an exercise Eisenstein started to engage in himself as early as 1927. Indeed, prior to Eisenstein's epic failures – his aborted film *Que viva México!* (1932) and destroyed *Bezhin Meadow* (1937) – several of his earlier projects, including *King Hunger* (1921), *Garland's Inheritance* (1923), *Patatras* (1923), *Red Cavalry* (1924) and *Dzhungo* (1926) came to nothing. Registering the pattern of his realized projects as 'odd', and unrealized as 'even', Eisenstein granted to this fragile regularity the status of a working method. For him, what was at stake in this classification was the nature of artistic creativity, the tension between a utopian, unrestricted quality of conception as a vision and the realities of the materially achievable. In Condren's reading, the figure of the 'unfinished' in Eisenstein's reflection is thus not only imbued with heavy symbolic burden but also stands for pure potentiality as such.

The following two chapters examine the role of the outside, the heterogeneous 'surround', in Eisenstein's work. Traditionally, Eisenstein's oeuvre was seen as tightly aligned with political issues, and in the words of Annette Michelson, as 'indissolubly linked to the project of the construction of socialism'.[9] As we move further away from the Soviet experiment, and as Eisenstein's previously unpublished and censored writings come to light, it becomes clear that he was operating on a different scale. What Eisenstein strove to address was the commensurability of human being, history and, ultimately, the universe. History didn't begin for him with the social, with human time – rather, it stretched further back, into deep cosmological time; and, correspondingly, the context of human life and artistic creation is not limited to social actions but must also embrace nature and environment.

Contributing to this re-examination, Joan Neuberger's chapter explores Eisenstein's complex view on the natural world, its representation in art and the imbrication of subjectivity and collectivity with both. Neuberger alerts us to a major insight of Eisenstein's in this area, which has previously passed unnoticed: namely, that he developed his understanding of nature and landscape in political terms. In theorizing landscape, Eisenstein approached the artistic representation of nature as an issue closely intertwined with that of power: both an artist's power to inflict violence and transform nature, and nature's own (certainly greater) power over us. As Neuberger argues, Eisenstein's singular concept of 'nonindifferent nature' speaks to the representations of nature and subjectivity in mutually constitutive terms, attending simultaneously to the active and autonomous role of nature and the creative and transformative efforts of an artist. At stake here was the issue of unity between subject and object, art and its creation, human beings and the universe. Neuberger further shows how Eisenstein's political philosophy of nature informed his understanding of social formations, individuality and community.

On a similar theme, Robert Bird's chapter reassesses Eisenstein's engagement with the environment in the light of recent eco-criticism and polemics on the issue of the Anthropocene. He asks whether Eisenstein's *Nonindifferent Nature* is consonant with Soviet and, specifically, Stalinist rhetoric on the transformation of the natural world; or whether, instead, it deploys Marxist language to ground a different, possibly antithetical understanding of the relationship between humans and their environment. Bird further proposes that *Nonindifferent Nature* can be seen as a speculative media ecology that accords a privileged position to cinema, which not only serves as a central instrument of mediation under the conditions of technological modernity, but can also provide a valuable guide to democratic governance.

Part Two, 'ced*Grundproblem*, Regress, Sensuality', engages with the central dichotomy at the core of Eisenstein's intended magnum opus *Method*, the relationship between progress and regress in human evolution and cultural history. For Eisenstein the tension between progress and regress represents nothing less than the major problem of art, which he defined, using German terminology, as the *Grundproblem*. This problem consists in the ability of a work of art to mobilize two opposing impulses: one towards a rational, intellectual insight and enrichment, realized mainly at the level of content ('progress'), and the other towards the engagement of the whole sensory, affective and emotional sphere, achieved mainly through form ('regress'). The latter only becomes possible, according to Eisenstein, because the language of form is based on a plethora of mechanisms developed throughout the cultural history of humankind and its evolutionary prehistory as a species. Eisenstein's principle hypothesis in *Method* was the idea that while art can deliver the highest intellectual ideas through its content, to achieve emotional engagement, aesthetic form needs to take on some regressive qualities. The *Grundproblem* became for him an exploration of such archaic forms of thinking and operating, which he describes as 'ways of regress' and 'shifts in time'. These mechanisms include such phenomena as synesthesia (a complex multimodal integration of the senses); the ability to perceive a part as representing the whole (expressed in the rhetorical formula 'pars pro toto'); rhythmical repetition; and so on – mechanisms that, working in combination with one another, create the 'magic' of art.

Chapters in Part Two explore implications of Eisenstein's binary model, regress–progress, for our understanding of a range of complex phenomena – from stream-of-consciousness as an aesthetic device to the relations between desire, eroticism, gender and sexuality. Ilaria Aletto's chapter offers a condensed introduction to the origin and development of the *Grundproblem*. Eisenstein's notion of regress turns out to be highly idiosyncratic, since he maintained that regressive characteristics of form (such as its subordination to the logic of free associative thinking) should always be balanced by the presence of a strong rational idea at the level of theme. Aletto explores how Eisenstein's view of regress contrasted with that of surrealism and various techniques practised by modernist writers. For Eisenstein, artists such as Proust and Bretonian surrealists failed to mobilize the potential of regress, merely valorizing the accidental or free-floating, while Joyce's use of stream-of-consciousness demonstrated the potential inherent in regressive aesthetic forms.

Ian Christie's chapter unearths deep and unexpected affinities between Eisenstein and D. H. Lawrence, going beyond their shared propensity to shock audiences with obscene and controversial material, albeit one publicly and the other in private. Christie suggests that Eisenstein found in Lawrence an alternative but equally powerful formulation of his *Grundproblem*. While Eisenstein described it as the problem of coexistence and tension between modern and archaic, rational and emotional elements, Lawrence cast it as the conflict between 'blood-consciousness' and 'mind-consciousness'. Christie's chapter also engages with Eisenstein's critique of Freud and psychoanalysis in general, seeking, like Lawrence, a more integrated and profound view of the sexual and erotic forces within the totality of the organism and its evolutionary development.

In the following chapter, Evgenii Bershtein compares Eisenstein's view of gender and sexuality with Alexander Sokurov's position on the politics and poetics of the body. For Eisenstein, the split into femininity and masculinity represents a late evolutionary achievement, which art can sometimes productively reverse to return viewers to the state of primordial unity, which *Method* posits as a point of origin, rehearsed in the mythological figure of the androgyne or the psychoanalytic concept of bisexuality. Sokurov, however, sees Eisenstein as a master giving free rein to unchecked masculinity and as such responsible for the glorification of aggression. Bershtein links Sokurov with a strong tradition in Russian literature and philosophy that draws on the legacy of Vasilii Rozanov in rejecting such an emphasis on masculinity, since by obliterating femininity it also obliterates soul. Yet, despite Sokurov's critique of Eisenstein – not untypical of many Russians of the later Soviet period – as Bershtein suggests, these two giants of Russian cinema can be seen as developing similar non-heteronormative positions, thus challenging a monolithic understanding of gender.

Part Three, 'Pathos, Immersion, Affect', focuses on Eisenstein's interest in psychology, emotions and the brain, and demonstrates how his groundbreaking work on creativity and film spectatorship can acquire new relevance and urgency in the context of the current turn towards bringing neuroscience into the humanities. Antonio Somaini's chapter explores the key question that runs through the entire corpus of Eisenstein's writings: 'how to understand the laws that govern the *effectiveness* of a work of art, its capacity to *act* on the mind, body and emotions of the spectator'.[10] Somaini traces how Eisenstein addressed this issue through such notions as 'expressive movement', 'montage of attractions', 'intellectual montage', 'imagicity', 'regression', 'pathos' and 'ecstasy' and points to an uncanny coincidence between Eisenstein's thought and that of the art historian and theorist Aby Warburg, who, despite having no knowledge of each other's work, developed strikingly similar interests in 'formulae' of pathos.

Somaini unravels a complex network of correspondences, shared influences and productive interpretations of the relationship between plastic form and extreme emotional states in the work of these two thinkers.

Shedding light on Eisenstein's little-known interest in hypnosis, Julia Vassilieva's chapter foregrounds the importance of Eisenstein's engagement with contemporaneous psychology in both his theoretical and his practical work. Eisenstein pursued his interest in hypnosis not only by following the work of the famous psychophysiologist and the key authority on hypnosis in Russia at the turn of the twentieth century, Vladimir Bekhterev, but also through his collaboration with cultural psychologist Lev Vygotsky, neuropsychologist Alexander Luria, psychoanalyst Yuri Kannabich and historian of Russian religious sects Dmitry Konovalov. Vassilieva further explores similarities and differences in the appropriation of the notion of trance and ecstasy in the work of Eisenstein and the Kiev-born Maya Deren, best known as a founding figure in American avant-garde film, who were both influenced by the Russian tradition of 'psychotechnics'. As Vassilieva argues, Eisenstein's interest in cinema's engagement with hypnosis goes beyond the currently topical phenomenon of 'immersion' to address the ultimately political issue of directorial control and spectator freedom.

Ada Ackerman's chapter traces the representation of a fundamental form of human expression, screaming, with complex emotional and psychological connotations, and its representation by artists ranging from Poussin and Goya to Eisenstein and Francis Bacon. Given that these representations in visual art and in Eisenstein's early (silent) films, including *The Battleship Potemkin* (1925), where we find arguably the most memorable example of screaming, are all effectively mute, such images raise the question of an intricate relationship between sensory modalities and expressive power. Ackerman demonstrates how Eisenstein's renditions of screams can be thought of as a limit case of the relationship between the visible and the aural, image and sound, mere representation and expressive depth.

Part Four, 'History, Representation, Montage', deals with the shifting ways in which Eisenstein theorized montage and used it in his efforts to model history. Håkan Lövgren's chapter focuses on an early stage of Eisenstein's work, his revolutionary tetralogy *The Strike* (1924), *The Battleship Potemkin* (1925), *October* (1928) and *The Old and the New* (1929). Specifically, Lövgren examines the extent to which *October* adheres to the canon and methods of (literary) allegory, and deploys distinctive imagery and symbolism to produce revolutionary spectacle. Aligning the film's greatest achievement – the introduction of intellectual montage – with allegory, Lövgren demonstrates how montage can operate as a system producing a predetermined meaning, governed by the imperative to create a heroic and glorifying myth. Yet Lövgren also suggests that it was the constantly shifting politics of the film's content which actually gave Eisenstein space, and incentive, to experiment with different forms of intellectual montage, thus proving to be a much more flexible method than its received understanding would suggest.

Felix Lenz's chapter interrogates Eisenstein's later theorization of montage and demonstrates that Eisenstein saw this not only as a flexible and evolving system but also as a fundamentally open one. Lenz argues that Eisenstein's view of montage was governed by two deeply contradictory impulses: the form-giving impulse aimed at creation, birth and proliferation of images and meanings, and an opposing, annihilating drive towards death, disintegration and liquidation of meaning. Lenz suggests that these tendencies in Eisenstein's theory and practice correspond to the pre-Socratic Greek philosopher Empedocles' cosmology, in which processes of decay and emanation, separation and fusion alternate. In this context, Lenz concludes, montage acquires fundamental generative qualities, as by animating images it bestows life.

Massimo Olivero detects similar tendencies in his chapter. Olivero traces the origins of Eisenstein's treatment of the concept of ecstasy to the myth of Dionysus, who was traditionally believed to have been born twice, killed, dismembered and then reconstituted into a new transfigured entity. Olivero suggests that Eisenstein employed the myth as both a political and an artistic model: the figure of Dionysus speaks to the unity of a community that is divided and reconfigured into a new, qualitatively superior form. As such, Eisenstein's reading recalls Hegel's emphasis on the negation of negation while simultaneously aiming towards a profound, synthetic unity.

Nikita Lary's chapter examines the echo of Dionysian myth in Eisenstein's *Ivan the Terrible* (1943–7). This echo found its way into Eisenstein's late masterpiece not directly but via Shakespearean tragedies. Tragedy, Eisenstein maintained, had its roots in the ancient ceremonial cults in which the ritual dismemberment of a deity or hero was followed by their resurrection. Lary observes that Eisenstein's work on the film coincided with his intensified examination of Shakespeare's tragic characters, their inner conflicts, their conflicts with the worlds they inhabited and, moreover, with the specific attention to Shakespeare's (often violent) treatment of the human body. But Eisenstein not only referred to the trope of dismembering of the human body and its subsequent reassembling in relation to the generic implications for staging tragedy on screen. More significantly, he saw the cycle of division and disintegration followed by reintegration as the 'Urphenomen' of cinema – its very condition of possibility, as by first disarticulating objects and figures into their parts, and then reintegrating them within the image on screen, cinema produces its central effect – the illusion of movement.

Part Five, 'Space, Place, Legacy', examines Eisenstein's critical reception and legacy as well as the geopolitical reach of his projects. Nariman Skakov's chapter analyses how Eisenstein's mobilization of the concept of 'national form' allowed him to expand his repertoire of modernist techniques and themes by engaging in stylistic experiments attuned to the cultural specificity of regions and nations ranging from Mexico to the Central Asian Soviet republics of Uzbekistan and Kazakhstan. Departing from Stalin's imperative to produce art which would be 'national in form, socialist in content', Eisenstein recodified the latter in accordance with his valorization of archaic, culturally and historically specific ways of aesthetic expression. In a desperate attempt to reconcile the logic of *Method* with the dominant ideology of his time, Eisenstein's engagement with the issue of the national attempted to pave the way for a number of interesting, yet unrealized projects, including 'The Great Ferghana Canal'.

Widening the context of critical discussions of the global impact of Eisenstein's oeuvre, Adrian Danks's chapter reconstructs how Eisenstein's films reached Australia. While earlier releases of Eisenstein's works, *The Battleship Potemkin* in particular, both in Europe and in the United States, produced political storms, their belated arrival in Australia at the end of the 1940s was met with a more measured, yet characteristically ambivalent response. Danks's analysis brings to the surface nuances of reception by mapping ebbs and flows in the Left political movement against the dynamics of the development of film culture in Melbourne.

Finally, Oksana Bulgakowa's chapter documents the changing practices of exhibitors of Eisenstein's multifarious output – the films, drawings, letters, diaries and memorabilia that are utilized to 'curate' an image of this prodigiously gifted artist. Beginning with the famous *Film and Photography* exhibition in Stuttgart in 1929 (commonly known as *FiFo*), and covering a wide range of exhibitions of Eisenstein's work during the twentieth century (including exhibitions of his drawings at the Cinémathèque Française in 1960 and at the Cineteca Italiana in Milan in 1961, *Example Eisenstein: Drawing Theatre Film* in 1987 in Düsseldorf and *Eisenstein: His Life and Work* in 1988 in Oxford, London and Manchester), Bulgakowa concludes with a survey of digitally enhanced exhibitions at the turn of the twenty-first century (such as the Daniel Langlois Foundation's web publication *The Visual Universe of Sergei Eisenstein* in 2000) and in the first two decades of the twenty-first century (for example, *L'Œil extatique: Serguei͏̈ Eisenstein, cinéaste à la croisée des arts* at the Centre Pompidou-Metz, which ran from September 2019 to February 2020). She shows how, by responding to successive 'turns' in the humanities, including emphases on textuality, visuality and objecthood, evolving curatorial practices have both reflected and reinforced the 'protean' nature of Eisenstein's achievement.

On the basis of these imaginative and innovative contributions to Eisenstein scholarship, there seems good reason to anticipate that his influence will continue to resonate powerfully for the foreseeable future. Eisenstein himself jokingly spoke of looking 'beyond the stars', meaning the Hollywood deities of his own era. But with vastly increased access to the full range of his legacy, new bearings are urgently needed to navigate this expanding universe, here provided by our authors.

* * *

Translation notes

A few words are needed about translation and terminological issues. Eisenstein's multilingual texts (his writing often switches between Russian, English, French and German), as well as his propensity for coining neologisms, often present difficulties and challenges for translators. We therefore feel the need to provide a rationale for the translation and transliteration choices of some of the key terms used by the authors in this collection.

Grundproblem. Following an emerging consensus, the German term *Grundproblem* that Eisenstein adopted to denote what he saw as the major problem of art is kept in its original spelling. The term is one of the key notions in Eisenstein's *Method* and was inspired by widespread use of the term *Grundproblem* in German-language scholarship around the turn of the nineteenth century. Arthur Schopenhauer's *Die beiden Grundprobleme der Ethik* (1880), Edmund Husserl's *Grundprobleme der Phänomenologie* (1910–11), Georgi Plekhanov's *Die Grundprobleme des Marsxismus* (1910), Hans Driesch's *Grundprobleme der Psychologie* (1929) and Ernst Cassirer's *Die Grundropleme der Aesthetik* (1932) persuasively demonstrate this trend.[11] The formulation of *Grundproblem* was publicly presented by Eisenstein only once – in his famous speech to a major Soviet filmmakers' conference, the First All-Union Creative Congress, in 1935. Eisenstein's speech was published in Russian in 1935, translated and published in English as 'Film Form: New Problems' first by Ivor Montagu in *Life and Letters Today* (September–December 1935) and, later, with Eisenstein's further clarifications, by Jay Leyda, in *Film Form* in 1949.[12] But while this important work has long been known to film scholars, the massive research that Eisenstein undertook for *Grundproblem* and summarized in *Method* was only published in Russia in 2002, followed by a German edition in 2008, and a selection of chapters translated into English in 2017 as *Art: The Primal Phenomenon*. Eisenstein's *Grundproblem* has been interpreted as an aporia inherent in the dual nature of art, addressing simultaneously rational and irrational, logical and emotional, modern and archaic, contemporary and evolutionary, the cognitive and intellectual, and the sensory and carnal. In contemporary psychological terms, it can perhaps be compactly described as the relationship between cinema, meaning-making and the brain-body system.

Sensual, sensuous, sensory. Another important term frequently used by Eisenstein in *Method* is *chuvstvennoe myshlenie*, a fundamental component of his *Grund*-problematics. Following Jay Leyda's early translation of Eisenstein's speech to the All-Union Creative Conference of Soviet Filmworkers in 1935 ('Film Form: New Problems'), *chuvstvennoe myshlenie* is most often translated as 'sensual thought'.[13] In the English translation of 'Conspectus of Lectures on the Psychology of Art', one of the last pieces of writing Eisenstein produced at the request of Alexander Luria in November 1947, *chuvstvennoe myshlenie* is rendered as 'sensuous thought'.[14] Yet, in Russian, the adjective *chuvstvennoe* can mean 'relating to or affecting the senses' or it can have erotic, libidinal connotations. As such, it encompasses the meanings of sensual, sensuous, sensory and sensorial. In adopting this term, Eisenstein was inspired by Hegel's and Plekhanov's epistemological ideas, which stressed the importance of the sensory fabric of knowledge or sensible objects.[15] The contemporary translation of *chuvstvennoe myshlenie* as sensory and emotional processes does justice to Eisenstein's inspiration. However, the erotic overtone which might be latent in Eisenstein's original usage of the term in Russian, but which is nonetheless still present, is erased in such an overly cognitivist rendering. Different authors in this collection have adopted a variety of translations, which we, as editors, have decided to retain; however, it is important to alert readers to the implications of Eisenstein's original terminological choice.

Pra-logical, primitive, archaic. Sensuous thought (*chuvstvennoe myshlenie*) was placed by Eisenstein in evolutionary and historical perspective and aligned with phylogenetically and ontogenetical earlier stages of human biological development, as well as with earlier stages of human cultural history.

He often associated mechanisms of 'sensuous thought' with what he described as *pra-logical* (commonly translated as pre-logical), *primitive* or *archaic* thinking. Eisenstein's anthropological inflection of the term had multiple sources: he followed a range of anthropological theories formulated by such researchers as Lucien Lévy-Bruhl, James Frazer, Richard Turnwald and Frank Hamilton Cushing; he was also interested in Nikolai Marr's linguistic palaeontology; and his collaboration with Vygotsky and Luria exposed him to the paradigm of cultural-historical psychology. The terms pra-logical, primitive and archaic were used widely in the anthropological discourse of Eisenstein's time, even if they may strike modern readers as derogatory. However, for Eisenstein, like his contemporaries, they did not seem to carry a value judgement; rather, he tried to capture the specificity and distinctive characteristics of historically and evolutionary varied forms of psychological operation.

Ecstasy, exstasis, ek-stasis represent different ways of translating Eisenstein's key notion in *Non-Indifferent Nature*: *ekstaz*. Adopting this Greek term, Eisenstein strove to conceptualize the process of engaging with the work of art in terms of rupture, arguing that at some climatic moments the viewer must 'leave himself behind', 'transcend himself' or 'lose himself'.[16] This meaning is similar, but not reducible, to the common contemporary sense of ecstasy as elation, since, for Eisenstein, it is not the specific emotional characteristics of the process – 'an overwhelming feeling of great happiness or joyful excitement' – but the shift towards a qualitatively different state that is crucial. As he explained in *Nonindifferent Nature*: 'The leap outside oneself (= *ek-stasis, ecstasy*) is necessarily the passage to something else, to something of a different quality, something contrary to what precedes.'[17] It is important to bear in mind that Eisenstein also drew on the uses of the term in philosophy, descriptions of religious experience and psychiatry, as in Russian exstasis can signify a variety of 'altered' states of consciousness, such as hypnotic exstasis, manic exstasis or even epileptic exstasis.

Notes

1 Peter Wollen, 'Eisenstein's Aesthetics', in *Signs and Meaning in the Cinema* (London: Secker & Warburg, 1969), 19–70.
2 Annette Michelson, 'Film and the Radical Aspiration', *Film Culture* 42 (1966): 415.
3 Alexander Solzhenitsyn, *One Day in the Life of Ivan Denisovich* (1962), trans. Ralph Parker (London: Victor Gollancz, 1963), 95.
4 Bulgakowa quotes Shklovsky, writing in 1985: 'What in Eisenstein's cinema had been a disdain for plot, and subsequently a parody of plot, now becomes a new

[kind of] plot' (Viktor Shklovsky, *Za 60 let: Raboty o kino*, ed. Efim Levin [Moscow: Iskusstvo, 1985], 167). Oksana Bulgakowa, *Sergei Eisenstein: A Biography* (Berlin: PotemkinPress, 1998), 78.

5   The New York Drawing Center exhibition, *The Body of the Line*, held in 2000, marked an important stage in the recognition of Eisenstein's drawings, following the publication of *Dessins Secrets* (Paris: Seuil, 1999). Ian Christie's contribution to the catalogue, in *Drawing Papers 4*, used the phrase 'The Third Text' to refer to the drawings, alongside films and writings.

6   Sergei M. Eizenshtein, *Metod*, ed. Naum Kleiman, 2 vols (Moscow: Muzei kino/Eizenshtein-tsentr, 2002), Sergei M. Eizenshtein, *Metod*, ed. Oksana Bulgakowa, 4 vols (Berlin: PotemkinPress, 2008); Sergei M. Eizenshtein, *Neravnodushnaia priroda*, ed. Naum Kleiman, 2 vols (Moscow: Muzei kino/Eizenshtein-tsentr, 2004–6).

7   Sergei M. Eisenstein, *Disney*, ed. Oksana Bulgakowa and Dietmar Hochmuth, trans. Dustin Condren (Berlin: PotemkinPress, 2011). Sergei M. Eisenstein, *Notes for a General History of Cinema*, ed. N. Kleiman and A. Somaini (Amsterdam: Amsterdam University Press, 2016); Sergei M. Eisenstein, *The Primal Phenomenon: Art*, ed. Oksana Bulgakowa and Dietmar Hochmuth, trans. Dustin Condren (Berlin: PotemkinPress, 2017).

8   Recent exhibitions: *Unexpected Eisenstein*, GRAD, London, 2016; Alexander Gray, New York, 2017, and Frieze London, 2018; *Sergei Eisenstein: The Anthropology of Rhythm*, Rome, 2017; *Shapeshifting: Eisenstein as Method*, Lodz, 2018; *Le Violin d'Ingres*, Villa Medici, Rome, 2018.

9   Annette Michelson, 'Eisenstein at 100: Recent Reception and Coming Attractions', *October*, vol. 88 (Spring, 1999): 69–85, 85.

10 Antonio Somaini, '*Formula pafosa*, *Pathosformel*: Eisenstein and Warburg', this volume, our emphasis.

11 Oksana Bulgakowa, 'Theory as a Utopian Project', in Sergei Eisenstein, *Metod*, vol. 1, ed. Oksana Bulgakowa, 4 vols (Berlin: PotemkinPress, 2008/16), 18–19.

12 Sergei Eisenstein, *Film Form: Essays in Film Theory*, ed. and trans. Jay Leyda (New York: Harcourt, Brace and Company, 1949).

13 Sergei Eisenstein, 'Film Form: New Problems', in Eisenstein, *Film Form*, 122–150, see 130–131.

14 Sergei Eisenstein, *The Psychology of Composition*, ed. Jay Leyda, trans. Alan Upchurch (Calcutta: Seagull Books, 1987), 23–27.

15 Eisenstein, 'Film Form: New Problems', in Eisenstein, *Film Form*, 130.

16 Sergei M. Eizenshtein, *Neravnodushnaia priroda* [Nonindifferent nature] (Moscow: Muzei kino/Eizenshtein-tsentr, 2004–6), vol. 2, 36–47, translated by the editors.

17 Ibid., translated by the editors.

Part One

Creativity, Nature, Politics

1

Odd and Even: Eisenstein and Unfinished Work

Dustin Condren

In November 1927, barely five years into his career as a filmmaker, Sergei Eisenstein was already beginning to feel the symbolic burden of a growing number of projects he had not been able to complete. In a diary entry from this time, amidst notes that show him considering what seems to be a book chapter on such 'unrealised' projects, he lists the major theatre and film endeavours of his young career chronologically. In compiling this list, he detects a strange pattern: all of the odd-numbered projects of this sequence – *The Mexican* (staged March 1921), *Wiseman* (staged April 1923), *Are You Listening, Moscow?!* (staged November 1923), *Gasmasks* (staged February 1924), *The Strike* (premiered April 1925), *The Battleship Potemkin* (premiered December 1925) and *The General Line* – had been successfully completed.[1] The even-numbered projects, however – *King Hunger* (1921), *Garland's Inheritance* (1923), *Patatras* (1923), *Triapitsyn* (date unclear), *Red Cavalry* (1924) and *Dzhungo* (1926) – had all failed to come to fruition. Eisenstein then bestows on these unrealized works the comical but ominous epithet, 'even-numbered productions' (*chetnye postanovki*).[2]

After meticulously charting this pattern – in which the transition from theatre to film happened also to fall in line with this odd/even alternation, making *The Strike*, for example, both the first (odd) work of film and the ninth (odd) work overall – the filmmaker pauses to wonder, with a kind of superstitious submission to this law of numbers, which of his three currently developing film projects – *October*, *The Glass House* and *Capital* – should, if the pattern were to continue, be placed in the list as odd and destined for completion and which designated as even, and thereby doomed to failure.[3] This instance of almost gnostic self-interrogation, even if half-playful, suggests a kind of superstitious view of the creative process in which not only is non-completion of projects *inevitable* but also *necessary* for the completion of the projects with which they alternate; without the even, the logic suggests, there can be no odd.

And yet, it would seem that the rigidity of this essentially dialectical system still allowed for the possibility of its manipulation. That Eisenstein meant to manoeuvre within the system he had himself outlined is demonstrated in a diary entry made almost one year later, on 12 September 1928, in which he records another hasty thought about two of the projects he currently had in parallel development: '*Ganz intim: Khap* will be an odd-numbered work. And *Glass House* will be even!!!! It is not worth it to do it in America – [where it would be] *not* even!!!'[4] Here there is a sense of hope (still highly exclamatory and, therefore, we must assume, best read with some irony) that a total change of location, from the USSR to the United States, might have enabled Eisenstein to restart the sequence, thus changing *Glass House* from an even-numbered to an odd-numbered work, as the first to be done in America, and therefore, by this magical thinking, possible to realize.[5]

The plunge into numerology aside, this diary analysis of the success of his own oeuvre demonstrates the extent to which the growing corpus of unrealized works had begun to embed itself in Eisenstein's creative self-concept, even at a relatively early stage and, perhaps more intriguingly, shows how the gravity of these unmade films triggered the abstract functions of his imagination. At the same time, the notes betray his stoic sense that the completed work almost demands the experience gained from planning the unrealized work to generate the momentum necessary for it to move towards its proper conclusion. This is not to suggest that Eisenstein maintained a rigid view of some law of strict alternation between the complete and the incomplete, as these notes might imply if taken in isolation, but it is to observe that his perception of a meaningful, productive and even dialectical relationship between the completed and the unachieved is undeniable.

As a specific instance, there are hints of such a belief in Eisenstein's formulation of the reciprocal relationship between two of his ambitious projects of the late 1920s, *The Glass House* and *Capital*, neither of which would reach fruition. Despite this fact of his filmography, in more than one sense the magisterial accomplishment of intellectual cinema that was the anticipated outcome of the *Capital* project was fully dependent on the discoveries to be made in pursuit of the *Glass House* project – itself ultimately intended to be a way station on the path towards *purely* intellectual film. In a note of 5 September 1928, in which he discussed in detail the synthesis upon which 'the new film' is predicated, he wrote, switching to German, '*Rein wird die Synthese erst in Marx-Eisenstein-Film "Kapital" sein!!!*'[6] The *Capital* project – here presented hyperbolically, almost absurdly, as a true collaboration between Karl Marx and Eisenstein – is given the burden of carrying the new 'pure' (*rein*) language of film into creation. Further down the notebook page, however, we see how *Capital* is dependent on *The Glass House*; as he writes, '(Just as *The Glass House* film must be maximally impure – through the clay bath of *The Glass House* to the sun of the Marx film!) Through "purgatory" to "paradise!"'[7] Again, Eisenstein makes the proper achievement of his goals in *Capital* contingent upon the 'dirty work' to be done in *The Glass House*, which, inevitably, was to include many elements of the old, non-intellectual cinema within its idiosyncratic structure. Though it would aspire towards 'pure' intellectual film, it would necessarily remain 'impure' in the particulars of its execution – this included a total reconstitution of the film frame and dalliance in an *unrein* implementation of the language of intellectual cinema, a process he characterizes here as a movement 'through "purgatory" to "paradise"'. Undoubtedly, the director would have liked to make both films, but there is a certain sense in his notes of 1927–8 that in the case of these simultaneously pursued projects, work on the one was oriented towards the realization of technique that would make possible the creation of the other.

In this treatment of the concept of the reciprocal relationship between works – of the odd and even, so to speak – and in the suggestion of a quasi-mystical view of creative sequencing, we may see the seed, still far from full development, of what would be expressed in Eisenstein's much later essay 'Even and Odd: Bifurcation of the Singular', included in the materials planned for the second volume of *Method*. Eisenstein opens that essay with a long passage quoted from Marcel Granet's 1934 book *La pensée Chinoise* that detailed the conceptual operation of Chinese dialectic: 'The Odd contains within itself and separates out from itself the Even, which is merely the external two-sided (right and left, Yin and Yang) manifestation of the Odd.'[8] The passage ultimately demonstrates the coexistence and interdependence of the two figures, Odd and Even, and suggests that what separates the one from the other is a question not of numerical *quantity* but of internal *quality*. This is also what unites each manifestation of the Odd with all others, and likewise each Even with every other manifestation of its kind. Following this long passage, Eisenstein writes:

> Is it not the case that this sounds like some kind of strange half-mystical raving? And at the same time, somewhere [and] somehow – I would say somewhere 'apart from' consciousness – you feel some sort of rightness in these assertions. Somewhere not in the brain, but in the region of the … tendons (!) you feel that somewhere in the dynamism of these concepts there is something real.[9]

These last observations, here on the Chinese sequential system, could just as easily have been written about the sequential system he proposed for his own creative biography – although it may sound like a sort of 'strange half-mystical raving', one senses something truly operative in the conceptual dynamic.

From a position of historical distance, these observations on the dialectical power of the even and odd sequence over his creative output cannot help but highlight the tragic *naïveté* of the young Eisenstein, writing in 1927 about his future endeavours in filmmaking. How was he to know, after all, that this steady pattern of completion and non-completion would break very soon, how it would break, and with what dramatic force? How different his interpretation of the pattern might have been had he known that every feature film project he would undertake in the decade between 1929 and late 1938 – between the compromised completion of *The General Line* and the release of *Alexander Nevsky* – would remain unstarted, unfinished or unseen. Already by 1933, in recognition of the tenth anniversary of his working in cinema, and having experienced a series of intense creative disappointments in his two-year sojourn in Europe, Hollywood and Mexico, along with some false starts in his first year back in the Soviet Union, the director took up the task of editing for publication the screenplays from these unmade projects in the hopes of demonstrating the quality of some of the work that he had done over the past few years. Though this publication project itself never came to fruition, thereby multiplying the layers of non-realization, Eisenstein did prepare the draft of a preface for the collection, which has been preserved in his archive and was published by Naum Kleiman in *Iskusstvo kino* in 1992 as 'Toward a Preface for the Unfinished Pieces'.[10] In its task of introducing the film scripts to the reading public, the essay also demonstrates Eisenstein's developing attitude towards his expanding corpus of unfinished work and its relevance for his artistic legacy.

In the essay, he characterizes some of the work done in the West as the development of a cycle of films around 'superhuman' characters such as John Sutter, Henri Christophe, Basil Zakharov, and the fictional Clyde Griffiths of *An American Tragedy*. This description culminates with a quotation from the nineteenth-century Austrian writer Franz Grillparzer, who wrote in his diary 'I would like to be able to write a tragedy in thoughts. It would be a masterpiece!'[11] The possibility of such an immaterial masterpiece was compelling for Eisenstein, who wrote, 'Alas, such a fate has befallen the second five-year period of my creative work. To what extent the compositions of this period are masterpieces I do not know, but that they remained … in the mind, unfortunately, is a fact.'[12] Eisenstein then goes on to make an outline list of the 'meteoric' proposals for films that had appeared fleetingly in the last years (a jubilee film for Belgian independence, a globe-trotting advertisement about the benefits of Nestlé cocoa, a film about the benefits of British colonial rule in Africa, and adaptations of Vicki Baum's *Grand Hotel* and Lion Feuchtwanger's *Jud Süß*, to name but a few) before coming to a list of eight more substantial unrealized projects, 'd'inachevés' to which Grillparzer's concept of the unmade masterpiece might apply:

1. *The Glass House*
2. *Sutter*
3. *Zakharov – Götterdämmerung*
4. *Haiti [Black Majesty]*
5. *An American Tragedy*
6. *Qué viva Mexico!*
7. *M M M*
8. *Moscow*[13]

The film projects enumerated here span the seven years between 1926 and 1933, and each represented an instance of Eisenstein's concerted passion and sustained labour towards the eventual emergence of a full filmic text. Though none ever made it to the screen, they yielded varying amounts of pre-cinematic material, such as brief but pointed initial notes for *Black Majesty*, dozens of pages of notes and drawings for *Glass House*, full screenplays and director's plans for *Sutter's Gold* and *An American Tragedy*, and tens of thousands of metres of unedited footage shot for *Que viva México!* Eisenstein's omission of *Capital* from this list of projects is notable, given the intensity of his devotion to the project over several months in 1927 and 1928. One reason for its absence may be that, apart from the most basic consideration of outright ideological prudence, in 1933 he had perhaps not fully given up on the possibility of pursuing the project and therefore did not quite want to consign it to a list of the unrealized.

Perhaps more compelling than the list itself is Eisenstein's assessment of the labour he devoted to these works. He writes: '[In this] series of unsuccessful projects ... [I experienced] all the delights and voluptuous tremblings of the creative process. But, alas, with one minor nuisance. Telepathy is still not a universally available instrument of knowledge. And therefore this *opus* is fated to remain kept tightly "to myself".'[14] Eisenstein's interiority features as the sole projection space for these works, his thoughts prove an unreliable medium for their transmission, and his continuing cinematic silence guarantees their unrealized status. And yet, Eisenstein asserts that much within these eight projects came very close to completion – almost full circle, in fact, and that 'as creatively fully developed pieces, [the projects] bring with them undeniable experience'.[15] Here, again, is an assertion of the productive artistic value of unfinished work, not just for its inscription into a subsequent (completed) project but more for the general development of the filmmaker's aesthetic machinery.

This premise, that the value of the unfinished work lies in its potential energy as both expansion of experience and refinement of process, is expressed somewhat differently in the essay's opening pages, when Eisenstein makes an elaborate self-correlation with Leonardo da Vinci. The bond with Leonardo was one that he considered 'deep' and 'fateful', and the very thing that led him into the world of art in the first place. Ironically, the same quality in Leonardo had the power to lead him occasionally out of that world:

> 'señor Leonardo sits for months at a time in front of the sketched lines of the fresco', we read somewhere.
> This is not laziness. It is not the deadliness of slow tempos.
> It is curiosity ...
> The ever-persisting curiosity of little boys who are willing to sacrifice the functioning of a clock in the name of uncovering the secret of that function.
> There is no sweeter poison. And none more disastrous for creation.
> For this secret, you must pay a bloody price.
> For years, your picture will not get off the ground.
> All around there will be smiles. The shrugging of shoulders.
> But the curiosity drills deeper and deeper into the depths, into the mastery of the principle.[16]

In this passage, the image of the incomplete work has changed slightly. The question as to why work is left unfinished has moved from the assumption of some sort of external cause (more urgent demands from other projects, financial unviability, studio disapproval, governmental censorship) to a strictly internal one. The emphasis is now on the fascination with process and 'peering into' it, with the theorization of principles, with the constant refinement, elaboration and complication of the work *towards its end*, rather than with *the end itself*. This might be taken to an extreme – indeed, to prolong the pleasure of the process one may even wish to avoid the end. Eisenstein himself provides the sexual metaphor here to close the loop encircling the figures of process, completion and creation: the Da Vincian 'shamelessness of curiosity' about the artistic process is 'a sidelong glance into the bedroom of creativity at the very moment of the "holy act"'.[17]

Although this metaphor operates rhetorically both as a perverse confession and as an unimpeachable justification – he is guilty, true, of losing himself in the process, but after all, this was also the affliction of the greatest artist of the Renaissance – it is the same 'fault' that the director was so emphatically accused of in 1935 at the All-Union Creative Conference of Soviet Filmworkers, most notably by Sergei Vassiliev and by Aleksandr Dovzhenko, who exclaimed that Eisenstein 'knows so much and has such a clear mind that he, apparently, will never make another film again. If I knew so much, I think I would die.'[18] What troubled Eisenstein's colleagues in the Soviet filmmaking establishment was their general assumption about the incompatibility of the theoretical and the practical. Eisenstein's response to all of this was, of course, to defend the importance of yoking together theory and practice, arguing that 'work should be conducted parallel to a similarly intense theoretical work and theoretical research.'[19]

For Eisenstein, the strain between theory and practice need not be, as his critics assumed, the cause of his protracted incapacity to complete a project but rather was to be seen as a necessary condition for the creative engine to propel his cinematic activity. The thought that this tension may work as a sort of creative dialectic, in which the discoveries and complications of the one can be tested, accepted or even rejected by the practical implementation of the other, becomes a compelling model for a practice of cinema in which both the 'academic' and the 'actual' are given equal priority. The Da Vincian danger, 'peering inside the process', only results in stagnation when such peering is indulged in at the expense of its productive counterpart – praxis. Cases in which, as Eisenstein would later write, having 'worked out the principle, I lose interest in its application!'[20]

In an unpublished 1945 essay with the provisional title 'Twenty Years Later', connected to the section of *Method* titled 'The Author and his Theme', the director surveyed the twenty years that had passed between *Potemkin* and *Ivan the Terrible* and wondered whether there might exist any pervasive thread running through all his works when perceived retrospectively. He approaches the question with a working premise which 'counts the realized on a level with the imagined', and points out a tendency towards an almost diametrical dissimilarity between the works of his earlier period (as typified by *Potemkin*) and those of his later one (as typified by *Ivan*).[21] If one takes Eisenstein at his word, counting the unrealized work to be on the same level as the fully realized, the value of continued research into his unfinished works becomes self-evident, especially when attempting to trace the development of his creative processes and aesthetic tendencies over the period between the apparently divergent *Potemkin* and *Ivan*. Not only does his extended period of non-completion provide the caesura between these periods, but it also carries within it the theme of their inextricable connection.[22]

This is especially true if we focus our sidelong glance into the 'bedroom' of Eisenstein's creativity. In *Method*, he writes of Van Gogh's brushstroke as providing a 'marvellous sense of the coming into being of forms' – the brushstroke, he writes, is 'a peculiar residue within the work itself of the creator's own gestural motion, an idiosyncratic, dynamic self-portrait of the artist's gesticulation', as accurate as any literal self-portrait.[23] These observations precede a brief analysis of the convergence of diffuseness and definition in the writing of James Joyce, and in the sculptural works of both Michelangelo and Rodin. According to Eisenstein, Michelangelo's works are 'a pure revelation. Especially those in which the trace of the chisel's path is left deliberately on the surface as it gives birth to these living forms from out of the stillness of stone nothingness.'[24] And here he compares this 'unfinished textural quality' of Michelangelo – a quality that was the product of historical necessity, as the works were literally left unfinished because of the artist's biographical circumstances – and the stylistic choice of Rodin to leave this trace of the chisel in the work intentionally. He concludes that the 'partially finished final form' of both sculptors is key to their work's aesthetic power:

> However, the effect, if different in force, is undoubtedly identical in nature. And the crushing sensual strength of Michelangelo's incomplete statues of slaves from the gardens of Boboli (1519), who 'rise up out of the stone', just as the first people traditionally arose from the dust, or the gently lyrical beings of Rodin, airy, like a fleeting pulsation by which the vivified stone seems to thaw. These are, both in equal measure, the stone image of the transition from the diffuse and undefined into the differentiated and defined.[25]

This thought, then, points back to the idea of Eisenstein's finished and unfinished work – that the consideration of these unfinished pieces can provide the 'effect' of viewing within a work the crucial moment of its coming into being, the creation of form from diffuseness. The tension between that which is complete, fully formed, and that which is still *in potentia*, undefined. It returns us also to Eisenstein's strange articulation of the odd and the even from both the earlier and later stages of his theoretical development. When he writes in *Method* of the odd and the even, as we saw earlier, it is as an entrée into Eastern models of dialectical thinking, the bifurcation of the singular – Yin and Yang, each part containing and determining the other. In a section of his *Memoirs*, also with the provisional title 'The Bifurcation of the Singular', Eisenstein returns to the idea of division as a primary figure in Judeo-Christian cosmogony as well – that Jehovah divided the light from the dark, the water from the dry land, Eve from out of Adam.[26] The articulation (*chlenenie*) of form in this instance becomes the most basic figure of creation, in which diffuseness and form exist simultaneously at the moment when they are divided, an instance of pure creative energy. The incomplete works, counted on the same level as the complete, exist simultaneously and in dialectical relation to them, so that their necessary counterparts become cinematic objects unto themselves, figures of a durational creative process, of an idea caught exactly between the diffuse and the defined.

Notes

1   Russian State Archive of Literature and Arts (RGALI) 1923-2-1104, l. 46. Of course Eisenstein's inclusion of *The General Line* in the list of odd and completed works is premature. At the time this note was written in 1927, *The General Line* had not actually been completed: the director had interrupted his work on the film to focus on *October* and would not finish the film until early 1929, and then only in a heavily reformulated shape bearing the ideologically safer title *The Old and the New*.

2   A brief summary of the odd (realized projects) follows: *The Mexican* was staged in the Second Central Studio of the Proletkult, though Valentin Smyshlaev was credited as director and Eisenstein credited as designer of sets and costumes, it is clear from this note and other sources that Eisenstein considered himself the true author of the play (see Rostislav Yurenev, *Sergei Eizenshtein: Zamysli, filmy, metod. 1898–1929* [Moscow: Iskusstvo, 1985], 44–5). Eisenstein staged Wiseman, co-adapted with Sergei Tretiakov from Alexander Ostrovsky's *Enough Stupidity in Every Wise Man*, in the First Workers' Theatre in April 1923. Tretiakov's original play *Are You Listening, Moscow?* premiered at the Operetta Theatre on Bolshaia Dmitrovka in November 1923. *Gasmasks*, a second original work by Tretiakov, was staged in the workspace of a Moscow gas factory in February 1924. Eisenstein's first feature film, *The Strike*, was given its initial public showing in March 1925, and *The Battleship Potemkin* premiered at the Goskino Theatre in January 1926. And a summary of the even (unrealized) works follows here: in the summer of 1921, following his successful conception for *The Mexican*, Eisenstein was invited to stage Leonid Andreev's play *King Hunger* in the Central Proletkult Theatre for Valentin Tikhonovich, but the project ran into ideological trouble and was abandoned after two months of preparation. A collaboration with Proletkult playwright Valerian Pletnev, titled *Garland's Inheritance*, was conceived in 1923, but was never staged. Eisenstein again partnered with Pletnev on a second ill-fated collaboration of 1923, a three-act detective story called *Patatras* that was never staged. Very little information

survives on Eisenstein's intention to direct a play about Yakov Triapitsyn, the infamous Red Army Commander responsible for the 1920 Nikolayevsk massacre. Between December 1924 and summer 1925, together with Grigorii Alexandrov, Eisenstein developed plans for a film about the Civil War that would be a partial adaptation of Isaak Babel's *Red Cavalry* stories, but the project was set aside in favour of making *The Battleship Potemkin*. In 1926 Eisenstein explored the possibility of a three-part film series with the working title *Dzhungo* that would address China's revolutionary movement, and which was to be written by Sergei Tretiakov.

3   RGALI 1923-2-1104, l. 47. '*Oktiabr, Glaßhaus, Kapital, kak + i – respredeliat'sia zdes?!!*'

4   RGALI 1923-2-1108, 1. 152. All English translations from archival sources are my own. '*Khap*' should be understood here as one of the working titles for a comedy Eisenstein had begun developing at that time with friend and collaborator Maksim Shtraukh, most often referred to as *M.M. mopgyem* [*M.M. Buys and Sells*], and which would later partially inform the 1932–3 comedy project *MMM*.

5   As Naum Kleiman writes of *Glass House*, 'Eisenstein is preparing to give battle to the enemy on its own territory!' See '*Stekliannyi dom* S.M. Eizenshteina: K istorii zamysla', *Iskusstvo Kino*, no. 3 (1979): 95. Indeed, the impulse to shoot *Glass House* in America was inherent in the project's design from its genesis. In notes he made for the film in January 1927, Eisenstein posits its twin purposes – to satirize the detachment of capitalist life in America and to make that film *in* America: 'I thought this up today – I must do an American film with [Upton] Sinclair. "Glass House" … a glass skyscraper. A view into America through the walls … Staged through parody, using material from the real America – the America of Hollywood clichés.' See RGALI, 1923-2-1103, l. 13 (b).

6   RGALI 1923-2-1108, l. 105. 'A pure synthesis will be achieved first in the Marx-Eisenstein film *Capital*!!!'

7   Ibid. '(*Ebenso wie maximal unrein der Film Glaßhaus sein muß – durch "Lehmbad" Glaßhaus zur Sonne des Marx-Filmes!) Durch "Fegefeuer" zum "Paradies".*'

8   Sergei M. Eizenshtein, 'Chet–nechet. Razdvoienie edinogo', in *Metod*, ed. Naum Kleiman, 2 vols (Moscow: Muzei kino, Eizenshtein-tsentr, 2002), vol. 2, 151.

9   Ibid.

10 Sergei M. Eizenshtein, 'K predisloviu dlia nesdelannykh veshchei', ed. Naum Kleiman, *Iskusstvo kino*, no. 6 (1992): 4–8.

11 'Ich möchte eine Tragödie in Gedanken schreiben können. Es würde ein Meisterwerk werden!'

12 Cf. Eisenstein's later statement during his speech at the 1935 All-Union Creative Conference of Soviet Filmworkers: 'A not insignificant and quite serious creative labor took place, a creative labor which, unfortunately, no one has seen and for

which you will have to take my word.' See *Izbrannye proizvedeniia v 6-ti tomach* [Selected works in 6 volumes], ed. Pera Atasheva (Moscow: Iskusstvo, 1964), vol. 2, 101.
13 Eizenshtein, 'K predisloviu dlia nesdelannykh veshchei', 6–7.
14 Ibid., 7.
15 Ibid.
16 Ibid., 5–6. The depth and fatefulness of Eisenstein's interest and identification with Leonardo da Vinci can be sensed not just from the multiple analyses the director makes throughout his later writings of Da Vinci's works (*The Last Supper* and *The Virgin and Child with St Anne*, for example), he also refers to the period just before he began his activities in theatre, saying that Da Vinci was 'the ruler of [his] thoughts at that time' and that he 'read through absolutely everything that related to [him]'. See *Metod*, ed. Naum Kleiman, 2 vols (Moscow: Muzei kino, Eizenshtein-tsentr, 2002), vol. 1, 393.
17 Ibid.
18 'Vystuplenie A. Dovzhenko', in *Za bol'shoe kinoiskusstvo* (Moscow: Kinofotoizdat, 1935), 72.
19 Ibid., 163.
20 Eizenshtein, *Isbrannye proizvedeniia*, vol. 5, 80–81. Here, he speaks of his failure to complete the comedy film *MMM*.
21 See RGALI 1923-2-979. I am grateful to Naum Kleiman for alerting me to the existence of this document, which represents a draft of some thoughts that would appear in altered form in the 'Avtor i ego tema' section of *Method*. See Sergei M. Eizenshtein, *Metod*, in *Metod*, ed. Naum Kleiman, 2 vols (Moscow: Muzei kino/ Eizenshtein-tsentr, 2002), vol. 1, 225–7.
22 Masha Salazkina has demonstrated in her extended study of Eisenstein's most celebrated unfinished work, *¡Que viva México!*, 'that it is possible to see both "early" and "late" Eisenstein sharing space in his Mexican project'. See Salazkina, *In Excess: Sergei Eisenstein's Mexico* (Chicago: University of Chicago Press, 2009), 32.
23 Eizenshtein, *Metod*, vol. 1, 336.
24 Ibid., 337.
25 Ibid., 37–8.
26 Sergei M. Eizenshtein, *Memuary*, vol. 2 (Moscow: Muzei Kino, 1997), 45–7.

2

Eisenstein's Collectives: The Politics of Nature

Joan Neuberger

In the summer of 1945, as the chaos of war was winding down and Eisenstein was trying to finish *Ivan the Terrible*, Part II, he wrote the first draft of his essay 'The Music of Landscape and the Fate of Montage Counterpoint at a New Stage'. This essay became the second (post-war) half of the book manuscript *Nonindifferent Nature*, which Eisenstein had begun in 1939–40.[1] Re-watching *The Battleship Potemkin* in preparation for teaching the film to his directing students in Alma-Ata during the war, Eisenstein was struck by the extraordinary functions that landscape and music shared in silent film: their ability to embody and evoke feelings and their consequent ability to represent the polyphonic, multisensory, embodied experience of nature. Freed from the burden of explicating character and freed from storytelling altogether, music and landscape are both capable of 'emotionally showing what is inexpressible by other means'.[2] Landscape, he found, is 'least of all a catalog of trees, lakes, and mountaintops. Landscape is a complex carrier of the possibilities for a plastic interpretation of emotions.'[3] Attention to this essay has mostly focused on these passages about the nonverbal, sensory-emotional elements that landscape shares with music.[4] But, for Eisenstein, the sensory-emotional, invisible, and idealist was always in dialectical tension with the rational, the narrative and the materialist. We see that dialectic in 'The Music of Landscape' in the way Eisenstein treats landscape as a 'plastic' object that does the work of materializing and making visible such immaterial and invisible entities as thoughts and emotions. In fact, he saw landscape as the consummate object for exploring this central dialectic. The material potential of landscape is an elaboration of the principle he set out as early as 1925–6 in the essay 'On the Play of Objects', that is, the 'affective expressivity of objects'.[5]

'The Music of Landscape', then, is an extensive study of landscape that ranges far from its starting point, that is its potential for 'emotionally showing what is inexpressible by other means'. In the essay, Eisenstein analysed the properties of landscape – as a form, as a thing – in many of the same ways he had analysed other objects in earlier writing and in film practice: as the animation of the inanimate, as the thing onto which inner conflict could be projected, as self-portraiture, as montage cell or unit, as stimulating in the viewer a swarm of associations in polyphonic, multipoint montage, and as effecting a dialectic of materialist and idealist conceptions of nature. But then he does something else, something unusual, that has gone entirely unnoticed. He discusses the properties and uses of landscape, the dialectics of form and formlessness, of idea and sensory-feeling, of material and ideal, in explicitly political terms.

* * *

The ideological turn in Eisenstein studies in the 1990s, and the publication of *Method* and the expanded publication of *Nonindifferent Nature* in the early 2000s, have revived interest in Eisenstein's work in the Stalinist period, but the political trajectory of his thinking is still underappreciated. Eisenstein is, of course, famous for the political commitment of his early writing and film work. In the years immediately following the Russian Revolution, in the 1920s when Eisenstein was in his twenties, he was outspoken about cinema's political impact on viewers: properly composed films could raise class consciousness, help build socialism in the Soviet Union, and propagate revolution elsewhere. Radical politics became muted in his later writing, as his interests widened and the frame for public discourse narrowed under Stalin. But while Eisenstein never joined the Communist Party, he continued to believe in the possibility of an egalitarian, perhaps utopian, collectivity. And he continued to write about socialism, often in oblique ways, in connection with his studies of the arts. When Stalin commissioned him to make a film about Ivan the Terrible, he could not avoid, or he chose not to avoid, questions of history, society and politics. In *Ivan*, that took the form of rethinking questions of historical materialism, the new Soviet subjectivity, the public and the private, and the individual and the collective.

When Eisenstein was rediscovered in Western Europe and the United States in the 1960s, and in Latin America in the 1970s, his admirers focused on the collective heroes of his early films and the political claims in his writings of the 1920s. This generation of artists and scholars often disparaged Eisenstein's later work as caving to the demands of Stalinist censorship or worse, toadying to the dictator. In fact, such views haven't changed much since 1966, when the renowned American film scholar, Annette Michelson, wrote her influential essay 'Film and the Radical Aspiration'.[6] She argued then that radical political thinking had become impossible once the revolutionary wave of the early twentieth century had subsided and socialism had been disfigured by the states where it was adopted. When this essay was widely republished and anthologized, after the global failures of 1968, socialism seemed to have become nothing more than a subject for nostalgia and frustration. Eisenstein was Michelson's key witness:

> [Eisenstein's] energy, courage, and intellectual passion which sustained both theory and work were, of course, among the noblest of our century – in his defeat as in his achievement, and down to the very fragmentary quality of his work! One's sense of his defeat, visible in *Alexander Nevsky*, is so particularly agonizing because it constitutes a unique example of what one might call the pathos of dissociation [between the radical formal and the radical ideological] pushed to an extremity.[7]

And this is understandable. It is easy to dismiss Eisenstein's statements on the great achievements of the Soviet Union, on our 'inimitable country and epoch' on 'the Great Genius Stalin' as throw-away lines, as a noble-tragic necessity for survival. It is easy to assume that he is not serious when he writes things like: 'Here in our country [...] Our cinema, as the most progressive of the arts has this great task before it: to reveal in its works that profound unity and harmony, and that profound worldview that our socialist era has brought to humanity.'[8] But there is more to see here. I argue that Eisenstein took seriously the discursive framework of striving for a utopian world of 'unity and harmony'. At times, he conceptualized 'unity and harmony' in artistic terms as one form of dialectical synthesis; but in *Method* and especially in *Nonindifferent Nature*, he is writing about a socialist collective that both echoed and departed from official Soviet discourse.[9] In 1945, as the long and unthinkably destructive war was finally coming to an end, and Eisenstein was writing 'The Music of Landscape', we find the lines quoted above. More than an isolated and coerced conformist mask, these lines appear in a long concluding passage on the possible merging of materialism and idealism, on the interpenetration of contemplation and action, of the future and the past, and the past in the present, on the historical possibilities for the creation of a harmonious society and the ways various previous artists and thinkers had approached those possibilities. And he found the models for this society in the ability of human beings to immerse themselves in nature, in landscape. It's time we took another look.

* * *

Since the 1980s, a vast literature has appeared to examine landscape, nature, the environment, the Anthropocene, the human, non-human and post-humanist interactions with nature that places those relationships and representations in a social, cultural and political context that was missing from earlier art history and naturalism. The pioneers – Denis Cosgrove in geography, Simon Schama in history, Raymond Williams and the literary scholars and art historians who contributed to W. J. T. Mitchell's generative anthology on landscape and power – explored the ways landscape is constructed, represented and experienced in social and political terms.[10] Eisenstein prefigured some of this literature and he also diverged significantly from some of it. His view of nature stood in direct opposition to these authors' focus on modernization – both communist and capitalist – that saw nature as something to be conquered, dominated or managed; and that saw representations of landscape as contributing to those projects of social engineering. In choosing to see the power of landscape to express human feelings and shape human experience, Eisenstein was rejecting the detached, disembodied individual of both the Western and the Soviet imperialist modernizing male gaze.[11] For him, landscape is more than something seen with our eyes or constructed and represented for the purpose of colonization, or domination, or reinforcing class hierarchy and property ownership. Indeed, he prefigured the next generation's writing on landscape and nature in the late twentieth and twenty-first century, which recognized nature's own power over us and saw representations of nature as what might be called mutually constitutive. He comes closer to this later generation of writers who explore the active and autonomous character of nature and landscape. Although not particularly interested in gardens, for example, he is interested in the effect that James Elkins attributes to gardens: their ability to cast a spell on us, to make us feel and to make inadequate the words we use to describe our experience of nature.[12] Eisenstein saw the landscape as something that has power over us even as we remake it. But he saw that power ironically: the spell that it casts on us also confers freedom from social constraints, freedom from the weight of rationality, freedom from alienated, isolated individuality and even freedom from the bonds of human form.[13] His analysis of the political context in which art can be liberating shares some elements with today's activist artists who are asking how art can contribute to environmental justice and political and social equality.[14] In Eisenstein, landscape is both materialist and idealist. Cultures, political structures, individual and national memory are shaped by nature, and by our interactions with it, specifically with particular forms nature takes in a given region, as Kenneth Olwig and Simon Schama have both shown. But while these writers posit the material and the ideal, the embodied, multisensory experience and the construction of culture and memory based on the hard rock, flowing rivers and cultivated fields of our communities, they still fundamentally focus on human agency.[15] Eisenstein's dialectic of landscape – our experiences and representations of nature – is rooted in our ability to immerse ourselves in nature, to feel ourselves transfigured into elements of the natural world. And it is this experience – our embodied immersion in nature, our interaction with geographically determined nature – that is the model for human representations of landscape in art. Nonindifferent nature serves human needs in Eisenstein, but on its own terms.

Such a view of nature as something that human beings both use for their own ends and dissolve into or submit to entirely, is at the centre of 'The Music of Landscape'. *Nonindifferent Nature* is only partly a work of analysis. It is primarily – even more than *Method* (Eisenstein's other major work of the early 1940s) – a study of method in art concerned with the question: 'How to do it?'[16] If *Method* analysed and explicated the essential expressivity of objects and art works, *Nonindifferent Nature* sought to discover how films (and other works of art) can best convey the artist's ideas and feelings to the viewer. Eisenstein thought that landscape – both in nature and on screen – was especially good at this. *Nonindifferent Nature* can be seen as primarily about the ways we – living, breathing, thinking, feeling beings – interact with things outside ourselves. Landscape, at times standing in for all things, as the consummate thing, is nonindifferent because it interacts with us as we project on to it our desires for nature to interact with us. As Anne Nesbet noted, landscape in Eisenstein is '"inner monologue" made visible'.[17]

* * *

These concepts, Eisenstein tells us, derive from his experience of the interweaving of form and formlessness that occurred when he sailed through the early morning fog in the Odessa harbour to film scenes for *The Battleship Potemkin* with cinematographer Eduard Tisse. 'The general combination of motifs moves from the airiness of the mist through the barely perceptible outline of objects – through the lead-gray surface of the water and gray sails – to the velvety black hulks of the ships and the hard rock of the embankment. The dynamic combination of separate lines of these elements flows together into a final static chord.'[18] That 'chord' is a series of shots that express both the feeling and the concepts of the scene in transitioning from landscape to mourning for the martyr Vakulinchuk: the harbour seen from inside the tent with

Vakulinchuk's body through the triangle opening; the triangle of the top of the tent from the outside with two triangles of mourning crepe, and a medium shot of the tent with more triangles of ships' sails surrounding it. Mist, water, ships, sails, harbour: this linear, multipoint progression from dispersed materials to a harmonious chord is also a multipoint, dialectical process that accounts for each material piece and the dynamic transformation that brings them all together, and produces a concept/feeling of mourning for the martyred sailor.

Much of the rest of the essay then examines the ways other artists have used landscape to convey feeling and thoughts to viewers and readers, and ultimately to 'serve as a concrete image of the embodiment of whole cosmic conceptions, whole philosophic systems'.[19] Eisenstein amends that a little later to make it less unilateral, and encompass both the sensory-emotional and the conceptual: 'Everywhere this was the emotional landscape, dissolving into itself the human being, or more precisely: Everywhere the emotional landscape turns out to be an image of the mutual absorption of human and nature into one another'.[20] Artists are able to invest landscape with philosophy and feelings because human beings can immerse themselves in nature.

In this way, 'landscape', he wrote 'is largely a portrait, and very often a self-portrait, [...] self-portrait, that [...] dissolves the human into itself'.[21] This dissolution of self into the landscape is, of course, yet another example of one of the central components of Eisenstein's thought. It is the undifferentiation of the womb, the transfiguration into animals, the interpenetrating melting of boundaries between people and things, the animation of the inanimate, originary bisexuality, and the culmination of dialectical conflicts of all kinds in the ecstatic, transformative, dialectical synthesis. It is also the combination of all these points of synthesis into the immersive, polyphonic montage we see in *Ivan the Terrible*. In his memoirs, Eisenstein wrote that he was passionate about what he called 'the mutability of form'; this dissolution into landscape is the primary 'mutability of form'.[22]

Anne Nesbet, Yuri Tsivian, Mikhail Iampolski, and others have focused on this dissolution as the death that precedes life, one of the 'savage junctures' that animates so much of Eisenstein's work.[23] Nesbet has also shown that the figure dissolving in the landscape – and emerging from it – originated in Eisenstein's reading of Andrei Bely's book on Gogol: 'Gogol's landscapes', claims Bely, 'produce the figures who inhabit them'.[24] The following key passage in *Nonindifferent Nature* shows how Eisenstein links Bely's reading of Gogol with his own study of Chinese landscape painting, and his focus on landscape itself:

> This immersion into self, into the 'great Nothing', which at the same time 'gives birth to Everything', is, of course, basically an 'imagistic' [*obraznaia*] interpretation of that exalted state that seizes every person when they remain completely alone with nature. In such moments they are seized by an unusual feeling as if a dissolution [*samorastvorenie*] in nature and a merging [*sliiania*] with it, that feels like a removal of the contradictions between the universal and the individual, usually opposing each other, just as humans oppose the landscape [...] Moreover, we especially experience this feeling, not only in its early 'pantheistic' form but in its highest and most perfect form – on the social stages of development. This is what the feeling of merging with the collective and merging with class is like; the experience of indestructible unity with one's nation, with the best part of humanity as a whole.[25]

In other words, it turns out that this dialectic of 'Nothing', the 'death that leads to life', and 'Everything', or 'the womb that gives birth to Everything', is intimately related to something Eisenstein considers even more fundamental and profound: this dissolution into nature, and the merging of the self and the landscape. And then also, not to be missed, the feeling of merging with the collective. This merging into nature is so fundamental for Eisenstein that he sees it as the origin of all dialectics, but, in a crucial turn, it is a dialectics that will evolve into a non-violent, non-binary dialectics of immersion.[26]

The path from dissolution into nature to the individual into the collective begins with the self-portrait. The immersion that makes landscape a self-portrait is not a metaphor. Eisenstein is not talking about a metaphorical likeness when he writes that he saw his *Ivan the Terrible* merging with the landscape, when he finds 'an unexpected harmony' between the 'plastic images' of Ivan and the 'plastic images' of the landscape. He sees this self-portrait as the same process as the human being dissolved into the landscape.[27] Ivan is not *like* the landscape, he *is* the landscape, and when Eisenstein calls this image of Ivan his own 'self-portrait' this is not representation: that depiction of Ivan *plus* landscape *is* Eisenstein, himself, transformed into the image – a primary example of the mutability of form. This is what Eisenstein means when he says in his memoirs that he is 'fascinated by the artist who is *present in the rhythms of his experience as he produces a work of art*'.[28]

What makes this particular mutation of form, this dissolving into landscape, and so producing a self-portrait – possible? First landscape can only become a carrier of emotion in silent film as mentioned above, when it is properly composed – and that composition has to be what he calls musical. His analysis of the mists of *Potemkin* and the uncoiling of East Asian landscape scrolls is a structural, formal analysis of compositions that function like music. That is, they aren't just somehow 'lyrical' or 'operatic' but are composed with rhythm, counterpoint and other musical properties. Only in those cases does immersion become possible. This section of the chapter includes detailed discussion of *Potemkin* and *Ivan* Part I, in particular the contributions of Sergei Prokofiev, Eduard Tisse and Andrei Moskvin to evoke feeling and sensation in viewers, to create 'the graphic interpretation of the inner flow of the music'.[29] Take, for example, the scene where Ivan is dying (or seems to be dying) and wants everyone to pledge loyalty to his baby son Dmitri, while Efrosinia wants the *boyars* to pledge to her son Vladimir, and Ivan realizes for the first time that there is serious opposition to his rule and his plans. In this scene, the score traces the horizon of a landscape as it follows Ivan and his entourage around his bedchamber and then down the hall. The points where the score's individual figures are repeated delineate the forms of Ivan's vulnerabilities and his exercise of power while at the same time tracing Ivan's emotional ups and downs as he moves around the room. This is an emotional and semantic landscape: 'the graphic interpretation of the inner flow of the music'.

Second, he explores the ways that a variety of early modern and modern painters and thinkers depicted and wrote about the dissolution into landscape. And he finds dozens of examples. Here's George Sand:

> There are moments when I crawl out of myself, when I live in vegetation, when I feel like the grass, the birds, the top of a tree, a cloud, running water, the horizon, a flower, form and feelings, changing, transforming, indistinct; moments when I run, fly, swim, drink the dew, spread out in the sun, sleep under the foliage, fly with the swallows, crawl with the lizards, twinkle with the stars and planets, when I, in short, live in what composes the milieu of evolution, seeming to appear as the extension of one's own being.[30]

And Guy de Maupassant:

> I think, sir, that I am quite open, that everything enters into me, forces me to cry or gnash my teeth. Well now, when I look at the slope opposite us, at this large green fold, at these hordes of trees climbing up the mountain, the whole forest in my eyes; it penetrates all of me, seizes me, flows in my blood, and I even think that I am eating it, that it fills my insides; I myself have become the forest.[31]

One more lyrical, the other quite frightening and violent. If they can reproduce this mutation of form in their work they will have effected what Eisenstein calls 'self-portraiture in landscape'.[32] Or 'the "inner monologue" made visible'.[33] The replication of the writer's experience of dissolution and immersion materializes their inner experience in words, which in turn allows readers to immerse themselves in the text, transforming the material thing into their own related thoughts and feelings and merge with the writer. But even better is the embodiment on screen or canvas.

He also finds scores of examples of visual artists making their inner monologue visible. According to Eisenstein, El Greco does this better than anyone: in *Storm over Toledo* he mutates into the landscape: 'one of the first "pure" landscapes, that is one where for the first time any realistic depiction of human semblance has slipped away [...] possibly the most ardent self-portrait of the "soul" of the human being – its creator'.[34] Here Eisenstein quotes from an early twentieth-century study of *Storm over Toledo* by the German art historian Hugo Kehrer, that captures the dissolution which produced a self-portrait that enables the viewer feel what El Greco felt:

> With the infallible precision of a sleepwalker's movements, El Greco paints the lightning, how it creeps along, burning homes, churches, and bridges. Everything is lost in this dizzy summer lightning: forms spread, running into ephemeralness. The spirit obeys the material completely and turns nature into the image of its own experience. In the foreground, the painter's brush bursts into flames, burning up what is concrete; the crags lose their sharp outline and strict form [...] Thus everything concrete dissolves, become the grandiose embodiment of the inner states of El Greco.[35]

Eisenstein includes a long passage from Friedrich Engels's 1840 article on landscape that brings together many of his ideas about the ways landscape embodies 'plastic emotions' and the ways that the material, the sensory-emotional and the intellectual come together, as happens to artists like El Greco, Sand and Maupassant in their immersion into nature.[36] In citing Engels, Eisenstein draws attention to the cultural differences that derive from natural geographic landscape formations, and he adds a cultural complication. He makes a distinction between the *opposition* of the universal and the individual determined by cultural differences, and the *immersion* of the individual into the universal determined by human physiology and biology. Engels was describing the experience of hiking the north German moors as a fantastical, mythic, nightmarish episode. Walking the moors on dark nights, Engels experienced the return of scary memories of childhood, when, 'at nightfall the human element vanishes and the terrifying shapeless creations' – the forms of landscape – become otherworldly. In losing 'shape' (the mutability of form!) they take on magical qualities, neither human nor natural; the physical features of the landscape become 'the tangible embodiment of feelings aroused in the solitary heath'. The human element that vanishes here is the illusion of human control over nature, or human detachment from the natural world, or the natural world as indifferent, inanimate, inert. The physical forms of the dark landscape are emptied of human elements to become organic and living but uncontrollable monstrous forms, that can absorb and materialize human feelings. This is key because it is a dynamic process of transmutation of both the landscape and the viewer – that enables the merger of the individual into some whole, some universal, or some collective. By placing this experience in a specific cultural context, Eisenstein is creating a dialectic that places differences of geography and cultural formation against psychological and biological similarity.

But what kind of merger, dissolution, 'undifferentiatedness' is this? Eisenstein addresses these questions in the last section of 'The Music of Landscape', titled 'Becoming' (*Stanovlenie*). Here he switches mode, tone and subject matter. Up to this point in the text, the dissolution into nature and the dialectic of 'Nothing' and 'Everything' has been examined in artistic forms; now he turns to the conditions that make that dissolution possible. If the first interpretation was 'imagistic', this one is the political. At the end of this chapter of *Nonindifferent Nature*, his discussion of conditions that allow for the mutual absorption of self and landscape, individual and universal, self-portraiture, is all about politics and history.

First, he discusses artists who fail to properly reflect the historical context in which they are living or who are living in places where politics prevent the full expression of the dialectic of art and politics. Michelangelo, Shakespeare, George Sand, Victor Hugo, Leo Tolstoy, Pablo Picasso and Hui Tsung (the eighth-century Song emperor and calligrapher) could elevate and transform us with their unique individual visions that reflect the social structures of the time and place, but they can only *suggest* the paths towards 'the actual realization of those basic universal aspirations for unity and harmony of the future'.[37] These magnificent writers and artists of genius could only point the way to a desirable future, they couldn't take us there. And that is what Eisenstein wants them to do. The 'Becoming' of the title of this section refers to social-political transformation as well as individual becoming.

After this detour into the shortcomings of artists trapped in flawed societies, or who, like Picasso, try to keep their art and radical politics separate, Eisenstein returns to landscape in the culmination of the essay. Only three countries, he tells us, have made it possible for someone to feel immersed in nature in a way that would be transformative: the USSR, the United States and Mexico. Only these three 'make you feel, as if in three different phases and experience, the *great principles of the dynamics of completion – of formation and becoming*.³⁸ He quickly disposes of the United States and the USSR, in each case with an ideological cliché. Modernization and collectivism in the Soviet Union saved the nomad and the peasant 'through social becoming'. Modernization and industry, reaching into the skies with fabulous skyscrapers in the urban landscape of the United States, described with ecstatic enthusiasm, embody technical and material becoming. These are caricatures, but they are caricatures with a purpose. In both cases, the United States and the USSR, history moves in only one direction: forward. 'Becoming' there is defined as leaving the past behind. When Eisenstein turns to Mexico, the world he describes is dialectical and immersive: the past isn't left behind, it is fully felt, seen and materialized in the present.

At first Eisenstein's descriptions sound much like the detached, colonializing male observer, as Masha Salazkina has shown, presenting a series of Orientalist observations. He calls Mexico a timeless land in perennial childhood: 'It is as if the organic world looked just like this in the first days of creation.'³⁹ But he then rejects the Orientalist insistence on timelessness and the binary of traditional and modern, and with it a view of Mexico as static, mired in the past or disqualified from participating in the modern world. Eventually, Eisenstein arrives at the opposite understanding: in Mexico the present is everywhere in dialogue with the past, the modern with the traditional, the urban with the rural, the male with the female. Or, as he put it: 'the cradle in each sarcophagus [...] the constant mixture of life and death, appearance and disappearance, dying and being born, at every step'.⁴⁰

Eisenstein's time in Mexico, spent working on his unfinished film *Que viva México!*, coincided with a period when the government and much of Mexico's intelligentsia sought to elevate 'traditional', indigenous culture as the origin of Mexican national identity and a source of national pride, a policy called *indigenismo*.⁴¹ Eisenstein befriended the great artists of the period (he met Diego Rivera in both in Moscow and in Mexico City), but he did not share their *indigenismo*. Even his most stereotypical images of indigenous Mexicans as tokens of the past are always paired with or in complex dialogue with images of the present: 'existing in the same space as that occupied by the post-revolutionary modern Mexico [...] the pre-modern always haunts the modern [in *Que viva México!*]', as Andrea Noble puts it.⁴² The structure of *Que viva México!* is both teleological and circular. The narrative follows a path from the tyrannies of the past towards revolution and liberation, but at the same time Eisenstein wanted to show the many ways that the past always lives on in the present, both in Mexican culture and society, and inside all of us.

These immersive dialectics make all other essential dialectics possible, including that which enables art to be truly transformational. The political interpretation of the dissolution into nature was the merging of individual in the collective, which could only come about in a place where the modern hadn't eradicated the historical. Unlike any of the other contexts he has described in *Nonindifferent Nature* – where Tolstoy, Picasso, etc., were working – his Mexico is in a state of *becoming*: 'in this feeling [this dissolution in nature and union with it] there seems [...] to be a removal of the contradictions between the universal and the individual, usually opposing each other, just as human opposes the landscape'.[43] Eisenstein ends the main text of 'The Music of Landscape' here. Immersion in nature and the immersion of the past in the present not only model other forms of immersion but, in this case, make it possible for the individual to become immersed in the collective.

Then, just as he seems carried away with the utopian possibilities of the immersive dialectic of the human and nature, he snaps back to his more familiar ironic and cynical self. As Naum Kleiman wrote in the introduction to his edition of *Nonindifferent Nature*, the Epilogue to 'The Music of Landscape' provides a safety valve for would-be utopians, the reminder Eisenstein always gives us when the dialectic seems to work out too perfectly in a longed for 'unity'. Too much balance – too perfect a unity and harmony – is as dangerous as an over-powerful state. Eisenstein's landscape is dialectical, which means that it is a tense dynamic of becoming that occasionally gives us the experience of intense feeling (*pathos*), out-of-body transformation (*ek-stasis*), out-of-body dissolution into nature and feeling of transcendence, synthetic unity, harmony and transformation. But that experience is always dynamic and temporary. In the political references at the end of *Nonindifferent Nature*, he warns against every form of collectivity or merger or dissolution that is reified in ideology or political sloganeering. 'Unity and harmony' may be attainable – as he experienced in Mexico in the form of immersion into nature – but this is fleeting, a momentary joining of material and ideal, yet always worth pursuing no matter how ephemeral.

Notes

1   Parts of *Nonindifferent Nature* were written in 1939 and 1940 and parts were translated into English in *The Film Sense*, ed. and trans. Jay Leyda (New York: Harcourt, Brace and Company, 1942) and *Film Form: Essays in Film Theory*, ed. and trans. Jay Leyda (New York: Harcourt, Brace and Company, 1949). Eisenstein

conceived the book as a discrete text in 1945 and one version of that manuscript, which included texts written between 1939 and 1947, was published in his collected works (*Izbrannye proizvedeniia v 6-ti tomach* [Selected works in 6 volumes], ed. Pera Atasheva (Moscow: Iskusstvo, 1964–71), vol. 3, 33–432); this is the text Herbert Marshall used to translate the book into English (Cambridge: Cambridge University Press, 1987 [*NN*]). In 2004–6 Naum Kleiman published another, more complete version of the text with a second volume of related materials (2 vols, Moscow: Muzei kino/Eisenstein Center, 2004–6 [*NP*]). On the complicated publication history of *Nonindifferent Nature*, see *NP*, vol. 1, 613–15. The best introductions to *Nonindifferent Nature* are Naum Kleiman, 'Pafos Eizenshteina', *NP*, vol. 2, 5–32; and Herbert Eagle, 'Introduction', in *NN*, vii–xxi.
2 *NP*, vol. 2, 311; *NN*, 217.
3 *NP*, vol. 2, 459; *NN*, 355; Russian State Archive of Literature and Arts (RGALI), 1923-2-1169, l. 44–8, [21 May 1942].
4 Francesco Finocchiaro, 'Sergei Eisenstein and the Music of Landscape: The "Mists" of Potemkin between Metaphor and Illustration', in *The Sounds of Silent Films*, ed. Claus Tieber and Anna Windisch (Basingstoke: Palgrave Macmillan, 2014), 172–91; Massimo Olivero, 'La Musique du paysage, ou de la non-indifférence de la Nature', in *The Flying Carpet: Studies on Eisenstein and Russian Cinema in Honor of Naum Kleiman*, ed. Joan Neuberger and Antonio Somaini (Paris: Éditions Mimésis, 2017), 295–306; Robert Robertson identifies additional themes in *Eisenstein on the Audiovisual* (London: I.B.Tauris, 2009), 85–139.
5 Sergei M. Eizenshtein, 'Ob igre predmetov' [On the play of objects], *Kinovedcheskie zapiski* 36/37 (1997/8): 34–8.
6 Annette Michelson, 'Film and the Radical Aspiration', *Film Culture* 42 (1966): 404–21. On Eisenstein in Latin America, see Masha Salazkina, 'Eisenstein in Latin America', in *The Flying Carpet: Studies on Eisenstein and Russian Cinema in Honor of Naum Kleiman*, ed. Joan Neuberger and Antonio Somaini (Paris: Éditions Mimésis, 2017), 343–65.
7 Michelson, 'Film and the Radical Aspiration', 415.
8 *NN*, 376.
9 For example, 'Poslednee slovo o forme. Form as urge k besklassovosti', Sergei Eisenstein, *Metod*, ed. Oksana Bulgakowa (Berlin: PotemkinPress, 2008), vol. 1, 259–67.
10 There is of course a long history of writing about landscape, nature and representations of landscape and nature; here my departing point is works that address the social and political formations of nature and landscape and their critics: Raymond Williams, *The Country and the City* (Oxford: Oxford University Press, 1973); Denis Cosgrove, *Social Formation and Symbolic Landscape*, 2nd edn (Madison: University of Wisconsin Press, [1984] 1998); Simon Schama, *Landscape*

and Memory (New York: Knopf, 1995); W. J. T. Mitchell, ed., *Landscape and Power* (Chicago: University of Chicago Press, 1994).

11 Cosgrove, *Social Formation and Symbolic Landscape*, xvii-xviii.
12 James Elkins, 'On the Conceptual Analysis of Gardens', *Journal of Garden History* 13, no. 4 (1993): 189–98.
13 For the contemporary discussion of post-human landscape, see Rosi Braidotti, *The Posthuman* (Cambridge: Polity Press, 2013); Eduardo Kohn, *How Forests Think: Toward an Anthropology Beyond the Human* (Berkeley: University of California Press, 2013); Emanuele Coccia, *The Life of Plants: A Metaphysics of Mixture* (Cambridge: Polity Press, 2019).
14 Heather Davis and Etienne Turpin, eds., *Art in the Anthropocene: Encounters Among Aesthetics, Politics, Environments and Epistemologies* (London: Open Humanities Press, 2015), 3; Emily Eliza Scott and Kirsten Swenson, eds., *Critical Landscapes: Art, Space, Politics*, (Berkeley: University of California Press, 2015).
15 William Cronon, *Changes in the Land: Indians, Colonists, and the Ecology of New England* (New York: Hill and Wang, 1983); Kenneth Olwig, *Landscape, Nature, and the Body Politic* (Madison: University of Wisconsin Press, 2002); Schama, *Landscape and Memory*.
16 Sergei Eisenstein, *Beyond the Stars: The Memoirs of Sergei Eisenstein*, ed. Richard Taylor, trans. William Powell (London: British Film Institute, 1995), 430.
17 Anne Nesbet, 'Gogol, Belyi, Eisenstein and the Architecture of the Future', *The Russian Review* 65, no. 3 (2006), 498; citing RGALI, 1923-2-250, l. 1.
18 *NP*, vol. 2, 327; *NN*, 228.
19 *NN*, 355; *NP*, vol. 2, 460.
20 *NN*, 359; *NP*, vol. 2, 470, translation slightly revised.
21 *NN*, 252–254 and 358; *NP*, vol. 2, 354–358, and 470, translation revised.
22 Sergei M. Eizenshtein, *Memuary* (Moscow: GARAJ, 2019), 1, 336.
23 Anne Nesbet, *Savage Junctures: Eisenstein and the Shape of Thinking* (London: I.B.Tauris, 2007); Yuri Tsivian, *Ivan the Terrible* (London: British Film Institute, 2002); Mikhail Iampolski, 'Drawing As Will and Representation', in *The Body of the Line: Eisenstein's Drawings: Drawing Papers*, no. 4 (New York: Drawing Center, 2000).
24 Nesbet, 'Gogol, Belyi, Eisenstein', 497.
25 Ibid., 498; *NN*, 356 and 358; *NP*, 467–8 and 469. Marshall's translation of this passage into English is based on the version published in *Izb. Proiz.* 3, 391 and 393; but that passage appears in a slightly revised and repositioned version in *Neravnodushnaia priroda* (2004–6); this last version is the basis for my translation. Critically, the word 'poetic' has been replaced by the word 'imagistic'. The original placement of the text and the switch from 'poetic' to 'imagistic' make it clear that here Eisenstein is discussing a specific convention of painterly representation

that occurs in Chinese landscape painting, and in the immersive effect of placing religious shrines high up on the top of mountains or pyramids; that these experiences are all related to 'whole philosophic systems', specifically ancient Chinese yin and yang, and not only to Western conventions of the 'death that leads to life'.

26 NN, 358. On dialectics of landscape see Mikhail Iampolski, 'Point–Pathos–Totality', *Notes for a General History of Cinema*, ed. Naum Kleiman and Antonio Somaini (Amsterdam: Amsterdam University Press, 2016), 357–73.
27 NN, 357.
28 Eisenstein, *Selected Works: Beyond the Stars*, 309, emphasis in the original.
29 NN, 389.
30 Ibid., 357.
31 Ibid., 357.
32 Ibid., 359; NP, 470.
33 Nesbet, 'Gogol, Belyi, Eisenstein', 498; citing RGALI 1923-2-250, l. 1.
34 NP, 470 (NN, 359); translation slightly revised.
35 NN, 361.
36 Friedrich Engels, 'Landshafty', *Sochinenie* 2 (1936): 55–7; first published *Telegraph für Deutschland*, no. 122 (July 1840), quoted in NN, 376–8.
37 NN, 376.
38 NN, 378; NP, 490, emphasis in the original.
39 NN, 380.
40 NN, 380; Masha Salazkina, *In Excess: Sergei Eisenstein's Mexico* (Chicago: University of Chicago Press, 2009).
41 Though, as Alan Knight noted, *indigenismo* did not produce much in terms of concrete improvements in lives of the poor, indigenous or other; see 'Racism, Revolution, and Indigenismo: Mexico, 1910–1940', in *The Idea of Race in Latin America, 1870–1940*, ed. Richard Graham (Austin: University of Texas Press, 1990), 71–115, cited in Andrea Noble, 'Seeing Through ¡Que viva México!: Eisenstein's Travels in Mexico', *Journal of Iberian and Latin American Studies* 12, nos. 2–3 (2006): 177–8.
42 Noble, 'Seeing Through ¡Que viva México!', 184.
43 NN, 356 and 358; NP, 467–8 and 469; see note 25.

3

The Politics of Nonindifference in Eisenstein's Dialectics of Nature

In memoriam Hannah Frank

Robert Bird

In the 'Postscriptum' to his unfinished book project *Nonindifferent Nature*, Eisenstein defines its titular concept as an 'emotional' or 'musical landscape' that captures the mutual reshaping of human and environment: "'nonindifferent nature'", he writes, 'is primarily not nature around us, but our very own nature – the nature of a person who is not indifferent, but who passionately, actively and creatively approaches the world which he re-creates'.[1] With this ambitious remit, *Nonindifferent Nature* implicates a multitude of discourses, from psychology to art history, but it might most consistently be read as a work of ethics; in many of its sections, especially in the long part entitled 'Pathos', *Nonindifferent Nature* espouses a posture of ecstatic openness towards the world. Ultimately, with its focus on the mediation between human and world under the conditions of technological modernity, *Nonindifferent Nature* is also a theory of cinema; in the words of Naum Kleiman, *Nonindifferent Nature* was to be 'a book about the universal laws [*zakonomernosti*] of cinema, which reflect the fundamental bases of Being'.[2] Landscape, ecstasy, cinema, ontology: in its many and diverse parts Eisenstein's *Nonindifferent Nature* amounts to a speculative media ecology.

But Eisenstein's *Nonindifferent Nature* also amounts to a politics, one that embeds aesthetic creation in the real world outside, while also representing real-world agency as a form of aesthetic creativity: here, cinema emerges as a means of governance. Although Eisenstein does not articulate his media ecology in explicitly political terms, he is aware of the need to position cinema amidst properly political forces. In his 'Afterword' to the book Eisenstein describes the Soviet cinema as a medium of history and nation, and therefore as a fundamentally democratic force:

> Our nation and our time dictate to us what we shoot.
> The nation and time dictate how we view phenomena.
> And the view of things and our relation to phenomena dictate the look and form in which we clothe them.
> The structure of the work, the principles of its resolution and the development of our methods are born wholly out of the nature of the theme and its interpretation.
> This defines the vitality of the theme.[3]

Cinema channels its historical environment; the historical moment dictates the aesthetic medium. But what happens if the moment is one not of Soviet democracy but of Stalinist tyranny? Is the cinema then merely a passive tool of political terror, repeating and imposing its dictates, or can cinema exert resistance within its historical world?

There are moments where, in its synthesis of aesthetics and politics, *Nonindifferent Nature* comes troublingly close to mimicking the Stalinist project for the transformation of nature, and for the recruitment of art as a contributing force to this project. Eisenstein explicitly seeks common cause with the Stalinist remaking of the natural environment as a 'second nature', the thrust of which is captured in a common paraphrase of Marx in Soviet discourse of the 1930s, that 'by transforming nature man transforms himself'.[4] At its worst, the Stalinist project for transforming nature embraced the mass deployment of convict labour as a means of reforging both humanity at the same time as the landscape; even at its best, it has caused vast and lasting ecological damage. About his unrealized film *The Ferghana Canal* (1939), set at a major construction project of the late 1930s, a site of great human and ecological devastation, Eisenstein writes that it culminates in a story told by a Central Asian worker that characterizes 'the only struggle that remains to the fate of a man who is free from exploitation, freed from the chains of slavery, a man who is creating communist society – the struggle with the elements, the victory over nature, and the subordination of natural forces to the creative genius of free man'.[5] Eisenstein also accepts the ways that the Stalinist struggle with nature was transforming the position of art:

> Here in the USSR the builders of real life have overtaken the creators of artistic values, and the creators of our country's and our epoch's art face an unprecedented problem – not to be above their time or ahead of it, for neither is possible here – but to attain the level and prove worthy of their time, their epoch, their nation.[6]

In the concluding words of the 'Postscriptum', Eisenstein declares that 'the nonindifference of our own human nature, as it participates in the great historical deed of the best part of humanity, is an indestructible pledge of the undying essence of the great arts that have used all of their means to glorify the majesty of Man'.[7] In these passages Eisenstein positions himself as a foot soldier – at times, even as a general – in the Stalinist campaign for dominance over the physical and cultural environment.

Even more sobering than Eisenstein's appeal to the Stalinist rhetoric of the 'struggle with nature' (*bor'ba s prirodoi*), because in its flagrant originality it is more difficult to discount as enforced ideological necessity, is the way that *Nonindifferent Nature* also embraces the atomic age that dawned as Eisenstein was at work on the book. In a brief essay from October 1945, included in the recent Russian edition as a preface to the second volume of *Nonindifferent Nature*, Eisenstein heralds the first atomic explosion not only as signalling the end of the war and the beginning of the United Nations, and thus the beginning of a new governance for global humanity, but also as the springboard for a qualitatively new understanding of nature and also of artistic production:

> The weapons of super-destruction must forever destroy our very tendency of destroying each other.
> Of course, this is mostly words.
> Good intentions.
> And often not even good [intentions], but simple hypocrisy.
> But the uttered word lives. It forms consciousness. It creates conceptions, born from the declared word.
> The conceptions seek paths for realization.
> Time passes, and conceptions break into reality.[8]

Referring back to the 'ore' that he mined in *The Battleship Potemkin* and continues to 'process', Eisenstein refers to his work thus far as a 'compendium of humanity's ambitions in the epoch leading up to the invention of the bomb'.[9] Like the bomb itself, what follows is by definition unpredictable:

> The revolutions [*perevoroty*] in consciousness and thought that will follow
> from the social shifts engendered by this [i.e. the bomb] are unaccountable.
> But one way or another, we will need to gather the accumulated experience of
> problems, through which we proceed to the solution of new ones, at the foot of
> the new cultures that will be engendered by this new era.
> The problems I touch upon here aspire to nothing more.
> But also to nothing less, if only because they are constantly transfixed by
> the image of Man, who in his works reflects what [ascends] in nakedly
> consummate forms out of the departing storm clouds of war, like the scarlet
> fiery balls from the *Qualm* [German for 'clouds of smoke'] over the ruined
> Hiroshima.[10]

This new science confirms Eisenstein's basic premise that the mutually conditioned state of human and world can be instantaneously transformed into a new quality through an image-based chain reaction. The violence of this breakthrough, the human and natural devastation it wreaks, and the political relations it implies, do not at this moment seem to worry Eisenstein.[11]

In its embrace of both Stalinism and the atomic age, Eisenstein's politics of nonindifference verges on political romanticism, in the conception of Carl Schmitt. Schmitt identified romanticism as a form of occasionalism: it dwells on antitheses in the phenomenal realm (subject/object, man/nature) only as 'occasions' for the manifestation of some third, absolute power (community, God), in which 'the concrete antithesis and heterogeneity disappear'.[12] Since romantics see the activity of this 'third' element in art, manifest conflicts become occasions merely for the experience or 'mood' of the individual artist, for his personal 'activity and productivity':[13] 'The assent of the romantic occasionalist weaves a web for itself that is not touched by the real external world, and thus it is not refuted either.'[14] As a consequence, the romantic excuses himself from elucidating causes and effecting ends in reality; action is reduced to the creative subject's assent or rejection of the occasion from outside.[15] Schmitt's critique highlights how Eisenstein's ecstatic posture – a posture of radical assent to event – threatens to become indistinguishable from political indifference, or at least ambivalence (which in Russian is the same word: *ravnodushie*, literally 'equanimity'). It is this threat of indifference (or, to extend Eisenstein's terminology, non-nonindifference) that I ultimately want to assess by working through the implications of Eisenstein's media ecology for his political self-fashioning under Stalin and under the new, scientific regime of the Cold War. I begin by examining the ethical, aesthetic and cinematic dimensions of Eisenstein's media ecology to gauge how cleanly it can be separated from the historical contexts within which it took form, before returning, in conclusion, to an assessment of its politics to determine whether nonindifference in Eisenstein's conception can ever make good on its promise of democratic governance to become a form of agency, and even of resistance.

Landscape

The symphonic and ecstatic interaction between human and world is exemplified for Eisenstein by several kinds of landscapes, including Chinese scroll painting, El Greco's oil paintings and Giovanni Battista Piranesi's etchings.

In *Nonindifferent Nature* Eisenstein approaches these landscapes from a range of theoretical standpoints, but most conspicuous is the way he treats them as 'eye music':[16]

> I am interested not only in the *emotionality* of landscape, but primarily in its *musicality*, that is to say, the variety of 'nonindifferent nature' when the emotional effect is achieved not only *by a selection of represented elements* of nature, but primarily and mainly by the *musical development and composition* of what is represented.[17]

As an example of musical landscape Eisenstein cites the winter landscapes of Wang Wei (699–759) for their rhythmic selection and distribution of natural elements: mountain, tree and water. Eisenstein goes so far as to see a kind of 'musical notation' in these scroll paintings, as if they are not viewed by spectator, but performed as a score, sweeping across the image from left to right. Specifically, Eisenstein insists on the landscape's seriality, namely, the artful repetition of elements across the long pictorial scroll, which the viewer performs sequentially in the act of viewing.

This serial quality is even more pronounced in the overtly synaesthetic landscapes of fin de siècle Lithuanian painter Mikolajos Čiurlionis (1875–1911), a favourite of the Russian symbolists, whose works often bore musical titles. Here, Eisenstein writes:

> Repeated motifs of pyramids and palms, repeating in various planes and various vertical and horizontal sections [*chleneniia*], provide a picture of the plastic excesses in the area of abstracted plastics that would have been reached by the compositional system of Chinese landscapes had their authors taken one step further and broken with the representational logic of their natural landscapes in the name of musicality.[18]

Čiurlionis stands for the heightened seriality of modernist landscapes, which discard any fidelity to figurative realism in the name of total eye-music, at the very border of abstraction.

But music alone proves inadequate for a comprehensive definition of the serial principle at the base of these landscapes. Drawing on Marcel Granet's *La Pensée chinoise* (1934), Eisenstein establishes a set of yin and yang dichotomies at work in landscape art: flow vs stillness; softness vs hardness; bared surfaces vs vegetation.[19] In Chinese landscapes, for instance, Eisenstein finds emotion distributed across the surface in a flow, out of which emerge forms, colours, volumes and other aesthetic characteristics. The first principle at the basis of this kind of landscape seriality is that of diffuseness.

By contrast, Eisenstein's treatment of Piranesi's seriality stresses the strategy of 'discontinuity and jumpiness',[20] or what here, to highlight connections to important aesthetic debates contemporary to Eisenstein, I will call disarticulation (*raz-raschlenenie*). He writes:

> The composition of architectural ensembles [...] is built on (perspectivally diminishing) repetitions of one and the same architectural motif, which are as it were ejected out of each other as they constantly grow smaller.
>
> As if stretching out in length, diminishing to the diameter of a section of a single telescope, these arches thrust into the depths, born of arches of a closer plane; these ascents of steps, which erupt upwards into these progressively diminishing new marches – all of this is thrust into the deep distance. Bridges generate new bridges. Columns – new columns. Vaults – new vaults. And so *ad infinitum*. As far as the eye can follow.
>
> [...] It is as if Piranesi is pushing the fugue of sequentially deepening volumes and spaces further into the depths, one link further each time, bound and sliced by staircases.
>
> Plane is torn from plane and is thrust into the depths with a system of explosions.[21]

Each layer in this deepening image seems to have its own perspective and scale, making the series into 'disjointed links of independent spaces, linked not for their unified perspectival continuity, but as sequential conflicts of spaces of various qualitative intensity and depth'.[22] Eisenstein finds an analogous telescopic seriality in Russian nesting dolls, in Gertrude Stein's 'a rose is a rose is a rose' and in many other sources.[23] Today we might call them fractals. Eisenstein identified them with the atomic chain reaction that in his day had just recently been christened fission (Rus. *rasshcheplenie*).

Eisenstein is eager to relate the two kinds of serial representation to one another. He compares Piranesi's disjointedly layered dungeons to Chinese (and Japanese) vertical landscapes. Both kinds of vertical landscape feature a kind of 'ascent' (or perhaps, given the mystical implications, 'ascension'). While Piranesi showcases 'dynamism, whirlwind, a mad tempo of immersion into the depths and inside', the Chinese landscape expresses 'peacefully solemn ascent to clear heights'.[24] Piranesi deepens, while the Chinese landscape flattens. Piranesi disarticulates; the Chinese landscape diffuses.

Relying on rather clichéd cultural associations, Eisenstein develops the two distinct principles of landscape seriality into corresponding postures of ecstasy: passionate and enlightened. Diffusion is expressive of pantheistic quietism, which is characteristic of the ecstatic contemplation of the East, which seeks dissolution of the self in the whole. The disarticulation typified by Piranesi and Stein, by contrast, expresses the 'explosiveness' typical of 'active' ecstasy, one of the deviations of 'western' ecstasy, in which the self and the whole seek mutual penetration.[25] As two basic principles of Eisenstein's media ecology, diffuseness and disarticulation merge aesthetic and ethical criteria into a single comprehensive dichotomy, as two modes of being in and of representing the world.

Landscape in motion

As suggestive as Eisenstein's analyses of painting and etching might be, static landscapes provide merely the starting point for the kinds of transformations that Eisenstein wants to see in the art of his day. 'Eye music' was present in silent film, indeed to a greater degree than in subsequent sound film, which has subordinated formal composition to narrative and dramatic development. 'Silent film', Eisenstein writes, 'wrote music for itself. Plastic [music]. And this was a distinctive "leaving of the self" [i.e. ecstasy], a leaving into another dimension. The plasticity of silent film had also to *resound*.'[26] Eisenstein now calls for an accelerated transition to a mode of audiovisual film in which sound and image will work together to produce a unified musical effect. In the meantime, however, Eisenstein fails to find any worthy examples of nonindifferent nature in sound film.

The reasons for film's failure become clearer in the course of Eisenstein's discussions of Émile Zola, whom Eisenstein calls 'the great teacher of visual music'[27] and whom he credits with a formative influence on the musical landscapes of Soviet silent cinema. In the section of *Method* entitled 'Diffuse Perception', Eisenstein compares Zola's contextualized vision to that of a spider, who 'perceives ("perceives", and doesn't "see") a fly "as a fly", i.e. as an object of consumption, as "a victim", only in the context of the spider web [...] The spider's affective-aggressive behavior takes place only when the fly is immersed into the appropriate special environment.'[28] Zola's spider-like, diffuse vision links him to gestalt psychology.[29] Eisenstein argues that Zola's characters are 'inseparable from the environment [*sreda*]' in which they are found, on which score he contrasts them with the characters of Balzac, who are '"extracted" from the contextual diffuseness of their environment'.[30]

> You can't perform such a 'separation' and reverse 'immersion' of the person in Zola's novels [as you can in Balzac]. With regard to the person and environment [*sreda*] they have the same kind of fluid immersion [*vplyvanie*] into each other as one finds in Gogol in regard to separate areas – 'sections' of form.³¹

Eisenstein links Zola's 'painting-like diffuseness' to his friendship with painter Paul Cézanne, which parallels Gogol's friendship with the painter Aleksandr Ivanov. Crucially, for my further argument below, Eisenstein acknowledges the 'limited nature of both authors' social conceptions' and admits the possibility that their diffuse 'method of writing' might reflect 'the picture of diffuseness of social ideas' in both writers. Perhaps unsurprisingly, given the quietistic overtones of diffuse ecstasy in Eisenstein's conception, Zola's (and Gogol's) diffuse nonindifference to nature is of a piece with political indifference.

Still, in *Nonindifferent Nature*, Eisenstein faults 'modern cinema stagings of Zola' for 'absolutely ignoring this striking and deeply musico-cinematic feature of the great Frenchman'.³² He singles out Jean Renoir's adaptation of Zola's *La bête humaine* (1938), in which

> we saw nothing of the striking symphony of railways, locomotives, rails, engine oil, coal, steam and traffic lights – all that is so exciting in the novel with its rhythms, tempos, color, texture and sound.
>
> Several grey train journeys, shot like a newsreel ... several inexpressive corners of train stations ... two or three empty platforms ... perhaps they respond to the scholastic notions of obsolete 'slogans' of the naturalist school, but they contain not a gram of the fire and murmur, passion and lyricism of the pages of the great magician, wizard and, most of all, poet Zola.³³

Any viewing of *La bête humaine* will suggest that Eisenstein may not have been entirely fair to Renoir; Eisenstein might have felt obliged to overstate his case to defend Zola against accusations of flat naturalism, for instance, at the hands of Georg Lukács, who markedly preferred the realism of Balzac and Tolstoy on the basis of their elaborately and elegantly structured narration of a world.

If Jean Renoir failed to produce an equivalent of Zola's diffuse world on screen, then equally culpable is Walt Disney, especially since animation provides 'absolutely limitless possibilities for the elements of the landscape – while being deformed – to live and pulsate in unison with the tone and emotions of the remaining action'.³⁴ In fact, Eisenstein previously had attributed a kind of ecstasy to Disney's animation. In *Method* Eisenstein speaks of Disney's world as 'a revolt against fragmentation',³⁵ a world dominated by what

Eisenstein calls 'co-possession', a concept that defines the comic: 'a picture that formally-mechanistically reproduces the dialectical proposition about the unity of opposites, in which "each individual" opposite exists at the same time in unity, which is possible only in process, in movement, in dynamism'.[36] This movement and dynamic unity of opposites are 'characteristics of a transfigured world, a world that has stepped out of itself',[37] specifically, a world in ecstasy or, to use Eisenstein's word, plasmaticity.

In *Nonindifferent Nature*, by contrast, Eisenstein critiques Disney for failing to extend this diffuse ecstasy to the landscapes. He singles out *Skeleton Dance* (1929), 'where the naturalistically-shaded dead background is especially ugly and unpleasant'.[38] This failure is particularly regrettable since, unlike live-action filmmakers who have to 'chase after effects of real nature and beg it on their knees for elements of symphonies of sunsets and sunrises', Disney is 'the complete master of the atmosphere and elements of his landscape'.[39] If in *Method* Eisenstein cites *Bambi* as an example of Disney's 'turn towards ecstasy – serious, eternal ecstasy',[40] at least in its narrative, then in *Nonindifferent Nature* he shreds *Bambi* for its failure to make good on this promise:

> [In animation] it is possible to convey the real *flow* and *factual* genesis of the landscape and the transitions from one element of the landscape to another not only by means of a dumb pan past it or by means of the camera simply tracking back from the crude naturalistic daub of the background [...] This is accompanied also by a complete conflict in the stylistic manner between the flat drawing of *supposed volume* in the figures and the *fake three-dimensionality of the setting*.[41]

Eisenstein finds this failure particularly lamentable given the early design sketches for *Bambi*, which show 'a complete harmony between the outlines of the character and the background, while the very manner of drawing both and the color resolutions closely held to' Eisenstein's preference.[42] (This observation is all the more remarkable that, in basing his judgement solely on the illustrations in Robert Feild's book *The Art of Walt Disney* [1942], Eisenstein could not have known that the author of these sketches was Chinese American artist Tyrus Wong.[43]) Eisenstein laments that *Bambi* turned away from Chinese landscape, which conveys 'an emotionally saturated "atmosphere"' by 'de-materializing' its elements, 'soft spots of color with diffuse edges' as 'hints' of emotion.[44]

Unexpectedly, then, diffuse ecstasy proves a safeguard against naturalism and, thus, a guarantor of true realism, but it remains unclear how diffuse ecstasy might look in the cinema, or whether it is even possible. Moreover, Eisenstein's remarks about Zola's (and Gogol's) 'social ideas' cast doubt on whether diffuse ecstasy can ever provide a sound basis for a political art, that is, an art that achieves or even projects social agency in the real world.

Eisenstein's landscapes

When he turns to identifying positive examples of nonindifferent nature in film, Eisenstein decides that what is needed is a synthesis of the two principles of ecstasy, diffuseness and disarticulation. The cinema, Eisenstein writes, is capable of achieving

> the correct combination of both tendencies: both *continuity* (characteristic of early thought) and articulation (by means of developed consciousness) [...] Only here – in the cinema – is there the possibility of realizing all the hopes and tendencies of other arts – without sacrificing *realism*.[45]

Tellingly, however, the sole cinematic examples of 'discontinuous' or 'disjointed' landscapes come from Eisenstein's own films, in which diffuse, atmospheric settings build a tension that is then marshalled for an explosive breakthrough into a new quality, invariably some variation on revolution. I will return below to the question of what Eisenstein means by articulation and how it relates to realism.

The 'founder of the genre of nonindifferent nature' is *The Battleship Potemkin* (1925), which begins with static, pale seascapes, which are succeeded by shots of the murdered sailor Vakulinchuk lying in state for baleful mourners.[46] These shots gradually build oppressive, high-contrast tension, only to break through into a flash of colourful revolt in the scene on the Odessa steps. As Eisenstein describes it:

> The action starts with 'nonindifferent nature' in its pure form and gradually passes to the mournful silence of the city dwellers who approach Vakulinchuk's corpse, where individual groups and individual close-ups combine along the very same musical principles as the beginning of the scene was constructed.[47]

The diffuse (or 'pure') ecstasy of the opening becomes distributed among individuals and groups, repeating (and articulating) itself in each serial repetition. Ecstatic revolt is generated not by the diffuse atmosphere of the mournful morning, but by the director's montage, which analytically divides the scene into components and builds up to a new quality. Recalling Eisenstein's description of Piranesi's etchings, here 'plane is torn from plane and is thrust into the depths with a system of explosions', culminating in revolt.

Similar dialectical progressions are found in Eisenstein's subsequent films. The transition of *The Old and the New* (1929) is formulated by its title, allegedly bestowed on the film by Stalin himself, but the key moment of dialectical transition comes with the sexual ecstasy suggested by the scene of Marfa Lapkina operating the milk separator. This ecstasy is represented not as diffusely atmospheric but as disjointedly dynamic. Similarly, the tripartite narrative of *The Ferghana Canal* follows a principle that Eisenstein identifies as telescopic, with the historical scale diminishing in size as the narrative proceeds through three phases of the development of Central Asia: Tamerlane, tsarism and collectivization. 'How to combine these three epochs, which stand centuries and decades apart, in a dynamic unity?', Eisenstein asks. 'The device here is the "triple self-expulsion", a double ecstasy, grouped in retrospective sequence.'[48] Thus ecstatic transition becomes not only a visual but also a narrative principle, which dictates the serial presentation of times and modes of historical ruptures, building to a crisis that resolves into revolution. As his final example Eisenstein highlights *Ivan the Terrible, Part II* for the 'gigantism' of its sets and their '"ecstatic" method of construction according to the scheme of ... a telescope',[49] which is amplified by the film's dialectical transition into full colour.

To understand how this principle of articulation relates to realism, it is useful to consider how Eisenstein's analysis deploys a vocabulary that had been developed in the course of early debates about socialist realism, specifically in Georg Lukács's readings of Zola. In his 1936 essay 'Narrate or Describe?' Lukács established an influential theory of literary realism and a schematic definition of its antipodes, formalism and naturalism. His analysis begins with the coincidence of two parallel scenes in contemporaneous novels named for anagrammatic heroines; namely, the horse races in Émile Zola's *Nana* (1880) and Lev Tolstoy's *Anna Karenina* (1873–8). Zola's 'brief monograph' about horse racing is a symbolic insert into his novel about the prostitute Nana, while Tolstoy makes Frou-Frou's fatal fall into a turning point for multiple plotlines centred on the adulteress Anna. Zola's horse race is an exterior appendage to the central story, while Tolstoy's is a fully integrated limb. Lukács concludes: 'In Zola the race is *described* from the standpoint of an observer; in Tolstoy it is *narrated* from the standpoint of a participant.'[50] Lukács judges *Nana* and *Anna Karenina* by their starkly different treatments of chance in the horse race scene: Tolstoy's horse race is an 'exceptional' event, but one that is so closely coordinated with the novel's major plotlines that Frou-Frou's fall reads like a death sentence pronounced on Anna herself.[51] Zola's horse race scene, by contrast, is self-contained and easily separable from the rest of the novel. For Lukács, Tolstoy exemplifies how truly realist artists 'das Zufällige in die Notwendigkeit aufheben' (elevate chance to the inevitable).[52] Lacking this air of inevitability, Zola's horse race is merely a naturalistic 'hypertrophy of real detail', as Zola himself describes his method.[53] For Lukács, Tolstoy's narration 'provides quite another mode of artistic inevitability [*künsterliche Notwendigkeit*] than is possible with Zola's exhaustive description'.[54] Lukács concludes: 'Narration establishes proportions [*gliedert*], description merely levels.'[55] The established English translation of this line obscures the central concept in Lukács's theory of realism – articulation (Ger. *Gliederung*; Rus. *raschlenenie*) – which does not merely establish proportions and arrange them into hierarchical order but also elevates chance to the status of necessity. True to its etymology in Latin and German (*artus* and *Glied* mean a joint, limb or member), articulation raises details to the status of members in a unified organism. A consistent opponent of seriality, Lukács is most interested in how narrative articulates isolated occurrences as events in history, understood in a Marxist vein; he argues that narrative articulation 'conforms to the laws of historical development and is determined by the action of social forces'.[56] Thus the 'artistic inevitability' of the narratively articulated event (*Ereignis*) coincides with historical necessity, intuited by the artist and transposed into fiction. Lukács even goes so far as to argue that history itself 'objectively articulates' (*gliedert*) the fictional world and the characters that the realist artist depicts.[57] Although both Eisenstein and Lukács see realism as a synthetic image, or *Gestalt*, Lukács defines this composite image primarily in terms of narrative articulation, whereas Eisenstein privileges the discontinuous repetition of its distinct sections. Whereas Lukács stresses the event as a fused concentration of historical totality, Eisenstein sees it as a series of explosions. Instead of cogent articulation (*raschlenenie*), Eisenstein proposes a principle of disarticulation (*raz-raschlenenie*, or *rasshcheplenie*).

It is clear from his examples that the dialectical transition or 'explosion' that Eisenstein is looking for occurs beyond the realm of ethical judgement, namely, beyond categories of good and evil, truth and falsehood, etc. Politically, the problem is no longer the 'diffuseness of social ideas', as it was with ecstatic writers such as Gogol, but precisely the way this diffuse tension resolves into distinct, decisive and sometimes violent actions: the rebellion on the Odessa steps, the orgasmic thrill of technology or the Terror. Eisenstein seems to value the ability of film to act as a trigger but doesn't seem particularly bothered about the gunman or the aim. Accordingly, the diffuse danger of political romanticism here resolves into the threat of aestheticized politics, moreover, a politics judged by the aesthetic attraction of a violent explosion.

The passages I have been quoting had already been written when the first atomic bomb exploded over Hiroshima, but Eisenstein immediately found in this event the crystallization of the dialectic he had been examining across so many mediums and epochs of art. He immediately reformulates his idea about seriality as a universal homology uniting nature at all scales, from atom to galaxy, like the golden proportion.[58] And he discovers a new term for what I have christened disarticulated seriality: fission, a process that unites montage with rocket science and cell division, as a dialectical leap that cuts through proportions, dimensions and temporalities in its explosive ecstasy. The clearest example is the ending of Gogol's *Dead Souls*, which demonstrates 'an ecstatic movement from quality to quality as the sequence of explosions of a rocket warhead, like the chain reaction of an atom bomb'.[59] In *Ivan the Terrible, Part II*, which was in production as the war reached its final crescendo, Eisenstein's 'nonindifferent nature' goes nuclear, and his politics of indifference become an outright celebration of violence.

Control

At the close of *Nonindifferent Nature*, Eisenstein seems to recognize the dangers of ceding wholly to ecstasy, so he tempers the ecstatic engine of action by introducing a mechanism of ideological control. Again, the source of this control is aesthetic and is best exemplified by Eisenstein's own films. Eisenstein recalls that in *Potemkin* he even wanted screenings to culminate in the bow of the ship physically breaking through the screen, but he held back. For all of its blatant symbolism, the eroticism of *The Old and the New* stops just short of being pornographic. *Ivan the Terrible*, Eisenstein admits, 'barely restrains itself on the border of slipping into a slow succession of dream visions, past the spectator's perception, following its own laws, its own moods, almost only for itself, in "plastic solipsism"'.[60] But still, even *Ivan* stands back from the precipice of outright terror.

Eisenstein formulates the principle of this restraint playfully, in terms derived from an advertising campaign for Gillette razors, which counsel 'a light half-turn that one must make in the opposite direction immediately after [the razor] is turned to the limit'.[61] Gillette's golden rule of light restraint illustrates how the artist translates his own agency over the medium into viewers' governance over their environment, by enabling viewers to hold back at the edge of full disclosure, and empowering them to finish the image in the real world. It is the image of a chain reaction that never quite trips into explosion, remaining a positive and productive transfer of potentiality. Gillette's rule explains how it was that Eisenstein thought he might be transferring control over his explosive image worlds to the nation, thereby making them a means of democratic governance, making them not a passive tool of terror but its cathartic defusing. By bringing the action to a head, but restraining it from tipping over into ecstasy, agency would be distributed among viewers.

This note of restraint is unlikely fully to quell the disquiet we might feel at Eisenstein's vision of distributed ecstasy in the immediate wake of Stalin's Terror. The governance that Eisenstein conveys might as well be tyrannical, as democratic. Mostly, he seems to celebrate life on the razor's edge of controlled nuclear reaction, or of a violence that is ready to be conscripted to any cause, for any reason, as likely erotic as despotic. In the final analysis Eisenstein's *Nonindifferent Nature* itself proves startlingly indifferent to the political environment that it absorbs and explodes. But perhaps this indifference renders it just as available as a resource for media ecology in our own very different time and place, for the making whole of an exploded world, as it was when the damage was still just beginning to be done.

Notes

1 Sergei M. Eizenshtein, *Neravnodushnaia priroda*, 2 vols (Moscow: Muzei kino/ Eizenshtein-tsentr, 2004–6 [*NP*]), vol. 2, 507. Future references will be given to this edition and where possible to the relevant page of the published English translation, which was made from a less complete previous edition of the Russian source texts: Sergei Eisenstein, *Nonindifferent Nature*, trans. Herbert Marshall (Cambridge: Cambridge University Press, 1987 [*NN*]).
2 *NP*, vol. 1, 614.
3 *NP*, vol. 2, 499.
4 See Karl Marx, *Capital*, vol. 1, ch. 7; in Robert C. Tucker, ed., *The Marx-Engels Reader*, 2nd edn (New York: W. W. Norton, 1978), 344.
5 *NP*, vol. 2, 185.
6 Ibid., 487.
7 Ibid., 507.
8 Ibid., 8.
9 Ibid., 9.
10 Ibid., 9, cf. 541.
11 In another introduction to *Nonindifferent Nature* from August 1946, after the onset of Cold War antagonism, Eisenstein strikes a very different tone about the atom

bomb, highlighting its place in Western militarism and the injustice of the American monopoly on atomic weapons: 'Having fallen into madness, drunk on the dangerous toy of the wonderworking destructiveness of atomic energy, humanity moves further and further away from the ideals of peace and unity, and closer and closer to summoning to life the image of militarism in even more monstrous forms, in even more terrifying forms, than the recently toppled idol of Fascist misanthropy and obscurantism' (*NP*, vol. 2, 41). Eisenstein proceeds to draw an analogy between the atomic technologies and the progress of cinema art, calling on his foreign counterparts, 'unlike those who jealously guard the "Udolfian secrets" of modernity – the atomic secrets – behind seven seals, constantly and stubbornly collaborating with each other, we resolve to contribute to the good of our common task everything that we learn from our surprising art [of the cinema]' (*NP*, vol. 1, 42).

12 Carl Schmitt, *Political Romanticism*, trans. Guy Oakes (Cambridge, MA: MIT Press, 1986), 89.
13 Ibid., 96.
14 Ibid., 103.
15 Ibid., 94.
16 *NP*, vol. 2, 315.
17 *NP*, vol. 2, 321; *NN*, 226, emphasis in the original.
18 *NP*, vol. 2, 335; *NN*, 234. Eisenstein's analysis is somewhat self-contradictory, in that 'sections' are considered as producing an effect that Eisenstein elsewhere describes as 'diffuse'. Eisenstein explicitly contrasts these categories with regard to Zola: 'Such diffuseness within a work is not at all obligatory. On the contrary, classical art, for example, presupposes precise divisions [*chleneniia*] and the clarity of each element's treatment'; Sergei M. Eizenshtein, *Metod*, ed. Naum Kleiman, 2 vols (Moscow: Muzei kino/Eizenshtein-tsentr, 2002), vol. 1, 333. It would seem, though, that there are various kinds of 'sectioning' (*chlenenie*), some of which are not tantamount to 'clarity' in the sense of classical art or 'articulation' (*raschlenenie*) in Lukács's theory of realism, on which see below. Cf. also Eisenstein's quotations from Curt Glaser's *Die Kunst Ostasiens* in *NP*, vol. 2, 333–4, 348.
19 *NP*, vol. 2, 336; *NN*, 236.
20 *NP*, 180.
21 *NP*, vol. 2, 179; *NP*, 147.
22 *NP*, vol. 2, 180.
23 *NP*, vol. 2, 264; *NN*, 266.
24 *NP*, vol. 2, 181.
25 Ibid., 183.
26 Ibid., 311, emphasis in the original.
27 Ibid., 506.
28 Eizenshtein, *Metod*, vol. 1, 329.

29 Ibid., 330.
30 Ibid., 328.
31 Ibid., 329.
32 *NP*, vol. 2, 506.
33 Ibid.
34 Ibid., 501.
35 Eizenshtein, *Metod*, vol. 2, 257.
36 Ibid., 290.
37 Ibid., 263.
38 *NP*, vol. 2, 501.
39 Ibid.
40 Eizenshtein, *Metod*, vol. 2, 295.
41 *NP*, vol. 2, 501, my emphasis.
42 Ibid., 502.
43 Daniel McDermon, 'How Bambi Got Its Look from 900-Year-Old Chinese Art', *The New York Times*, 5 January 2017, available online: https://www.nytimes.com/2017/01/05/arts/design/how-bambi-got-its-look-from-900-year-old-chinese-art.html (accessed 27 November 2020).Hannah Frank would have pointed out that Wong's anonymity was ensured not only by his ethnicity and profession but also by his role in the 1940 animators' strike against Disney.
44 *NP*, vol. 2, 501–2.
45 *NP*, vol. 2, 352, emphasis in the original.
46 *NP*, vol. 2, 354; *NN*, 253.
47 *NP*, vol. 2, 346; *NN*, 242.
48 *NP*, vol. 2, 185.
49 Ibid., 184.
50 Georg Lukács, 'Narrate or Describe?', *Writer and Critic and Other Essays*, ed. and trans. Arthur D. Kahn (New York: Grosset and Dunlap, 1971), 111, emphasis in the original; Georg Lukács, 'Erzählen oder Beschreiben? (Zur Diskussion über Naturalismus und Formalismus)', *Internationale Literatur*, no. 11 (1936): 102. For a fuller account of this essay in its original, Soviet context, see: Robert Bird, 'Articulations of (Socialist) Realism: Lukács, Platonov, Shklovskii', *e-flux journal*, no. 91 (May 2018), available online: https://www.e-flux.com/journal/91/199068/articulations-of-socialist-realism-lukcs-platonov-shklovsky/ (accessed 27 November 2020).
51 Lukács, 'Narrate or Describe?', 112, 125; Lukács, 'Erzählen oder Beschreiben?', 101, 111.
52 Lukács, 'Narrate or Describe?', 112; Lukács, 'Erzählen oder Beschreiben?', 102.
53 Lukács, 'Narrate or Describe?', 116; Lukács, 'Erzählen oder Beschreiben?', 104.
54 Lukács, 'Narrate or Describe?', 112; Lukács, 'Erzählen oder Beschreiben?', 102.

55 Lukács, 'Narrate or Describe?', 127; Lukács, 'Erzählen oder Beschreiben?', 112.
56 Lukács, 'Narrate or Describe?', 122; Lukács, 'Erzählen oder Beschreiben?', 108.
57 Ibid.
58 *NP*, vol. 2, 190.
59 Ibid., 191.
60 *NP*, vol. 2, 498.
61 *NN*, 385.

Part Two

Grundproblem, Regress, Sensuality

4

Regress–Progress in Proust, Surrealism and Joyce

Ilaria Aletto

This chapter analyses notes found in Sergei Eisenstein's copy of *Axel's Castle: A Study in the Imaginative Literature of 1870–1930* (1931), a collection of essays by the American journalist, critic and editor Edmund Wilson (1895–1972).[1] The nine sheets of pink and beige paper with writings in Russian, English and French were reflections on *Axel's Castle* written by the director in 1931 in Mexico and initially kept in the library of the Eisenstein Cabinet in Moscow.[2] When the condition of the Smolenskaya apartment was deemed detrimental to the preservation of these fragile materials, the notes were transferred to the Russian State Archive of Literature and Arts (RGALI) in 2014.[3]

First transcribed by the critic Annette Michelson but not released until they were published by Natalia Riabchikova, these annotations not only summarize the content of Wilson's book but also contain the ideas that Eisenstein started to develop while reading it.[4] Appropriating words, sentences and paragraphs from Wilson's essays which, as Naum Kleiman points out, he studied 'attentively',[5] gave Eisenstein the basis for his own observations on a source text that acquire meaning beyond it.

Before turning our attention to the notes, it is interesting to mention the still uncertain circumstances in which Eisenstein acquired Wilson's book. The fly-leaf bears the inscription: 'To Hart from Malcolm & Peggy Cowley. Bun [*sic*] Voyage.' As Riabchikova explains, this dedication reveals that the book was a gift to the poet Harold Hart Crane (1899–1932) from Malcolm Cowley (1898–1989) – a literary critic and editor of *The New Republic* from 1929, when Wilson left that position to devote himself to the writing of *Axel's Castle* – and his wife Peggy (née Baird, 1890–1970), a painter and activist in the women's suffrage movement.[6] Through the wordplay between the French 'bon' (good) and the English 'bun' (buttocks), the couple wishes Crane, who was known for his turbulent life, to enjoy a pleasantly transgressive journey. Although Crane and Eisenstein were in Mexico during the same years and had common acquaintances (such as the writer Anita Brenner (1905–1974) and the painter and muralist David Alfaro Siqueiros (1896–1974)), there is no evidence of any meeting between them. Riabchikova hypothesizes that Eisenstein had the intention of returning the book, because all underlining had been carefully erased and his notes on the text were not written in the margins of the pages but on separate paper. However, some graphic symbols drawn by the director are still visible in this copy.[7]

The creative process of Eisenstein's reading and writing that Anne Nesbet describes as 'flexible' and 'intensely plastic' draws on *Axel's Castle* with the same originality that distinguishes the director's theoretical thinking.[8] His notes develop through sudden intuitions, productive conjectures, crucial questions, seemingly final remarks then reconsiderations, in a tireless reshaping of assumptions previously expressed in different terms. Eisenstein's comments refer to writers mentioned in *Axel's Castle*, notably D. H. Lawrence, Honoré de Balzac, André Gide, Sherwood Anderson, Blaise Cendrars and Eugene O'Neill, in addition to Marcel Proust, James Joyce and Arthur Rimbaud, who are the subjects of three chapters of the book. But they also include others – such as the writer Theodore Dreiser, the painter Paul Gauguin, the lithographers and caricaturists Honoré Daumier and Paul Gavarni, and the dramatist Nikolai Evreinov – who are not cited by Wilson. As a result, the references in the essays in *Axel's Castle* are broadened through heterogeneous and, at times, unexpected connections that allow these notes to evoke numerous original suggestions.

This chapter investigates three such annotations, each introduced by a number indicating the page of Eisenstein's copy of *Axel's Castle* they pertain to. They have not been grouped according to a chronological principle but rather in accordance with themes, since they reflect Eisenstein's thoughts on the works of Proust and Joyce, which are often mentioned in his notes, as well as on surrealism. The sixth and the eleventh note – on the first and in the second page of Eisenstein's annotations, respectively – place Proust and Joyce in opposition:

> *Note n. 6*: '166. Hysteria of Proust 166. Neurotic asthma |Blindness of Joyce|'[9]
> *Note n. 11*: '204. Joyce & Proust quand-même [illegible] d'un trait
> As unpardonable as Daumier & Gavarni in one "Studio"isme'.[10]

The tenth – written on the first page of the notes – contains a reference to the surrealist movement:

> *Note n. 10*: '184. "Surrealism" of Proust's technique – describing the basis of automatic "psychoanalyt[ical]" writing [cf. 179].'[11]

To unpack these notes, it is helpful to refer to *Regress–Progress*, one of the preliminary drafts for *Method* that Eisenstein wrote in 1934 when debate on Joyce, Proust and other Western 'bourgeois' writers was at its height in the USSR. This draft is dated 17. IX. 1934, one month after the First All-Union Congress of Soviet Writers began on 8 August.[12] While references to Joyce, Proust and the surrealists can be found throughout Eisenstein's writings, it is in *Regress–Progress* that he brings them together in the same analysis. Here, he develops more extensively themes only touched on in his annotations in *Axel's Castle*.

In the introduction to *Regress–Progress*, he writes: 'Proust gives us a pure example of *regressive nostalgia*. Not only for method itself, but also because of a conscious tendency of method to affirm that precisely this [regressive nostalgia] should be its condition.'[13] Eisenstein then quotes an extract from an essay by Elena Galperina that was published in the same year, 1934, in the journal *Literaturnyi kritik*:

> Proust endeavoured to stage creative mechanisms (and prove the exceptional role of intuition) in the very imagery of the novel. A remarkable description of the creative process is provided in the first volume, *Swann's Way*, and the last volume, *Time Regained*, which itself represents a complete theory of art. For Proust, the creative act is always accidental. In the first volume, the passing and, more importantly, involuntary perception of taste, the taste of cake, immediately brings Marcel into a state of creative remembering. One memory is followed by another childhood memory which resurfaces from his unconscious ... All this is occurring without the will or awareness of the writer. He simply needs to surrender to his intuitive flow of thoughts in an entirely passive and involuntary way. And then, Proust assures us, such creative remembering will generate extraordinary happiness, supreme ecstasy, which will take over Marcel's grey and miserable everyday life.[14]

It is not surprising that Galperina's references to features of artistic creation – involuntary memory, the writer's role and ecstatic experience – captured Eisenstein's attention, while also providing him with an opportunity for criticism. In Eisenstein's view, all these elements exist in the 'healthiest' artistic process, 'especially when they are not rigidly limited to the stages of "childhood" but understood as *everything* that can be perceived even before childhood.'[15] Nonetheless, he argues that these aspects 'are not exhaustive' but only 'a part of the whole process. A substantial one. But only a part.'[16]

Describing 'this peculiar characteristic' through a schematization, Eisenstein locates Proust's *À la recherche du temps perdu* in an intermediate position between two lines: one heading 'towards the extreme limit of the absurd and the disintegration of method', the other 'towards the point of complete junction with what was consciously organised through an intentional elaboration'.[17] Thus, according to the director, in À la recherche these points of connection are not sufficiently structured or elaborated in an entirely conscious manner. Consequently, Eisenstein regards them as a vehicle for 'regressive nostalgia', a concept that is very different from what he considers genuine regression.

To understand how these two trends differ, it is worth emphasizing that the title of the draft, *Regress–Progress*, should be interpreted in light of Eisenstein's theoretical objectives in *Method*. According to his plan, the book would include an analysis of the different forms of art across the centuries' that 'seem to strive towards cinema', since 'a backward glance at these arts helps cinema to understand their method in many ways.'[18] In fact, one of the main purposes of *Method* was to study how primordial layers of sensory-emotional thinking manifested themselves throughout history and to analyse how they could be recovered in the present, on account of their intense effectiveness on the viewer:

> For art (the real thing) artificially returns the spectator to the primitive stage of sensuous thinking, to its norms and types, and this stage is in reality a stage of magical connection with nature.
> When you have achieved, *par exemple*, a synaesthetic merging of sound and image, you have subjected the viewer's perception to sensuous thinking conditions, where the synaesthetic perception is the only possible one – there is still no differentiation of perception.
> And you have the spectator 're-oriented', not to the norms of today's perception, but to the norms of a primordially sensuous one – he is 'returned' to the magical stage of sensation.[19]

Regress is one of the essential features of the *Grundproblem* of the artistic form, representing a downward and backward movement, able to effectively reactivate the profound layers of the pre-logical and primitive in the present. For Eisenstein, a genuine work of art simultaneously demonstrates regress and progress, an idea that he expounded in January 1935 at the All-Union Creative Conference of Soviet Filmworkers during a speech that outlined the new theories he intended to develop in *Method*.

The key issue addressed in the speech – and badly received by the conference participants – was the 'dialectic of works of art', which Eisenstein proposed is 'built upon a most curious dual-unity':

A progressive rise along the lines of the highest explicit steps of consciousness and a simultaneous penetration by means of the structure of the form into the layers of profoundest sensual thinking. The polar separation of these two lines of flow creates that remarkable tension of unity of form and content characteristic of true art-works. Apart from this there are no true art-works.[20]

This tension, aimed at unity and provoked by opposing tendencies (regress and progress, pre-logical and logical thinking), manifests itself in different fields: the 'inner speech' that preserves 'the forms of sensual, pre-logical thinking [...] among the peoples who have reached an adequate level of social and cultural development';[21] 'in paintings and drawings, where two colour spots and a flowing curve give a complete sensual replacement of the whole object';[22] in the beliefs of the Bororo Indians, who, in their totemic images maintain the 'simultaneous double existence of two completely different and separate and, none the less, real images' (that of a human being and, at the same time, of a kind of red parakeet).[23] This kind of 'dual-unity' is also reflected in the constructions of other indigenous people's speech (the Bushmen and the Klamath, studied by Wundt and Lévy-Bruhl, respectively), a 'long' and almost 'asyntactic series' of 'descriptive single images', which 'show how, the moment we have to pass from informative to realistic expressiveness, we inevitably pass over to structural laws corresponding to sensual thinking, which plays the dominant role in representations characteristic of early development'.[24] Moreover, according to Eisenstein we can find the same duality in the 'different versions of a writer's manuscript. Between the earlier drafts and the final version';[25] and in 'nature at large, or the history of mankind' as described by Engels – 'the picture of an endless entanglement of relations and reactions, permutations and combinations, in which nothing remains what, where, and as it was, but everything moves, changes, comes into being and passes away'.[26] Lastly, it is possible to observe this tendency in cases of 'psychic regression' after brain surgery, when 'phenomena of approach and return to forms characteristic of earlier levels' of thinking can occur.[27] As an example, Eisenstein mentions the case of a patient of the Moscow Neuro-Surgical Clinic, who 'immediately after the operation [...] showed his verbal definition of an object going gradually and clearly through the phases outlined above: [...] objects previously *named* were then identified by the *specific verbs indicating an act performed with the aid of the object*'.[28]

If regress and progress are the two extremes of the dialectical artistic process, then, according to Eisenstein, Proust's work is positioned in the middle, between the dissolution of form – typical of surrealism's fascination with automatic writing – and a conscious organization of narrative material. Only the latter technique can prevent a mere regressive nostalgia that would create a loss of reference to reality and diminish the novel's status as a genuine work of art. For these reasons, the dialectical process in À la recherche is only partially implemented.

However, one could ask which works of art would exemplify the intentional elaboration of artistic material that, as Eisenstein points out, 'because of its exterior features, to a myopic observer it may not appear to belong to a new quality'.[29] Entering the heated debate on Modernism, he opposes the prevailing critical tendency that relates Joyce's work to that of Proust and the surrealists, a connection that is made 'with the most unjustified superficiality'.[30] He writes:

> Based on the fact that all the three types of writers have paid attention to the inner flow of thoughts, emotions and consciousness, they are thrown into the same pile, without anyone care to understand what place each author occupies in relation to this 'flow'. Whether the author flounders in a muddy riverbed, like the Surrealists, or floats on Moses' willow basket of memories, or goes with the flow, like Proust. Or, if the author conducts a wise passage downstream and upstream, like Joyce, who has both a sly knowledge of how to reach the ford through the stream, and a firm, deeply objective point of observation from a solid rock of a river bank.[31]

The schematization previously mentioned – the 'two lines' illustrating the dynamics of the creative process – is amplified by Eisenstein through a series of evocative aquatic and nautical metaphors. The two extremities are occupied by surrealist writers representing the '*reductio ad absurdum* of the disintegration of artistic elements that interest us' and Joyce's works which exemplify 'an accomplished achievement revealing the right solution to the problem'.[32] Proust, as already noted, is placed in an intermediate position. For Eisenstein, any critic like Galperina, who brackets together Proust, Joyce and surrealism is a 'myopic observer' conducting a superficial analysis, and unable to see the structural differences underpinning new works of art.

Speaking of sight, it is worth considering the sixth annotation, which reads: '166. Hysteria of Proust. Neurotic asthma |Blindness of Joyce|.' On the page of *Axel's Castle* indicated by Eisenstein, Wilson affirms that, although the author and the protagonist are not identical, it is possible to detect the pathologies suffered by Proust (asthma and neurasthenia) in the hero of À la recherche.[33] Even though Joyce was not named here by Wilson, the topic of illness brings to Eisenstein's mind the Irish writer's near-blindness – an association of images to which he would return some years later.

In fact, Eisenstein's sixth annotation concisely expresses a concept that he would develop in *Regress–Progress*:

> The fact that in his old age Joyce is cast into the darkness of blindness. The fact that Proust spends the rest of his days in the darkness of his isolated cork-lined room (because of his asthma), never leaving it. The fact that Surrealists are blind, and that their skulls are made of two cork walls, which makes them even more isolated than the first two poor wretches, doesn't allow us to throw them all in one pile.[34]

It is well known that the director was not on good terms with the surrealists, or more exactly with André Breton's leadership of the group. On the occasion of his lecture at the Sorbonne in 1930, while admitting that 'on one level' they and he might seem to operate 'on common ground', Eisenstein highlighted their 'diametrically opposed' ways of working: 'The Surrealists seek to expose subconscious emotions while I seek to use them and play with them to provoke emotions.'[35] However, he felt close to the 'left (democratic) wing of Surrealists, which had broken away from the Breton faction'.[36] Ethnography and experimentation on the effectiveness of montage were interests shared by the circle of dissident surrealists, mainly represented by Georges Bataille, and Eisenstein, who in 1930 published thirty frames from *The General Line* in the French writer's journal *Documents*.[37]

In 1937, Eisenstein made another reference to surrealists in *Montage*, now contrasting them with Joyce, to whom a section of the chapter *Laocoön* is dedicated. Written at a delicate moment of his life and career, Eisenstein's attacks on bourgeois literature that open the text (Joyce is 'the last of the bourgeois writers' and *Ulysses* 'the final peak attained by bourgeois literature'[38]) do not disguise his obvious admiration for the Irish author, or hinder his astute interpretation of *Ulysses* ('All this is … a miniature encyclopaedia of all the forms and genres of literary composition, which arise from the complex of chapters that go to make up the image of "Literature"'[39]). Bringing surrealism into his analysis, Eisenstein insists that Joyce's method and that of surrealists are 'completely different': surrealist 'automatic writing' is 'a type of purposeless meditation', while Joyce aims at 'unity and wholeness'.[40]

Later, between 1942 and 1946, in his memoirs Eisenstein returned again to Proust: 'I have never enjoyed Marcel Proust. And that has nothing to do with snobbery – deliberately ignoring the terribly fashionable interest in Proust',[41] and to the surrealists: 'My relations with this group of the Surrealists, which centred on their leader, André Breton, remained quite cool.'[42] Eisenstein also recalled how he met Joyce, stressing his uneasiness when he first noticed Joyce's failing vision. While struck by 'how blind this man' was, Eisenstein argued that Joyce's 'outer' blindness was 'a condition for his "inner" perspicacity when describing "inner life" in *Ulysses* and *A Portrait of the Artist as a Young Man*.'[43]

Infirmity was also a key issue in Eisenstein's tenth annotation: '184. "Surrealism" of Proust's technique in describing the basis of automatic "psychoanalyt[ical]" writing.' In his essay on *À la recherche*, Wilson connected features of Proust's artistic method to the writer's illness, stating: 'The book itself had been undertaken, as he [Proust] says, "on the eve of death", at least late in life [...] The penalties for this were long sentences and tiresome repetitious analyses that make Proust so exasperating to read.'[44] Wilson's verdict in effect describes the surrealist aspects of Proust's technique that in *Regress–Progress* Eisenstein saw as lacking 'intentional elaboration' in the 'irrational stream' of thought, which are fundamental to genuinely dialectical works of art. However, despite the filmmaker's harsh criticism of surrealist writers, in Kleiman's view it is appropriate to compare Eisenstein's drawings with both the surrealists 'spontaneous automatic writings' and 'the bold experiments of his beloved Joyce', who 'contrived to interweave records of everyday life with mythological reminiscences and the reconstruction of interior monologue'.[45]

The eleventh annotation – '204. Joyce & Proust *quand-même* [illegible] *d'un trait*. As unpardonable as Daumier & Gavarni in one "Studio"isme' – provides further evidence of key ideas that Eisenstein would develop some years later. The comparison between the 'unpardonable' tendency to group Joyce, Proust and the surrealists without any distinction, and the attitude of those who include Honoré Daumier (1808–79), and the lithographer and caricaturist Paul Gavarni (1804–66) in the same artistic school resurfaces in *Regress–Progress*. Maintaining that Daumier is superior to Gavarni,[46] Eisenstein defines the linking of the two artists as 'purely mechanical', arising from 'the same kind' of association that is made when mentioning the Japanese Ukiyo-e painters Tōshūsai Sharaku (active 1794–5) and Katsushika Hokusai (1760–1849):

> Sharaku is the Daumier of the Japanese, similarly far from their Gavarni-Utamaro (or Hiroshige?). Not to mention Hokusai, who has nothing more in common with Sharaku than the fact that their name can be found in the same monograph, just as with the French illustrators, who both drew with a lithographic pencil on a stone.[47]

Eisenstein's notes on *Axel's Castle*, extract themes from the book and 'enrich' them with personal evaluations and original associations. They essentially point away from Wilson's essays, revealing a writing practice that, as Ada Ackerman has argued, fosters systematic recourse 'to the digression and the association of ideas – a strategy of suspension and short-circuiting of the text'.[48] In the case of the annotations in Wilson's book, this tension between 'suspension' and 'short-circuiting' can be seen constantly renewing itself, as it recurs in different writings. These short but incisive notes allow us to glimpse the inner mechanics of Eisenstein's writing, demonstrating how a few brief thoughts could serve as a blueprint to be greatly expanded in *Regress–Progress* as a fundamental aspect of *Method*.

Notes

1   Wilson's first work of literary criticism, *Axel's Castle* traces the origins and the development of the ideals and method of symbolism in the writings of some of the author's contemporary and most representative novelists and poets: W. B. Yeats, Paul Valéry, T. S. Eliot, Marcel Proust, James Joyce, Gertrude Stein and Arthur Rimbaud. See Edmund Wilson, 'Symbolism', in *Axel's Castle: A Study in the Imaginative Literature of 1870–1930* (New York: Charles Scribner's Sons, 1931), 1–25.

2   The second of the nine sheets of paper is dated '21.XII.31' in red crayon. In December 1931, Eisenstein spent Christmas holidays at the Hacienda Tetlapayac. See Oksana Bulgakowa, *Sergei Eisenstein: A Biography*, trans. A. Dwyer (Berlin: PotemkinPress, 2001), 138–9.

3   The annotations, which were being catalogued at the time of this writing, will be available in the new inventory n. 4 of the Eisenstein fund (n. 1923) in RGALI. I would like to thank Naum Kleiman and Vera Rumiantseva-Kleiman, who generously provided me with this and other crucial information about Eisenstein's notes as well as invaluable suggestions about my research.

4   See 'Eisenstein-Uilson: dialog na poliach knigi' [Eisenstein-Wilson: Dialogue in the margins of a book], *Kinovedcheskie zapiski* [Cinema Studies Notes] 87 (2008): 30–53. My sincere gratitude goes to Natalia Riabchikova, who kindly made a copy of her essays on Eisenstein and Wilson available to me.

5   Naum Kleiman, '"Gospodinu Eizenshteinu, kotoryi mne simpatichen …". Ob avtografach na knigach iz biblioteki S. M. Eizenshteina' ['"To Mr. Eisenstein, who I like … ". On the autographs in the books of the library of S. M. Eisenstein'], *Kinovedcheskie zapiski* 85 (2007): 79–95.

6   See Natalia Riabchikova, 'Sergei Eizenshtein and Edmund Uilson: istoriia odnogo dialoga' [Sergei Eisenstein and Edmund Wilson: Story of a dialogue], *Kinovedcheskie zapiski* 85 (2007): 53–65.

7 By kind permission of Naum Kleiman, I had the opportunity to work at Eisenstein's Cabinet on the annotations for my doctoral thesis, which examines the influence of Joyce's works – in particular, *Ulysses* – on Eisenstein's aesthetics (Ilaria Aletto, "'L'ürphanomen del cinema … fuori dai confini del cinema": James Joyce e Sergej Ejzenštejn' [The cinematic ürphanomen … outside cinema: James Joyce and Sergei Ejzenštejn], PhD thesis, Roma Tre University, Rome, 2017). Using the autograph materials I compared the original version of the director's notes to the Russian transcription published by Natalia Riabchikova ('Eisenstein-Uilson: dialog na poliach knigi', *Kinovedcheskie zapiski* 87 [2008]: 30–53), which omits some numbers of the pages of *Axel's Castle* and punctuation marks noted down by the director.

8 Anne Nesbet, *Savage Junctures: Sergei Eisenstein and the Shape of Thinking* (London: I.B.Tauris, 2007), 1.

9 In English in the original. Here and further in the texts of the two other annotations, quotation marks, capital letters and graphic symbols are shown as they were used by Eisenstein.

10 In French and English in the original text.

11 This annotation is mainly written in Russian: '«Surrealism» техники Prousta – выписыват[ь] основы «психоаналит[ического]» автомати[ческого] письма' (cf. 179).

12 See Sergei Eisenstein, *Regress–Progress*, in Eisenstein, *Metod, tom 2, Tainy masterov* [Method, vol. 2, The secrets of the masters], ed. N. I. Kleiman (Moscow: Muzei kino/Eizenshtein-tsentr, 2002), 352–8.

13 Eisenstein, *Regress–Progress*, 352. Here and henceforth, the provided translations of extracts from *Regress–Progress* is my own with Eisenstein's italics reproduced from the original.

14 Ibid., 352.

15 Ibid., Eisenstein's italics, 352.

16 Ibid., 352.

17 Ibid., 352.

18 Sergei Eisenstein, *Krupnym planom (vmesto predisloviia)* [On the close-up (in place of a foreword)], in Sergei M. Eisenstein, *Metod, tom 1*, ed. N. I. Kleiman (Moscow: Muzei kino/Eizenshtein-tsentr, 2002), 38.

19 Sergei Eisenstein, *Magiia iskusstva* [The magic of art], in Eisenstein, *Metod, tom 1*, p. 46n (trans.Julia Vassilieva, in *Culture as organization in early soviet thought: Bogdanov, Eisenstein, and the Proletkult*, ed. Pia Tikka [Aalto: Crucible], available online: http://crucible.org.aalto.fi/spherical/index.php [accessed 28 November 2020]).

20 Sergei Eisenstein, 'Film Form: New Problems', in *Film Form: Essays in Film Theory*, ed. and trans. J. Leyda (New York: Harvest, 1977), 144–5.

21 Ibid., 131.

22 Ibid., 133–4.

23 Ibid., 136.
24 Ibid., 138.
25 Ibid.
26 Ibid., 140.
27 Ibid., 140–1.
28 Ibid., 141, italics in original translation.
29 Eisenstein, *Regress–Progress*, 352.
30 Ibid., 352.
31 Ibid., 353.
32 Ibid., 353.
33 'We begin to feel less the pathos of the characters than the author's appetite for making them miserable. And we realize that the atrocious cruelty which dominates Proust's world, in the behavior of the people in the social scenes no less than in the relations of the lovers, is the hysterical sadistic complement to the hero's hysterical masochistic passivity [...] The hero of *À la Recherche du Temps Perdu* is not the same person as the author – the man who is supposed to be telling the story represents only specially selected aspects of the man who is actually composing the novel, and he is kept strictly within certain limits [...] Proust's chronic asthma developed, like that of his hero, very early; and [...] Proust himself was aware from the beginning of the neurotic character of his ailment [...] Proust had evidently come to use his illness as a pretext for escaping the ordinary contacts with the world', Edmund Wilson, 'Marcel Proust', in *Axel's Castle: A Study in the Imaginative Literature of 1870–1930* (New York: Charles Scribner's Sons, 1931), 166–7.
34 Eisenstein, *Regress–Progress*, 353.
35 Sergei Eisenstein, 'The Principles of the New Russian Cinema', in *Selected Works. Volume I: Writings, 1922–1934*, ed. and trans. Richard Taylor (London: BFI Publishing, 1988), 201–2.
36 Sergei Eisenstein, 'Épopée', in *Beyond the Stars: The Memoirs of Sergei Eisenstein. Part I: The Boy from Riga*, ed. Richard Taylor, trans. William Powell (London: Seagull Books, 2018), 231.
37 On the relationship between Eisenstein and the branch of dissident surrealists, see Antonio Somaini, 'Metod: *le vie del regresso*' [*Metod*: Paths of regression], in Somaini, *Ejzenštejn: Il cinema, le arti, il montaggio* [Eisenstein: The cinema, the arts and the montage] (Turin: Einaudi, 2011), 219–228; and Marie Rebecchi, 'The Unlimited Montage: Eisenstein's Anthropological Gaze', in *Sergei Eisenstein and the Anthropology of Rhythm*, ed. Marie Rebecchi and Elena Vogman (Rome: NERO, 2017), 21–34.
38 Sergei Eisenstein, 'Laocoön', *Selected Works. Volume II: Towards a Theory of Montage*, ed. Michael Glenny and Richard Taylor (London: BFI Publishing, 1991), 193.
39 Ibid., 196.

40 Ibid., 197.
41 Eisenstein, 'Foreword', in *Beyond the Stars: The Memoirs of Sergei Eisenstein. Part I: The Boy from Riga*, ed. Richard Taylor, trans. William Powell (London: Seagull Books, 2018), 5.
42 Eisenstein, 'Épopée', 268.
43 Sergei Eisenstein, 'Vol'ter'ianskim nedugom … ' [Voltairian disease …], *Izbrannye proizvedeniia v 6-ti tomach* [Selected works in 6 volumes], ed. Pera Atasheva (Moscow: Iskusstvo, 1964), vol. 1, 486.
44 Wilson, 'Marcel Proust', 184.
45 Naum Kleiman, *Eisenstein on Paper: Graphic Works by the Master of Film* (London: Thames & Hudson, 2017), 21.
46 'Daumier Was [*sic*] a genius. His greatest pictures can be hung beside works from art's greatest epochs. But Gavarni was no fuore [*sic*] than an elegant *boulevardier* of a lithographer, for all that the Goncourts sang their friend's praises' (Eisenstein, 'Foreword', 5).
47 Eisenstein, *Regress–Progress*, 352–3.
48 Ada Ackerman, *Eisenstein et Daumier: des affinités électives* (Paris: Arman Colin, 2013), 16.

5

'The Old IT': Eisenstein and D. H. Lawrence

Ian Christie

Eisenstein's early immersion in classic English literature is well known. He was familiar from youth with Charles Dickens, Rudyard Kipling, Lewis Carroll, G. K. Chesterton and the Sherlock Holmes stories. No doubt he also knew at least the narratives of Shakespeare's plays, long a cornerstone of Russian culture and an integral part of the bourgeois culture in which he grew up. Later he would discover Shakespeare's near-contemporaries Ben Jonson and John Webster, and perhaps typically express a preference for these, while also becoming familiar with advanced Shakespeare criticism.[1] Among contemporary English writers, he knew George Bernard Shaw from having designed a 1922 Moscow production of *Heartbreak House*, originally described as 'a fantasia in the Russian manner', before meeting the author on his visit to England in 1929.[2] However, he was more excited by meeting James Joyce in Paris during the same trip, after the banning of *Ulysses* in Britain and America had created one of the great post-war cultural controversies. Joyce he found 'so real (and uniquely real) ... that all other names "had no appeal".[3] Controversy was undoubtedly attractive to Eisenstein, as was the access to celebrity that his own fame provided after *The Battleship Potemkin*. The passage quoted above continues: 'After Joyce came Lawrence, on the basis of the censor's banning first *Ulysses* and then *Lady Chatterley's Lover*.'

Among all Eisenstein's literary enthusiasms, D. H. Lawrence is perhaps the most surprising, and also the least remarked upon before the 1990s. In her early biography, Marie Seton quoted verbatim a 1932 letter to the editor of *Close Up*, Kenneth Macpherson, in which Eisenstein listed the six works by Lawrence that he had, while asking for five more and for 'the best things written *about* Lawrence'.[4] But she did not explore this evident fascination, continuing instead to stress Eisenstein's interest in Frazer's *Golden Bough* and the parallel with his '*alter ego* Da Vinci', which formed the leitmotif of her biography. There are single references to Lawrence in Yon Barna's 1973 biography and in Herbert Marshall's 1985 edition of the *Memoirs*, both lacking any further comments.[5]

Not until Ronald Bergan's 1997 biography, which was able to make extensive use of Richard Taylor's new edition of the *Memoirs* (1995), was Eisenstein's fascination with Lawrence fully acknowledged.[6] And since the publication of his unfinished *Method*, with its profusion of references to Lawrence, scoping it more fully becomes both possible and essential.[7]

The 1932 letter to Macpherson is evidence of a serious interest that would have been unusual anywhere at this time, showing that Eisenstein had already assembled a library of Lawrence's writings and was aware of the first books to be published about the writer.[8] My contention is that this attraction may well be the most significant of all his 'elective affinities', considering that it cut across obvious political differences, and stimulated not only extensive theoretical and even critical writing by Eisenstein, but also drawings directly inspired by Lawrence's fiction that have only been seen and discussed in recent years.[9] And among the more 'respectable' figures with whom Eisenstein has been associated – Da Vinci, Pushkin, Luria – Lawrence remains still controversial.[10]

At the time of his death in 1930, Lawrence was perhaps a uniquely scandalous figure among twentieth-century writers, and would remain so for decades. Not only was his *Lady Chatterley's Lover* (1928) banned from unexpurgated publication in Britain until 1960, when a landmark trial freed it from the stigma of obscenity, but both of his previous novels, *The Rainbow* (1915) and *Women in Love* (1920), were also banned in Britain.[11] Eisenstein was clearly aware of the author's notoriety when he reached western Europe during 1929 – indeed this may have been what first attracted him to Lawrence, given his interest in sexual scandal.[12]

Eisenstein recalled meeting the 'still young' André Malraux in Paris, when Malraux was writing a preface to the French translation of *Lady Chatterley*, after the original had been privately printed in Italy in 1928.[13] Perhaps symptomatically, in view of the work's notoriety, Eisenstein gave two contradictory accounts of when he read the 'original' *Lady Chatterley*, dating this to either before or after his visit to America and Mexico. According to one chapter of the *Memoirs*, 'I read it as I rested after my ordeals in Paris on the deck of the *Europa* … crossing the Atlantic to America.'[14] But in another chapter he wrote

> I turned a deaf ear to it.
> I bought *Lady Chatterley* on board the SS Europe on my way to America.
> Not to read it, but out of snobbery.
> It was a long time before I read it.
> And it was not on board a ship. Nor in the USA. Not even straight away in Moscow.[15]

In the later account, Eisenstein described how he had initially 'resisted', before being 'bowled over', presumably by *Lady Chatterley*, and then developing a 'mad attraction'. This led him to order *Women in Love* (1920), already banned in Britain throughout the 1920s, and *The Plumed Serpent*, along with essays and travel writings.[16] In his second account, Eisenstein added that he bought an American psychologist Joseph Collins's book, *The Doctor Looks at Literature*, for its chapter on Joyce, only to discover it contained 'a malicious attack on Lawrence'.[17]

Why these two accounts? The narrative of Eisenstein's growing infatuation with Lawrence, threaded through the *Memoirs*, is written to suggest a process of seduction – as if he has reluctantly been drawn to this controversial figure. Despite 'stubborn' resistance, he falls helplessly under the writer's spell, seemingly to adopt Lawrence in place of the more reputable avant-garde figure of Joyce, and defending him against charges of obscenity by describing a poor Russian translation of *Lady Chatterley* as 'sheer filth and pornography', compared with the original 'highly poetic work by one of the best writers in English'.[18] The 'malicious attack' deplored by Eisenstein was a diagnosis by the above-mentioned Joseph Collins, that Lawrence was a repressed homosexual, based on his earlier writings. This, of course, was a sensitive subject for Eisenstein, the complexity of which can be fully understood only in the context of *Method* and Eisenstein's idiosyncratic approach to the issue that he termed 'bi-sex'.[19] This complexity is betrayed in Eisenstein's letter to Macpherson (himself homosexual) requesting 'psychoanalytic things as well', but adding that 'in the case of Lawrence they must be very vulgar and flat and the case as such is much more profound and interesting'.[20]

Working with Lawrence

The last of Lawrence's public clashes with British prurience took place near the end of his life in June 1929, and arose not from his writing but from the interest in painting that he developed in his final years. An exhibition of his paintings at a small gallery in central London attracted twelve thousand visitors before it was raided by the police after a visitor's complaint, and thirteen works were confiscated on grounds of obscenity. The resulting trial ordered that the pictures should never again be exhibited in Britain.[21] Eisenstein could hardly have been unaware of this latest scandal surrounding the writer when he recalled how Ivor Montagu had 'valiantly' tried to introduce him to Lawrence in London just five months after the trial.[22]

Such a meeting would have been unlikely, since Lawrence had not visited England since 1926, and very likely contentious. If there had been any direct contact, Eisenstein could hardly have failed to discover Lawrence's hostility to cinema, and indeed to the legacy of the Bolshevik Revolution. Unlike Shaw, Joyce and other writers he met, who were impressed at least by the impact of Eisenstein's films (which they had yet to see), Lawrence had attacked the 'mechanistic' nature of cinema in his novel *The Lost Girl* (1920). Here, the effect of 'the pictures' on audiences in a Midlands town is deplored: 'they cost the audience nothing, no feeling of the heart, no appreciation of the spirit'.[23] Later, he would broaden his attack to brand film along with all other 'popular amusements' as 'obscene', existing 'to provoke masturbation'.[24]

Given his fundamental antipathy to cinema, and indeed his peripatetic travels in remote regions, it seems unlikely that Lawrence had seen many films. His few written references are essentially generic: 'a lovely woman must look like Lilian Gish, a handsome man must look like Rudolph Valentino'.[25] *Aaron's Rod* (1921) included a withering denunciation that implies he had seen some Arctic exploration films and perhaps the official British war film *The Battle of the Somme* (1919):

> Alas, the cinema has taken our breath away so often, investing us in all the splendors of the splendidest American millionaire, or all the heroics and marvels of the Somme or the North Pole, that life has now no magnate richer than we, no hero nobler than we have seen, on the film. Connu! Connu! Everything life has to offer is known to us, couldn't be known better, from the film.[26]

Might he have taken a different view if he had seen anything by Eisenstein? In a review of Dos Passos's *Manhattan Transfer*, he invoked the idea of 'a movie picture with an intricacy of different stories and no close-ups and no writing in between', apparently without disapproval, which might suggest his potential openness to a montage-based cinema.[27] But this can only be speculation, while what Eisenstein discovered in Lawrence's writings during the 1930s and 1940s he interpreted as support for his own developing preoccupation with 'prelogical sensuous thought', and guidance towards like-minded sources.[28]

An entry in the 'Disney' section of *Method*, written while recuperating from a collapse during the production of *Ivan*, recorded this associative process in a diaristic format:

> *Lawrence, St Mawr.*
> As usual. As soon as I read something new, breathless with delight, it turns out that it fits *perfectly* somewhere into my research material. It's understandable.

The things that are thrilling for me tend to be of a particular nature. And they are also the things that interest me from a research perspective. It's pleasant, however, that this kind of stuff usually comes to me 'par l'amour'. That gives it a certain suavity, vigour, emphasis instead of academic dryness. Something youthful, not to say boyish!

Anyhow, I'm intoxicated by D. H. Lawrence's St. Mawr.[29]

St Mawr belongs to a period in the early 1920s when Lawrence discovered the short novel or novella form, and which also saw him preoccupied by the theme of male supremacy and female passivity, often described as his 'leadership' period.[30] This reached its climax in the full-scale novel set in Mexico: *The Plumed Serpent* (1925).[31] The novella that so entranced Eisenstein was written between two drafts of the Mexican novel, and is aptly summarized by Keith Sagar as 'about a woman who does *not* meet a man capable of transforming her life', but who nevertheless achieves this 'with the help of first a horse [St Mawr] and then a landscape'.[32]

For Eisenstein, Lawrence's invocation of a stallion 'looming like some god out of the darkness' to awaken his heroine to the triviality of her life was equivalent to *St Mawr*: 'Lawrence's totemic animal epic ... [sticking] its head into my Disney', as he struggled to probe the roots of his fascination with Disney's 'humanised animal' figures.

> St Mawr jumps like a fish, sits, spreads his legs wide like a lizard. Horses glide over the fields like playful butterflies [...] this is reminiscent of Disney's *Merbabies* with its metamorphosis of animals into other animals. [...] The collapse of worlds through the eyes of St Mawr and the countless stages of the gradual domestication of animals is an intersection with the Disney theme – the humanisation of animals ... and the domestication of men according to Lawrence.[33]

What follows in this intensive period of work on the projected *Method* text, of which 'Disney' would form a part, might be described as *using* Lawrence's tale to structure Eisenstein's exploration of the 'animal theme', not only in Disney's animation but also in his own work, and in a diverse range of other writers, including Tolstoy, Gogol, Lewis Carroll, Poe and Lautréamont. Indeed, the sensuality of Lawrence, not only in *St Mawr* but in other stories mentioned here, also prompted Eisenstein to recall his own erotic initiation with Agniia Nikolaevna Kasatkina ('the first I slept with', in English in the original) when he was working at the Proletkult Theatre.[34] Although he observed that 'Lawrence's entire opus is *animalisé*', the analysis of *St Mawr* is remarkably detailed and rigorous, with many passages transcribed, and far-reaching questions raised.

Why is the horse named St Mawr?[35] Because, Eisenstein suggests, 'Lawrence seems to identify all things manly and sensuous with Moors',[36] citing Paulina's lover in 'The Lonely Lady' (Mawro) and even exploring the possibility that the other meaning of 'moor' – 'an area overgrown with heather' – might be relevant to 'a background in primitive passions' in such works as Lawrence's 'England, My England', and Emily Brontë's classic Romantic novel *Wuthering Heights* (1847).

Figure 5.1 D. H. Lawrence's *Studies in Classic American Literature*, first published in the United States in 1923, had a lasting influence on literary scholarship, and on Eisenstein when he discovered it in the 1930s.

The parallels between men and animals in Lawrence took Eisenstein far beyond his attempt to explore the roots of what fascinated him in Disney, originally chosen 'as the purest specimen of the inviolably spontaneous element present in all art, here displayed in its chemically distilled form'.[37] Specifically, he offered a penetrating analysis of *St Mawr*, identifying as its 'fundamental motif ... the theme of Samson and Delilah', with the horse seeming to Lou nobler than any man she has seen. But probably the most important discovery that Eisenstein owed to Lawrence was from the latter's *Studies in Classic American Literature* (1924) (see Figure 5.1). This 'strange, brilliant and maddening' book, as a modern reviewer described it, was a pioneering account of American literature which effectively helped create a new canon, at a time when that field was dominated by Oliver Wendell Holmes, John Greenleaf Whittier 'and other Boston, Concord, and Cambridge worthies'.[38] Lawrence's subjects ranged from Benjamin Franklin, Fenimore Cooper and the largely forgotten Hector St John de Crevecoeur, to Hawthorne, Melville and Whitman. The tone is far from detached or even-handed: it is often outspokenly critical, ridiculing some of America's sacred names, such as Franklin, while giving high praise to Poe, Melville and Whitman, who at this time still lacked critical recognition.[39]

Eisenstein dramatized his discovery of Lawrence's *Studies* while searching for a text by Melville in the Moscow Library of Foreign Literature in December 1944, a year after his epiphany with *St Mawr*.

> I ploughed through all the chapters on Melville and was left *bouche bée* [aghast]
> It was so close to the themes of my *Grundproblem* of Melville *vu par* Lawrence – utterly astounding.[40]

Grundproblem was Eisenstein's alternative title for, and the central 'research question' of, *Method*. The *Grundproblem*, or the major problem of art theory and practice, as Eisenstein saw it, was posed by a split between modern and archaic, rational and emotional, progressive and regressive in the contemporary psyche, and the challenge to mobilize and integrate these opposing poles in the process of artistic creation and reception.

Eisenstein had started to work on *Method* while in Mexico in 1932. It has been widely assumed, following his own narrativization in the *Memoirs*, that the impetus for this ambitious project came from discovering Lucien Lévy-Bruhl's *La mentalité primitive* and James Frazer's *The Golden Bough*, both of which he acquired on the journey across Europe and America that would eventually bring him to Mexico. However, as Julia Vassilieva observes, he would have already known of Lévy-Bruhl from Alexander Luria's and Lev Vygotsky's account of his work in their book *Ape. Primitive. Child*, which offered a comprehensive account of anthropological research up to the late 1920s. Although this was not published until 1930, Eisenstein must have been introduced to the earlier explosion of anthropological thought by the pair who had become his mentors in matters related to psychology and other human sciences since the mid-1920s.[41]

If Eisenstein was already aware of Lévy-Bruhl's concept of the 'pre-logical', as a distinguishing feature of what was then commonly termed 'primitive thought', and fascinated by Frazer's massive compilation of myths describing fertility cults, he was further exposed to current anthropological thinking by Anita Brenner's *Idols Behind Altars* (1929), and by discussions with Brenner while encountering the reality of Mexican life during his travels and filming of *Que Viva México!* in 1931, which, like *Method*, was ultimately left unfinished. Masha Salazkina has explored at length the extent to which Eisenstein made use of anthropological perspectives, without sharing their authors' scientific goals, to structure a view of Mexican folklore that he believed could be politically and artistically progressive.[42] Like several of his Mexican guides, notably Adolfo Best-Maugard, he found a wealth of mythic and anthropological rituals which appeared to underpin modern artistic practice.[43] However, back in Moscow after the collapse of the Mexican film, his first attempt to present the core idea, 'that mythological thought can serve as a reservoir of artistic method', at the All-Union Conference of Film Workers in 1935, met with derision and hostility from his colleagues.[44]

It was not until his wartime evacuation from Moscow in the 1940s that he was able to work intensively on *Method*, alongside the production of *Ivan the Terrible*. After a breakdown brought on by overwork on *Ivan* at the end of 1943, he returned to the manuscript, in a fragmentary, often cryptic series of notes, which have been compared to Benjamin's procedure in his (similarly unfinished) *Arcades* text. During January 1944, as we can now see from the 'Disney' section of *Method* in Bulgakowa's extended edition, Eisenstein was heavily influenced by Lawrence's chapters on Nathaniel Hawthorne and Melville. Indeed, this section of the text amounts to an annotated gloss on Lawrence's account of Hawthorne and Melville, with reminders to himself such as: 'Need to write about [Melville] at the start of the Lawrence quote.'[45]

In the chapter of *Studies* discussing Melville's Pacific islands tale *Typee*, Eisenstein found Lawrence expressing rhapsodically his own sense of how 'primitive societies' offer access to the primordial 'sensuous thought' that underpins creativity.[46]

Tahiti, Samoa, Nukhueva, the very names are a sleep and a forgetting ... 'Trailing clouds of glory' ... echoes from the world once splendid in the fullness of the other way of knowledge ... the sleep and the forgetting of this great life, the very body of dreams. And to this dream Melville helplessly returns. He enters first in *Typee*. Nothing is more startling, at once actual and dream-mystical, than his descent down the gorges to the valley of the dreadful Typee. Down this narrow, steep, horrible gorge he slides and struggles as we struggle in a dream, or in the act of birth, or in some cloacal apprehension, to emerge in the green Eden of the first, or last era, the valley of the timeless savages.[47]

In another version of this passage, Lawrence commented that 'this is a bit of birth-myth, or re-birth myth, on Melville's part – unconscious no doubt', adding that his 'running under-consciousness was always mystical and symbolical'.[48] Eisenstein merely notes

Ib. 199 Birth and re-birth
Myth in Typee
A connection with the 'retournons' of J. J. Rousseau.[49]

Several pages later, after noting that 'According to Lawrence, Moby Dick is the basic phallic blood origin and "Jesus"', Eisenstein emphatically underscores the parallels between Lawrence's ideas and his own thinking when he writes the single word, '*Grundproblem*', followed by the exclamation 'Very important!' (in English).[50] A quotation from Lawrence's discussion of *The Scarlet Letter* follows 'We are divided in ourselves, against ourselves. And that is the meaning of the cross-symbol'.[51] Eisenstein then transcribes two pages of Lawrence's chapter ('in full'), which consist of a diatribe against 'ghastly Americans, with their blood no longer blood'.[52] This passage is based on Lawrence's preoccupation with a supposed conflict between 'blood consciousness' and 'mind-consciousness', which he traces back to the Garden of Eden and the Fall:

we fell into knowledge when Eve bit the apple ... Wanting to UNDERSTAND. That is to intellectualize the blood. The blood must be shed, says Jesus. Shed on the cross of our own divided psyche.[53]

Throughout this part of *Method/Grundproblem*, Eisenstein quotes and paraphrases Lawrence almost continuously, clearly finding his idiosyncratic and irreverent handling of what are usually solemn themes highly congenial. Indeed, the effect is of Eisenstein speaking *as* Lawrence, although it is of course impossible to know how this note form might have been revised in a finished text.

Despite his infatuation with the author, Eisenstein's appreciation of Lawrence's fiction was not uniformly favourable. In the *Memoir* chapter 'Encounters with Books', he judged *Aaron's Rod* 'just as surprisingly poor as *Sons and Lovers*'. He also admitted to not having been able to finish Lawrence's Mexican novel *The Plumed Serpent*, attributing this to 'knowing the country' (although others might point to its quasi-Fascist doctrines and their 'longwinded doctrinaire' formulation as reasons for rejecting this).[54] But he singled out for praise two qualities characteristic of Lawrence's shorter fiction. One is 'the "animal epic" running through his novellas', which seems to hinge on the example of St Mawr being compared metaphorically with a fish, lizard and butterfly (as noted above), compared with the *formal* metamorphosis of animals into others in Disney.[55] Critics have noted this as a feature of Lawrence's handling of pain: 'the most common reactions to physical trauma are conveyed through animal imagery and images of madness', according to Shirley Rose, listing examples from a number of stories and novellas.[56] For Eisenstein though this speaks to a broader issue of *plasticity* for which Disney provides an ultimate example.

The other quality Eisenstein admired in Lawrence's stories was 'their abundance of latent action'.[57] A case in point here is 'The Prussian Officer', an early story in which simmering tension between a frustrated, sadistic officer and the orderly he takes pleasure in persecuting leads eventually to the orderly killing his superior before meeting his own solitary death on a mountainside. There is little external narrative in the story, which consists almost entirely of describing the officer's mounting irritation at the 'instinctive sureness of movement of an unhampered young animal', then jealousy at the orderly having a girlfriend, and his 'mute and expressionless demeanour' in the face of provocation; and finally of the orderly's mounting delirium after the killing. The story must have impressed Eisenstein as, quite exceptionally, we have four Lawrence-related drawings that he made during one day in January 1944, and one is titled 'The Prussian Officer'.[58]

Unlike two other drawings that refer to *Lady Chatterley's Lover* and *Women in Love*, and only portray pairs of characters, 'The Prussian Officer' is formally titled and visualizes the arc of the story, from the stiff Captain, seated before a grid which might be a table, the doe-eyed orderly, carrying a precarious stack of plates (which the captain causes him to drop), to the corpse of the officer in the bottom corner, with a red V signifying his broken neck. The drawing is unusual in providing a thematic summary of the story, as most of Eisenstein's numerous 'literary' drawings capture only a character or a relationship. But here it seems that the brooding 'latent' tensions of the story led him to express these graphically, which may also provide a clue to what Eisenstein found most attractive in Lawrence's stories – the pressure of the flow beneath their narrative surface (Figure 5.2).

Figure 5.2 A drawing that illustrates Eisenstein's analysis of the early D. H. Lawrence Story 'The Prussian Officer', made in January 1944 when he was working on the Disney section of *Method*.

Why should Lawrence have been so vividly present in Eisenstein's imagination on 14 January 1944? Thanks to his custom of dating both manuscripts and drawings, we know from the expanded 'Disney' portion of *Method* that on that day, Eisenstein was wrestling with the attempt to bring 'high' and 'low' instances of ecstasy together.[59] Referring to the history of his own theorizing on montage, he writes:

> we can see Mickey as 'ecstatic' and – ritually corresponding to [the] Dionysian canon!
>
> … The mystery of Mickey is comical, but there is also the mystery of Bambi, a pure one![60]

And in the course of this densely referenced passage, Lawrence's 'animal epos' appears:

> The plastic metaphor of the animal via plant elements, like how Lawrence has people compared to plants or animals, different animals compared to animals of earlier stages: the horse St Mawr as a fish, horses as butterflies, Disney's underwater circus; horses as snakes in *Taras Bulba*.[61]

After noting William Blake's poem *The Marriage of Heaven and Hell*, and one of its sources, the Swedish mystic Emanuel Swedenborg's *Heaven and Hell*, Eisenstein makes a cryptic equation '(Lawrence – Mickey)?'[62]

If the drafts of *Method* show Eisenstein effectively 'thinking with Lawrence', in the *Memoir* that he worked on intensively in June 1946 while convalescing from a heart attack, he explained the appeal of Lawrence as offering a 'broader' alternative to Freud's 'purely sexual' focus on 'the personal, biographical adventures of human individuals'.

> Sex is no more than a concentrate, a tight knot; but through its innumerably repeating spirals it recreates rings of regularity which have an unimaginably large radius.
>
> Which is why I like D. H. Lawrence's conceptions that obliged him to step outside the parameters of sex and into (inaccessible for a limited being) a cosmic, universal confluence.[63]

In two essays published in 1921 and 1922, Lawrence marshalled his growing opposition to Freudian psychoanalysis, claiming that Freud brought back from the unconscious 'nothing but a huge, slimy serpent of sex', and revealed 'the serpent of sex coiled around the root of all our actions'.[64] He had been influenced by contact with the American Jungian Trigant Burrow, who wrote about modern sexuality as 'a replacement for the organic unity of personality arising naturally from the harmony of function that pertains biologically to the primary infant psyche'.[65]

Eisenstein had his own disagreements with orthodox psychoanalysis, despite the profound impact that reading Freud had first had on him. He believed that the Oedipus complex had been 'blown up out of all proportion to its place in Freud's teaching',[66] and in a continuation of the passage quoted above, he wrote

> Which is why I find pre-logic so attractive: it grants the subconscious sensuality, but does not subordinate it to sex.
> Which is why the subconscious itself appears first of all as a reflection of one's earliest and most undifferentiated stages of social existence.[67]

After his immersion in Frazer's folklore and Lévy-Bruhl's 'primitive mentality', he undoubtedly found Lawrence's 'deepest self', 'the old IT', invoked in the first chapter of *Studies*, a congenially poetic conception of the organic unity he constantly sought.[68]

> We cannot see that invisible winds carry us, as they carry swarms of locusts, that invisible magnetism brings us as it brings the migrating birds to their unforeknown goal. But it is so. We are not the choosers and deciders we think we are. IT chooses for us [...] If we are living people, in touch with the source, it drives us and decides us.[69]

Posthumous paths

To link Eisenstein with Lawrence as closely as I have suggested is inevitably to raise wider issues. There are undeniable parallels. Both were groundbreaking artists who gathered worldwide audiences, challenged taboos and attracted controversy. Both died young, with much of their prodigious output censored or inaccessible. Both have become 'classics' in their respective fields, with substantial academic industries devoted to their exegesis, even if there are still strong passions in play, for and against.

But there are also obvious differences. Most of what Lawrence wrote for publication was available for Eisenstein to collect and read during the 1930s. By contrast, the full corpus of Eisenstein's writing and drawing is still in process of being published, and remains comparatively little known among those who know his films. It has only been recent editorial work and publishing that reveals the full extent of Eisenstein's engagement with Lawrence. But already it seems clear that Lawrence provided an instructive point of comparison and an inspiring example for the embattled Soviet filmmaker and theorist. Eisenstein must have been attracted by Lawrence's fearless independence and refusal to be cowed by criticism, the refusal that Eisenstein himself had fought to control and supress in his own constant battles with the authorities. They both rejected a conventional Freudianism and looked for other ways of understanding the unconscious and sensuality, in which their life-changing visits to Mexico undoubtedly played a central, though not identical, role. Eisenstein confessed to his dislike of Lawrence's *The Plumed Serpent*, tactfully recommending *Mornings in Mexico* as 'deeper', meaning no doubt that it was closer to his own lived experience of Mexico. But if Eisenstein's *Que Viva México!* had emerged as its creator hoped, might we also have had to question its portrayal of this legendary land by yet another idealizing pilgrim?

If we think about their reputations, Lawrence's was at a comparatively low ebb when he died, after the bannings and prosecutions that had dogged his career. Although most obituaries, at least in the mainstream press, cast him as little more than a pornographer, there were a number of defensive eulogies, some by notable English literary figures such as E. M. Forster and Rebecca West.[70] Throughout the 1930s and 1940s, Lawrence was hardly considered one the great authors of English literature, who had been canonized as Austen, Eliot, James and Conrad by the influential Cambridge critic F. R. Leavis in his 1948 manifesto *The Great Tradition*. Yet in 1955, Leavis would publish his *D. H. Lawrence: Novelist*, which staked a claim for the one-time maverick as worthy of entering the canon. This was the result of Leavis's reassessing Lawrence's novels as essentially dramatic poems, with *The Rainbow* and *Women in Love* as exemplary. In the 1950s, Leavis became increasingly preoccupied with Lawrence – in terms that somewhat recall Eisenstein's own confession of his infatuation a decade earlier. Leavis contrasted Lawrence with the life-denying Christianity of T. S. Eliot, and he would write of the importance of 'life' for Lawrence – 'a necessary term, far from meaningless, and used by Lawrence "without inner resistance"'.[71] 'Nothing is important but life', he quoted appreciatively. In a glowing contemporary review of Leavis's *Lawrence*, John Wain singled out this passage:

> Lawrence's work ... is an immense body of living creation in which a supreme vital intelligence is the creative spirit – a spirit informed by an almost infallible sense for health and sanity. Itself it educates for the kind of criticism that here and there it challenges – it provides the incitement and the criteria ... There is no profound emotional disorder in Lawrence, no obdurate major disharmony; intelligence in him can be, as it is, the servant of the whole integrated psyche.[72]

This verdict on Lawrence by his most ardent English supporter would certainly have appealed to Eisenstein. And as Eisenstein's own tortured, complex work on his *Method* emerges, it may well express what he hoped to achieve in his search for the key to its central challenge: to integrate the divisions summed up under the banner of *Grundproblem*.

Notes

1. On Eisenstein's awareness of contemporary Shakespeare scholarship, see Nikita Lary, '*Ivan the Terrible* in the Context of Shakespearean Tragedy', this volume.
2. On Eisenstein in England, see Ian Christie, ed., *Unexpected Eisenstein* ([exhibition catalogue] Kino Klassika Foundation Publishing, 2016), available online: https://simplebooklet.com/8U8Bac6myLQNASv87sjyIY#page=0 (accessed 28 November 2020).
3. Sergei Eisenstein, *Beyond the Stars: The Memoirs of Sergei Eisenstein*, ed. Richard Taylor, trans. William Powell (London: British Film Institute, 1995), 358 [hereafter *BTS*].
4. Letter from Eisenstein to Macpherson, dated 13 October 1932, quoted in Marie Seton, *Sergei M. Eisenstein: A Biography* (New York: Grove Press, 1960), 357–8, emphasis in the original.
5. Yon Barna, *Eisenstein: The Growth of a Cinematic Genius* (Boston: Little, Brown and Company, 1978), 189; Herbert Marshall, ed., *Immoral Memoirs* (Boston: Houghton Mifflin Company, 1984), 29.
6. Ronald Bergan, *Eisenstein: A Life in Conflict* (London: Little, Brown, 1997), 186–187.
7. Sergei Eisenstein, *Metod*, ed. Naum Kleiman, 2 vols (Moscow: Muzei kino/Eizenshtein-tsentr, 2002) and Sergei Eisenstein, *Metod*, ed. Oksana Bulgakowa, 4 vols (Berlin: PotemkinPress, 2008). Sergei Eisenstein, *The Primal Phenomenon: Art*, ed. Oksana Bulgakowa and Dietmar Hochmuth, trans. Dustin Condren (Berlin: PotemkinPress, 2017) offers two chapters from the unfinished manuscript of *Method*.
8. The first of these, *D. H. Lawrence: A First Study*, by Stephen Potter – later to become famous as the inventor of 'one-upmanship' – had appeared within weeks of Lawrence's death. Frederick Carter's highly personal memoir, casting Lawrence as a fellow-mystic, *D. H. Lawrence and the Body Mystical*, was being advertised in *Close Up* in 1932, as Eisenstein remarked.
9. Four drawings attributed to a cycle titled 'The themes of D. H. Lawrence' appear in Naum Kleiman, *Eisenstein on Paper* (London: Thames & Hudson, 2018), 258. Other drawings are included in Mark Cousins' film *Eisenstein and Lawrence*, made for the exhibition *Unexpected Eisenstein*, GRAD gallery, 2016.

10 In his polemic, *The Intellectuals and the Masses* (London: Faber 1992), 12, the widely published reviewer and critic John Carey devoted considerable attention to Lawrence's Nietzschian views, including a 1908 call for mass euthanasia of 'society's outcasts' by means of a vast lethal gas chamber, with 'the Cinematograph' helping to lull victims into compliance.

11 In 1960, Penguin Books sought to publish an unexpurgated edition of *Lady Chatterley's Lover*, and was prosecuted under Britain's Obscene Publications Act. After a six-day trial, during which many eminent writers gave evidence, the book was judged not obscene, and over 200,000 copies of a new edition were sold.

12 During his travels in Europe in 1929–30, Eisenstein visited nightclubs and brothels, and collected many of the era's notorious 'banned books', gleefully mentioned throughout the *Memoirs*. See Oksana Bulgakowa, *Sergei Eisenstein: A Biography*, trans. Anne Dwyer (Berlin: PotemkinPress, 2001), 99, 107.

13 BTS, 216.

14 Ibid., in a chapter now assembled as 'Épopée' in BTS dating from May 1946.

15 In the chapter 'Encounters with Books', also written in mid-1946, and with a working title 'Lawrence, Melville. *Love for Three Oranges*' (BTS, 358).

16 BTS, 357; *Immoral Memoirs*, 360.

17 Joseph Collins's *The Doctor Looks at Literature: Psychological Studies of Life and Literature* was published in 1923 in New York.

18 BTS, 216.

19 See Evgenii Bershtein, 'Sokurov contra Eisenstein: The Balance of Gender', this volume.

20 Letter from Eisenstein to Macpherson, dated 13 October 1932, quoted in Seton, *Sergei M. Eisenstein*, 357–8.

21 Lawrence's paintings were in fact not exhibited again in Britain until 2003, when a London bookshop showed them, despite the ban being theoretically still in place. See Daniella Demetriou, '"Obscene" Art of DH Lawrence Goes on Show after 70-year Ban', *Independent*, 4 December 2003, available online: https://www.independent.co.uk/news/uk/this-britain/obscene-art-of-dh-lawrence-goes-on-show-after-70-year-ban-81065.html (accessed 28 November 2020).

22 BTS, 357.

23 D. H. Lawrence, *The Lost Girl* (Harmondsworth: Penguin, 1969), 183.

24 D. H. Lawrence, *Phoenix*, 178, quoted in Sam Solecki, 'D. H. Lawrence's View of Film', *Literature Film Quarterly*, January 1973.

25 Ibid., 325.

26 D. H. Lawrence, *Aaron's Rod* (New York: Thomas Selzer, 1921), ch. 12.

27 Ibid., 364–5.

28 'Sensuous thought' recurs through *Method*, as well as one of the last texts that Eisenstein completed, a 'Conspectus of Lectures on the Psychology of Art', written

at the request of Alexander Luria in November 1947. See Jay Leyda, ed., *The Psychology of Composition*, trans. Alan Upchurch (Calcutta: Seagull Books, 1987), 23–7. See also many of the contributions to this collection, and a discussion of the difficulty of translating Eisenstein's terminology in the Introduction, this volume.

29 Sergei Eisenstein, *Disney*, ed. Oksana Bulgakowa and Dietmar Hochmuth (Berlin: PotemkinPress, 2011), 66, emphasis in the original [hereafter *Disney*].
30 See Keith Sagar's 'Introduction', in *The Complete Short Novels* of Lawrence (London: Penguin, 1982), 26–7.
31 *BTS*, 361.
32 Sagar, 'Introduction', 27, emphasis in the original. Sagar comments that 'no other Lawrence heroine is denied her saving man', adding that 'for the only time in his major fiction, Lawrence denies himself the opportunity to approach his religious vision ... through sexual metaphor'.
33 *Disney*, 67–8.
34 Ibid., 66.
35 Ibid., 68.
36 Ibid.
37 Ibid., 11.
38 See the review of a new edition of Lawrence's book by William E. Cain in the journal *Resources for American Literary Study*, vol. 30 (2005): 342–4.
39 *Studies* is also a complex text, consisting of many different chapters and versions. 'Tracing a clear textual history is almost impossible', according to the editors of the Cambridge edition of Lawrence's works, vol. 2, 'Background', xxiii. Since it is not clear which version Eisenstein read in 1944, I quote here from the Intermediate Version of 1919, Cambridge text, 337.
40 *BTS*, 360.
41 Julia Vassilieva, 'Eisenstein and Cultural-Historical Theory', in *The Flying Carpet: Studies on Eisenstein and Russian Cinema in Honor of Naum Kleiman*, ed. Joan Neuberger and Antonio Somaini (Paris: Éditions Mimésis, 2017), 421–41.
42 Masha Salazkina, *In Excess: Sergei Eisenstein's Mexico* (Chicago: University of Chicago Press, 2009), see ch. 2, 'Sandunga', especially pp. 72–4.
43 Ibid., 28–34.
44 Oksana Bulgakowa, 'Psychology of Form', Afterword to Eisenstein, *The Primal Phenomenon*, 253.
45 *Disney*, 101.
46 On Eisenstein's relationship to contemporary anthropological studies, see Introduction, this volume.
47 D. H. Lawrence, *Studies in Classic American Literature* (Cambridge: Cambridge University Press, 2003), 337, ellipses in the original.
48 Ibid., 125.

49 *Disney*, 97.
50 *Disney*, 98.
51 D. H. Lawrence, *Studies in Classic American Literature* (London: Penguin Books in Association with William Heinemann, 1971), 90.
52 Ibid., 99.
53 Ibid.
54 *BTS*, 361. The critical view of *Aaron's Rod* comes in an introduction by Cedric Watts to the 1995 Wordsworth Classics edition, p. xxi.
55 *Disney*, 67.
56 Shirley Rose, 'Physical Trauma in D. H. Lawrence's Short Fiction', *Contemporary Literature* 16, no. 1 (Winter 1975): 7.
57 *BTS*, 361.
58 Kleiman, *Eisenstein on Paper*, 258.
59 See Massimo Olivero, 'The Two-Headed Ecstasy: The Philosophical Roots of Late Eisenstein', this volume.
60 *Disney*, 117.
61 *Disney*, 118.
62 *Disney*, 118. Both Blake's poem and Swedenborg's book belong to the late eighteenth century.
63 *BTS*, 437.
64 D. H. Lawrence, *Psychoanalysis and the Unconscious* (New York: Thomas Seltzer, 1921), 201–3.
65 Trigant Burrow, 'Psychoanalysis in Theory and in Life', *Journal of Nervous and Mental Disease* 64, no. 3 (1926): 209–24; 210; quoted in Bruce Steele, 'Introduction', in D. H. Lawrence, *Psychoanalysis of the Unconscious and Fantasia of the Unconscious* (Cambridge: Cambridge University Press, 2004), xxxiii.
66 *BTS*, 105.
67 *BTS, Wie Sag Ich's meinem kinde?*, 437.
68 See Eisenstein, *Metod*, vol. 1, 225–50.
69 D. H. Lawrence, *Studies in Classic American Literature* (Cambridge: Cambridge University Press, 2003), 18.
70 A study of more than two hundred obituary notices for Lawrence in Britain, Europe, America and Australia showed that most obituaries throughout the world were journalistically fair, despite received opinion that he was generally reviled. Discussed in James C. Cowan, 'Elegies for D. H. Lawrence', in *The Spirit of D. H. Lawrence: Centenary Studies*, ed. Gamini Salgado and G. K. Das (London: Palgrave Macmillan, 1988), 311.
71 F. R. Leavis, *Thought, Words and Creativity: Art and Thought in Lawrence* (London: Chatto and Windus, 1976).
72 John Wain, 'Leavis on Lawrence', *The Spectator*, 7 October 1955.

6

Sokurov contra Eisenstein: The Balance of Gender

Evgenii Bershtein

During his lifetime, Sergei Eisenstein was both officially lionized and officially condemned in the Soviet Union, occasionally at the same time. The government repeatedly applied to him a peculiar formula by which the latest film of this 'Honored Artist' was declared a 'grave error'. Paradoxically, these opposite poles of Eisenstein's status coincided in the final year of his life, after Stalin rejected Part II of *Ivan the Terrible*. To quote Oksana Bulgakowa, in this period, 'Eisenstein found himself in an odd situation. His film was banned, but his person enjoyed highest favor.'[1] Eisenstein's ambiguous reputation as both iconic and suspect persisted into the post-Stalin era, albeit now undergoing a dramatic reconfiguration. As a canonized Soviet classic, he became an object of official reverence (a Moscow street was named after him in 1968) and a subject of compulsory study in film schools. At the same time, as Naum Kleiman has recently pointed out, some prominent members of the emerging 'Thaw' generation of Soviet filmmakers were put off by what was perceived as Eisenstein's place of honour in official Soviet culture.[2] These younger artists had been raised on Eisenstein's films and readily acknowledged their artistic power, but resented their explicit political messages.

In the Thaw period, Alexander Solzhenitsyn (1918–2008) produced an important early case of the moral and political rejection of Eisenstein, coupled with aesthetic indebtedness to him. Solzhenitsyn's groundbreaking prison camp novella *One Day in the Life of Ivan Denisovich* (1962) included two memorable scenes in which prisoners debate Eisenstein's work: the novella's eponymous protagonist, a peasant arrested during his wartime military service, overhears two conversations about Eisenstein, each initiated by a youngish Muscovite named Tsezar, an unsympathetically depicted cosmopolitan aesthete, filmmaker and Eisenstein enthusiast. Tsezar's interlocutors, meanwhile, are critical of

Eisenstein's work. One of them, a former naval officer, attacks *The Battleship Potemkin* as packed with falsehoods about the treatment of sailors in the tsarist navy. The other, a prisoner numbered X 123, discusses *Ivan the Terrible*. When Tsezar praises the director's genius as manifest in the cathedral scene and the oprichniks' dance, his interlocutor explodes:

> 'Ham,' said X 123 angrily [...] 'It's all so arty there is no art left in it. Spice and poppyseed instead of everyday bread and butter! And then, the vile political idea – the justification of personal tyranny. A mockery of the memory of three generations of Russian intelligentsia.
>
> [...] Don't call him a genius! Call him an ass-kisser, obeying a vicious dog's order. Geniuses don't adjust their interpretations to suit the taste of tyrants!'[3]

Solzhenitsyn's story takes place in early 1951; it is thus hardly plausible that the long-serving prisoner X 123 could have seen the second part of *Ivan the Terrible* discussed here, as the film was not released until 1958. (It was however screened to Moscow filmmakers in 1946–7, so Tsezar could have seen it before his arrest.) Solzhenitsyn prided himself on being meticulous about historical detail, but here his disregard, likely intentional, of chronological veracity conveys the urgency he felt to articulate, through a minor character, his rejection of Eisenstein.

These two Eisenstein-centred conversations deliver separate blows to Eisenstein's oeuvre and creative personality: one attacks his main early work as mendacious, and the other targets his final work for its alleged subservience, political conformism and empty aestheticism. Yet remarkably, as Ilya Kukulin has shown in detail, the Eisensteinian technique of 'montage of attractions' had a significant direct influence on Solzhenitsyn's own poetics, especially in his screenplays and his epic historical novel *The Red Wheel*.[4]

Similarly, Andrei Tarkovsky kept returning to Eisenstein in his theoretical musings, while reiterating a categorical rejection of the master's poetics. Despite describing *Potemkin* as 'full of life and poetry' and *Ivan* as 'astonishingly powerful in its musical and rhythmic composition',[5] Tarkovsky declared: 'I reject the principles of "montage cinema" because they do not allow the film to continue beyond the edges of the screen: they do not allow the audience to bring personal experience to bear on what is in front of them on film [...] The construction of the image becomes an end in itself, and the author proceeds to make a total onslaught on the audience, imposing upon them his own attitude to what is happening.'[6] Further, 'Eisenstein's montage diktat [...] deprives the person watching [...] of the opportunity to live through what is happening on the screen as if it were his own life.'[7] Tarkovsky's aesthetic objections to Eisenstein's method have decidedly political undertones: he rebels against the director's perceived manipulation and indoctrination of the viewer.[8]

In a mirror reflection of Eisenstein's bifurcated official reputation under Stalin, there formed something of a tradition among the independent-minded intelligentsia of the late Soviet period of taking a negative view of Eisenstein on moral and political grounds, while acknowledging his significance for film and art history. This was how the influential Soviet cultural historian and literary scholar Yuri Lotman (1922–93) positioned himself in relation to Eisenstein. Even while engaging with Eisenstein's semiotic ideas, Lotman did not hesitate to express his aversion for a director he saw as 'very talented [...] but entirely indifferent to truth and morality'.[9]

'The aesthetic canonization of cruelty'

Born in 1951, Alexander Sokurov is our contemporary and one of the most celebrated film auteurs today. A prolific director, he has cemented his international reputation by making sixteen fiction films, including *Moloch* (1999), *Russian Ark* (2002), *Father and Son* (2003), *Alexandra* (2007) and *Faust* (2011), as well as some three dozen documentaries, including *Conversations with Solzhenitsyn* (1998) and earlier *Moscow Elegy* (1987), a memorial to his friend and patron Andrei Tarkovsky. In Russia, Sokurov is widely seen as his generation's most significant highbrow film director and a national treasure. In addition to his authority as a filmmaker, he has become one of Russia's leading public intellectuals, a frequent presence in the national media. For a period of time in the 1990s, he tutored President Boris Yeltsin in history; nowadays he meets regularly with President Putin (whose policies he often challenges in his media appearances).

Eisenstein is present in Sokurov's films intertextually, at times in an openly polemical way. Sokurov filmed his entire *Russian Ark* at the Hermitage, the museum occupying the same Saint Petersburg Winter Palace that figured so prominently in Eisenstein's *October*. Set in the very location of some of Eisenstein's most iconic and radical montage sequences, Sokurov's fantastical costumed presentation of Russian imperial history, featuring a cast of over two thousand, consists of a single continuous 98-minute shot. The film's storyline breaks off in 1913, anticipating the advent of the new era of violent revolutionary fragmentation celebrated in *October*.

In a nod to *The Battleship Potemkin*, one of Sokurov's most ambitious 'semi-documentaries', *Confession* (1998, 260 mins), takes place on a naval ship in the Barents Sea, and includes exceptionally long shots of young sailors asleep in their berths. In *Potemkin*, Eisenstein imagined this part of the ship as a birthplace of violence and social fury, and edited the scene of the sailors' interrupted sleep explosively. Unlike his predecessor in sailor-obsession, Sokurov presents *his* sleeping servicemen in a tender and melancholy extended contemplation of youthful masculinity.[10]

In what follows, I focus on what I believe is very significant aspect of Sokurov's critique of Eisenstein, presented in his essay 'Hands: Thoughts on Professional Growth', first published in 2009 and specifically devoted to Eisenstein.[11] Sokurov's text is a long, meandering, and intellectually and philosophically intense overview of Eisenstein's artistic personality and his oeuvre. It is obvious from this text that its author not only remembers Eisenstein's films, drawings and biography in great detail, but that he defines himself as an artist through (and in opposition to) Eisenstein. The essay's analytical narrative is subjective and lyrical in intonation, but rich in knowledge of Eisenstein's creative biography. It follows the Soviet-era pattern of censuring Eisenstein while acknowledging his exceptional significance, with some of its theses representing Thaw-era and late-Soviet commonplaces of this approach (for instance, Sokurov refers in passing to Eisenstein as 'an artist of a totalitarian society').[12] However, a number of Sokurov's thoughts are highly idiosyncratic and worthy of closer examination. For me, the essay is particularly intriguing in that it reveals an important intellectual overlap in the two directors' metaphysical and anthropological ideas, especially in their modelling of gender and sexuality. I argue that this overlap and its intellectual genesis provide a vital context for understanding Sokurov's 2007 film *Alexandra*.

In a gesture characteristic of psychological autobiography, Sokurov begins with an analysis of his own childhood response to Eisenstein's films. *Potemkin* and *The Strike*, he says, had a strong and traumatic impact on him as a schoolboy, triggering rejection and protest: 'too much pathos [...] too much cruelty'.[13] He found Eisenstein's fascination with violence deeply troubling and describes its consequences in hyperbolic, almost horrific terms: Eisenstein's cinematic representations of violence, he argues, helped legitimize it for this new medium. According to Sokurov, cinema learned from Eisenstein how to show extreme brutality, and this in turn made murder acceptable to viewers. Much of the real-life cruelty in today's world, Sokurov believes, is caused by movies:

The masses' instruction in methods and means of destroying human life, an instruction provided first by film and later by television, produced, for an enormous audience, the habit of death as a public spectacle [...] There are phenomena that you can approach but should not look at directly. And one should not display them for public viewing. Eisenstein and his associates were 'playing' with this.[14]

Sokurov rejects Eisenstein's fascination with the regression, both of individuals and of civilization, the bestialization of men and their concomitant brutality. As he sees it, life is already full enough of 'terrible struggle': 'All day long, the TV channel *Animal Planet* shows, in great detail, everyone hunting everyone and everyone eating everyone. It shows living creatures dying in terrible pain, seeing the eyes and jaws of their killer.'[15] According to Sokurov, the purpose of art should be to counteract this situation – to humanize life.

Sokurov views Eisenstein's depictions of brutality, in *The Strike* in particular, as based in 'erotic aggression extended into all spheres of life – social, religious, family, state [...] *Strike* is a chain of violent acts by some people over others, with pleasure being received [...] One side temporarily prevails and enjoys victory [...then] the violated side gets satisfaction in the next episode. The victor rapes the vanquished, and the vanquished thrusts himself upon the victor.'[16] It is not that art has no place for the representation of violence; but Sokurov believes that, unlike the depictors of cruelty among great writers such as Émile Zola and Anton Chekhov, Eisenstein lacked empathy and compassion – his unquestionable genius was ethically indifferent and fuelled by aggression. An examination of Eisenstein's drawings, including his still largely unpublished 'sex drawings', proves to Sokurov that, as a graphic artist, Eisenstein likewise focused on hyperbolically presented acts of aggression – sexual and political in equal parts.[17]

Sokurov outlines a gender mechanism at work in Eisenstein: the masculine and feminine, he believes, were insufficiently balanced in this Soviet master, with masculinity so dominant that it left Eisenstein utterly indifferent to the life of the soul:

> The masculine and feminine elements which are mutually complementary and co-exist in every person, are characterized, in Eisenstein's case, by the obvious predominance of masculinity and the possibly total absence of femininity, that is, of the soul. Active aggression [...] was the essence of [his] epoch and it facilitated the catastrophic development of Eisenstein's 'dialectics'.[18]

> His soul had none of the feminine element that is [otherwise] present in men as well. He was a man only. His every image gives the sense of male aggression, devoid of any counterbalance.[19]

Sokurov suggests that Eisenstein's disproportionally developed masculinity not only caused his fascination with violence but also determined his indifference to the life of the soul, 'the sphere of the feminine'.[20] Eisenstein's gender-unbalanced nature, in this view, is reflected in his artistic methods, which are entirely constructivist and lacking in visual contemplation or lyricism. Sokurov finds these latter qualities in the other, parallel tradition in Russian cinema, which he associates with the works of Aleksandr Dovzhenko, Andrei Tarkovsky and, implicitly, his own. The essay reads as Sokurov's artistic manifesto, albeit a negative one.

Eisenstein's 'bisex'

One striking feature of this text is Sokurov's reading of Eisenstein's artistic persona through the prism of androgyny. Yet the vision of both genders coexisting in a single person comes from a theoretical matrix that was absolutely crucial for Eisenstein himself, even if he did not readily display it in public. Sokurov's analysis suggests a model of sexual and gender intermediacy that is closely akin to the one deployed by Eisenstein, yet Sokurov turns it against his predecessor.

The model itself was first and famously articulated by the Austrian Otto Weininger in his 1903 book *Sex and Character: A Principled Investigation*, an international bestseller that mixed neo-Kantian philosophy, contemporary biological science (which had not yet discovered sex hormones) and popular psychology to develop the philosophical theory of *Geschlecht* (German for both 'sex' and 'gender'). Weininger argued that a combination, in varying proportions, of the masculine and feminine elements was present in every person, both biologically and psychologically – a phenomenon he called 'bisexuality', and from which he drew far-reaching philosophical and anthropological conclusions. These conclusions were pessimistic: the masculine element was in decline, and therefore the faculty of reason and such phenomena as culture and creative genius, all seen as paradigmatically masculine, were also declining. Shortly after publishing his book, its 23-year-old author committed suicide in the very house where Beethoven had died. His death was covered by the international press and, in the ensuing years, much of the reading public of the entire Western world devoured the book by this tragic 'young genius from Vienna'.[21]

Over the years, Eisenstein, who read Weininger in 1919–20 while serving in the Red Army, would add many theoretical layers to the theory of bisex (or bisexuality, or 'b.s.' – he used these terms interchangeably), borrowing in particular from the sexologists Richard Krafft-Ebing and Magnus Hirschfeld, and the psychoanalytical philosophers Sigmund Freud and Carl Jung.[22] He was especially influenced by Freud's disciples Sándor Ferenczi and Otto Rank, who helped him see bisex as an evolutionary and developmental phenomenon of regress. In Eisenstein's view, bisexual individuals are connected to both primordial and prenatal states – states as yet untouched by sexual differentiation – and marked by a strong sense of themselves as possessing a 'superhuman essence'.[23] From around 1928 until his final days two decades later, Eisenstein discussed bisex in his theoretical writing and self-analysis, thematized it in his films and imagined it in his drawings. In his diary, he explained the foundations of his early film poetics as 'produced entirely' by 'a sex[ual] ecstatic catastrophe based on b.s. [bisex, bisexuality]'.[24]

As Eisenstein developed the central categories of his theoretical system – pathos, ecstasy and dialectics – he postulated bisex as a 'physiological prerequisite' for genius, insofar as any genius must necessarily be attuned to dialectical processes and experience them as ecstatic creativity.[25] He put the same thought in different words thus: 'The dialectical principle in sex is bisexuality [...] this is why almost all ecstatic persons [*ekstatiki*] have a distinct element of bisexuality'.[26] He reiterated that 'bisexuality is [...] the dynamic unity of opposites in the sphere of sex'.[27] He even called his own sexualized theoretical system *khuëvaya dialekticheskaya kontseptsiya* which could be roughly translated as 'dick dialectics', albeit with the loss of the pun on the first word's dual meaning of 'shabby'/'penile', noting that he used the obscene epithet 'in the full sense'.[28] Eisenstein did not identify as a homosexual, and was largely celibate throughout his life, although he did have traumatic infatuations with men and experienced powerful attraction to them.[29] Analysing himself in his diaries, Eisenstein explained every instance of his same-sex attraction with reference to his own bisexual constitution. In general – which is an important point to remember – Eisenstein firmly believed homosexuality to be just an extreme and potentially antisocial manifestation of bisex.[30] In the drawings that accompanied his self-analysis, Eisenstein frequently represented himself as a bisexual being: for instance, in a 1932 drawing, he imagines himself as a man and a women contained in a single two-headed bisexual body, the two tongues simultaneously kissing and stinging (Figure 6.1).

Figure 6.1 Eisenstein's self-portrait, pasted into his diary (1932). Russian State Archive of Literature and Arts (RGALI), by permission.

Bisexual dialectics provided a recurrent theme for Eisenstein's graphic artworks, which he claimed to produce 'almost in a trance and in the strongest *sensualité*.'[31] Thus, his numerous drawings of Gospel subjects turn Christ's Passion into the story of a love triangle between the bisexual Jesus, his favourite disciple John and the jealous lover Judas. One drawing from this series depicts two haloed figures: the feminine Jesus, with the face, hair and physique of Oscar

Figure 6.2 Eisenstein, 'Le Christ & Johnnie' (1932). RGALI, by permission.

Wilde, embraces the sweet-looking youth 'Johnnie', who in turn touches Jesus's voluptuous body in a sexual way. The picture is entitled 'Le Christ & Johnnie' (Figure 6.2).

Eisenstein obsessively drew many images of St Sebastian and the biblical (as well as Wildean) Salome, presenting them as ecstatically bisexual: St Sebastian here is an effeminate, sexually receptive, submissive martyr; Salome, a masculine, aggressively phallic rapist.[32] In describing Eisenstein's sex drawings as almost invariably violent and political, Sokurov certainly has a point.

Yet Sokurov's bisexual model of Eisenstein would likely have come as a surprise to its subject. Not because of its condemnation of cruelty – after all, Eisenstein discussed his own sadistic tendencies frankly in his memoirs – but rather with regard to the *ratio* involved.[33] When Eisenstein himself contemplated Weininger's formula, which allowed for a numerical calculation of masculine (M) and feminine (F) elements in each person, he assigned himself the traditional proportion of 50/50. This is the figure given in a diary entry from 1928, and it is also how he appears in his self-portraits – evenly split between M and F.[34] This is how he described his creative persona generally – as divided equally between what he viewed as the masculine impulse to attack and penetrate the world with a camera and, on the other hand, the feminine impulse to gather and collect artefacts and knowledge.[35] Obviously, the concept of 'soul' did not figure in this scheme.

'Baba Sasha', or femininity unleashed

Debating the gender of the 'soul' was however a fairly common exercise in Russian religious philosophy of the Silver Age, an intellectual tradition perhaps marginal for Eisenstein, but important for creative artists of the late and post-Soviet periods. Unsurprisingly, this tradition readily appropriated Weininger's model.[36] In 1915, the writer Vasilii Rozanov famously described a surge of erotic excitement he experienced – a 'girlish infatuation' – at the sight of a mounted regiment moving through the streets of Saint Petersburg. From this, Rozanov concluded that 'the essence of the army is that it turns us all into women – weak, trembling, air-embracing women. Some experience it more, some less, but everyone does to some degree.'[37] The philosopher Nikolai Berdyaev, another Russian reader of Weininger, responded to Rozanov's pronouncement with an article memorably entitled 'On the "Eternal *Baba*" in the Russian Soul'. *Baba* does not translate well into English: it can mean 'peasant woman', or 'grandma'; and can also stand as an informal, even affectionate synonym for 'woman', or a derogatory one, like the English 'broad'. In his article, Berdyaev, appalled by Rozanov's patriotic outburst and its psychosexual implications, used the word pejoratively. Rozanov's soul, he suggested, is feminine in a purely negative sense, harbouring a typically *baba*-ish mixture of irrationality, strong-but-submissive lust and occasional pity. Berdyaev went on to generalize that the collective soul of all Russia had been weakened and disfigured by the same pedestrian femininity.[38]

This philosophical background is relevant for both of our directors' creative work. Like Eisenstein, Sokurov delights in the male form. Indeed, one of the most prominent visual similarities between the two masters' work lies in their preoccupation with portraying (and deploying non-diegetically) athletic young male bodies. Yet a careful examination of how Eisenstein and Sokurov treat these magnificent bodies reveals a significant difference. Eisenstein routinely presents his semi-naked muscular youths in the process of being humiliated, tortured or butchered, or ecstatically baring themselves as if accepting martyrdom in the manner of St Sebastian. In such scenes, the camera is emphatically an instrument of masculine aggression: the shots are extremely brief, and the changing angles create a vision of youths fragmented and dissected (recall the famous episode of the sleeping sailors in the beginning of *Potemkin*, which culminates in a young sailor being brought to tears by a petty officer's abuse and the title 'Hurtful!'). In contrast to Eisenstein, Sokurov photographs his soldiers and sailors with an almost motionless camera and in long takes, as if absorbing these lads contemplatively in real time. In his *Confession*, the lighting and music, as well as the captain's voiceover diary (read by Sokurov himself), render a range of emotions, from mournful pity for his sailors to heart-warming tenderness for them. The setting and composition of some scenes are not unlike those of Fassbinder's *Querrelle*, except that the ship and most of the sailors depicted in this quasi-documentary are real, and there is no onscreen sex (although plenty of undressing and bathing, carefully observed almost in real time). Having diagnosed Eisenstein with a pathological masculinization of the soul, Sokurov builds for himself an epistemological model of a very different balance. In this model, what he identifies as the compassion-based, feminine type of cognition prevails. While still a bisexual model, it constitutes a reversal of Eisenstein's, in which male aggression ran unchecked.

Sokurov's alternative to Eisenstein's violent, masculine-dominated bisex was fully revealed in his 2007 feature *Alexandra*. In this rare case of Sokurov himself writing the screenplay for one of his fiction films, he not only gives the female protagonist Alexandra Nikolaevna the grammatically feminized version of his own name and patronymic, but sends her into the all-male world of a military base in wartime. A supremely authoritative yet fully feminine Alexandra Nikolaevna, played by the eighty-year-old opera singer Galina Vishnveskaya, visits her grandson Denis, a Russian officer stationed in war-torn Chechnya. Alexandra Nikolaevna spends two days at the makeshift base, observing the sleepy, fatigued young soldiers and feeding, pitying and studying them. In the screenplay, her officer grandson calls her '*Baba* Sasha' (combining an echo of Berdyaev's 'eternal *baba*' with the informal variant of Sokurov's first name).[39]

It is perhaps worth recalling that Eisenstein performed a similar regendering of names in *October*, likening the first name and patronymic of Alexander Fedorovich Kerensky to Alexandra Fedorovna, the dethroned empress. Eisenstein's pun here, however, dripped with malice; it figuratively castrated Kerensky, and its mockery seems particularly brutal in light of Alexandra Fedorovna's actual fate: her and her whole family's murder by the Bolsheviks in 1918. As if rescinding the celebration of such (masculine) violence, Sokurov reverses the direction of the pun, gifting his own name to a regal old lady – his film's protagonist and his alter ego.

Alexandra Nikolaevna admires the smells and sights of condensed masculinity, but sternly excoriates men for their brutality – the cause of war, death and destruction. Critics have described the relationship between this stately and imperious grandmother (often seen as symbolically standing for Grandmother Russia) and her tough sweaty grandson as 'the utopian construction of absolute intimacy' (Mikhail Iampolski) and an 'unlikely romance' (Jeremi Szaniawski).[40] In her love for Denis, Alexandra is shown as needing his physical closeness, and this motif finds its culmination when, in a maternal and comforting gesture, he lays her head on his chest and fondly embraces her. Supported by his sculpted bare arm, Alexandra takes in his masculine scent and praises it ('How good men smell sometimes!').[41] Denis may smell like a man, but in this scene he evinces a tender, feminine compassion. He offers to braid his grandmother's

Figure 6.3 Alexander Sokurov's *Alexandra* (2007).

hair, and does so, like one of her girlfriends, in a folkloric gesture of returning youth and girlhood to the old woman (Figure 6.3). In this moving scene, a powerful, authoritative woman and a compassionate, soulful man are united in love.

In making *Alexandra*, Sokurov filmed at an actual military base and an actual Chechen city devastated by war, and many of the soldiers depicted were real servicemen. Alexandra sees much misery at the base and devastation outside it. Leaving the base and going to the market, she easily befriends Chechen women. Compassion and connection come naturally to her: she pities local women, she pities Russian conscripts, she pities angry Chechen youths, she pities (and loves) her grandson, hardened in bloody search-and-destroy operations. It is through the practice of patient, receptive feminine cognition that Alexandra, Sokurov's fictional feminine side, tries to bring people together politically. Both Alexandra and the film as a whole condemn violence and war, albeit not without a supplement of visually poeticized martial masculinity. Here Sokurov's notion of androgyny, as if challenging that of Eisenstein, helps build a practical poetics by which to articulate the director's humanitarian position. It must have taken some fearlessness for Sokurov – a public figure in a socially conservative society – to expose his highly developed feminine aspect and adopt a feminine gaze. The end result, in any case, is a rejection of Eisenstein's ethics and aesthetics of the violent affirmation of power, understood as a characteristically masculine trait. Like Eisenstein in his many theoretical writings, Sokurov in *Alexandra* integrates the model of 'bisex', but in this case not by staging moments of regress – of 'return to the beast[ial]', in Eisenstein's quip – but rather constructing a counterweight to the extreme brutality that, in his view, has spread from the movie theatre to the theatre of war.[42]

* * *

Alexander Sokurov and Sergei Eisenstein, the subjects of this chapter, and even the briefly mentioned but significant Vasilii Rozanov, have all produced epistemological perspectives that challenge a static monolithic understanding of gender. Their 'bisexual' theories informed, even shaped their poetics, enabling them to develop distinctly non-heteronormative artistic models of reality in general, and of its political dimensions in particular. Both Eisenstein and Sokurov approached the task of reimagining gender in an intense and philosophically grounded way. Despite their many fundamental differences, one can view both of these filmmakers as beacons in a specific tradition within Russian culture. This tradition has taken shape within a predominantly statist and nationalist discourse, and in full view of the cultural mainstream; and for this reason, it has long escaped being recognized as a queer one. Queer 'in the full sense of the word', as Eisenstein could say.

Acknowledgements

Early versions of this chapter were presented as talks at UC Berkeley, Willamette College, Bowdoin College, and the First Eisenstein International Network symposium in Paris. I am grateful to the audience members who contributed to the discussion of this paper, to Ian Christie, Naum Kleiman, Ilya Kukulin and Roman Utkin, who made specific suggestions, and to Avram Brown, who helped edit the manuscript.

Notes

1. Oksana Bulgakowa, *Sergei Eisenstein: A Biography*, trans. Anne Dwyer (Berlin: PotemkinPress, 2001), 230.
2. I paraphrase the remarks Naum Kleiman made on 15 October 2019 in discussing my talk at the Eisenstein International Network conference in Paris. Kleiman suggested Tarkovsky's and Sokurov's negative views of Eisenstein could be further explained by their insufficient knowledge and understanding of the master's life and full legacy.
3. Alexander Solzhenitsyn, *One Day in the Life of Ivan Denisovich*, trans. Eric Bogosian (New York: Penguin Putnam, 2009), 80–1. I have slightly edited the translation for precision.
4. Ilya Kukulin, *Mashiny zashumevshego vremeni: kak sovetskii montazh stal metodom neoficial'noi kul'tury* (Moscow: Novoe literaturnoe obozrenie, 2015), 299–340. See also Kukulin, 'A Prolonged Revanche: Solzhenitsyn and Eisenstein', *Studies in Russian and Soviet Cinema* 5, no.1 (2011): 73–101.
5. Andrey Tarkovsky, *Sculpting in Time: Reflections on the Cinema*, trans. Kitty Hunter-Blair (Austin: University of Texas Press, 1986), 68, 67.
6. Ibid., 118.
7. Ibid., 183. I have edited the translation of this passage, replacing the obscure 'montage dictum' with 'montage diktat' to more clearly convey the obvious political connotations of the original Russian *montazhnyi diktat*. I have used the original Russian text, see Andrei Tarkovskii, *Zapechatlennoe vremya*, available online: http://tarkovskiy.su/texty/vrema/vrema8-2.html (accessed 5 May 2020).

8   Tarkovsky, *Sculpting in Time*, 183.
9   Cited from Mikhail Trunin, '"Ochen' plokho otnoshus' k etomu deyatelyu": Lotman ob Eizenshteine kak predshestvennike sturkturalizma', *Novoe literaturnoe obozrenie* 3 (2016): 97. See also I. Z. Belobrovtseva, 'Kak izobrazhat' Eizenshteina: polumemuary o Yu. M. Lotmane', *Russkaya literatura* 4(2012): 70–9.
10 On visual representations of masculinity in Sokurov, see Evgenii Bershtein, 'Melankholicheskie atlety Aleksandra Sokurova', *Neprikosnovennyi zapas* 2(2011): 81–93.
11 Aleksandr Sokurov, 'Ruki. Razmyshleniya o professional'nom razvitii', in *V tsentre okeana* (Saint Petersburg: Amfora, 2012), 267–300. The essay was first published in the 2009 Italian edition of the same book: Aleksandr Sokurov, *Nel centro dell'oceano* (Milan: Bompiani, 2009).
12 Sokurov, 'Ruki. Razmyshleniya o professional'nom razvitii', 281.
13 Ibid., 267–8.
14 Ibid., 271–2.
15 Ibid., 290.
16 Ibid., 286.
17 Ibid., 279. I have borrowed the expression 'sex drawings' for Eisenstein's sexually explicit sketches, of which he created thousands, from Joan Neuberger's 'Strange Circus: Eisenstein's Sex Drawings', *Studies in Russian and Soviet Cinema* 6, no.1 (2012): 5–52.
18 Sokurov, 'Ruki. Razmyshleniya o professional'nom razvitii', 279.
19 Ibid., 283–4.
20 Ibid., 284.
21 See Chandak Sengoopta, *Otto Weininger: Sex, Science and Self in Imperial Vienna* (Chicago: University of Chicago Press, 2000). On the Weininger craze in Russia, see Evgenii Bershtein, 'Tragediya pola: dve zametki o russkom veiningerianstve', *Novoe literaturnoe obozrenie* 1, no.65 (2004): 208–28.
22 Sergei Eisenstein, *Beyond the Stars: The Memoirs of Sergei Eisenstein*, ed. Richard Taylor, trans. William Powell (London: British Film Institute, 1995), 484. In a 1928 diary entry, Eisenstein provides a detailed recollection of how he read and absorbed Weininger's book (Russian State Archive of Literature and Arts [RGALI], 1923-2-1109, l. 132–3).
23 Sergei Eizenshtein, *Metod*, ed. Naum Kleiman, 2 vols (Moscow: Muzei kino/Eizenshtein-tsentr, 2002), vol. 1, 285–6.
24 RGALI, 1923-2-1137, l. 139–40.
25 RGALI, 1923-2-1123, l. 139.
26 RGALI, 1923-2-1136, l. 90.
27 Cited in Yuri Tsivian, *Ivan the Terrible* (London: British Film Institute, 2002), 65. Tsivian's indispensable study includes a section on Eisenstein's use of bisexual imagery in *Ivan the Terrible*, 60–73.

28 RGALI, 1923-2-1126, l. 83.
29 RGALI, 1923-2-1136, l. 139.
30 Oscar Wilde, whose works and biography Eisenstein studied in detail, was a case in point; see Eizenshtein, *Metod*, vol. 2, 357.
31 RGALI, 1923-2-1140, l. 2.
32 Some of the drawings I discuss here have been reproduced in various publications, both print and online. See, for instance, Naum Kleiman, *Eisenstein on Paper: Graphic Works of the Master of Film* (London: Thames & Hudson, 2017), 184, 185; Kleiman, *A Mischievous Eisenstein* (Saint Petersburg: Slavia, 2006), 58; see also the catalogue of a recent exhibit of Eisenstein's sex drawings: Alexander Gray Associates, 'Sergei Eisenstein: Drawings 1931–1948', 7 January–11 February 2017, available online: https://www.alexandergray.com/exhibitions/sergei-eisenstein (accessed 5 May 2020).
33 Sergei Eisenstein, 'To the Illustrious Memory of the Marquis', in Eisenstein, *Beyond the Stars*, 510–66.
34 RGALI, 1923-2-1109, l. 131–3.
35 Ibid., l. 131: Eisenstein uses the formula 'banditry of camera work' (*makhovshchina razboya kino-apparatom*) for his 'manly' activities. See also Sergei Eisenstein, 'Monsieur, madame et bébé', in Eisenstein, *Beyond the Stars*, 505.
36 See Evgenii Bershtein, 'The Notion of Universal Bisexuality in Russian Religious Philosophy', in *Understanding Russianness*, ed. Risto Alapuro, Arto Mustojaki, Pekka Pesonen(London: Routledge, 2012), 210–31. On philosophical and artistic treatments of sexuality in Russian Silver Age culture, see Olga Matich, *Erotic Utopia: The Decadent Imagination in Russian Fin-de-Siècle* (Madison: University of Wisconsin Press, 2005).
37 Vasilii Rozanov, *Poslendie list'ya* (Moscow: Respublica, 2000), 340.
38 N. A. Berdyaev, 'O "vechno bab'em" v russkoi dushe', in *V.V. Rozanov–pro et contra: Lichnost' i tvorchestvo Vasiliya Vasil'evicha Rozanova v otsenke russkikh myslitelei i issledovatelei. Antologiya*, ed. V. A. Fadeev, vol. 2 (Saint Petersburg: Russkii Khristianskii gumanitarnyi institut, 1995), 41–51.
39 Aleksandr Sokurov, 'Aleksandra. Kinematogracheskii rasskaz', in Sokurov, *V tsentre okeana*, 64. Note that Sokurov's 'cinematographic story' is published under the same cover as his essay on Eisenstein.
40 Mikhail Iampolski, 'Truncated Families and Absolute Intimacy', in *The Cinema of Alexander Sokurov*, ed. Birgit Beumers and Nancy Condee (London: I.B.Tauris, 2011), 110; Jeremi Szaniawski, *The Cinema of Alexander Sokurov: Figures of Paradox* (New York: Wallflower Press, 2014), 244.
41 Sokurov, 'Aleksandra. Kinematograficheskii rasskaz', 67.
42 Sergei Eizenshtein, *Disnei* (Moscow: Ad Marginem, 2014), 70.

Part Three

Pathos, Immersion, Affect

7

Formula pafosa, Pathosformel: Eisenstein and Warburg

Antonio Somaini

'An unexpected juncture'

In an essay written in 1928, after having seen some Moscow performances of the Kabuki theatre troupe led by Ichikawa Sadanji II, Sergei Eisenstein underlined the 'unexpected juncture' that linked the archaic, centuries-long tradition of Kabuki with the latest stage in the technological development of cinema: sound cinema.[1] He would further develop these ideas in the 1929 essay 'Beyond the Shot',[2] stating that the 'monistic' approach to the interweaving of music, stage design, acting, dancing and singing found in Kabuki – the fact that all these expressive registers were treated as 'equivalents' rather than hierarchically subordinated to one another – could provide a model for the future of audiovisual 'montage thinking'.[3]

Beyond the cross-cultural and cross-temporal correspondences that interested Eisenstein in 1928–9, and would increasingly preoccupy him throughout the 1930s and 1940s, we could describe as an 'unexpected juncture' another set of correspondences: between some of Eisenstein's key ideas and those of various art historians, cultural critics and philosophers who were writing in the same period, but who Eisenstein never had a chance to meet or read. Among these is the 'unexpected juncture', still somewhat understudied, that links Eisenstein with Aby Warburg (1866–1929).[4] Without being aware of one another, Eisenstein and Warburg both found in the idea of a 'formula of pathos' – *Pathosformel* in Warburg, *formula pafosa* in Eisenstein – a concept which was to play a crucial role in their understanding of the history, agency and power of images and artistic forms.

Eisenstein mentions the concept of a *formula pafosa*, sometimes called *formula ekstaza* (formula of ecstasy),[5] in various sections of his unfinished book project *Nonindifferent Nature* (1939–47): in particular, in two chapters of the section 'Pathos' (1946–7) entitled, in the English translation, 'Superconcreteness' and 'On the question of suprahistory'. These two chapters, and the section they are part of, are preceded by a first section entitled 'On the structure of things' (1939), in which Eisenstein presents the three notions of *organicity*, *pathos* and *ecstasy* as the pillars of the entire theoretical construction of *Nonindifferent Nature*. As in most of Eisenstein's writings, the key question is how to understand the laws that govern the effectiveness of a work of art, its capacity to act on the mind, body and emotions of the spectator.[6] Having tackled this issue through notions such as 'expressive movement', 'montage of attractions', 'intellectual montage', 'imagicity' and 'regression' in *Nonindifferent Nature*, Eisenstein presents the idea that the most effective artworks are those structured according to a 'formula of pathos' that endows them with the capacity of capturing and giving form to the energy and the dialectical dynamism that pervades the natural environment, to release such energy onto the spectator.

Warburg mentions the concept of a *Pathosformel* for the first time in an essay written in 1905 entitled 'Dürer and Italian antiquity'.[7] The concept then became a cornerstone of the psychological and energeticist approach to the cultural history of images that guided his work on the picture atlas *Mnemosyne* (1924–9).[8] This was to be a series of rectangular plates with black backgrounds and various montage-like arrangements of photographic reproductions which were supposed to map the 'survival' [*Nachleben*] and the spatio-temporal 'migration' [*Wanderung*], mainly from Greek and Roman antiquity to the Italian Renaissance, of a series of *Pathosformeln*, a series of recurring 'heightened gestures' [*erregte Gebärde*] that Warburg considered to be expressive of a number of intense prototypical emotions and affects.

In converging towards the same idea, Eisenstein and Warburg also converged in some cases on the same works of art: for example, the sculptural figure of the Laocoön and the painting entitled *Laocoön* (1610–14) by El Greco, discussed in Eisenstein's essay 'El Greco and the cinema' (1937–9),[9] and included by Warburg as plate n. 41a of *Mnemosyne*, dedicated to the 'pathos of suffering' and to the 'death of the priest'.

How to explain such an 'unexpected juncture'? How to explain that both Eisenstein and Warburg, independently and in different phases of their intellectual itinerary, decided to assign a central role in their writings to the same, slightly oxymoronic concept of a *formula of pathos*? 'Slightly oxymoronic' since it associates the turbulent, unstable energy of *pathos* with the fixed, schematic nature of the *formula*.[10]

This coincidence raises a number of questions that will be tackled in the following pages: What role do the concepts of *formula pafosa* and *Pathosformel* play in Eisenstein's and Warburg's interpretation of the history of images and artistic forms? What understanding of art, psychology, memory and history explains for both of them the *transhistorical, transmedial nature* of the *formula pafosa* and the *Pathosformel*, with their recurrent manifestations and their active dimension? What temporal models were their visions of history based on? What epistemological tools did they use to compare and analyse the different historical manifestations of the *formula pafosa* and the *Pathosformel*? Finally, can we identify, in both Eisenstein's and Warburg's intellectual itineraries, a common source that might explain such unexpected convergence? Before tackling the first three questions, we may suggest an answer to the fourth.

New Mexico and Mexico

Behind this unexpected convergence towards the same concept of a *formula of pathos* there is, in both Eisenstein's and Warburg's intellectual itinerary, the experience of a direct encounter with 'ancient' energies and affects which seemed to have survived through history before reappearing in the present. This encounter took place for Warburg during his journey to New Mexico in 1895–6 to study the serpent ritual of the Hopi indians, as we know from the notes and the photographs that he used for a lecture given in 1923 in the psychiatric clinic of Kreuzlingen, after a six-year stay in Paul Binswanger's institution.[11] For Eisenstein, it was his travels in Mexico between December 1930 and March 1932, for the aborted *Que viva México!*, which we can study through the unedited rushes and various attempts by others to edit these, the diary entries and the drawings produced while in Mexico, as well as through the many references to the Mexican journey in Eisenstein's later writings, including his *Memoirs*.[12] There are indeed analogies between these two journeys which may well have created a common interest in the idea of a *formula of pathos*.

In the first place, the journeys were travels *in space* which were experienced by both Warburg and Eisenstein as travels *in time*, reaching back to earlier, deeper strata of culture, in which Warburg hoped to find the origins of symbolic thought and action, and Eisenstein believed he could observe the surviving forms of 'prelogical' and 'sensuous thinking'.[13]

Furthermore, these journeys made possible encounters with cultures perceived by both Warburg and Eisenstein as intertwining different historical layers, so that deeper, older strata seemed to have survived and mingled with later ones. Warburg saw such intertwining in the 'contaminated' culture of the Hopi which, like a 'stratified' multilayered 'palimpsest',[14] was characterized by the coexistence of 'imaginative magic' and 'rational utilitarianism',[15] by a 'transitional state [...] between magic and logos'.[16] In Mexico, Eisenstein discovered a country where 'history had been replaced by ... geography', as he wrote in the commentary to another unfinished film project, *The Ferghana Canal* (1939), so that moving between different regions one had the impression of travelling 'in time, across centuries of history', across 'shifts' [*sdvigi*] from one epoch to another.[17]

Both itineraries through New Mexico and Mexico provided direct contact with rituals and ceremonies in which bodies in a state of ecstatic frenzy experienced some kind of transformation, as if pathos and ecstasy had an intrinsically *dynamic* and *performative* nature. Warburg saw this not only in the Hopi's serpent ritual but also in the 'dance of the antelope' which he photographed in San Ildefonso – two rituals that he interpreted as a kind of 'danced mythological causality',[18] aimed at producing effects such as the coming of rain. Eisenstein saw it in Catholic processions reenacting the Via Crucis in the town of Amecameca, and in the hybrid ceremonies of *danzantes* during the celebration of the Virgin of Guadalupe in Mexico City.

Such encounters convinced both Warburg and Eisenstein that the cultural history and psychology of images, their *migration* across epochs and cultures, and their *agency*, their capacity to act on the body, mind and emotions of the spectator, could only be understood within a cultural-anthropological perspective.[19] And this pointed to an archaeologically stratified, non-linear understanding of history, locating the present within a complex 'deep time', within a *longue durée* conceived in archaeological and anthropological terms.[20]

In both cases, finally, it was the practice of *montage* – the display of black-and-white photographic reproductions of works of art against the black velvet background of the plates in Warburg's *Mnemosyne* atlas, the sequencing of examples and references in Eisenstein's writings from the 1930s and 1940s, often accompanied by drawings, diagrams and photo-collages – that seemed the most appropriate way of organizing and comparing images stemming from different historical layers, conceived by both Warburg and Eisenstein as a crucial *morphological tool* for the study of images and artistic forms.

Warburg's *Pathosformel*

The term *Pathosformel* appears for the first time in Warburg's writings in the 1905 essay 'Dürer and the Italian Antiquity', in which he wrote that what the Italian artists of the Renaissance were searching for in the art of classical antiquity were not examples of a classicism based on the Apollinean values of 'noble simplicity and silent greatness' praised by Winckelmann in his famous *History of Ancient Art* (1764), but rather the models of an art inbued with a Dionysian energy of pathos: an art in which the protagonists of the Italian Renaissance could find, as Warburg writes, a series of 'prototypes of heightened pathetical gestures'.[21]

Warburg's interest in such 'heightened gestures' – which were for him the 'embodiment' [*Verkörperung*] of a broader understanding of life 'in movement'[22] – dated back at least to 1893, the year in which he wrote 'Sandro Botticelli's *The Birth of Venus* and *Spring*'. In this, he highlighted the presence of a number of figures in Botticelli's mythological paintings, such as Venus, characterized by a series of 'moving accessories' [*bewegtes Beiwerk*]:[23] garments, veils, draperies, hair, which seem to be set in motion both by the figures's own inner emotional states, and by the turbulence of the natural *milieu* that surrounds them, emphasized by an intense wind. This is true not only of *The Birth of Venus* (1482–3) but also of another, highly symbolic painting by Botticelli, *Spring* (1485–7), in which the nymph Chloris (visible on the extreme right) is pursued by a flying figure personifying the first wind of spring, Zephyr. We find further examples of 'moving accessories' in other nymph-like figures studied by Warburg: the running, almost flying servant in Ghirlandaio's *The Birth of the Saint John the Baptist* (1486–90) in the Tornabuoni Chapel of Santa Maria Novella in Florence, and the dancing Salome in Fra Filippo Lippi's *The Death of Saint John the Baptist* (1460–4) in the Cathedral of Prato.

These 'moving accessories' were for Warburg not only a stylistic trait that Italian painters of the late fifteenth century had found in models from classical antiquity, but also the signs of an understanding of pathos as a force that becomes visible at the intersection between inner bodily states and the natural, sensible *milieu* or *medium* surrounding the body itself.[24]

As Georges Didi-Huberman wrote in his *Ninfa fluida: Essai sur le drapé-désir*:

> The 'moving accessories' that Warburg talks about are much more than something 'accessory'. Warburg saw them as the *very texture of animation* in the art of the Quattrocento. As the operator of a conversion between the intangible *air* and the visible *bodies*, but also between the visible *movements* and the *motions* of the soul. If sails agitated by the breeze, those 'billowing sheets', proliferated

so remarkably during the Renaissance, it is because they provided artists with an invaluable figurative and pathetic tool: a kind of interface that bodies could have, at their edges, between the 'external causes' (relating to the space outside, to the atmosphere) and the 'internal causes' (relating to the space inside, to the mood) of their movements.[25]

In the essay on Dürer, the 'formula of pathos' manifests itself in the 'pathos-laden, heightened gestures'[26] of the figures of two furious maenads caught in the act of killing Orpheus, both in Dürer's drawing *The Death of Orpheus* and in its source, an engraving from the circle of Andrea Mantegna. In both these images, Warburg saw examples of how 'forcefully' an 'archaeologically authentic *Pathosformel*' of murderous fury had 'migrated', thanks to some kind of 'survival' followed by a 're-entry', from classical antiquity to the Italian and the northern Renaissance, travelling across a kind of 'pathetic current' [*pathetische Strömung*] that carried a series of 'prototypes of heightened pathetic gestures' and acted as a powerful 'style-building' factor.[27] The term 'current' – like other crucial terms in Warburg's later writings, such as 'polarity', 'magnetisation', 'conservation' or 'inversion' of energy, or the Latin 'transformatio energetica' – refers to electricity and magnetism, and is part of an 'energetic theory of human expression', or an 'historical phenomenology of the energetic formation of expressive values',[28] which was the basis of Warburg's cultural history of images.[29]

Twenty years after the essay on Dürer, the concept of *Pathosformel* would become a cornerstone of Warburg's *psychological* and *energeticist* approach to the cultural history of images that was deployed throughout the plates of atlas *Mnemosyne*. The sixty-three plates that have survived stem from the final version of an atlas which Warburg considered a work in progress, to be exhibited periodically in the oval room of the library of the Warburg Institute in Hamburg. In each plate, a series of black-and-white photographic reproductions chosen from Warburg's vast photographic archive were arranged in different configurations against a black background which, like the statues of the 'Gods' in Eisenstein's *October*, acted as a 'medium' to decontextualize each image and treat it as an element of a carefully planned montage.[30] Warburg's intention, as we know from the 'Introduction' he wrote in 1929, the year of his death, was to establish an 'inventory' of 'pre-coined expressive values' concerning the 'representation of life in motion'.[31] In mapping the *Pathosformeln* linked to emotions, gestures and actions such as 'fight', 'defeat', 'victory', 'triumph', 'fury', 'murder', 'destruction', 'lamentation', 'sacrifice', 'ascension' and 'apotheosis', the atlas was to become a *mnemotechnical tool*: an instrument to help visualize manifestations of the intense pathos-laden emotions that were preserved in the collective memory as 'engrams of affective experience'.[32]

Warburg had found the term 'engram' in the theories of memory as a function of 'organized matter' developed by Ewald Hering and Richard Semon.[33] According to both of these, memory was not a mental activity specific to human consciousness, but a property of all organized, organic matter that explained many processes of reproduction and transmission between an organism and its environment. Human collective memory was considered by them to be a part of such processes. Warburg reformulated this idea by considering collective memory as a collection of 'engrams of emotional experience'[34] produced by intense emotions experienced in the early, archaic stages of the history of humanity – such as the Dionysian rites with their states of mass orgiastic exaltation and phobic furore – which could remain for long in a state of latency, but once reactivated could release the emotional energy they had accumulated.

The hundreds of black-and-white photographic reproductions that Warburg planned to include in the plates of the published version of the atlas, were conceived by him as 'dynamograms':[35] that is, visual diagrams or 'seismographs'[36] of emotional energy flowing across time and space, oscillating, through a constant 'transformatio energetica', between the 'schizophrenic' and 'manic-depressive'[37] poles of 'calm contemplation' and 'orgiastic fury',[38] 'vita activa and vita contemplativa',[39] and coagulating at different moments in various *Pathosformeln*. Organized in clusters and constellations within the rectangular space of the plates, the photographic reproductions allowed these to be identified and studied through 'comparative observation',[40] allowing the 'psycho-historian'[41] of images to develop what Warburg called an 'iconology of the interval' or of the 'in-between space' [*Ikonologie des Zwischenraums*]:[42] an iconology or 'dynamology' of 'life in movement' tracing the trajectories of expressive emotional energy and the different spatio-temporal manifestations of the *Pathosformeln*.

What interested him in particular, in the context of his psychological approach to the cultural history of images, was how in certain cases the same *Pathosformel* manifested itself through a sort of 'energetic inversion' in figures lying at opposite emotional poles. This unstable, polar dimension of the *Pathosformel* was particularly evident in the figure of the nymph, of which Warburg had found a prototype in a servant in the already mentioned fresco by Ghirlandaio, *The Birth of St. John the Baptist*. With her 'lively mobility', her 'loose hair and fluttering garments',[43] the nymph could be found in various examples throughout Greek and Roman antiquity, notably in representations of the wind goddess Fortuna. From the mid-fifteenth century, it began to reappear, with its polar oscillating energy, during the Italian Renaissance and the Baroque, as a murderous maenad dismembering the body of Orpheus, as in Dürer's drawing, and as a mourning Mary Magdalen at the foot of the Cross, in Bertoldo di Giovanni's *Crucifixion* (1485). Warburg underlined this oscillation in various plates of the atlas: in plate 42, the nymph appears as a 'Maenad at the Cross';[44] in plate 47, as a 'protective angel' in Guercino's *Tobias and the Angel Raphael* (1624–6), and as a 'head hunter' in Filippo Lippi's *Salome Dancing Before Herod* (1464).

Eisenstein's *formula pafosa*

The various texts by Eisenstein that have been assembled under the title *Nonindifferent Nature* were not the first in which he engaged with questions of pathos and ecstasy.[45] The artistic and political dimension of pathos had already been tackled in 1926, in the context of the German reception of *The Battleship Potemkin*, which Eisenstein described in the essay 'Constantsa' (1926) as characterized by a 'new psychologism', moving away from the 'montage of attractions' which had played a key role in *The Strike* (1925).[46] In an interview published in the *Berliner Tagblatt* under the title 'Eisenstein on Eisenstein, Director of *Battleship Potemkin*', he defended *Potemkin* from accusation of being 'too full of pathos'.[47] Cinema, writes Eisenstein, is about 'tendentiousness', about 'speculating' on 'latent moods and passions', and directing them towards the desired goal through a form that acts as a 'lightning-conductor' and avoids any 'dissipation of energies'.[48]

In 1929 the question of pathos and ecstasy recurs in an essay entitled 'How Is Pathos Made?' in which Eisenstein interprets the viewer's emotional response to film as 'an ecstatic, trance-like state'.[49] During his three-year journey abroad from 1930 to 1932, he would further explore the condition of ecstasy through texts of the mystics Teresa of Avila, St John of the Cross and, most importantly, Ignatius Loyola. Another 1929 essay, 'The Dramaturgy of Film Form', stated that the 'emotional dynamisation' of the spectator derives from the capacity of film form to capture and reproduce 'in concrete forms' the tensions and conflicts that characterize 'the dialectical system of objects' to transmit their transformative energy to the spectator.[50] As Eisenstein writes, the 'dynamisation of material' which constitutes film form 'produces, not in the spatial but in the psychological, i.e. the emotional, field' a form of 'pathos', with the last pages of the essay offering examples from the end of *The Strike* (1924) and from various passages of *October*.⁵¹

The connection between *pathos*, *ecstasy* and *dialectics* is crucial to understanding the concepts of 'formula of pathos' and 'formula of ecstasy' that we find in *Nonindifferent Nature*. In the texts that make up this book, Eisenstein considers nature to be essentially *ecstasic* because of its *dialectical* structure and *pathos* to be the emotion that accompanies the feeling of embodied participation in the dialectical processes of nature. Artworks organized according to these 'formulae' provide one of the ways of experiencing such embodied participation.

After the publication in 1925 of Engels's *Dialectic of Nature*, Eisenstein considered the realm of natural phenomena to be characterized by constant quantitative and qualitative transformations. Such dialectical 'shifts' and reversals render nature 'ecstatic' in the sense of being 'non-static', or 'out of a state of stasis' – the literal translation of the ancient Greek *ek-stasis* – and therefore 'nonindifferent'.[52] This 'non-indifference', this dialectical turbulence, even 'frenzy' [*isstuplenie*], is felt emotionally by the artist as 'pathos'. The artist experiences this emotion and injects it into a work of art which is itself in a state of continuous 'ecstasy', a leap of each separate element or sign of the work of art 'from quality to quality',[53] in such a way that each 'leap' becomes a dialectical reversal, 'a diapason leap into the opposite'.[54] From the work of art, the ecstatic flow of dialectical energy that runs across the natural phenomena then reaches the spectator, who 'feels organically tied, merged and united with a work of this type, just as he feels himself *one with and merged with* the organic environment and nature surrounding him'.[55] Experiencing a work of art characterized by a 'structure of pathos', the spectator experiences in the form of pathos and ecstasy 'the moments of culmination and becoming of the norms of the dialectical processes'.[56]

It is from this *sensory* and *empathic* bond that unites the spectator, the work of art and the organic environment which surrounds them that Eisenstein derives the definition of pathos and the idea of a 'formula of pathos', which all effective works of art have or *should* have (the notion has a normative dimension). Such a formula, he argues, is a principle that is 'in action and active', infusing in the work of art the dialectical turbulence of the natural environment, producing an emotional, embodied and kinesthetic reaction in the spectator.[57] In the part of *Nonindifferent Nature* entitled 'On the structure of things' (1939), he sets out to define pathos starting from the effects that it has on the spectator:

Pathos is what forces the viewer to jump out of his seat. It is what forces him to flee from his place. It is what forces him to clap, to cry out. It is what forces his eyes to gleam with ecstasy before tears of ecstasy appear in them. In a word, it is everything that forces the viewer to 'be beside himself'' [*vykhodit iz sebya*].

Putting it more elegantly, we might say that the effect of the *pathos* of a work consists in bringing the viewer to the point of ecstasy. Such a formula adds nothing new, for three lines above we said exactly the same thing, since *ex stasis* (out of a state) means literally the same thing as 'being beside oneself' or 'going out of a normal state' does.

All the signs mentioned strictly follow this formula. Sitting – he stood up. Standing – he jumped. Motionless – he moved. Silent – he shouted. Lusterless – began to gleam (eyes). Dry – became moist (tears). In every case there occurred a 'going out of a state', 'being beside oneself'.

But this is not sufficient: 'To be beside oneself' in not 'to go into nothing'. To be beside oneself is unavoidably also a transition to something else, to something different in quality, to something opposite to what preceded it (no motion – to motion, no sound – to sound, etc.).[58]

The four sections of *Nonindifferent Nature* examine different examples of creating pathos and ecstasy in works of art predating cinema – drawing, painting, architecture, theatre and literature – from the most varied cultural and historical traditions. In all of these, Eisenstein searches for examples of such 'being beside oneself', leading from a state to its polar opposite, which constitute the essence of 'the ecstastic scheme of the construction of pathos'.[59]

In some cases this ecstatic 'frenzy' manifests itself as an 'explosion' that propels forms in all directions, triggering some kind of dialectical transformation.[60] As often in his writings, Eisenstein cites examples from his own films and describes 'the pathos of the milk separator'[61] in *The Old and the New*: a scene that stages the 'qualitative transformation' of a drop of milk 'into a drop of cream' as a symbol of a 'gigantic qualitative leap in the area of social progress, from individual landownership to collective agriculture'.[62] In the same film, he finds an ecstatic dimension in the perspective distortions produced by the 28mm lens used for deep-focus shots that 'propel objects [...] *to go beyond themselves*'.[63] In painting, Eisenstein finds examples of pathos and ecstasy in the work of El Greco, already examined in the essay 'El Greco and the cinema'. In *The Resurrection from the Grave* (c. 1595–8), he highlights a truly ecstatic 'explosion' of forms that propels upwards, in the upper part of the painting, the figure of the resurrected Christ with its 'flight to heaven', while pushing downwards, in the lower part of the painting, the figure of a naked human body, 'amazed, turned completely upside down, with feet up ... in stunned fall'.[64] Leonardo's *St. Anne, the Virgin, and Child* (1503–19) displays a different kind of *ek-stasis*, in which a sort of telescoped series of explosions seems to propel the three figures one out of the other, following 'a scheme of the "ejection of the next out of self"', as happens also in some of Saul Steinberg's drawings.[65] In the field of architecture, Eisenstein finds examples of ecstatic forms in the multilayered, labyrinthine spaces of Piranesi's *Prisons* (particularly in the series dated 1745 and 1761–5) and in the 'telescoped' interior spaces of his own *Ivan the Terrible*, as well as in the upward thrusts of Gothic cathedrals and in the 'vertical landscapes' of Chinese and Japanese paintings.

In yet other cases, 'being beside oneself' appears in works which describe or visualize some kind of *immersion* or *dissolution* of a subject into the surrounding natural environment: a *merging* of the self and the landscape, a *blurring* of the limits that separate individuals from their encompassing *milieu*.[66] This may happen when the pathos of a character radiates 'beyond the limits of the human being' and spreads 'both to the milieu and the surroundings of the character'.[67] A prime example of this occurs in Shakespeare's *King Lear*, in the storm scene, where the 'frenzy' of the protagonist turns into the 'frenzy' of nature itself:

> Blow, winds, and crack your cheeks! rage! blow!
> You cataracts and hurricanoes, spout
> Till you have drench'd our steeples, drown'd the cocks!
> You sulphurous and thought-executing fires,
> Vaunt-couriers to oak-cleaving thunderbolts,
> Singe my white head! And thou, all-shaking thunder,
> Smite flat the thick rotundity o' the world!
> Crack nature's moulds, all germens spill at once,
> That make ingrateful man![68]

Eisenstein also found examples of this overspill of pathos from a literary character in the way that Émile Zola compels the 'surrounding environment' [*sreda*] and 'atmosphere' to resound 'in unison' with the emotional tonality of a given moment in his 'realist' depictions of human existence.[69]

In the section entitled 'Nonindifferent Nature', this idea of an ecstatic 'going out of oneself' is further developed in the idea of an 'emotional landscape', which for Eisenstein designated 'an image of the mutual absorption of human and nature into one another'.[70] This he considered as equivalent to the idea of a 'nonindifferent nature', since it refers to a situation in which the landscape acts as 'a complex carrier of the possibilities for a plastic interpretation of emotions', 'resonating' with some kind of affective tonality or 'atmosphere'.[71] Eisenstein found examples of this in the 'symphony of the mist' in his own *Potemkin*[72] and in the 'stormily emotional landscape' of El Greco's *Storm over Toledo*, in which the German art historian Hugo Kehrer saw a scene where 'everything concrete dissolves, becoming the grandiose embodiment of the inner states of El Greco'.[73] He mentions also a whole series of literary and pictorial works, in which what is at stake is a kind of 'dissolution in nature and a union with it'.[74] Examples include the longing for withdrawal into the natural world that emanates from Chinese landscape paintings of the Song dynasty (960–1279), with their depiction of an 'immersion into Nothing',[75] and late-Romantic literary passages conveying an 'ecstastic feeling of a merging with nature'.

At the end of the section entitled 'Pathos' of *Nonindifferent Nature*, Eisenstein asks himself what unites all these different examples: is it a simple analogy, a simple formal resemblance, or do we find in all of them 'the same laws' the same 'formula'?[76] The response to this question comes in the chapters 'Superconcreteness' and 'On the question of suprahistory', in which Eisenstein explains the foundations of the *transmedial, transhistorical* nature of pathos and the ecstasy:

> We selected our examples to be as colorful and varied as possible, without taking into account time, place, nationality, or theme of the works chosen …
>
> And we discovered everywhere that one and the same formula by which, without person, epoch, or field, the fundamental ecstatic explosion is achieved, which lies at the basis of the *pathos* effect of the whole.
>
> The question naturally arises – what is this extrahistorical, extranational, extrasocial 'panacea' with certain immanent features 'outside of time and space'?
>
> And how can it be that with the greatly varied and incompatible contents in these most diverse examples of the principle of 'pathosization', the principle of their pathos exposition, the conditions of the pathos quality of their sound, they suddenly turn out to be exactly the same?[77]

The question was a difficult one, for anyone writing in the cultural and political context of the Soviet Union just after the end of the Second World War, dominated by a strong nationalism and a teleological vision of history. Eisenstein answers it by saying that what explains the 'suprahistorical', 'supranational' and 'supra-social' nature of the 'formula of pathos' is the fact that, in the works of art that follow it, the spectator experiences 'a sense of participation in the laws governing the course of natural phenomena'.[78] He adds:

The norms of this state, as we have already said, are known to us.

They are single and unchanging.

These are those basic laws according to which the formation of everything that exists flows.

The 'obsession' related to them.

The structure of its psychic state is tuned in unison to it.

And through it this system becomes the basic structure of the work and 'the formation of its material'.

And in a vivid experience, those perceiving this structure, through the system of images of the work, participate in the operating of the norms of motion of the whole existing order of things and, experiencing it in dizzy ecstasy, participate in the state of being possessed by pathos.[79]

Connecting these ideas to those being developed at the same time for the book project *Method* (1932–48), Eisenstein presented this 'psychic state' of ecstasy and pathos as something that is located below and before any form of activity by the intellect or the imagination. It is a state that precedes the formation of an image or a concept: it is both 'aniconic' and 'pre-iconic', rooted in sheer 'sensation' and in the symptoms of that sensation.[80] To experience the state of pathos and ecstasy means, therefore, to experience 'a transport out of concepts, out of representation, out of images, out of any rudiments of consciousness whatsoever, into the sphere of "pure" effect, feeling, sensation, "state"'.[81] In this way, pathos and ecstasy become two of the 'paths of regression' that Eisenstein had been exploring, ever since the Mexican journey, for the unfinished book project *Method*: regression 'towards the origins', that is, 'from a phase of development to one considered contrary to evolutionary development'.[82] 'In the process of ecstasy, he writes, the ecstatic person "ascends" to the earliest phases, and therefore must inevitably find himself experiencing "Essence" and "*Être*" [being], becoming and the principle of becoming', in a form of pre-logical 'vibration' and 'participation'.[83]

Conclusion

We may finally draw some conclusions on the analogies and differences between Warburg and Eisenstein in their use of the same concept of a *formula of pathos*. Warburg was, of course, writing as a cultural historian of images, searching for the psychological principles that could explain the survival and the reappearances of *Pathosformeln* through time, while Eisenstein wrote primarily as a filmmaker, searching the history of the arts and a wide array of disciplines, including philosophy, ethnology, psychology, physiology and biology, for laws that might explain the effectiveness of different art forms, to apply these in his own film and theatre projects.

In fact, Warburg never gave a definition of the *Pathosformel*, even though the concept played a crucial role in his understanding of the cultural history of images. Eisenstein, however, defined the *formula pafosa* as the characteristic of a work of art that renders it capable of both capturing the dialectical energy that pervades the natural environment and releasing such energy onto the spectator. For him, the effectiveness of the *formula pafosa* is reached when the artist, the artwork and the spectator experience that same state of 'being beside oneself' [*vykhod iz sebya*] which is constitutive of all natural phenomena.

For both Warburg and Eisenstein, the effectiveness of the 'formula of pathos' is rooted in the process of 'empathy' that ensures its transmission across time. Warburg mentions 'empathy' [*Einfühlung*] as a 'style-building force' at the beginning of his 1893 Botticelli essay, while Eisenstein, from the beginning of the first section of *Nonindifferent Nature* entitled 'On the structure of things', emphasizes that the spectator, by being exposed to an artwork organized according to the 'formula of pathos', experiences the feeling of being '*one with and merged with* the organic environment and nature surrounding him'. In both cases, it is the empathetic, lived experience of the 'pathetic current' that runs through history and the dialectical turbulence of a 'nonindifferent nature' that render the 'formula of pathos' a principle 'active and in action'.

Again, for both Warburg and Eisenstein, the 'formula of pathos' has a *transmedial, transhistorical* dimension. Warburg's *Pathosformeln* 'migrate' across a non-linear, non-progressive history conceived in terms of 'survival' and 're-entry', and what explains their persistence is their being rooted in 'engrams' engraved in the material fabric of collective memory. Eisenstein's *formula pafosa*, as we saw, is 'suprahistorical', 'supranational' and 'supra-social' because such are the dialectical laws of nature that it captures and transmits.

For both, it is an unstable, metamorphic principle, even though such instability is conceived by Warburg and Eisenstein in different terms. Warburg's energeticist approach to the cultural history of images leads him to think in terms of 'currents', 'polarities' and 'inversions', focusing on the ways in which the same *Pathosformel* might oscillate, throughout history, between opposite magnetic poles, as we saw in the case of the nymph. Eisenstein's understanding of the instability of the *formula pafosa* relies, instead, on a *dialectical*, rather than a *magnetic*, model. The *formula pafosa* is moved by the same dialectical principles that produce, within the world of natural phenomena, a series of 'shifts', 'leaps' and reversals, which in turn cause analogous dialectical transformations in the viewer.

Both the *Pathosformel* and the *formula pafosa* exist at the threshold between bodies and their surrounding natural environment. They manifest themselves in *gestures* – the 'heightened gestures' that Warburg pinpointed in the 1893 Botticelli essay, and never ceased studying thereafter, and the 'jumping out of his seat' that Eisenstein observes in the viewer acting under the force of pathos – but such *gestures* are closely related to the dynamism and turbulence of the natural *milieu* that surrounds them. Warburg underlines the connection between 'heightened gestures', 'moving accessories' and 'transitory movements'[84] produced by an intensely blowing wind already in his 1893 essay on Botticelli, where he studies the literary sources of *The Birth of Venus*, from the birth of Aphrodyte in the second Homeric Hymn to its reinterpretation in Angelo Poliziano's *Stanze per la giostra* (1475).[85] Loose undulating garments, veils and hair blown by the wind then become defining features of the nymph, in all its historical appearances, and all the 'heightened gestures' of each *Pathosformel* seem to take place in a fluid *milieu* that is itself in a 'heightened' state, characterized by an 'exterior mobility of forms'.[86] Eisenstein's *formula pafosa* calls for artworks that stage their forms within an 'environment' [*sreda*] that is itself in a state of turbulent 'non-indifference', and we might note that incessant wind plays a central role in *The Old and the New*, in which Eisenstein also finds an emblematic manifestation of the *formula pafosa*: the 'pathos of the milk separator'.

For both authors, finally, the tool used to study the 'formula of pathos' is montage: the open, variable montage of photographic reproductions that Warburg practised in the plates of the atlas *Mnemosyne*, and the literary montage that Eisenstein deploys in his writings, through the endless sequences of examples, digressions and citations that become increasingly prominent in the 1930s and 1940s, sometimes also supplemented by drawings, schemes, cut-out reproductions and even photo-collages. In montage – which Eisenstein considered a 'correlational and comparative activity' [*sootnositelnaya – sopostavitelnaya deyatelnost*] and Warburg a 'comparative observation' [*vergleichende Betrachtung*][87] – both believed they had found a heuristic and morphological tool to study the restless migrations and metamorphic manifestations of the 'formula of pathos'.

Notes

1. Sergei Eisenstein, 'An Unexpected Juncture', in Sergei Eisenstein, *Selected Works*, vol. 1: *Writings, 1922–1934* (London: I.B.Tauris, 2010), 115–22 [hereafter *SW*].
2. Ibid., 138–50.
3. Ibid., 117, 122.
4. On Eisenstein and Warburg, see Sylvia Sasse, 'Pathos und Antipathos. Pathosformeln bei Sergej Ejzenštejn und Aby Warburg', in *Pathos: Zur Geschichte einer problematischen Kategorie*, ed. Cornelia Zumbusch (Berlin: Akademie Verlag, 2010), 171–90; Antonio Somaini, *Ejzenštejn: Il cinema, le arti, il montaggio* (Turin: Einaudi, 2011), 363–6; Antonio Somaini, 'Cinema as "Dynamic Mummification", History as Montage: Eisenstein's Media Archaeology', in Sergei M. Eisenstein, *Notes for a General History of Cinema*, ed. Naum Kleiman and Antonio Somaini (Amsterdam: Amsterdam University Press, 2016), 61–77; Elena Vogman, *Sinnliches Denken. Eisensteins exzentrische Methode* (Zurich: Diaphanes, 2018), 425–30.
5. See Sergei Eisenstein, *Nonindifferent Nature*, ed. Herbert Marshall (Cambridge: Cambridge University Press, 1987), 183. On *Nonindifferent Nature*, see Naum Kleiman's introduction to the Russian edition (Naum Kleiman, 'Pafos Eizenshteina', in Sergei M. Eizenshtein, *Neravnodushnaia priroda* [Moscow: Muzei kino/d Eizenshein-tsentr, 2004], 5–32) and Pietro Montani's introduction to the Italian edition (Pietro Montani, 'Introduzione', in Sergej M. Ejzenštejn, *La natura non indifferente*, ed. Pietro Montani [Venice: Marsilio, 1981], IX–XLI).
6. For an analysis of how this key question runs through the entire corpus of Eisenstein's writings, see Somaini, *Ejzenštejn* and Antonio Somaini, 'Pouvoir des images et efficacité du montage', in *Serguei Eisenstein: L'Œil extatique*, ed. Ada Ackerman (Paris: Éditions du Centre Pompidou-Metz, 2019), 21–32.
7. Aby Warburg, 'Dürer and Italian Antiquity' (1905), in Aby Warburg, *The Renewal of Pagan Antiquity*, intro. Kurt W. Forster, foreword Gertrud Bing (Los Angeles: The Getty Research Institute for the History of Art and the Humanities, 1999), 553, 558.
8. Aby Warburg's *Mnemosyne* atlas can now be studied in a new edition: Aby Warburg, *Bilderatlas Mnemosyne: The Original*, ed. Roberto Ohrt and Axel Heil (Berlin: Hatje Cantz, 2020). Online access to the individual plates, with commentary, is available through journal *Engramma*: http://www.engramma.it/eOS/core/frontend/eos_atlas_index.php (accessed 2 June 2020).
9. Sergei Eisenstein, 'El Greco y el cine', in Sergei Eisenstein, *Cinématisme: Peinture et cinéma*, intro., notes and commentary François Albera (Dijon: Les presses du réel, 2009), 65–128.

10 Georges Didi-Huberman underlines this point in his *L'Image survivante: Histoire de l'art et temps des fantômes selon Aby Warburg* (Paris: Les Éditions de Minuit, 2002), 198.
11 The text of the lecture that Warburg presented, with numerous slides, at the Belle-Vue clinic in Kreuzlingen on 21 April 1923 is entitled 'Bilder aus dem Gebiet der Pueblo-Indianer in Nord-Amerika' and can be found in Aby Warburg, *Werke in einem Band*, ed. Martin Treml, Sigrid Weigel and Perdita Ladwig (Frankfurt: Suhrkamp, 2010), 525–66.
12 On Eisenstein's Mexican travel, see Masha Salazkina, *In Excess: Sergei Eisenstein's Mexico* (Chicago: University of Chicago Press, 2009). A new translation, by Natalie Ryabchikova, of excerpts from the diaries that Eisenstein wrote during the Mexican travel can be found in Marie Rebecchi and Elena Vogman (in collaboration with Till Gathmann), *Sergei Eisenstein and the Anthropology of Rhythm* (Rome: Nero, 2017), 37–64.
13 The exploration of the different forms of 'prelogical' and 'sensuous thinking' is at the centre of the unfinished book project *Method* (1932–48), which is accessible today in editions in Russian and translation of selected chapters in English. The two Russian editions are *Metod*, ed. Naum Kleiman, 2 vols (Moscow: Muzei kino/Eizenshtein-tsentr, 2002) and *Metod*, ed. Oksana Bulgakowa, 4 vols (Berlin: PotemkinPress, 2008). English translation by Dustin Condren of selected chapters of *Method* are available in *The Primal Phenomenon: Art*, ed. Oksana Bulgakowa and Dietmar Hochmuth (Berlin: PotemkinPress, 2017). Besides these two different editions, the most extensive study on *Method*, at present, can be found in Vogman, *Sinnliches Denken*.
14 Aby Warburg, 'Reise-Erinnerungen aus dem Gebiet der Pueblo Indianer in Nordamerika', in Warburg, *Werke in einem Band*, 572.
15 Warburg, 'Bilder aus dem Gebiet der Pueblo-Indianer in Nord-Amerika', 526.
16 Ibid., 538.
17 Sergei M. Eisenstein, 'Commentary on the Film *The Ferghana Canal*', in *Voprosy kinodramaturguii*, ed. Ilya Weissfeld (Moscow: Iskusstvo, 1959), 327–53.
18 Warburg, 'Bilder aus dem Gebiet der Pueblo-Indianer in Nord-Amerika', 557.
19 On the question of the *agency* of images, see David Freedberg, *The Power of Images: Studies in the History and Theory of Response* (Chicago: University of Chicago Press, 1991); Alfred Gell, *Art and Agency: An Anthropological Theory* (Oxford: Clarendon Press, 1998); and Horst Bredekamp, *Image Acts: A Systematic Approach to Visual Agency* (Berlin: De Gruyter, 2017).
20 On the tendency, during the 1920s and 1930s, of locating the present within the context of a *longue durée* conceived in archaeological and anthropological terms, see Erhard Schüttpelz, *Die Moderne im Spiegel des Primitiven* (Munich: Fink, 2005); the catalogue of the exhibition *Neolithic Childhood: Art in a False Present,*

c. 1930 (Berlin: Haus der Kulturen der Welt; Zurich: Diaphanes, 2018); and Maria Stavrinaki, *Saisis par la préhistoire: Enquête sur l'art et le temps des modernes* (Dijon: Les presses du réel, 2019).

21 Warburg, 'Dürer and Italian Antiquity', 176. Warburg marks his distance from Winckelmann in the essay 'Florentinische Wirklichkeit und antikisirender Idealismus' (1901), in *Werke in einem Band*, 225.

22 Aby Warburg, 'Sandro Botticellis *Geburt der Venus* und *Frühling*' (1893), in Warburg, *Werke in einem Band*, 63.

23 Ibid., 45.

24 On the concept of 'medium' as a sensible *milieu* see Antonio Somaini, 'Walter Benjamin's Media Theory: The *Medium* and the *Apparat*', *Grey Room* 62 (Winter 2016): 6–41.

25 Georges Didi-Huberman, *Ninfa fluida, Essai sur le drapé-désir* (Paris: Gallimard, 2015), 36, emphasis in the original.

26 Warburg, 'Dürer and the Italian Antiquity', 176.

27 Ibid., 176–7.

28 These ideas are particularly developed in the writings that accompany the work on the picture atlas *Mnemosyne*, between 1927 and 1929. See both the 'Mnemosyne Einleitung' in Warburg, *Werke in einem Band*, 629–39, and the 'Mnemosyne I. Aufzeichnungen, 1927–29', in Warburg, *Werke in einem Band*, 640–6.

29 On Warburg's cultural history of images in particular, see Andrea Pinotti, *Memorie del neutro: Morfologia dell'immagine in Aby Warburg* (Milan: Mimesis, 2001) and Georges Didi-Huberman, *L'Image survivante: Histoire de l'art et temps des fantômes selon Aby Warburg* (Paris: Éditions de Minuit, 2002).

30 On the black background of the atlas's plates as a 'medium', see Didi-Huberman, *L'Image survivante*, 495–6.

31 Warburg, 'Mnemosyne Einleitung', 630.

32 Ibid., 631.

33 Ewald Hering, *Über das Gedächtnis als allgemeine Funktion der organisiertes Materie* (1870); Richard Semon, *Die Mneme als erhaltendes Prinzip im Wechsel des organischen Geschehens* (1904).

34 Warburg, 'Mnemosyne Einleitung', 631.

35 Warburg, 'Mnemosyne I. Aufzeichnungen', 640.

36 Cf. Didi-Huberman, *L'Image survivante*, cit., the chapter entitled 'Sismographie des temps mouvants', 117–25. Warburg presented himself as a 'seismographer' in one of the texts written in 1923 and related to the travel to New Mexico: see 'Reise-Erinnerungen aus dem Gebiet der Pueblo Indianer in Nordamerika', 573.

37 Warburg, 'Mnemosyne I. Aufzeichnungen', 641, 644.

38 Warburg, 'Mnemosyne Einleitung', 629.

39 Warburg, 'Mnemosyne I. Aufzeichnungen', 645.

40 Warburg, 'Mnemosyne Einleitung', 630.
41 Warburg, 'Mnemosyne I. Aufzeichnungen', 645.
42 Ibid., 643.
43 Warburg's analysis of the fresco by Ghirlandaio and of the nymph can be found in the essay 'Florentinische Wirklichkeit und antikisierende Idealismus', 226ff.
44 In 2012 and 2014, first at Le Fresnoy - Studio national des arts contemporains in Tourcoing, and then at the Palais de Tokyo, Georges Didi-Huberman, in collaboration with the artist Arno Gisinger, curated two exhibitions entitled, respectively, *Histoire de fantômes* and *Nouvelles histoires de fantômes*. Both exhibitions were conceived as a reflection on the *dispositif* of the picture atlas, and included a video installation that dealt with the main theme of Warburg's plate n.42 – the pathos of mourning, its representations and its energetic inversions – by creating a new kind of atlas plate made of a series of video projections turned from the ceiling towards the floor. The result was a montage of scenes of mourning and lamentation, taken from the history of art and the history of cinema, and inviting the spectator to exercise a form of 'comparative observation' similar to the one that Warburg envisioned for the plates of *Mnemosyne*.
45 On the question of pathos in Eisenstein, besides the already quoted introductions to *Nonindifferent Nature* by Naum Kleiman and Pietro Montani, see also Natascha Drubek, 'Ejzenšteins Pathos. Verweltlichtes Wunder und ekstatische Dialektik', in *Ethos und Pathos: Mediale Wirkungsästhetik im 20. Jahrhundert in Ost und West*, ed. Riccardo Nicolosi and Tanja Zimmermann (Cologne: Böhlau, 2017), 203–22.
46 Sergei Eisenstein, 'Constantsa (Whither *The Battleship Potemkin*)', in *SW*, vol. 1, 69.
47 Sergei Eisenstein, 'Eisenstein on Eisenstein, the Director of *Potemkin*', in *SW*, vol. 1, 75.
48 Ibid.
49 Sergei M. Eisenstein, 'Kak delaetsia pafos?' (How Is Pathos Made?) (1929), Russian State Archive of Literature and Arts (RGALI), 1923-2-793, quoted in Ana Hedberg Olenina, *Psychomotor Aesthetics: Movement and Affect in Modern Literature and Film* (Oxford: Oxford University Press, 2020), 179.
50 Sergei Eisenstein, 'The Dramaturgy of Film Form (The Dialectical Approach to Film Form)' (1929), in *SW*, vol. 1, 161. On this essay see the revised and republished book by François Albera, *Eisenstein et le constructivisme russe* (Milan: Mimesis, 2019).
51 Ibid., 177.
52 On the theoretical and political implications of this 'nonindifference', and on Eisenstein's *Nonindifferent Nature* as 'a speculative media ecology', see Robert Bird, 'The Politics of Nonindifference in Eisenstein's Dialectics of Nature', this volume.
53 Eisenstein, *Nonindifferent Nature*, 38.

54 Ibid., 35.
55 Ibid., 12, emphasis in the original.
56 Ibid., 24.
57 Ibid., 168. See also Hedberg Olenina, *Psychomotor Aesthetics*.
58 Eisenstein, *Nonindifferent Nature*, 26–7.
59 Ibid., 185.
60 Ibid., 38.
61 Ibid., 39.
62 Ibid.
63 Ibid., 48, emphasis in the original.
64 Ibid., 118.
65 Ibid., 193.
66 On this topic, see Joan Neuberger, 'Eisenstein's Collectives: The Politics of Nature', this volume.
67 Eisenstein, *Nonindifferent Nature*, 39.
68 Shakespeare, *King Lear*, Act 3, Scene 2.
69 Eisenstein, *Nonindifferent Nature*, 60.
70 Ibid., 359.
71 Ibid., 355.
72 Ibid., 219.
73 Ibid., 361. On the painting *Storm over Toledo*, see also 121.
74 Ibid., 356.
75 Ibid., 355.
76 Ibid., 198, 165.
77 Ibid., 165–6.
78 Ibid., 168–169.
79 Ibid., 169.
80 Ibid., 187.
81 Ibid., 178–9.
82 Ibid., 173.
83 Ibid., 173–4.
84 Warburg, 'Sandro Botticellis *Geburt der Venus* und *Frühling*', 46.
85 In the essay, Warburg deploys a dense web of literary references for the analysis of Botticelli's *The Birth of Venus*, citing various literary descriptions of the way in which the wind produces the impression of a mobility and fluidity of forms both in the garments of the female figure of the nymph, with its various manifestations, and in the natural environment. On the connection between wind, nymph and the fluidity of forms across a whole series of artistic representations, from Botticelli and Leonardo to Man Ray, Victor Sjöström and Jean Vigo, see Didi-Huberman, *Ninfa fluida*. On the representations of the wind in the history of painting and in the

history of cinema, see Alessandro Nova, *The Book of the Wind: The Representation of the Invisible* (Montreal: McGill-Queen's University Press, 2011) and Benjamin Thomas, *L'Attrait du vent* (Crisnée: Yellow Now, 2016).

86 Warburg, 'Sandro Botticellis *Geburt der Venus* und *Frühling*', 58.

87 Sergei Eisenstein, *Prospectus of Additions to the Stuttgart Article*, in Albera, *Eisenstein et le constructivisme russe*, 260; Warburg, 'Mnemosyne Einleitung', 630.

8

Hypnosis, Psychotechnics and Magic of Art

Julia Vassilieva

While the appeal of hypnosis as a trope of mind-control has significantly diminished in the popular imagination, film studies have recently experienced a marked resurgence of interest in hypnosis. Works by Stephan Andriopolous, Raymond Bellour, Ruggero Eugeni and Andreas Killen have turned to a re-examination of hypnosis, echoing early film theory's fascination with hypnosis both as a subject of representation and as a cinematic trope.[1] We would have to look hard, however, to find any reference to Eisenstein's oeuvre in this context, and yet, as I argue in this chapter, hypnosis was central to Eisenstein's work, albeit a hypnosis singularly rethought for uniquely Eisensteinian purposes.

In fact, Eisenstein's entry into cinema took place under the aegis of hypnosis. We now know that prior to filming *The Strike* in 1924, he helped Esfir Shub re-cut Fritz Lang's *Doctor Mabuse, The Gambler* (1922) for Soviet release earlier in the same year.[2] Lang's film is, of course, one of the paradigmatic examples of cinema's mobilization of hypnosis, on multiple levels. Not only does its protagonist, the master criminal Dr Mabuse, use his hypnotic skills to control people's will and agency as part of a giant criminal machination, but the film also uses cinematic devices such as close-ups, shifting camera movements and editing techniques to construct what has been called 'its specific "hypnotic" address of the audience'.[3] As Andreas Killen has noted, *Dr Mabuse* 'appropriates for its purposes a medicalized narrative of postwar German society, while at the same time also foregrounding the act of enunciation that produces such narratives'.[4] In this sense, *Dr Mabuse* serves as 'the embodiment of the "hypnosis myth" and its function in the modern era', aligning the anxiety about control and manipulation of individuals and masses with the cinematic medium's capacity to 'cast a powerful spell over its audience'.[5]

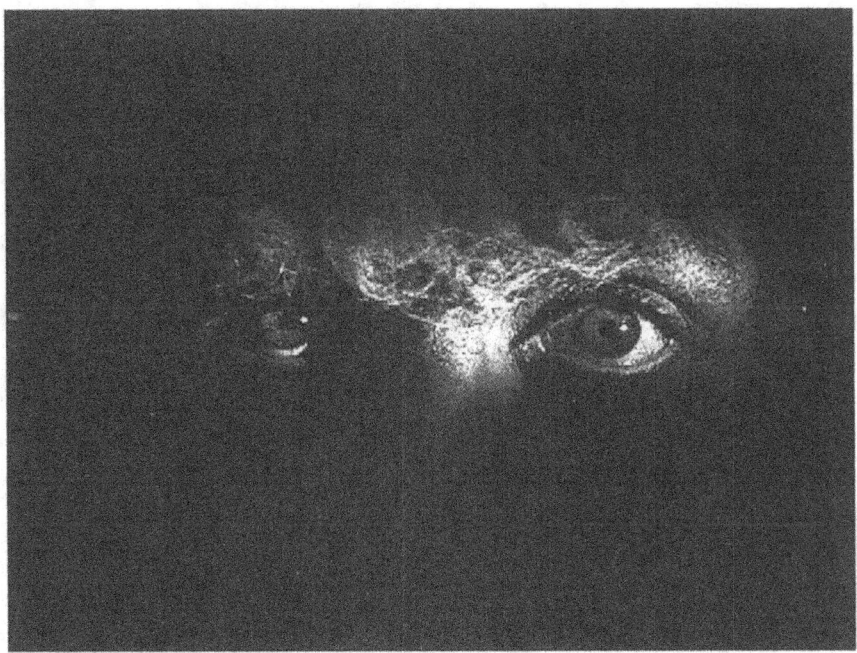

Figure 8.1 *Doctor Mabuse, The Gambler* (1922).

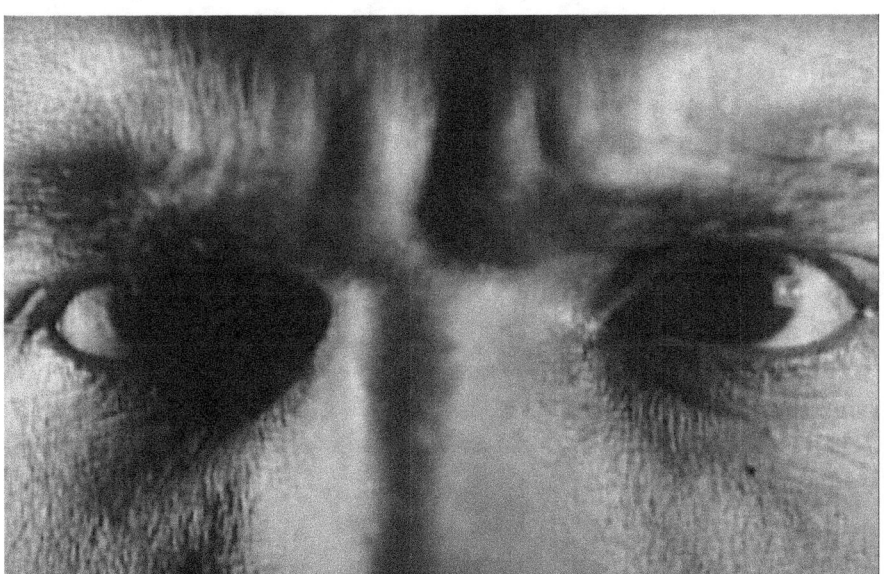

Figure 8.2 *The Strike* (1924).

Eisenstein's work on *Dr Mabuse* may have influenced him more profoundly than is commonly realized. Consider this comparison: the powerful final shot in *The Strike*, an extreme close-up of the worker Strongin's face (Figure 8.1), so often characterized as enigmatic, anomalous or even 'violently incongruent'[6] with the rest of the film, may be a direct intertextual reference to *Dr Mabuse* (Figure 8.2). Eisenstein presents Strongin's face in exactly the same manner as Lang presented the face of Dr Mabuse, who is seen from the point of view of his hypnotized subject, Wenk: both directors use lighting and framing to model the reduced peripheral attention and the concentration on the hypnotist's eyes typical of the hypnotized subject. However, if Shub and Eisenstein infamously had to transform *Dr Mabuse* through re-cutting for the Soviet censors, investing the film with a meaning contrary to that of Lang's story, characters and message, Eisenstein's appropriation of Lang's shot likewise recodifies its intention. The function of Strongin's hypnotic gaze in *The Strike* is not to put audiences to sleep, or into a trance, but to awaken revolutionary consciousness and agency in them.

Such a paradoxical approach to hypnosis would continue to inform Eisenstein's engagement with the phenomenon throughout his career. The desire to recodify hypnosis was clearly reflected in his interpretations of the crises he experienced in his understanding of the psychological mechanisms of art. The first crisis occurred in the 1920s when Eisenstein came to see art as 'fictive' activity bringing to the viewer a sense of participation and accomplishment through vicarious experience. In the early 1930s he experienced his second crisis, when, starting to work on his late major research project *Method*, he came to associate the mechanisms of art with regress. Nonetheless, in his accounts of these crises of aesthetic conscience or consciousness Eisenstein carefully avoided connecting his problematic understanding of art with hypnosis, despite the fact that the received view of hypnosis would readily link it to both fictive satisfaction and to regress, while the moral panic aligning hypnosis with manipulation, brainwashing and moral corruption would certainly have reinforced its negative connotations. Yet, reflecting on his second crisis and providing a list of medical conditions analogous to regress, Eisenstein conspicuously doesn't mention hypnosis; instead, he writes:

> It suddenly became clear that [...] through the use of form, art pushes both its creator and its viewer into the deepest chasms of primitive barbarism, which can be placed alongside alcoholism, with early dementia (with its chiming Latin name of *dementia praecox*, reminding one of rooster fights) or menacing schizophrenia.[7]

For, in Eisenstein's conception, hypnosis is similar to an altered and, indeed, augmented state of consciousness and subjectivity. His aim, thus, was to demystify hypnosis by uncovering an objective, scientific explanation of the phenomenon and repurpose it for the transformative and empowering aims of his cinema.

Eisenstein's views of hypnosis were formed in the context of his intense engagement with contemporary developments in the *psy* disciplines – psychology, psychoneurology and psychotechnics – and, specifically, his collaboration with the celebrated Russian psychologists Lev Vygotsky and Alexander Luria, which started in mid-1920s. Considering the variety of psychological schools in Russian psychology in the 1920s – 'objective' psychology represented by Ivan Pavlov (1849–1936) and Vladimir Bekhterev (1857–1927), 'idealistic' psychology advocated by Georgy Chelpanov (1862–1936), religious and philosophical psychology, and psychoanalysis – it is significant that Eisenstein came to form his most enduring collaboration with Luria and Vygotsky precisely at the time when they were laying down the foundations for what would become known as cultural-historical theory.

Cultural-historical theory would emerge as the most original and, arguably, the most valuable perspective elaborated in Russian social sciences.[8] As Jerome Bruner observes, it represented nothing less than a 'meta-psychology that encompassed the phylogeny, cultural history, ontogeny, and moment-to-moment dynamics of human functioning as a life-long process of becoming'.[9] This paradigm was forged in the short period between 1928 and 1934, yet the project was ultimately left unfinished: Vygotsky died from tuberculosis in 1934, while in 1936 the theory became effectively banned in a climate of growing ideological pressure on science and the demand to elaborate a 'true Marxist psychology'. Remarkably, Eisenstein's collaboration with Luria, and therefore his engagement with cultural-historical theory, continued through this turbulent era and then through the Second World War until his death in 1948.

Received accounts of Eisenstein's initial contacts with Luria and Vygotsky note their shared interest in aesthetic issues such as expressive movement and the nascent language of cinema. However, in his still-unpublished diary Eisenstein outlines a different context for his first meeting with Luria: he recalled that they met through Alexander Tygai and that their first conversation focused on 'tests for cinematographers'.[10] Tygai was head of the educational films section at the Mezrabpom Studio, where he was responsible for selecting themes for such films as well as for connecting scientists and filmmakers. The networking successes of this energetic entrepreneur included his introduction of Vsevolod Pudovkin to Pavlov to produce *The Mechanics of the Human Brain* (1925), a film intended to popularize Pavlov's theory of conditioned reflexes.[11] The fact that Eisenstein met Luria through Tygai, and the topic of their first conversation, point towards a different framework for understanding the joint agenda of Eisenstein later collaboration with Luria and Vygotsky, namely, towards the field of psychotechnics that was gaining momentum in the USSR at this time.

Psychotechnics arose in the early 1920s, facilitated by the shift towards new economic policies (NEP), and was supported by a wide range of influential figures, including Lenin, his wife Krupskaya and Trotsky.[12] The psychotechnic movement encompassed organizational psychology and the rationalization of labour; the use of psychotherapeutic methods in a clinical context; penal psychology, such as assessment of testimonies; and the use of psychology in pedagogical settings. Vocational and clinical testing – the subject of Eisenstein and Luria's first conversation – was a central part of this development.

In her groundbreaking study, *Psychotechnics and the Avant-garde*, Margarete Vöhringer demonstrated how the psychotechnic framework also encompassed a diverse range of interdisciplinary projects such as Pudovkin's *The Mechanics of the Human Brain* – the film that went beyond merely illustrating Pavlov's theory and tried to mimic the operation of various reflexes and 'condition' soviet audiences; Alexander Bogdanov's blood transfusion experiments to cure insanity, which blended psycho- and bio-technologies; and Nikolai Ladovski's 'Psychotechnic Laboratory' for testing and training future architects using a set of tools designed to simultaneously test and modify vision and perception. As such, argues Vöhringer, the psychotechnic paradigm cut across the divide between theory and practice, social and natural sciences, avant-garde experiments and optimization of labour, entangling them all in one common, experimental set-up encompassed by the aim to build a new world for the new, post-revolutionary human being.[13] The period of mass infatuation with psychotechnics was short-lived though and came to an end in the mid-1930s amidst the massive campaign to abolish testing and resort to more brutal methods of increasing labour efficiency, such as the Stakhanovite movement.[14]

Yet, due to Vygotsky's intervention the psychotechnic framework was rethought and repositioned as a foundational part of cultural-historical theory, which allowed these ideas to continue exerting influence beyond the organizational defeat of the movement. The essence of this intervention was outlined in his *Psychology of Art* (1925) and *The Historical Meaning of Crisis in Psychology* (1927). In these studies Vygotsky not only expanded psychotechnics from a set of narrow, practice-oriented methods into an overarching paradigm, but also turned the psychotechnic approach into a new onto-epistemology, forging his unique 'transformative' perspective in psychology.[15] In this paradigm, experiment serves not as a diagnostic but as a formative tool, knowledge is always provisional and functions as a 'project', and psychological structures and mechanisms are plastic, emergent and are mediated by constantly evolving cultural tools. Significantly for our discussion, the implications of the psychotechnic paradigm were visible first and foremost in the psychology of art. For, as Puzyrei explains, the first reality with which a psychotechnic approach to art should deal is 'the reality of the transformation or transfiguration of man's mental or spiritual organization, the transfiguration by means of particular instruments or organs (pieces of art) – the transfigurations that one may even picture as a particular kind of "action", which may provisionally be called a "psychotechnic action"'.[16]

The psychotechnic approach also influenced Eisenstein's work, as is evident from his attempt to create a psychotechnic laboratory in 1928, as well as his adoption of the psychotechnic theoretical framework, in the sense introduced by Vygotsky.[17] This can be traced from his early, still-unpublished study, 'How is Pathos Made?' (1929), through the fragment 'Stanislavsky and Loyola' (1937), to his late essay 'Rodin and Rilke' (1945)[18] and *Nonindifferent Nature*. In 'How is Pathos Made?' Eisenstein described Ignatius Loyola (1491–1556), Spanish Catholic priest and theologian, and the author of 'The Spiritual Exercises' – a step-by-step manual on how to achieve religious ecstasy – as 'Gastev of Catholicism', revealing simultaneously his broad familiarity with psychotechnic approaches in the USSR – Alexei Gastev was the head of Central Institute of Labour, one of the major centres of psychotechnic research and practice – and an ability to expand his understanding of psychotechnics to a range of practices that have psychological transformation at their core. In 'Stanislavsky and Loyola' Eisenstein compared Loyola's exercises to another practice that he insightfully conceptualized as psychotechnic – namely, Konstantin Stanislavsky's system of actor training. Finally, in 'Rodin and Rilke' Eisenstein constructed a psychotechnic genealogy of his own cinema, tracing this genealogy through Loyola's exercises and Stanislavsky's system, while defining all these practices as *psychotechnic apparatuses*, and, directly echoing Vygotsky, as 'similar types of "machines" designed to work on the psyche'.[19]

In this context, hypnosis was seen as one of the psychotechnic devices, a calculated intervention aimed to produce an altered state of consciousness. And it was through collaboration with Luria that Eisenstein came to see and participate in experiments using hypnosis in 1928. From 1923 to 1930 Luria was working on a massive experimental research project on the relationship between emotions, affects and human motorics.[20] In this research, Luria aimed to explore the dynamics and the effect on the overall behaviour of the individual of strong emotions and affects, as well as an individual's ability to control and regulate affective states. Luria frequently relied on the skills of Yuri Kannabich, a renowned psychiatrist and psychoanalyst, to place his subjects into hypnotic trances. But there were several features that sharply differentiated Luria's use of hypnosis from that of his contemporaries and that reflected the distinctive features of cultural-historical theory, above all its central assumption that language represents the key to the formation of higher psychological functions and the primary instrument for controlling and organizing behaviour, both the subject's own and others' behaviour. This fundamental principle was formulated gradually in the latter 1920s and would inflect Luria's use of hypnosis in his experiments. Hypnotic practices of the time tended to privilege the motor component in hypnotic induction, such as rhythmical movement of the pendulum or the ocular element in trance: the gaze of the hypnotist or the placing and removing of the (invisible) veil over the subject's eyes. By contrast, Luria posited that verbal injunction was the crucial component of hypnotic intervention: having placed a subject in a trance, Luria would proceed to deliver a hypnotic injunction by telling the subject a story, a fictional narrative in which the subject was positioned as a protagonist acting towards a set of goals.[21] Furthermore, Luria placed his subjects in a situation in which they were compelled to act while retaining a degree of choice, and hence free will in *how* they acted.

Eisenstein drew two important conclusions from observing and participating in Luria's experiments. On the one hand, their set-up challenged and subverted the received association of hypnosis with physical movements and gestural actions; and on the other hand, it questioned the ocular focus of the hypnotic set-up. These considerations have often been used to give weight to the idea that hypnosis and the cinematic dipositive are inherently connected.[22] By contrast, Luria's experiments demonstrated the central role of speech, in its semantic and pragmatic functions, which considerably expanded the understanding of hypnosis as a phenomenon restricted to its visual and motor components. In

Luria's experiments speech was used as the main instrument of achieving sensory-motor psychosynthesis, putting into practice a multimodal model of hypnosis commensurate with Eisenstein's intermedial understanding of cinema. Secondly, these experiments confirmed for Eisenstein that it was possible to be hypnotized into initiating volitional actions, which, for all intents and purposes, could be characterized as agentic and self-determined – precisely the possibility that Eisenstein had earlier tried to trigger in his final shot for *The Strike*, with its close-up of Strongin's hypnotic face.

Subsequently, Eisenstein accorded a major role to hypnosis in his early attempts to theorize cinema via psychology, while simultaneously rethinking hypnosis along several important lines. In his working notes contained in a folder dated 'November 1928', Eisenstein foregrounds the importance of hypnosis alongside two other psychological phenomena – eidetism and motor coordination in Parkinsonian patients, as researched at the time by Luria and Vygotsky – and he argues that these three experimental phenomena 'confirm my theory of cinema'.[23] Following Vygotsky and Luria in privileging the role of speech in hypnosis, Eisenstein aligns hypnosis with the 'linguistic method' and stresses the power of language as a foundational dimension in art. He further argues that eidetism, a vivid recall of images which allows a person to scan an image preserved in their memory as if it were materially present, creates a condition of possibility for rhythmic organization in art. Parkinsonian movement, which requires an obstacle to be placed in front of the patient to induce her/his forward movement, is seen as a paradigmatic example of dialectics, and is linked with Eisenstein's favourite type of expressive movement, *otkaz* (recoil).[24]

Furthermore, Eisenstein stressed the fact that under hypnosis an individual perceives stimuli more acutely than under normal conditions. In his essay 'How is Pathos Made?' he referred to the results obtained by Professor Ioffe, indicating that sensitivity to sound increases twenty-fivefold under hypnosis.[25] Most likely Eisenstein had in mind experiments conducted by the celebrated physicist Abram Ioffe as well as Leon Theremin, a multidisciplinary researcher and inventor of the famous electronic music instrument bearing his name.[26] According to Theremin, these experiments demonstrated that under hypnosis sensitivity to visual stimuli increases by forty to sixty times, while sensitivity to auditory stimuli increases by thirty times. Referring in his diary entries of the same period to experiments conducted by Professor Gurevich and reported by Luria, Eisenstein enthusiastically seized upon similar findings indicating that hypnosis amplifies perception by twenty-five to thirty times, an observation that challenged the more commonly assumed tendency of hypnosis to dull perception or produce hyposensitivity – as evident in its use as an analgesic or for anaesthetic purposes in surgical procedures.[27]

In exploring this surprising range of hypnotic effects, Gurevich was following in the footsteps of Bekhterev, under whose supervision he had worked earlier and completed his dissertation. Bekhterev's work on hypnosis rejected his predecessor Charcot's hypothetical explanation of hypnosis as a phenomenon analogous to hysteria, and instead aimed to provide an 'objective' understanding of hypnosis within his own overriding framework of reflexology. Gathering evidence about the experimentally verifiable characteristics of hypnosis, Bekhterev acknowledged both *hypo*sensitive and *hyper*sensitive effects of hypnosis, namely, the possibility of both reduced and amplified sensations under hypnosis (for example, earlier experiments by James Braid, who demonstrated that the senses of hearing, touch and smell could be increased twelvefold under hypnosis).[28] This line of research, which in contemporary neuroscience is defined as active-alert hypnotic induction,[29] has remained largely overshadowed, both before and after Bekhterev's intervention, by a traditional model linking hypnosis with a state of passivity. Indeed, Bekhterev himself favoured the latter model, as would Pavlov, formulating his understanding of hypnosis unambiguously in terms of inhibition rather than amplification. Bekhterev wrote: 'What we term hypnosis represents an artificially induced instance of a general reflex of inhibition in the form of a dream-like trance in different degrees.'[30]

Around the same time, Eisenstein himself began to experiment with techniques of altered states of consciousness. In a diary entry in March 1928 he mentioned that he experienced states akin to 'half-sleep' or even 'sleep' while working with Dr Konovalov.[31] Dmitry Konovalov (1876–1947) was a historian of Russian religious sects, who researched trance as an element of religious ecstasy. As Alexander Etkind showed, Konovalov's work drew on comparative ethnography and his knowledge of psychiatry, acquired while completing a degree in the Department of Medicine of Moscow University. In 1908 Konovalov defended a dissertation entitled 'Religious ecstasy in Russian mystical sects'. While the dissertation was condemned by conservative theologians, it quickly gained recognition in wider intellectual circles, due to both its subject matter and its methodology. Konovalov approached ecstasy not as an ideological phenomenon but as a psychological and physiological one, and he shifted the emphasis onto how ecstasy is produced. He defined ecstasy as 'A particular subjective turmoil, an instance of neuro-psychological excitation, produced by the artificial religious exercises, facilitated by the ascetic regime and [...] determined by the psycho-physiological organisation of the sect members.'[32] Konovalov analysed religious rituals that focused on 'the bodily manifestations of religious ecstasy in their progressive development': namely, motor components (whirling, shaking, jumping), changes in blood pressure and breath rhythms, and peculiarities of speech (moaning, yelling and glossolalia). Using a broad comparative analysis to advance his arguments, Konovalov drew on evidence beyond Russian religious sects to demonstrate not the peculiarities or unique character of religious rituals but rather what he considered universal mechanisms underlying the production of ecstasy. Comparing Russian religious sects with other traditions, he identified analogous elements of ecstasy among Shakers, early Quakers and other Protestant sects, and further demonstrated that non-Christian religious movements – Dervishes, Sufis, shamans – use similar techniques or practices (e.g. swirling). Stressing the comparative range of Konovalov's work, Alexander Etkind notes: 'On the same page he analysed the ecstatic processes among Russian south klysts, American Shakers, French hysterics, Mohamed and, in addition, Katherina in Dostoevsky's novel *The Landlady*.'[33]

I suggest that in effect, Konovalov advanced a psychotechnic understanding of ecstasy: not as an external manifestation of a religious experience but as a *techne* that is used to produce an experience which may be construed afterwards as 'grace', as the 'presence of Holy Spirit in the body', or even direct contact with God. Drawing an analogy between ecstasy and hysteria, and arguing that what is typically understood as a symptom is in fact an artificially produced psycho-physiological reaction, Konovalov anticipated the performative reading of hysteria proposed by Georges Didi-Huberman in his famous *Invention of Hysteria*.[34]

Eisenstein's encounter with Konovalov was crucial in establishing for him the connections between ecstasy, trance and hypnosis. From this point, Eisenstein's interest in hypnosis became closely intertwined with his study of ecstasy – a state which can be seen as the opposite of hypnotic sleep, yet at the same time sharing some important features with trance. In August 1929 he asked Luria to help him to locate materials on religious ecstasy which led Luria to refer him to Roza Averbuch, the head of the section of religious ideology at the Communist Academy, with this message: 'S.M. Eisenstein is working at the moment on the range of issues which are concerned with religious ecstasy. If you could give him materials which would be helpful in this incredibly interesting work – books and suggestions – I would be very grateful.' On the reverse side of this letter Eisenstein jotted some notes about Averbuch's recommendations: '1) Buddha's speeches, 2) Ignatius Loyola's instructions, 3) Tables of incarnations that a human being goes through according to the belief in the reincarnation of souls.'[35]

The exploration of ecstasy and its mobilization in cinematic practice became one of the central vectors of Eisenstein's later work, culminating in the theoretical studies *Nonindifferent Nature* and *Method* (1932–48). Developing his understanding of ecstasy, Eisenstein problematized simultaneously the received understanding of both hypnosis and trance, challenging their association with emotional numbing and abdication of will-power. The extent of this problematization, and the effect it had on his directorial practice, can be demonstrated by comparing his theory and practice to those of Maya Deren, the founding figure of American avant-garde film whose intellectual trajectory paralleled Eisenstein's own in striking ways, ranging from their shared exposure to the Russian *psy* disciplines to their common interest in ethnographic research into ekstatic rituals and their sustained attempts to use mechanisms of trance, hypnosis and ecstasy in their cinematic practice.

Deren was born Elenora Derenkowsky in Kiev in 1917, and she left Ukraine, fleeing pogroms, with her family in 1922. She changed her name to Maya, the Hindu word for illusion, in the 1940s when her career as a filmmaker began after meeting the Czech-born filmmaker Alexander Hammid. Her father, Solomon Derenkowsky, was a psychiatrist who had studied under Bekhterev in the Psychoneurological Institute in Saint Petersburg and later practised the treatment of alcoholics under hypnosis in Kiev, a treatment developed by Bekhterev.

Following their migration, Solomon Derenkowsky continued to work as a psychiatrist in America, not only practising as a clinician but also giving frequent lectures and talks. As Deren acknowledges in her writings, her father's work influenced her research significantly. A case in point is her paper, *Religious Possession in Dancing*, written in 1942, just before she made her first film, *Meshes of the Afternoon*, which explicitly acknowledges the help of Dr S. D. Deren. As Ute Holl argues, Derenkowsky, as a former student of Bekhterev, thus functioned as a bridge between the Russian *psy* disciplines and Maya Deren's understanding of the psyche and subjectivity.[36] Arguably, Bekhterev's privileging of social determinants over individual agency underlay Deren's insistence on 'the vital necessity to decenter our notions of self, ego and personality'.[37] Bekhterev's legacy could also have been instrumental in Deren's rethinking of such phenomena as hysteria and possession in social terms, and her attempt to explain them as ritualized forms of behaviour. This line of enquiry would lead Deren from her trance films, produced between 1943 and 1946, to her late ethnographic project in Haiti, from 1947 to 1954, supported by the Guggenheim Foundation. Drawing on such authors as Lévy-Bruhl, James Frazer and Eugen Bleuler, Deren planned to research three types of ritualized behaviour: children's games, Balinese performances and Haitian Voodoo rituals. Some of the results of this work were presented in her book *Divine Horsemen* (1953), as well as in the film of the same title, completed after her death.[38]

As Eisenstein's intended magnum opus *Method* demonstrates, a similar combination of ethnographic, anthropological and psychological frameworks came to dominate his research agenda from early 1930 until his death.[39] Significantly, *Method* was conceived as a collaborative project with Luria and Vygotsky, and cultural-historical theory exerted significant influence on the study's conceptual framework and selection of materials.[40] This influence is particularly visible in Eisenstein's adoption in *Method* of a tripartite framework of analysis which Vygotsky and Luria had previously introduced: the evolutionary, focusing on humans' development as a species and the prehistory of this development in 'deep' time of the universe; the historical, drawing on a vast quantity of anthropological and ethnographic material; and the ontogenetic, tracing the vicissitudes of individual psycho-social formation.[41] Eisenstein also expanded the cultural-historical theorization of the brain, as composed of different historical layers, to apply to understanding the organization of works of art, arguing that their structures are similarly multilevelled, and always bear traces of earlier stages of historical development.

Accordingly, Eisenstein began searching for such a prehistory of aesthetic techniques, and among hundreds of observations made by him from this perspective, we find exactly the same three phenomena that Deren was planning to study in her Guggenheim project: children's imaginative activities, Balinese performances and Haitian Voodoo rituals. We also find him referencing the same scholars as Deren does: Lévy-Bruhl, Frazer, Bleuler.[42]

Luria started to share children's drawing with Eisenstein as early as 1930, and Eisenstein used to draw parallels between the peculiarities of these (dismembering entities into separate parts), verbal traits (displaying thinking in 'complexes') and montage techniques.[43] Following the same logic, in *Method*, Eisenstein approached Balinese dancing and Voodoo drums as phenomena demonstrating how early forms of psychological functioning create a foundation for later aesthetic devices. He believed he had discovered in Balinese dancing the origin of 'embodied thinking',[44] while Voodoo drumming provided him with an essential demonstration of the importance of rhythm as a structuring mechanism in art and, more specifically, a mechanism for producing an ecstatic effect.

In *Method* Eisenstein argues that 'rhythmic drum' is effective because it returns us to the primitive sensory-perceptual stage of human development:

> Everything in us that occurs *apart from consciousness* and will occurs *rhythmically*: the beating of the heart and breathing, peristalsis of the intestines, merger and separation of cells, etc. Switching off consciousness, we sink into the inviolable rhythm of breathing during sleep, the rhythm of sleepwalking, etc. And conversely – the monotony of a repeated rhythm brings us closer to those states 'next to consciousness', where only the traits of sensuous thought are capable of functioning fully.[45]

Yet rhythm is not equivalent to frequency and pulsations – to be perceived as rhythm pulsations need to be organized into a pattern, to be given form, and this can only take place through cultural mediation. So Eisenstein stresses the need to reconstruct the cultural history of rhythm by investigating the functions of rhythm in various forms of ritualized actions:

> Starting with the simplest and most literal – the ritual drums of the voodoo cult (in Cuba). Their measured beating, in a continuously accelerating tempo, leads the responsive listeners into a state of total frenzy. And they are totally in the power of the images flashing through their excited imagination, or of whatever their leader suggests to them [...] The rhythmic drum of the Catholic religious machine is described by Zola in *Lourdes* [...] For orthodox ecstasy – Gorky has left a description.[46]

Beyond the thematic overlap between the forms of ritualized behaviour – children's games, Balinese dancing and Voodoo rituals – that Deren sought to explore in her Guggenheim project and that Eisenstein researched in *Method*, there is a deeper affinity between Deren's ideas and Eisenstein's theorizing. Deren argued that all three forms of ritualized behaviour demonstrate an 'inviolable' configuration and suggested that such inviolability is central to artistic autonomy, for her, art's 'prestige [...] is contingent on satisfaction of the form itself'.[47] Deren then goes on to argue that rituals encapsulate a form of performance in which an individual is not the central protagonist or driving force, but rather a subordinated element of a larger whole, and that by participating in a ritual the subject transcends the bounds of personality and is liberated from the enclosure of individuality. By becoming an integral part of a social whole, the subject is augmented and empowered. And it is to this end that rituals mobilize both trance and ecstasy, which Deren sees as different stages of the same experiential progression. In her essay 'Anagram of Ideas', Deren writes:

> The ritualistic form treats the human being not as the source of the dramatic action, but as a somewhat depersonalized element in a dramatic whole. The intent of such depersonalization is not the destruction of the individual; on the contrary, it enlarges him [sic] beyond his personal dimensions and frees him from the specialization and confines of personality. He becomes part of a dynamic whole which, like all such creative relationships, in turn, endows its parts with a measure of its larger meaning.[48]

Furthermore, Deren understands art in the same terms as she understands ritual, describing it as a tool to engender transformation of the self.[49] She posits possession as a pivotal moment in such transformation, not as a means of 'decomposition or decay of personality but, on the contrary, growth and enlargement'. In this way, she comes close to Eisenstein's definition of ecstasy as 'the leap outside oneself' and 'necessarily the passage to something else, to something of a different quality',[50] as a climax of aesthetic experience.

Deren did not merely propose to investigate the origin of art through its connection with ritual; rather, she proposed a paradigm in which different media and ritualized forms are seen as instruments or techniques for producing experience, including aesthetic experience – in fact a psychotechnology, as Ute Holl describes it. As previous discussion has demonstrated, Eisenstein formed a similar view of art, developing a psychotechnic paradigm through his collaboration with Luria and Vygotsky. This paradigm responds not to the question, 'What does art mean?' but to another: 'What does art do?' And from the perspective of Russian psychotechnics, 'every piece of art is a particular "organ" of man's mental and spiritual development – an organ or "adjunct" that man uses to complete himself, until he becomes an integral entity that can only develop, this being the only way in which man can accomplish his own development'.[51]

For Deren, as Holl demonstrates, an understanding of cinema as psychotechnology had several important corollaries. First, she argued that 'the task of cinema or any other art form is not to translate hidden messages of the unconscious soul into art but to experiment with the effects contemporary technical devices have on nerves, minds or souls'.[52] This imperative was underwritten by Deren's more basic assumption that 'the reality from which man draws his knowledge and the limits of his manipulation has been amplified not only by the development of analytical instruments; it has increasingly become, itself, a reality created by the manipulation of the instrument.'[53] Holl further suggests that Deren's agenda was in fact forward-looking and has contemporary relevance: 'In this sense her understanding of "ritualistic" is not a (pseudo-) primitive one but refers to the media aspect of art: art forms [...] are historical techniques of transmission that produce reality. The technical reality of man produces the emotional reality as a secondary effect.'[54]

Not only were Deren and Eisenstein intimately familiar with developments in the Russian *psy* disciplines, but they both came to share a 'psychotechnological' view of art as a generative mechanism or instrument designed to alter or produce 'human mental or spiritual organization'. And yet, they mobilized this psychotechnic attitude in their directorial practice in very different ways, demonstrating how the phenomena of trance and ecstasy could be deployed in cinema to contrary ends.

For, despite Deren's overriding goal of the emancipation of the subject, her use of visual vocabulary in her cinematic rendering of 'the process of becoming'[55] (to which her films are, by and large, dedicated) remained firmly wedded to the conventional iconography of the hypnotic trance. She invariably mobilizes such devices as still images, slow and reverse motion, delays, repetitions, close-ups and fragmentation, as well as space crossing and doubling, to create a distinctive dream-like effect. She adopts the strategy of illustrating hypnotic phenomena with imagery of drifting and disempowerment, of a subject out-of-control, passive, submissive, floating. As such, Deren's arsenal of plastic and figurative expressions remains clearly indebted to Bekhterev's paradigm of hypnosis as a reflex of inhibition. In addition, placing trance and possession on the same continuum, Deren characterized the latter as a state in which 'the inhibitory effects of cerebral consciousness are minimized or altogether absent'.[56]

Eisenstein did something different in his cinema. While he aimed, like Deren, to repurpose hypnosis for loftier goals, in his practice as a filmmaker he managed to dissociate principles of hypnosis from the conventional graphic representation and illustration of trance. For Eisenstein, hypnotic effects can be achieved, instead, through rhythm and montage, repetition and seriality, and, above all, the instrumental power of the word – and all of these techniques can be entirely divorced from the traditional subject matter associated with hypnosis. The marching soldiers on the Odessa steps in *The Battleship Potemkin*, the firing of the machine guns in *October*, the frenzy of the dance of *oprichniki* in *Ivan the Terrible* all produce hypnotic effects, despite their subject matter being diametrically opposed to any view of hypnosis as a form of sedation.

Besides, hypnosis here spills over into ecstasy, revealing the affinity of the two phenomena when they are approached on a structural level, through patterning and organization of film material.

For Eisenstein, both hypnosis and ecstasy belong to fundamental mechanisms of art explored in *Method*, mechanisms such as rhythm, synaesthesia and plasticity, which are deeply rooted in the evolutionary development and cultural history of humanity, and supposedly universal in their effects. Eisenstein identified these mechanisms with phylogenetically early stages of human development, and evolutionary relationships within the animal kingdom, which are rehearsed or repeated, ontogenetically, in every childhood.

In this respect, his treatment of trance comes close to a recent account of the relationship between hypnosis and cinema proposed by Raymond Bellour, who has argued that 'Animality [...] embodies the inner element of hypnosis that is intrinsic to the emotional body [...] through an influence operating from body to body, as if through a mechanism that multiplies its most somatic affects many times over in the human organism.'[57] Bellour further proposes that there is a 'child who sleeps in every spectator' and is awakened by the cinematic apparatus precisely at the moment when s/he falls under the spell of the hypnotic effect of film.[58] Surrendering to hypnosis, this 'child-viewer' reveals the 'animal that he [or she] is', since a susceptibility to hypnosis is what human beings share with animals.

However, if Bellour does not consider surrender to the hypnotic apparatus of cinema as problematic, Eisenstein always did. For Eisenstein, an engagement with cinema and the experience of its hypnotic effect is never a matter of sliding into a primordial bliss, which would represent regress. It is always a dialectical repetition on a new level and for new purposes, and in the case of hypnosis, for the most paradoxical purpose of awakening consciousness and strengthening agency – the purpose so potently anticipated by his final shot in *The Strike*. Thus Eisenstein repeatedly renders the phenomenon of hypnosis as *aporia*, in which spectatorial freedom and directorial control, abdication of will and goal-directed actions, are both given equal weight. This tendency is foregrounded in one of Eisenstein's late manifestoes, 'The Magic of Art', in which the central argument of *Method*, the necessity to translate 'logical thesis' into an emotionally rendered form, is presented in a condensed manner. Eisenstein worked on 'The Magic of Art' between 1944 and 1948.[59] In 1944 he associated the state of trance with spectatorial submission, while casting the director as a 'magician' concentrating the 'active' power of art in his hands. At that time, he wrote: 'Because the feelings and consciousness in this case are submissive and regulated almost as if in trance. Yet art is not only passively magical but, simultaneously, actively magical in terms of overtaking and regulating the viewer by the magician-creator.'[60] Four years later, he reiterated that art operates by placing the subject in a state akin to a trance through unleashing the force of 'sensory-emotional thought':

> And you have the spectator 're-oriented', not to the norms of today's perception, but to the norms of a primordially sensory-emotional one – he is 'returned' to the magical stage of sensation.
> And the idea that has been realised by a system of such influences, embodied in a form by *such means* – irresistibly controls the emotions.
> For the feelings and consciousness in this case are submissive and manageable, almost as if one were in a *trance*.[61]

However, in the same text, Eisenstein insisted that the magic of art is simultaneously 'directly linked with [...] personality-formation' for the viewer, since art is a tool that can be applied to oneself to transform and generate new experiences, feelings and thoughts. This self-transformation and self-determination condense and incarnate the essence of becoming a human – which, for Eisenstein, as for his collaborators Vygotsky and Luria, was a matter of acquiring control over one's destiny, motivation and affects. Thus, for Eisenstein, art implies agency and freedom, not only on the part of the creator but also on the part of the viewer.

It would be all too easy for me to conclude by saying that Eisenstein's problematization of hypnosis reflected the vexed polemic between those who view hypnosis as a paralysis of will and those who consider it a means of enhancing mind-body control; or that it anticipated the current schism between proponents of hypnosis as an altered state of consciousness and socio-cognitive theories that see hypnosis as imaginative involvement. But I think Eisenstein's work does much more than just illustrate these opposing positions. In his epistemology, hypnosis functions as one of the phenomena that expose the unresolvable conflict between agency and control, modern and archaic, natural and constructed, the spectator's freedom and the director's propagandist agenda. As such, Eisenstein's theoretical account of hypnosis, which is fraught with contradictions, ambiguity and ruptures, arguably speaks to a fractured totality of the psyche that cannot be put right. Yet, what his cinema demonstrates persuasively is that even if this fractured totality cannot be put right, it can be put to work. In this sense, Eisenstein's oeuvre remains a positive challenge to, rather than a mere illustration of, the theoretical exploration of the relationship between art, mind and the brain.

Notes

1. Stephan Andriopolous, *Possessed: Hypnotic Crimes, Corporate Fiction, and the Invention of Cinema* (Chicago: University of Chicago Press, 2008); Raymond Bellour, 'From Hypnosis to Animals', *Cinema Journal* 53, no. 3 (2014): 1–24; Andreas Killen, *Homo Cinematicus: Science, Motion Pictures, and the Making of Modern Germany*, Intellectual History of the Modern Age (Philadelphia: University of Pennsylvania Press, 2017); Ruggero Eugeni, 'Imaginary Screens: The Hypnotic Gesture and Early Film', in *Screen Genealogies. From Optical Device to Environmental Medium*, ed. Craig Buckley, Rüdiger Campe and Francesco Casetti (Amsterdam: Amsterdam University Press, 2019), 269–91.
2. Alexander Deriabin, 'Sergei Eisenstein – Esfir Shub, "Gilded Rot, A cine-play in 6 parts"', *Kinovedcheskie zapiski* 58 (2002): 144–52.
3. Killen, *Homo Cinematicus*, 126.
4. Ibid., 130.
5. Ibid.
6. Luka Arsenjuk, *MOVEMENT, ACTION, IMAGE, MONTAGE: Sergei Eisenstein and the Cinema in Crisis* (Minneapolis: University of Minnesota Press, 2018), 89.
7. Sergei M. Eizenshtein, *Metod*, ed. Naum Kleiman, 2 vols (Moscow: Muzei kino/Eizenshtein-tsentr, 2002), vol. 1, 135.
8. See, Lev Vygotsky and Alexander Luria, *Obeziana. Primitiv. Rebenok* [Ape. Primitive. Child] (Moscow: Gosizdatel'stvo, 1930); Lev S. Vygotsky, *Sobranie sočinenej* [Collected works in 6 volumes] (Moscow: Pedagogika, 1982–4); Lev S. Vygotsky, *The Collected Works of L. S. Vygotsky*, ed. Robert W. Reiber, 6 vols (New York: Kluwer Academic/Plenum Publishers, 1987–99). In English the best publications on Vygotsky's legacy to date are Alex Kozulin, *Vygotsky's Psychology: A Biography of Ideas* (Cambridge, MA: Harvard University Press, 1990) and René van der Veer and Jaan Valsiner, *Understanding Vygotsky: A Quest for Synthesis* (Oxford: Basil Blackwell, 1991).
9. Jerome Bruner, *Actual Minds, Possible Worlds* (Cambridge, MA: Harvard University Press, 1986), 72.
10. Russian State Archive of Literature and Arts (RGALI) 1923-2-1143, lines 75–6.
11. On A. Tygai see Nikolai Lebedev, *Essays on the History of Cinema in USSR. Silent Cinema: 1918–1934* (Moscow: Iskusstvo, 1965).
12. At least two major platforms of psychotechnics existed at the time. One was associated with the Central Institute of Labor led by Alexei Gastev, encompassed by Gastev's 'man as machine' ideal and focused on optimization of specific labour processes. Another platform, developed by P. Kerjentsev, V. Radus'-Zenkevich, A. Stopani, I. Spielrein and I. Burdiansky developed a 'softer' model of psychotechnic encompassed by a more organic vision of man.

13 Margarete Vöhringer, *Avantgarde und Psychotechnik: Wissenschaft, Kunst und Technik der Wahrnehmungsexperimente in der frühen Sowjetunion* [Avant-garde and Psychotechnology: The Science, Art and Technology of Experiments on Perception in the Early Soviet Union] (Göttingen: Wallstein, 2007).
14 See Olga Artemieva, 'Soviet Psychotechnics: Social Biography of Scientific and Practical Movement', *Psychologist*, no. 2 (2014): 1–23.
15 Lev Vygotsky, *The Psychology of Art* (New York: MIT Press, 1971); Lev Vygotsky, 'The Historical Meaning of the Crisis in Psychology: A Methodological Investigation', in *The Collected Works of L. S. Vygotsky. Cognition and Language*, ed. Robert W. Rieber and Jeffrey Wollock (Boston: Springer, 1997).
16 Andrei Puzyrei, 'Contemporary Psychology and Vygotsky's Cultural-Historical Theory', *Journal of Russian and East European Psychology* 45, no. 1 (2007): 8–93, 38.
17 In 1928 Eisenstein became head of the cinema section within 'The laboratory for the study of mass behavior and mass psychotechnics' at the Moscow Polytechnic Museum, the program for the section's work and his work ID is preserved in RGALI 1923-1-2405.
18 Sergei M. Eizenshtein, 'Rodin and Rilke', in *Neravnodushnaia priroda*, ed. Naum Kleiman (Moscow: Muzei kino/Eisenstein Center, 2004–6), vol. 2, 509–36; Sergei M. Eizenshtein, 'Stanislavsky and Loyola', in *Neravnodushnaia priroda*, vol. 1, 485–511; Sergei M. Eisenstein, 'Kak delaetsia pafos?' ['How is Pathos Made?'] (1929), RGALI, 1923-2-793; 1923-2-794.
19 Eizenshtein, 'Rodin and Rilke', vol. 2, 525.
20 The results of this project were published in the United States in 1932 as *The Nature of Human Conflict, or, Emotion, Conflict, and Will: An Objective Study of Disorganisation and Control of Human Behaviour* (New York: Liveright Publishers, 1932). Luria further defended this study as his doctoral dissertation at the Institute of Tbilisi in 1937, yet in Russian the monograph was published for the first time only in 2002: Alexander Luria, *Priroda chelovecheskikh konfliktov* (Moscow: Cogito Centre, 2002).
21 Luria's unique approach to hypnosis in these experiments exerted a formative influence on Milton Erickson (1901–80), the founding president of the American Society for Clinical Hypnosis and one of the leading figures in the psychotherapeutic application of hypnosis. Erickson's famous mobilization of metaphors and stories evoking different psychological and life situations, often with examples of their resolution in his therapeutic use of hypnosis are the result of his early encounter with Luria's work, on which he drew in Paul E. Huston, David Shakow and Milton H. Erickson, 'A Study of Hypnotically Induced Complexes by Means of the Luria Technique', *Journal of General Psychology* 11, no. 1 (1934): 65–97.
22 See, for example, Ruggero Eugeni, 'Imaginary Screens: The Hypnotic Gesture and Early Film', in *Screen Genealogies: From Optical Device to Environmental*

Medium, ed. Craig Buckley, Rüdiger Campe and Francesco Casetti (Amsterdam: Amsterdam University Press, 2019), 269–91.
23 RGALI, 1923-2-1106. Eisenstein's diary, entry dated 23 December 1928.
24 Ibid.
25 Eisenstein, 'Kak delaetsia pafos?' ['How is Pathos Made?'], RGALI, 1923-2-793; 1923-2-794.
26 RGALI, 1923-2-1106. Eisenstein's diary, entry dated 23 December 1928.
27 Leon Theremin, '*Vospominania ob A.F.Ioffe*' [My memories of A. F. Ioffe] (Leningrad: Nauka, 1973).
28 Vladimir Bekhterev, *Gipnoz. Vnushenie. Telepatia.* [Hypnosis. Suggestion. Telepathy.] (Moscow, Misl', 1994).
29 Éva I. Bányai, 'Active-Alert Hypnosis: History, Research, and Applications', *American Journal of Clinical Hypnosis* 61, no. 2 (2018): 88–107.
30 Bekhterev, *Hypnosis*, 54–5, translated by the author.
31 RGALI, 1923-2-1107, l. 4.
32 Quoted in Alexander Etkind, *Tolkovanie puteshestvii* [The Interpretation of Travels] (Moscow: NLO, 2001), 79.
33 Ibid., 89.
34 Georges Didi-Huberman, *Invention de l'hystérie: Charcot et l'Iconographie Photographique de la Salpêtrière* (Paris: MACULA, 1982).
35 RGALI, 1923-1-1456.
36 Ute Holl, *Cinema, Trance and Cybernetics* (Amsterdam: Amsterdam University Press, 2017).
37 Bill Nichols, 'Introduction', in Bill Nichols and Maya Deren, *Maya Deren and the American Avant-Garde* (Berkeley: University of California Press, 2001), 10.
38 Maya Deren, *Divine Horsemen: The Voodoo Gods of Haiti* (New York: Vanguard Press, 1953). Deren died in 1961, at the age of forty-four. From the footage shot by Deren between 1947 and 1954, a film was completed by Deren's third husband Teiji Ito and his wife Cherel Winett Ito in 1977 under the title *Divine Horsemen: The Living Gods of Haiti*.
39 *Method* (1932–48), Eisenstein's unfinished study, had to wait for its publication for almost half a century and finally was brought to light by Naum Kleiman in 2002 as a two-volume publication: *Metod*, ed. Naum Kleiman (Moscow: Muzei kino/Eizenshtein-tsentr, 2002). Another edition, in four volumes followed in 2008: *Metod*, ed. Oksana Bulgakowa (Berlin: PotemkinPress, 2008). English translation of selected chapters of *Method* by Dustin Condren became available in 2017: *The Primal Phenomenon: Art*, ed. Oksana Bulgakowa and Dietmar Hochmuth (Berlin: PotemkinPress, 2017).
40 RGALI, 1923-2-1125, l. 26, Eisenstein's diary, entries 8 July–14 August 1931. See also Julia Vassilieva, 'Eisenstein and Cultural-Historical Theory', in *The Flying Carpet: Studies on Eisenstein and Russian Cinema in Honor of Naum Kleiman*,

ed. Joan Neuberger and Antonio Somaini (Paris: Éditions Mimésis, 2017), 421–41; Julia Vassilieva, 'The Eisenstein-Vygotsky-Luria Collaboration: Triangulation and Third Culture Debates', *Projections: The Journal for Movies and Mind* 13, no. 1 (2019): 23–44.

41 This framework was outlined in Vygotsky and Luria in *Obeziana. Primitiv. Rebenok.*
42 Eisenstein's interest in the ethnographic work of Lévy-Bruhl and Frazer is well known. Less known is the fact that he also kept a copy of Bleuler's book *Naturgeschichte der Seele und ihres bewusst-werdens: eine Elementarpsychologie* in his library. The book was given to him by Luria on 25 May 1932, with Luria's autograph. Paul Eugen Bleuler was a Swiss psychiatrist and eugenicist most notable for his contributions to the understanding of mental illness. He introduced several important psychiatric terms, including 'schizophrenia', 'schizoid', 'autism' and 'depth psychology'.
43 *Sergei Eisenstein: Selected Works. Volume II: Towards a Theory of Montage*, trans. Michael Glenny and Richard Taylor (London: I.B.Tauris, 2010), 97.
44 Eizenshtein, *Metod*, vol. 1, 236.
45 Ibid., vol. 1, 185, translated by the author, emphasis in the original.
46 Ibid.
47 Quoted in Annette Michelson, 'Poetics and Savage Thought: About *Anagram*', in Nichols and Deren, *Maya Deren and the American Avant-Garde*, 37.
48 Deren, 'Anagram of Ideas', Appendix, 20, in Nichols and Deren, *Maya Deren and the American Avant-Garde*, 20.
49 Holl, *Cinema, Trance and Cybernetics*, 167.
50 Sergei M. Eizenshtein, *Neravnodushnaia priroda* [Nonindifferent nature] (Moscow: Muzei kino/Eisenstein Center, 2004–6), vol. 2, 36, translated by the author.
51 Puzyrei, 'Contemporary Psychology and Vygotsky's Cultural-Historical Theory', 38.
52 Holl, *Cinema, Trance and Cybernetics*, 164.
53 Ibid.
54 Ibid., 167–8.
55 Massimiliano Mollona, 'Seeing the Invisible: Maya Deren's Experiments in Cinematic Trance', *October* 149 (2014): 159–80.
56 Vèvè A. Clark, Millicent Hodson and Catrina Neiman, eds., *The Legend of Maya Deren: A Documentary Biography and Collected Works* (New York: Anthology Film Archives/Film Culture, 1984), 493.
57 Bellour, 'From Hypnosis to Animals', 13.
58 Ibid., 18.
59 Eisenstein gave two pieces the same title, 'The Magic of Art', in 1944 and 1948. He gave the later one to Luria, and it remained in Luria's personal archive, where I discovered it and subsequently published it along some other fragments of *Method* preserved by Luria (including 'Structure as syuzhet') in *Kinovedcheskie zapiski* 8 (1990): 79–97. In the 2002 edition of *Method*, 'The Magic of Art' (1948)

opens volume 1. The earlier version is preserved in RGALI 1923-2-1172, l. 104–5. My translation of 'The Magic of Art' is available in *Culture As Organization in Early Soviet Thought: Bogdanov, Eisenstein, and the Proletkult*, ed. Pia Tikka (Aalto: Crucible, 2017).
60 RGALI, 1923-2-1172, l. 16, October 1944, 104–105, translated by the author.
61 Sergei Eisenstein, 'The Magic of Art', trans. Julia Vassilieva in *Culture As Organization in Early Soviet Thought*, emphasis in the original.

9

Eisenstein's Scream(s)

Ada Ackerman

What is 'humanism'? In what terms can we define it without engaging in the logos of a definition? In those terms that will remove it farthest from a language: the cry (that is to say the murmur), cry of need or protest, cry without word, without silence, ignoble cry where, perhaps, the cry writes the graffiti of high walls.

—Maurice Blanchot, 'Atheism and Writing: Humanism and the Cry', *The Infinite Conversation*, 1993 [1966]

Endowed with a prodigious visual memory, Sergei Eisenstein created his powerful images out of numerous multilayered references from art history. In turn, his iconic images have inspired many artists, including painters. The visual fortune of *Potemkin*'s screaming nurse,[1] one of Eisenstein's most famous motifs and a striking *pars pro toto* of his entire oeuvre, provides a clear example of such circulation and re-elaboration, from painting to cinema, and from cinema to painting.

Eisenstein's poetics of the scream

Eisenstein's films, especially from the silent era, have often been analysed and described in terms of screams. As his close friend the communist critic Léon Moussinac wrote as early as 1928: 'Eisenstein's films are like a cry.'[2] An enthusiastic Eisenstein approved this definition of his art, as shown by the reply he wrote to Moussinac: 'My warmest thanks for your book that I have received and which pleased me much. The difference you establish between Pudovkin and myself, between a song and a scream is astonishing and brilliantly apt.'[3]

Twenty years later, Georges Sadoul, another close friend of Moussinac, used the same simile in reference to *The Battleship Potemkin*, in a text symptomatically entitled 'The Scream Becomes a Hymn': 'in *Potemkin*, the cradle rolling down the stairs, the blood from the wounded eye, the clenched hands of the woman on her injured belly – all these elements present themselves as screams'.[4]

Umberto Barbaro claimed that Eisenstein's treatment of the scream in *Potemkin* profoundly transformed film history, in the same way that Caravaggio's screams drastically revolutionized art history. In Barbaro's eyes, *Potemkin*'s plastic achievements should be equated with Caravaggio's dramatic and expressive open mouths:

> A mere close up of a sailor at work, or of an intellectual woman looking through her glasses, a mere wide open mouth desperately shouting, a mere frame or continuity shot in *Potemkin* were enough to push into a past era every former cinematographic achievement, even the highest, and to announce new times. Just as four hundred years ago, the silent screaming mouths by Caravaggio [...] would weigh heavily on all painting to come.[5]

Interestingly, Barbaro drew on a pictorial model to describe Eisenstein's filmic achievements. Moreover, he describes Caravaggio's mouths as paradoxical objects, since they are silent *and* screaming, exactly like Eisenstein's screams in his silent films – screams that are not literally heard, but which nevertheless roar, and roar powerfully (Figure 9.1).

Screams play a pivotal role in Eisenstein's films, where they are explored in all their polysemy, ambivalence and diversity. The scream is a notion that is hard to define and which, according to Alain Marc in his book *Writing the Scream*, still awaits theorization.[6] On the one hand, screams can be a merely articulated sound, an emotional and physiological response of the body, often shrill and dissonant. As such, they can be perceived as a visceral, bestial and primitive expression. In that respect Greimas describes the scream as being at the limit of human language.[7] The transposition of this bestial and primitive scream to an open mouth in the visual sphere translates the sound into an abhorrent and formless image, according to the famous statement by Lessing in the *Laocoön*; hence his advice to not represent it, to avoid offending the viewer with the repulsive spectacle of a distorted and monstrous face. The wide open screaming mouth, which he calls a blot, comes as an intolerable and indecent hole in the representation 'of the worst possible effect'.[8] For these reasons, Bataille and members of the *Documents* circle, as proponents of 'base materialism', would

Figure 9.1 Caravaggio, *Medusa*, 1597–8.

express their interest in the motif of the wide open mouth as famously embodied in the photographic close-up by Jacques-André Boiffard, published with Bataille's entry on the mouth in *Documents*. There Bataille wrote:

> On important occasions, human life is still bestially concentrated in the mouth: fury makes men grind their teeth, terror and atrocious suffering transform the mouth into the organ of rending screams. On this theme, it can easily be observed that the overwhelmed individual throws back his head while frenetically stretching his neck so that the mouth becomes, as much as possible, a prolongation of the spinal column; in other words, it assumes the position normally occupied in the constitution of animals.[9]

Marking the degradation from human speech to animality, the visual motif of an open mouth blurs the boundaries between inside and outside, giving access to

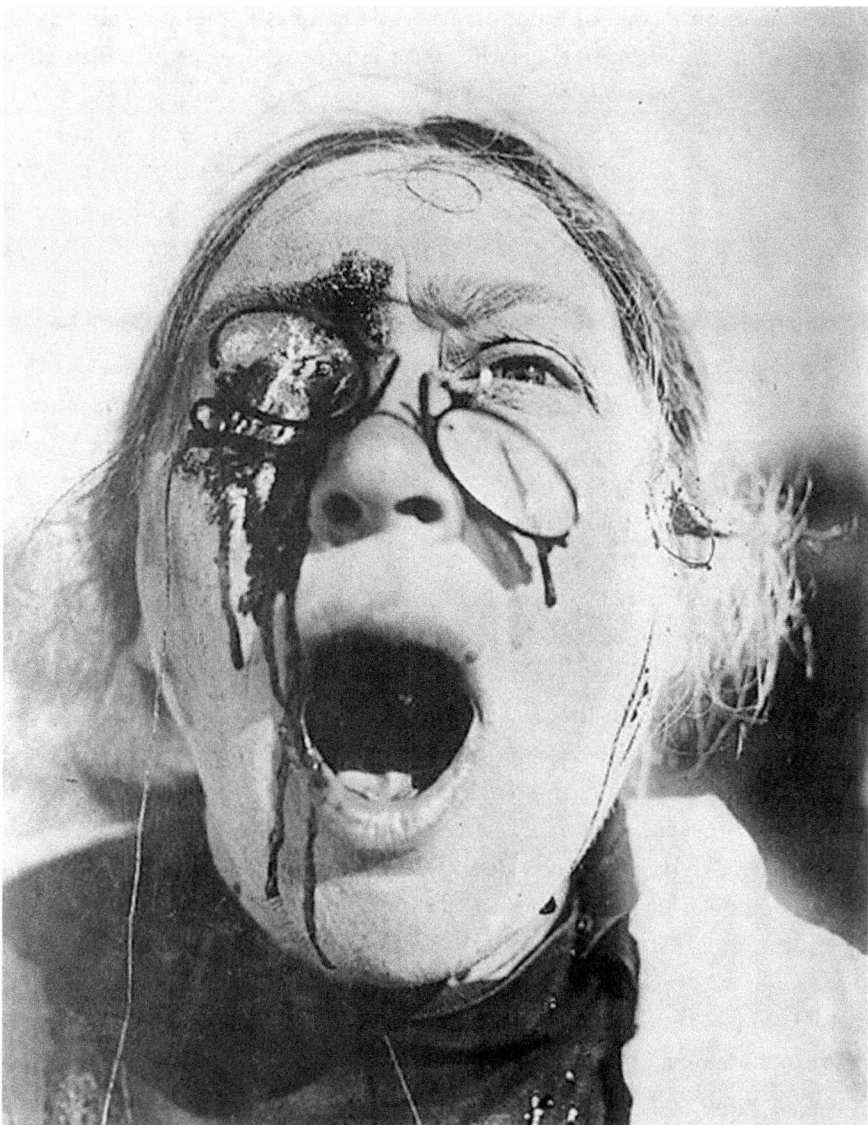

Figure 9.2 'The Screaming Nurse'. Still from Sergei Eisenstein's *The Battleship Potemkin* (1925).

shapeless (*informe*) flesh, to an intimate space usually unseen that is described by Nathalie Roelens as 'the face seen from inside'.[10]

These visceral and regressive dimensions make the open mouth an energetic and troubling form of excess, and a powerful source of affect. As such, it is hardly surprising that it caught Eisenstein's attention. In his films, numerous victims and innocent people scream while being molested and executed; as already mentioned, one of the most famous examples is the screaming nurse in *The Battleship Potemkin* (Figure 9.2). An efficient tool of pathos, their wide open mouths are intended to arouse viewers' indignation, to infect them with the need to scream in turn. And here we shift to another aspect of the notion of the scream.

A scream can also be construed as a positive and noble expression when associated with shouted articulate content. The scream functions then as a vehicle of indignation, as the expression of heart and soul. The verbal exclamation works as a powerful and a contagious stimulus, enabling people to join together as a community. In this respect, it is worth remembering that the word 'cry' is etymologically related to the Latin exclamation *quirites*, uttered by Roman citizens when help was needed.[11] This political aspect of the scream is quintessential in Eisenstein's poetics of riot and exaltation of the power of the masses, perfectly embodied, for instance, in the exclamations 'Brothers!' and 'One for all / All for one', which recur throughout the whole of *Potemkin*.

Eisenstein's intensive use of screaming figures, in all their diversity, is echoed in the numerous promotional posters for his films, which frequently include a wide open mouth. This is especially obvious in posters for *Potemkin*, which emphasize the role of this motif in the global economy of the film. Eisenstein's films are not only peopled by many screaming characters, but also encapsulate different kinds of 'roaring' cinematic material: expressive titles conveying emotions and, above all, complex and dynamic editing devices, converting the whole film into an extended scream. To create such roaring compositions, Eisenstein used pictorial models, especially in his silent films, where sound had to be suggested by visual means. He carefully studied how painters managed to materialize and express the phenomenon of voice. In the essay in which he conducted a post-theorization and analysis of *Potemkin*'s composition, Eisenstein drew a parallel between the latter and Vasily Surikov's painting *Boyaryna Morozova* (Figure 9.3), whose elaborate composition, based on the Golden Section, powerfully suggests by visual means what, according to Eisenstein, lies beyond representation – the 'plastic portrayal' of the voice of a woman known for her eloquence.[12] Similarly, when discussing the impact of the stone lions rising in *Potemkin* ('the roaring lions'), Eisenstein marvelled at Edvard Munch's *The Scream*, in which the scream is not only represented as an iconographic motif, an open mouth, but also as a visual reverberation that permeates the whole structure and composition of the work, because the painter sought to 'express in the picture's structure the feeling of a scream'.[13] Just as Munch's painting screams on every level, the whole of *Potemkin* is built upon ecstatic jumps from one quality to another, in which screams play a pivotal role as dialectical hinges.[14]

Figure 9.3 Vasily Surikov, *Boyaryna Morozova*, 1887.

Inspired by plastic representations of the scream, Eisenstein's films have in turn inspired painters, in a phenomenon of intermedial circulation which corresponds with Johanne Lamoureux's approach to the scream as an intermedial object.¹⁵ In that respect, *Potemkin*'s screaming nurse, an icon of a revolutionary pathos, functions as a peculiarly haunting image. Severed by the knife of montage, this filmic Gorgon has fascinated and petrified many viewers, not so much with her broken-glassed eyes but with the open gap formed by her screaming mouth. Eisenstein's Gorgon rises again in the work of Francis Bacon and Valerio Adami, who have taken different readings from this image and reworked it in diametrically opposed directions.

Encountering *The Battleship Potemkin*: The birth of 'the painter of the cry'?

Labelled by the French critic Gaëtan Picon as 'the painter of the cry', Francis Bacon viewed the scream as one of the loftiest objects to be painted.¹⁶ In a 1963 interview with the art critic David Sylvester, Bacon made a striking statement:

> I have always been very moved by the movements of the mouth and the shape of the mouth and the teeth [...] I like, you may say, the glitter and colour that comes from the mouth, and I've always hoped in a sense to be able to paint the mouth like [Claude] Monet painted a sunset.¹⁷

Eisenstein's *Potemkin* played a triggering role in Bacon's sensitivity to this motif, which pervaded all of his painted work. The ground was prepared by

Figure 9.4 Nicolas Poussin, *The Massacre of the Innocents*, 1625.

his discovery in 1927 of Poussin's painting *The Massacre of the Innocents* (Figure 9.4), which made a vivid impression upon him. As he recalls in the same interview with Sylvester: 'I remember I was once with a family for about three months living very near [Chantilly], trying to learn French, and I went a great deal to Chantilly and I remember this picture made a terrific impression on me.'[18] Poussin's painting creates not only a visual impression but also a powerful auditory effect thanks to its elaborate composition. As Nathalie Roelens notes, it is not enough to depict an open mouth to make the image heard and give it a voice.[19] In this work, described by Louis Marin as 'one of the most outstanding pictorial representations of a scream', Poussin unfolds an intricate play of correspondences between vision and sound; an elaborate orchestration of visual signs waiting to be deciphered as sounds:

> The intensity of the scream, the voice at its extreme range is visually 'noted' by the point of the raised sword and especially by the obelisk behind, above the head: their intersecting point is empty, conveying the scream's

shrillness while the non-realistic elongation of the woman's arm converts into visual terms its unbearable duration.[20]

Marin also highlights that the trajectory of voice is visually suggested and embodied through the loops formed by the arms of the soldier and the woman, and echoed and enhanced by the movement of the soldier's red cloak. The powerful impact of Poussin on Bacon was reinvigorated when he saw *The Battleship Potemkin*, probably in Paris during an illegal projection organized by the communist cine-club Les Amis de Spartacus.[21] As he explained to Sylvester:

> It was a film I saw almost before I started to paint, and it deeply impressed me – I mean the whole film as well as the Odessa Steps sequence and this shot. I did hope at one time to make – it hasn't got any special psychological significance – I did hope one day to make the best painting of the human cry. I was not able to do it and it's much better in the Eisenstein and there it is. I think probably the best human cry in painting was made by Poussin.[22]

In his diaries, Bacon further highlights the role of Eisenstein's film as a crucial trigger for his activity as a painter, writing: 'In my youth, I was strongly attracted to painting after having been struck by the remarkable visual imagery of Eisenstein's films, *The Strike* and *The Battleship Potemkin*.'[23] A passionate film viewer, Bacon confessed to the publisher and scholar Michel Archimbaud his amazement at the 'tremendous force of the silent era' and the expressive resources of cinema, and claimed that he would have liked to become a film director if he hadn't been a painter.[24] After Bacon's death, several loose black-and-white stills from the Odessa steps sequence were found in his studio (Figure 9.5a and b).[25]

Among these was a close-up of the nurse mounted on cardboard, which Bacon had altered and savagely covered with paint dots and lines, adding a layer of pictorial violence to the violence already encapsulated in the filmic image. This reproduction nurtured his obsession with the scream and the open mouth; as he explained, 'I attempted to use the *Potemkin* still as a basis on which I could also use these marvellous illustrations of the human mouth.'[26] Bacon alludes here to a medical volume he owned titled *Diseases of the Mouth* (1894), which included spectacular and quite repulsive pictures of buccal pathologies.

> Another thing that made me think about the human cry was a book that I bought when I was very young from a bookshop in Paris, a second-hand book which had beautiful hand-coloured plates of diseases of the mouth, beautiful plates of the mouth open and of the examination of the inside of the mouth, and they fascinated me, and I was obsessed by them.[27]

Figure 9.5a and b Materials from Francis Bacon's studio, 'Screaming Nurse' stills from Eisenstein's *The Battleship Potemkin* (1925). Courtesy of Hugh Lane Gallery, Dublin. © The Estate of Francis Bacon.

Bacon also had in his library a copy of Roger Manvell's 1944 book *Film*, in which a still with the bleeding and screaming nurse was reproduced.[28] Long after his striking early encounter with *Potemkin*, Bacon would acquire Eisenstein's writings, published in English in 1973 and in 1982.[29]

Bacon recycled the screaming mouth of the nurse in different paintings, including his variations on Velázquez's portrait of Pope Innocent X (1949, 1953), who, in Bacon's interpretation, wears broken glasses, a marker evidencing Eisenstein as a source, as suggested in a 1949 essay by Robert Melville, which underlined the proximity of Bacon's figures to actors' gestures and the powerful expressivity of silent cinema.[30] Interestingly, Bacon painted his first portrait of Pope Innocent in 1949, the year Helen Weigel performed her famous silent scream in Brecht's play *Mother Courage*. Some of Bacon's studies could also be seen as a condensation of several motifs from the Odessa steps sequence: a stair-structure, the screaming mouth, the umbrella, with the overtone of red saturating the whole scene with bloody associations. In his 1952 *Study for a Portrait*, Bacon again associated a screaming mouth with the motif of glasses, like a variation on the broken pince-nez of the nurse.

More explicitly, Bacon dedicated a painting to the nurse in 1957 in the *Study for the Nurse in the Battleship Potemkin*. In this work, he substitutes a whole body, absolutely naked, for the close-up of the nurse's face, as if he needed to give a surplus of flesh to the screaming mouth. As Gilles Deleuze noted, Bacon portrays not faces but heads, inasmuch as the 'face is a structured, spatial organization that conceals the head, whereas the head is dependent upon the body, even if it is the point of the body' (Figure 9.6).[31] In this operation, the scream plays a crucial role: 'The [open] mouth acquires this power of non-localization that turns all meat into a head without a face.'[32]

Extracted from its original context and placed in an abstract and non-localizable space, the screaming nurse appears in Bacon's treatment as a generalized embodiment of human suffering; the blood on the leg echoes the blood in the eye as well as the redness of the mouth, as if the mouth itself were a wound. Crystallized by the medium of painting, which abstracts it from its filmic and dynamic source, the scream of the nurse seems paradoxically suspended in eternity, a never-ending sound. What resonates particularly strongly with Bacon's paintings is Eisenstein's nurse's mouth in its uncanny dimension as a fleshy gulf akin to meat, since in his view, according to Deleuze, 'Every man who suffers is a piece of meat.'[33] Precisely this equation also appears in Eisenstein, especially in *The Strike*, in which not only are the strikers literally butchered in the final sequence but the worker who dies by suicide looks like a

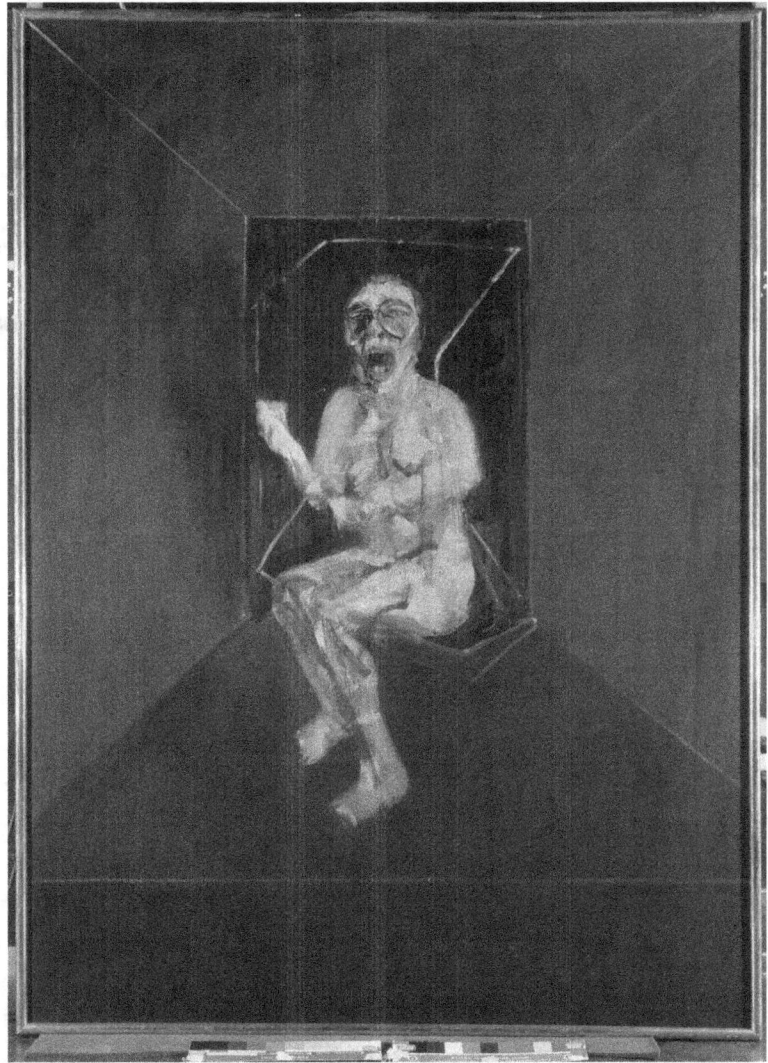

Figure 9.6 Francis Bacon, *Study for the Nurse in the film Battleship Potemkin by Eisenstein*, 1957. Courtesy of Städel Museum, Frankfurt am Main, U. Edelmann, ARTOTHEK.

hanging piece of meat, cut into pieces by the camera. As if to illustrate Deleuze's point that 'The head-meat is a becoming-animal of man', in Bacon's aesthetics meat fosters a zone of undecidability between man and animal.[34] The scream enhances this loss of fixed identity and contour, since 'Bacon's scream is the operation through which the entire body escapes through the mouth.'[35] Bacon's interest in the scream relates to its dynamic process of transformation or, better, of *deformation* of the body into animal, into pure meat and flesh. But what is at stake is also the need to capture the energetic movement which overwhelms the subject, to release presences beyond and beneath representation, to express the invisible forces 'that produce the scream, that convulse the body until they emerge at the mouth as a scrubbed zone'.[36] In Bacon's paintings of screaming figures, the characters' 'only function is to render visible these invisible forces that are making [them] scream'.[37] In that respect, while in Eisenstein people scream *about* and *in reaction to*, Bacon displaces this militant dimension of the scream and transforms it into a pictorial object per se, into a self-sufficient and absolute motif.

Valerio Adami's *Potemkin*: A radicalized political gesture

A totally different treatment and appropriation of the screaming nurse is to be found in the work of the painter Valerio Adami. Born in Bologna in 1935, Adami started his career in Milan before settling in Paris in 1970, where he established close contact with the intellectual and artistic avant-garde. His works have been analysed by Hubert Damisch, Jacques Derrida, Jean-François Lyotard and Jean-Luc Nancy, to name only a few, while they have been exhibited in such venues as the Paris Museum of Modern Art and the Centre Georges Pompidou.[38] During the 1970s, he became one of the major figures of a trend called 'narrative figuration' (*nouvelle figuration*), which claimed there was a need to return to narrative and figurative art, in opposition to abstraction as well as to the figuration practised in socialist realism. Adami's works are permeated with references to literature, music, pop art and film. He experimented with film in 1971, working with his brother Carlo Romani Adami on the film *Vacanze nel deserto*. When Adami moved to Paris in 1970, Eisenstein's writings and films were being intensively debated and discussed: *Cahiers du Cinéma* was publishing many new studies on his work (including Roland Barthes's article 'The Third Meaning'[39]). *Cahiers* was also running translations of Eisenstein's texts and dedicating special issues to him. The publisher Christian Bourgois initiated a cycle of translations of Eisenstein's texts including *Memoirs, Nonindifferent Nature* and others in its 10/18 series. Eisenstein became a key figure in aesthetic and artistic debates at that time, especially in the wake of several protests and uprisings that had shaken European countries at the end of the 1960s. It is not surprising, therefore, that in such a context, among Adami's various

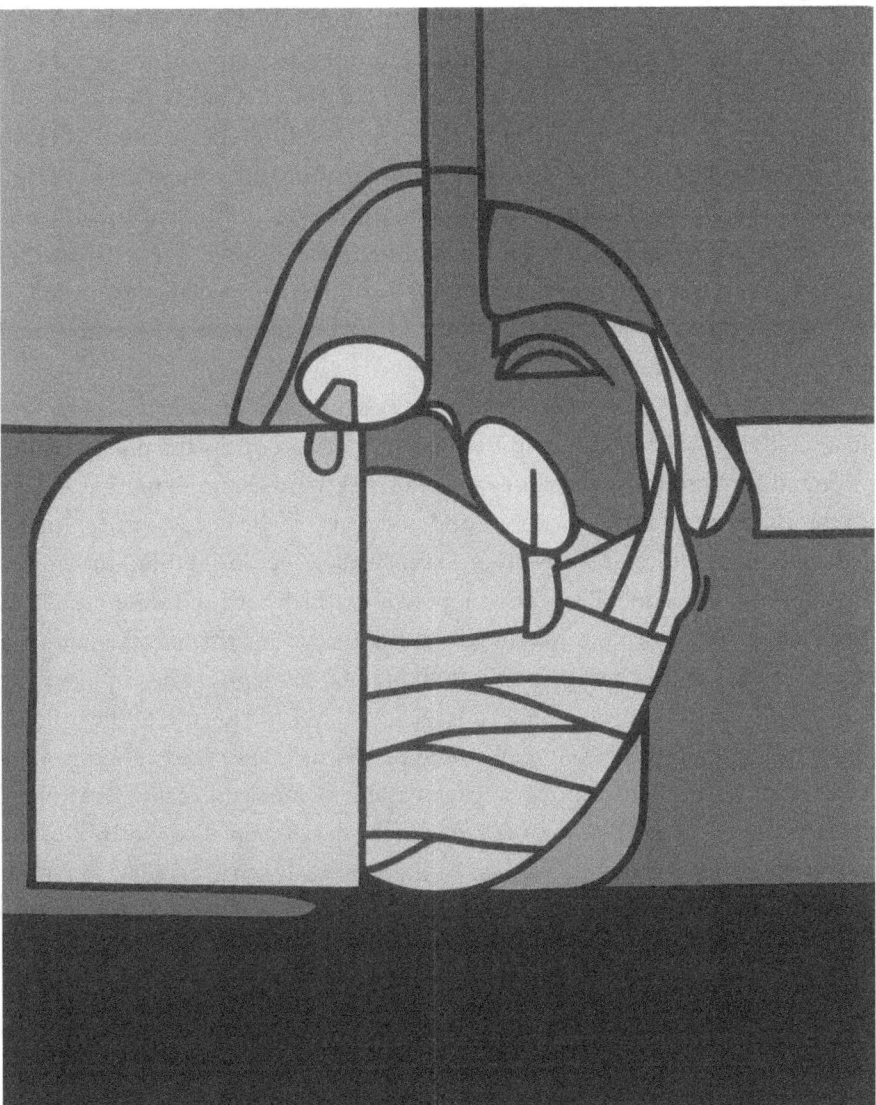

Figure 9.7 Valerio Adami, *The Battleship Potemkin*, 1971. Karouby collection.

works from the 1970s involving a filmic reference, he chose to dedicate one composition to Eisenstein. This was an intertextual gesture typical of his fellow artists from *nouvelle figuration*; Erro, for instance, would paste, rework and subvert famous images within new narratives. Between 24 September 1970 and 24 February 1971, Adami created a painting entitled *The Battleship Potemkin*.[40] The very fact that he would record and inscribe in the caption the time spent on the work stresses his concern with time, as if he wanted to convert the temporal flow of the film into the narrative of the process of pictorial creation, with a clear beginning and end.[41] Adami's filmic agenda also appears in one of his diaries, in which he lists different potential titles for the painting, among which is a list sounding almost like a scenario excerpt, or stage directions: 'People licking spits. Hysteria. Inhumane treatments. The mother asks desperately for news of her son.'[42] This list reveals Adami's mental associations with *Battleship Potemkin*. He is especially interested in moments of pathos, which he combines with images from his memory and imagination (Figure 9.7).

In his *Battleship Potemkin*, Adami reworked the motif of the screaming nurse in a totally opposite direction to Bacon: where Bacon opens the nurse's mouth wide and for eternity, Adami closes and obturates it in a climax of muting. Where Bacon is interested in the obscenity and organicity of the buccal orifice, Adami enhances the political dimension of Eisenstein's scene. In the film, the nurse's impotent scream symbolizes tsarist repression, which muzzled rioters and was unable to *hear* any protest. Adami goes further: covering the nurse's mouth – a wound hole – with a bandage; mummifying her, he deprives her of her voice and makes her definitively silent, adding a new layer of violence to the original image. Where Eisenstein's Gorgon would petrify the viewer, Adami gorgonizes the image itself. Representing a gag literally, Adami translates Eisenstein's imagery into a denunciation of contemporary censorship. The violence of the gesture is enhanced by the contrast of the grey with other colours, as a stain of silence invading the whole composition, which gives a peculiar stress to the broken glasses that are painted in acid pink.

Adami claimed that in this painting the use of colour is equivalent to the use of close-ups in cinema.[43] In addition, the inhumanity of the scene is reinforced by the smooth cold texture of acrylics and the stylized outlines, as well as by the ironic use of pop and vibrant colours. Everything in this cold, flat, metallic treatment contrasts with Bacon's vibrant, organic flesh. Adami answers Eisenstein's cruel filmic montage with a deconstructing assemblage of elements, a fragmented poetics which enhances the nurse's loss of speech and sight. The fragmenting process in itself is cruel, implying the sacrifice of some elements, as noted by Marc Le Bot: '[Adami's works] are like a scattered puzzle from which some pieces are lost, as if every image by Adami was initially cut in strips, these ones being then glued together at the expense of overlaps and lost fragments'.[44] Adami's aesthetics of 'montage-images'[45] relies upon a mutilation of the original image or model, and it never preserves faces' integrity or unity. When he draws,

Adami practises epidermal cuts: arbitrary cuts which echo the way a gaze itself cuts visible reality into arbitrary fragments.[46] It is not accidental that in many works from 1970 and 1971 Adami drew such particular attention to the motif of the glasses, not only in his reworking of *The Battleship Potemkin* nurse but also in his portraits of Freud, Gandhi and Joyce, where the motif of shattered glasses highlights the cruel operation of the fragmenting gaze, as well as the artist's violent and cruel gesture.

Remediated in painting, the scream of Eisenstein's nurse still remains vibrant and resonant, calling for new interpretations and re-elaborations across periods and media. In short, the nurse's voice demands to be heard and continues to reverberate.

Notes

1 I refer here to the screaming woman with broken glasses in the famous Odessa steps sequence. While nothing in the film leads us to assume that this woman is a nurse, she has been described as such by many commentators, although sometimes she is also described, more plausibly, as a teacher. There is also another female figure present in the same sequence, a nursemaid, who is shot in the stomach, before her pram careers down the steps. It is, however, the woman with broken glasses who has been referred to as a nurse by the artists I discuss here, Valerio Adami and Francis Bacon.
2 Léon Moussinac, 'Poudovkine', in *Le Cinéma soviétique* (Paris: Gallimard, 1928), 137, translated by the author.
3 Sergei Eisenstein to Moussinac, 15 October 1928, Bibliothèque Nationale de France/Arts du Spectacle/Fonds Léon Moussinac/4° COLIO/35 (1), translated by the author.
4 Georges Sadoul, 'Le Cri devenu hymne', *Les Lettres françaises*, 19 February 1948, quoted by Léon Moussinac, *Serge Eisenstein* (Paris: Seghers, 1964), 173, translated by the author.
5 Umberto Barbaro, 'Serghei Eisenstein maestro d'arte', in *Servitù e grandezza del cinema* (Rome: Editori Riuniti, 1962), 35, translated by the author.
6 Alain Marc, *Écrire le cri: Sade, Bataille, Maïakovski* (Paris: L'Ecarlate, 2000), 16.
7 Algirdas Julien Greimas, 'Pour une théorie du discours poétique', in *Essais de sémiotique poétique* (Paris: Larousse, 1972), 23.
8 Gotthold Ephraim Lessing, *Laocoön: An Essay upon the Limits of Painting and Poetry* (London: Dent, 1930), 13.
9 Georges Bataille, 'Bouche' (1930), *Documents*, II (Paris: Jean-Michel Place, 1991), 299.

10 Nathalie Roelens, 'La Bouche ouverte en peinture comme objet sémiotique: du cri au geste' [The open mouth in painting as a semiotic object: the cry of the gesture], in *Sémiotique et esthétique* [*Semiotics and Aesthetics*], ed. Françoise Parouty-David and Claude Zilberberg (Limoges: Presses Universitaires de Limoges, 2003), 381.

11 'Quirito', in Joseph Esmond Riddle, *A Complete Latin-English Dictionary*, 4th edn (London: Longman, Brown, Green and Longmans, 1844), 562.

12 See Sergei Eisenstein, *Film and the Structure of Things*, in *Nonindifferent Nature*, ed. Herbert Marshall (Cambridge: Cambridge University Press, 1987), 3–38.

13 Sergei Eisenstein, 'Sound in Painting', in *Notes for a General History of Cinema*, ed. Naum Kleiman and Antonio Somaini (Amsterdam: Amsterdam University Press, 2016), 140.

14 Gilles Deleuze, 'Montage', in *Cinema I: The Movement Image* (London: Bloomsbury Publishing, 2013), 60: 'Eisenstein attained the cry in the manner of a dialectician, that is as the qualitative leap which made the whole evolve.'

15 Johanne Lamoureux, 'Cris et médiations entre les arts: de Lessing à Bacon', *Protée* 28, no. 3 (2000): 13–21.

16 Gaëtan Picon, 'Le Cercle et le cri', in *Francis Bacon*, exhibition catalogue, ed. David Sylvester (Paris: Centre Georges Pompidou, 1996), 274–5.

17 David Sylvester, 'Interview 2' (1966), *Interviews with Francis Bacon* (London: Thames & Hudson, [1975] 2016), 57.

18 Ibid., 40.

19 Roelens, 'La Bouche ouverte en peinture comme objet sémiotique', 378.

20 Louis Marin, 'Aux marges de la peinture: voir la voix', *L'Écrit du Temps* 17 (1988): 69.

21 Émilie Bouvard, 'Pablo Picasso. Francis Bacon. Eléments de chronologie', in *Poussin, Le Massacre des Innocents, Picasso, Bacon*, exhibition catalogue, ed. Pierre Rosenberg (Paris: Flammarion, 2017), 126. Bouvard states that Bacon saw *The Battleship Potemkin* in Paris in 1927/8, while other authors claim it happened later, for instance Sylvester (*Francis Bacon*, 288), who reports the viewing occurred in 1935.

22 Sylvester, 'Interview 2', 40.

23 Bacon's autograph note, dated 4 June 1988, quoted in *Francis Bacon: Zhivopis* (Moscow: New Tretyakov Central House of Artists, 1988), 5.

24 Michel Archimbaud, *Francis Bacon in Conversation with Michel Archimbaud* (London: Phaidon, 1993), 16.

25 Margarita Cappock, 'Cinema', in *Francis Bacon's Studio* (London: Merrell Publishing, 2005), 119.

26 Sylvester, 'Interview 2', 40.

27 Ibid.

28 Émilie Bouvard, 'Poussin, Picasso, Bacon. Sur-réalité du Massacres des Innocents', in *Poussin, Le massacre des Innocents – Picasso, Bacon*, ed. Pierre Rosenberg, 133–137 (Paris: Flammarion, 2017), 143.
29 Cappock, 'Cinema', 119.
30 Robert Melville, 'Francis Bacon', *Horizon* 20, nos. 120–121 (December 1949–January 1950): 419–23.
31 Gilles Deleuze, *Francis Bacon: The Logic of Sensation* (London: Bloomsbury, [1981] 2017), 20.
32 Ibid., 26.
33 Ibid., 23.
34 Ibid., 27.
35 Ibid., 16.
36 Ibid., 60.
37 Ibid., 61.
38 On Adami's life and career, see Jacques Derrida, 'Extase, crise', in *Penser à ne pas voir: Écrits sur le visible, 1979–2004* (Paris: La Différence, 2015), 204–5.
39 Roland Barthes, 'The Third Meaning: Research Notes on Some Eisenstein Stills' (1970), in *The Responsibility of Forms* (Berkeley: University of California Press, 1991), 41–62.
40 Valerio Adami, *Œuvres récentes et portraits*, exhibition catalogue (Marseille: Musée Cantini, 1977), 47.
41 Dominique Païni, 'Valerio Adami. Le Cuirassé Potemkine. 1970–1971', *Art Press 2, Figuration Narrative* (February/March/April 2009): 82.
42 Hubert Damisch and Henry Martin, *Adami* (Paris: Maeght, 1974), 121.
43 Valerio Adami, *Dessiner: la gomme et les crayons* (Paris: Galilée, 2002), 32.
44 Marc Le Bot, 'La découpe et le vide', in *Valerio Adami: Essai sur le formalisme critique* (Paris: Galilée, 1975), 97.
45 Jean-Pierre Mourey, *Philosophies et pratiques du détail: Hegel, Ingres, Sade et quelques autres* (Paris: Champ Vallon, 1996), 104.
46 Ibid., 89.

Part Four

History, Representation, Montage

10

October: On the Cinematic Allegorizing of History

Håkan Lövgren

Allegories are the natural mirrors of ideology.

—Angus Fletcher, *Allegory*

October was Sergei Eisenstein's celebration of the tenth anniversary of the 1917 October Revolution or, as some might call it, the Bolshevik coup, notionally based on the American journalist John Reed's account *Ten Days That Shook the World*.[1] Conceptually it is his most sophisticated silent film, as it attempted to realize the principle of intellectual montage, which, as I propose here, can be understood as essentially an allegorical method. Eisenstein's proclaimed intention was to impart forcefully and conclusively Marxist revolutionary political ideas. In this sense, *October* may be regarded as the most extreme example of the period of 'multiple set-up cinema', as Eisenstein called the 'montage film' era of the 1920s, since the film sought to transcend ordinary storytelling in favour of a thesis-oriented narration of battling ideological concepts.[2] The ultimate goal of his intellectual montage project was complete control of the film audiences' responses to the spectacle. Despite the rather limited instances of intellectual montage in the film, as Eisenstein admitted,[3] *October* is marked by a culture that sought what Angus Fletcher has called the highest level of allegory: 'a symbolism that conveys the action of the mind'.[4] A thesis-antithesis form dominates the realization of the film, from the mass scenes down to the behaviour of the individual characters in the political conflict between the Kerensky government and its sympathizers on the one hand and the Bolsheviks on the other. Eisenstein portrayed the participants in this battle using a method of typecasting, typage (*tipazh*), based on physiognomics and supposed markers of social class and ideological affiliation.

This intellectual montage approach was clearly meant to counteract any doubts in the spectator's mind as to the logic and purpose of the revolutionary historical development he was witnessing. The 'allegorical thinking' in *October* sought to develop a clarity of intention similar to the one characterized by Fletcher:

> Allegory does not accept doubt; its enigmas show instead an obsessive battling with doubt. It does not except the world of experience and senses; it thrives on their overthrow, replacing them with ideas. In these ways allegory departs from mimesis and myth, and its intention in either case seems to be a matter of clearly rationalized 'allegorical levels of meaning.' These levels are the double aim of the aesthetic surface; they are its intention, and its ritualized form is intended to elicit from the reader some sort of exegetical response [...] In this way, oddly enough, allegorical intention is in general a simple matter. But since mythic and mimetic moments are always possible in the midst of a fable, we find that exegetical problems can always arise as to the specific intention of any particular work.[5]

In other words, while allegory represents a system of conceptual control, it also has a tendency to 'leak', to allow narrative and mythic 'impurities' to interfere with the process of properly interpreting the allegorical work, and so ultimately invite ambiguity. The issue here is perhaps contradictory inclinations in art and propaganda, one towards formal complexity and inscrutability, the other towards simplicity and ideological clarity and efficacy. *October* wanted to keep a foot in both camps, a fact that no doubt contributed to the numerous revisions and different versions produced around the time of the film's complicated release, as it aimed to be part of the celebration of the tenth anniversary of the October Revolution. Another contributing factor was the pressure on Eisenstein to attend to the shifting political landscape of the period, and particularly the power struggle between Stalin and Trotsky. Meanwhile, exegetical problems in the interpretation and reception of the film, which were recognized by contemporary Soviet critics, may be blamed on a lack of decoding skills in Eisenstein's working-class audience, or on the inherently 'leaky' or ideologically dubious quality of the intellectual montage sequences of this propaganda pageant.[6]

The players and stage of *October* could be described metaphorically as a giant game of social and political chess, in which the better organized and more ruthless side will win.[7] The ritualism of class struggle, from a Marxian standpoint, where the rules are set and the outcome is, if not inevitable, at least predictable, is reflected in the way that representatives of social classes and political groups of either the 'white' or the 'black' (actually 'red' in this case) side of the battle defeat one another's 'pieces' in the film. A major theme in the artistic embodiment of this class conflict is the dynamic interaction between human beings and statues – most often in a specific architectural setting – or figurines, a kind of metamorphosis of living and dead matter in the exchange between these two categories. The replacement of an obsolete political system by a new and vital one is allegorically reflected in this peculiar relationship between animate beings and their usually inanimate, although sometimes animated, sculptural representations.

For Eisenstein, the development of art in general and cinematography in particular was itself allegorical: it corresponded to the overriding historical dynamic, leading inevitably to communism through socialist development. In *October*, his mission was to give artistic form to this historical process that would lead to a classless Soviet society, a form that would similarly answer to a 'lawfulness' in the evolution and development of art, the pinnacle of which Eisenstein considered Soviet cinematography to be. In this scheme of things, he had identified the mass film as the 'new progressive phase of the theatre in the streets'.[8]

One celebrated example of monumental theatre in the streets staged after 1917 was Nikolai Evreinov's 1920 anniversary open-air mass spectacle, *The Storming of the Winter Palace*. This performance submerged reality in theatricality, creating a kind of ritual people's theatre, the structure of which may well have influenced the planning of *October*. Eisenstein admitted to being an ardent, even envious admirer of Evreinov's career and work.[9] In an interview for the newspaper *Life of Art*, published in the 30–31 September 1920 issue, Evreinov had said:

> The action will take place not only on the stages, but also on a bridge between them and on the ground, across which the Provisional Government will run attempting to escape from the pursuing proletariat, and in the air where aeroplanes will soar and bells and factory sirens will sound.
>
> Apart from ten thousand performers – actors and persons mobilized from the drama groups of the Red Army and Navy units – inanimate characters will also take part in the production. Even the Winter Palace itself will be involved as a gigantic actor, as a vast character in the play which will manifest its own mimicry and inner emotions. The director must make the stones speak, so that the spectator feels what is going on inside, behind those cold red walls. We have found an original solution to this problem, using a cinematographic technique: each one of the fifty windows of the first floor will in turn show a moment of the development of the battle inside.[10]

We can only speculate on the impact of these dramatic solutions on the emergence and development of cinematic montage, but in *October* Eisenstein certainly allowed the stones and other 'inanimate characters' of the Winter Palace and its surroundings to come alive in a manner Yevreinov never managed. After the period of War Communism (1917–20), mass spectacles in the format used by Evreinov became rarer and adopted a more rational and pragmatic approach to theatre, moving back onto smaller stages. This was intended to maximize the performance's impact upon an audience of ideal working-class spectators.[11] And it was the context in which Eisenstein's 1923 'Montage of Attractions' pamphlet as well as his 'Montage of Film Attractions', 'The Problem of the Materialist Approach to Form' and 'The Method of Making Workers' Films' of the following two years were written.

The year 1927 saw a renewed emphasis on the transformation of man and mass culture. At a Leningrad Agitprop meeting in May that year, theatre was again accorded a central role in the increasingly more instrumental and agitation-oriented view of culture. Mass spectacles were once more considered workable. One of the first to be performed was the 1927 revolutionary jubilee, *Ten Years*, under the leadership of a handful of veterans from Evreinov's 1920 production, including Sergei Radlov, Adrian Piotrovsky and N. V. Petrov as directors and scenarists. This time, however, the spectacle was located on the other side of the Neva River, opposite the Winter Palace, and the spatial scale and distribution set the tone of the performance rather than the number of participants. Of the spectacle, Katerina Clark writes, 'The audience alone stretched over one and a half kilometers.' She continues:

> Similarly remarkable was the sense of stage. *The Storming of the Winter Palace* had been largely set on two specially constructed stages on the Palace Square, with a bridge structure joining them. *Ten Years* was given its 'stages,' too, but they were not specially constructed ones. The set designer, Valentina Khodosevich, identified as the 'proscenium' a large stretch of the Neva River between two bridges, while she called the 'main stage' the Peter and Paul Fortress, with the Mint nominated as the 'rear stage' and the Kronversky Canal functioning as 'wings.' The auditorium, she claimed, was 'the entire population of Leningrad'.[12]

The space of action had thus expanded considerably and the theatre of mass spectacle laid claim to a major part of the city. The stage and backdrop were no longer specially constructed but 'expropriated' from Leningrad's existing architectural and urban setting. This space would also be used by Eisenstein in his version of the revolution, but most of the action in *October* would centre on the area of the Winter Palace and Palace Square, where architecture, architectural details, statues and figurines were consciously converted into allegorical participants in the battle for revolutionary power, the 'last and decisive battle', as one of the film's intertitles declared.

Eisenstein's contrasting use of statues and miniatures in *October* can be compared with Hillel Schwartz's observations in his book on the culture of copying and reproducing. Schwartz writes 'Colossal figures, by their very mass, assert that someone has *taken place*', by their presence 'they maintain the indelibility of power'. To these colossi, he counterposes

> miniatures, subtle with the playfulness of character, [which] extend us toward second chances, times ahead and remediable. Egyptian dolls, Roman puppets, jointed manikins in the studios of Renaissance artists were less mass than energy, always *trading places*, being changed or exchanged. The scale of the miniature encourages impromptu affections, banter, fantasy [...] The colossus is entirely dependent upon an external story; the miniature is that figure through which we collude with personable doubles.[13]

In Eisenstein's film one can see a similar stratification of colossi versus miniatures, an opposition of the world of 'heavy action', of manly deeds in the realms of giant statues, columns and immovable sphinxes to the intimate, 'effeminate' and obsolete sphere of tsarist power and reformist politics – *replaceable* entities – in which the manipulation of figurines, gadgets and trinkets of the imperial palace's internal space signals impotence in all senses of the word.

In the symphonic structure of *October*, the opening sequence is of great importance; a series of medium and close shots, where the 'pawns' go directly for the 'king', shows the torso and imperial implements in the hands of the tsar, the statue of the seated Aleksander III.[14] The angry crowds of the February Revolution surge up the steps leading to the statue, a ladder is raised and agile peasants and workers climb the torso, limbs and head of the statue to attach heavy ropes around it. The bunched ropes around the tsar, now looking like a fettered Gulliver, are stretched and tightened as if the crowd were ready to pull it down. There is a cut to a shot of a forest of raised scythes, obviously symbolizing the peasantry, followed by shots of similarly raised rifle butts to indicate soldiers renouncing war. We then see the statue mysteriously starting to disintegrate without any trace of ropes or people around it. It falls apart piece by piece, revealing an ordinary scaffold propping it up. Members of the bourgeoisie rejoice, a censer swings and an Orthodox priest performs a religious service in the shots that follow. What we witness in this sequence is thus essentially an assault on the statue of Aleksander III and its curious subsequent self-destruction.[15] This self-destruction in turn provides for the metaphoric reversal of the process later in the film, the 'cinematic' reconstruction of Aleksander III's statue as a symbol of political reaction.

The violent dismantling of statues representing dead or deposed rulers is a frequent historical phenomenon in both the real and symbolic struggle for political power. 'Consider how we are still drawn to images of crowds attacking gigantic statues of dead dictators', writes Kenneth Gross, 'statues that gain a striking, if sometimes forlorn sort of animation even in the process of being hacked, toppled, hung, burned, defaced; one feels here as if the violence done to such statues becomes an aspect of their peculiar life'.[16] Gross's point is that the violent attack on the statue, the attempt to demystify the idol's 'magic hold' on its subjects, may result in a re-mystification of that same power as well as of the motives behind the attack. As he explains:

> Since the iconoclastic stance depends on its own reductive, projective parody of idolatry, and on a radical mystification of the power that undoes that idolatry, the text's disenchantments remain unsettlingly ambiguous. One result of this ambiguity is that the 'enemy' will tend to be pictured as a peculiar composite of idol and demon, as a thing at once dead and uncannily alive.[17]

A curious sort of contagion occurs in this interaction; qualities are lost and transferred; inanimate objects come alive while living beings turn to stone. Gross's *The Dream of the Moving Statue* primarily focuses on fantasies about animated statues in works of literature. Not surprisingly, he devotes considerable analytical attention to Aleksander Pushkin's most famous contribution to the genre, 'The Bronze Horseman' (1833) and Roman Jakobson's essay 'The Statue in Pushkin's Mythology' (1937). Any artistic effort to deal with the theme of 'animated' statues of Russian historical potentates, such as Eisenstein's *October*, must inevitably evoke Pushkin's poem.[18] This also relates to the traditional iconoclastic controversy and ambiguity surrounding representation in Russian religious art; the fact that in semiotic terms the 'signified' is still potentially alive in the 'signifier', that the 'sculpted' may still be part of the 'sculpture', that there may in fact be a basis for idolatry. In the light of Gross's discussion, by dismantling the statue and then reassembling it, Eisenstein seems paradoxically to impart more power and life to the statue than it ever had when left in peace; he awakens the dormant demon in the sculpture, so to speak. However, Eisenstein's de- and re-construction of Aleksander III's statue in *October* is more than merely a clever political metaphor. The treatment of the statue, the fact that it 'comes alive' while falling apart, bears on our perception of subsequent juxtapositions of sculpture/figurine/miniature and woman/man/living being.

Consider the shots immediately following the machine-gun attack on the demonstrators, the masterly sequence beginning with the intertitle '*spasaia znamiia*' (to the rescue of the banner) and ending with the First Machine Gun Regiment being herded off. This sequence was barely hinted at in the original script, but the artistic consideration and energy given to it by Eisenstein seem to underline its importance in the film. A young Bolshevik standard bearer is trying to escape from pursuing police along the Neva embankment. A series of medium and close-up shots follow. The young man halts, looking around, framed between a sphinx-like pharaoh bust in granite and a large urn presumably in the same material, both belonging to the ornamentation of the riverside. There is a cut to demonstrators dispersing under fire from the machine gun, then back to the young man with the banner. Next we see the figure of the Bolshevik and a rounded object with a surface resembling the pattern of the urn, a parasol: a transition, first, from granite to cloth and then to the human beings behind it. The significance of this montage sequence could be that the impassive stone face of despotic power (the granite pharaoh, a king in our political chess game) suddenly comes alive, as a living representative in the flirting cadet who begins the attack on the standard bearer that will rally other bourgeois individuals, all in appropriate *typage* garb. The young man dies the death of a martyr, pierced like Saint Sebastian in classical art. However, in this case he is stabbed by enraged bourgeois women whose lace underwear and exuberant attire make them unlikely warriors. The martyr sequence is intercut with the raising of the bridge, in which a woman demonstrator and a white horse perish – the horse and the young man as well as banners and issues of *Pravda* being symbolically claimed by the water of the Neva River. At the end of the sequence, Eisenstein shows a view of the raised bridge with a statue gazing indifferently over the scene. There are also two close-ups of the same impassive granite pharaoh that occurred at the beginning of the entire 'reaktsiia pobedila' (reaction has won) sequence. Thus, the whole sequence is 'framed' by historical sculpture that visually aligns members of the Kerensky bourgeoisie and military with the tsarist despotism that was overthrown in the February Uprising.[19]

If this sequence represents interaction with colossi, immovable statues which have assumed a permanent (political) location, the sequence with a gloomy Kerensky in Tsar Aleksander III's study, showing him with a plaster miniature of Napoleon and an army of tin soldiers, corresponds to Schwartz's idea of figurines trading places both with one another and with humans. When Schwartz speaks about the miniature as 'that figure through which we collude with personable doubles', he alludes to a certain intimacy. In the film, the close-ups of Kerensky fiddling with a four-part bottle and cap in the shape of a crown, tin soldiers, a series of devotional figurines in the 'For God and Country' sequence, and the many objects in the imperial bedchamber, all have an aura of intimacy that creates curiosity, perhaps even a certain empathy, through their sensuous immediacy. The effect is one of ambiguity and, to the extent that it is consistent and pervasive, must be considered counterproductive to Eisenstein's alleged desire to debase these objects and images, as well as the people associated with them.

The toppling of Aleksander III's statue in the film is a striking image of the revolutionary imperative to *svergat' s prestola*, 'to depose' or literally 'to remove from the throne'. That the throne and deposition theme is a major consideration in Eisenstein's realization of this scene becomes clear from the fact that the statue is not actually pulled down with the ropes of the crowd. Instead, as already noted, Aleksander mysteriously disintegrates to reveal his hollow chair-like foundation and then topples over in a typical Eisensteinian triple jump-cut, with partial overlap and repeated shot. Likewise, the later reversal of the falling and disintegrating statue is free from backwards-moving humans and ropes which would have weakened its metaphoric effect to convey the idea of political reaction when General Kornilov approaches. The throne motif is obviously why Eisenstein chose the statue of Aleksander III in Moscow rather than the equestrian version in Petrograd/Saint Petersburg, which would have brought unwanted associations with Falconet's statue of an aggressive and, in the eyes of the Bolsheviks, possibly also progressive tsar, Peter the Great.

The symbolic series of seating arrangements running through the film, sometimes coinciding and intersecting with crowned objects, birds and people, constitutes a strong allegorical theme. It could be said that the specific forms of the tsars' 'seat of power' motif represent a declining series in terms of both height and status, from the elevated position of the Aleksander statue to the near floor level of the chamber pot in Nikolai's palace bedroom. The strictly regal and religious theme of the throne – the overthrow of the seated Aleksander, the chair left empty by Kerensky in the tsar's apartment and the appropriation of Tsar Peter's throne by the little boy at the end of the film – could be associated with the idea of regicide and parricide, as well as the scriptural Second Coming and icons of the Trinity. The first two are ubiquitous in alchemical myths and prevalent in psychoanalytic theory: the empty chair or throne is a symbol of God or the Second Coming in Byzantine art, and the Trinity is sometimes depicted as the Father, Son and the Holy Spirit simultaneously seated on or in the Throne, as this often acquires architectural features and dimensions. Dmitrii Popov has suggested that the chair motif in Eisenstein's personal photographs around the time of the shooting of the film symbolizes different meanings of the words 'victory' and 'conquest', a kind of 'Don Juan register'.[20] In the context of the film, this motif of royal chairs is perhaps intended as an expression of male self-reproduction or fecundation. Eisenstein's preoccupation with rifles and machine guns, his prime phallic symbol, misogynistic renditions of murderous bourgeois females and of members of the Women Death Battalion further underscore this theme of male 'self-reliance'.

The visual metaphor of political reaction – the restoration of Aleksander's statue in *October* – is also an image with mnemonic implications. It is striking and original, including 'magic' movement, which is bound to make a lasting impression on the spectator. Other image constellations in the film, such as the 'Napoleon' and 'For God and Country' sequences, obviously aspire to similar effect. Mnemonics interested Eisenstein, who maintained that the rules of this technique were based on the specifics of the earliest layers of human consciousness. The fundamental idea was that by applying these rules, the appearance of a single element would generate the entire gestalt or constellation to which this element belonged. This was one of Eisenstein's favourite notions, 'the extremely popular artistic device … *pars pro toto*'. He quipped, 'Nobody, receiving a button from a suit, would imagine that he was wearing a three-piece suit.'[21] Yet, argued Eisenstein,

> as soon as we enter the sphere where emotional and figurative constructions play a decisive role, the sphere of artistic constructions, this same tool of *pars pro toto* immediately comes into force. The pince-nez, offered in lieu of the whole doctor in *The Battleship Potemkin*, not only fulfils his role and place entirely: they do so with a colossal emotional and sensory gain in intensity of effect that is significantly greater than could have been obtained by the reappearance of the entire doctor![22]

Noting that '*pars pro toto*, in literary form, is what is termed *synecdoche*', Eisenstein continues:

> what we are dealing with here is not individual devices, peculiar to this or that area of art, but rather the specific progress and condition of thinking that gives form to things – with emotional thinking, for which the given construction is one of the laws. 'Close-up' used in a special way, synecdoche, a dot of colour or a line – these are only individual cases where the same law of *pars pro toto* (characteristic of emotional thinking) is present, depending on which particular area of art it acts in as the embodiment of the creative design.[23]

Steps and stairways, specifically ascending and descending figures, are of great importance in Eisenstein's films. Certainly these stairs often serve the purpose of graphically enhancing and dynamically reinforcing the mise en scène and action. But in addition, they provide what I would call an allegorical vertical emphasis which includes the transcendence of boundaries, movement along stairways, climbing and stepping over spatial and symbolic demarcations such as thresholds and doorways. In a word, there is a 'threshold crossing' symbolism that is crucial for the film's central theme, and important in relation to cultural tendencies generally in Soviet society at the time.[24] The feeling of labyrinthine claustrophobia in *October* is primarily associated with the use of architecture and architectural space, the propensity to tightly control the perception and limits of space, to 'enclose' and 'pile up' shots and restrict the viewpoint that seem to follow from the *pars pro toto* technique of intellectual montage.[25]

The issue I want to raise here is to what extent Eisenstein's understanding of myth, allegory and the psychoanalytic image of the labyrinth can be applied to *October* and intellectual montage, even though his discussion of these concepts occurs mostly in the 1930s and 1940s, some years after the film was conceived and produced. In terms of historical description *October* is, not unexpectedly, a mixture of fact and fiction. The opening sequence has already been discussed; and the rendition of the storming of the Winter Palace is largely mythical, since historically the attack was disorganized and the military cadets in the palace had already given up by the time the Red Guards and sailors were penetrating it.[26] But, we may wonder, did Eisenstein consciously strive for a mythical or allegorical form? In 'Perspectives' (published in 1929), the essay that tried to sum up the idea of the intellectual film, Eisenstein spoke of the moment when even the driest facts of a lecture on mathematics are enthusiastically absorbed by the audience due to the personality or personal method of the lecturer. He wrote, 'A dry integral is recalled in the feverish brightness of the eyes. In the mnemonic of *collectively* experienced *perception*.' 'What is the difference', he later asks, 'between a perfected method of oratory and a perfected method of acquiring knowledge? The new art must set a limit to the dualism of the spheres of "emotion" and "reason" [...] Only *intellectual* cinema will be able to put an end to the conflict between the "language of logic" and the "language of images". On the basis of the language of the cinema dialectic.'[27] There is only one obstacle in this process, which he defines as 'living man', a figure primarily associated with the culture of Moscow Art Theatre performances; that is, naturalism in style of acting and thinking. Quoting a speech by Molotov that referred to 'inappropriate progress' in agriculture, Eisenstein continues:

Filling the screen with 'living man' would mean precisely the same 'inappropriate progress' towards the industrialization of our cinema culture. Cinema can – and consequently must – convey on the screen in tangible sensual form the pure, dialectical essence of our ideological debates. Without recourse to intermediaries like plot, story or living man.[28]

This ambition seems to resemble the aforementioned 'symbolism that conveys the action of the mind', the highest level of allegory.[29] Eisenstein's intention in *October* was to present a historical process, the events leading up to the storming of the Winter Palace in 1917, shown in accordance with Marx's principles of historical and dialectical materialism. Far from offering his own interpretation of the revolutionary upsurge, Eisenstein strove to convey in visual terms (with a minimum of intertitles) the abstract categories and principles determining it. The result is ritualistically repeated and abstracted behaviour on the part of the actors and participants who tend to become walking concepts, *figurae*, or, in Eisenstein's terminology, *typage* figures. The intellectual montage which is meant to generate the highest level of abstraction consists typically of the combination of diegetic and non-diegetic images to form a trope, a metaphoric relationship, the content of which serves to justify both the treatment of specific historical characters (ironic caricature) and the historical process as a whole. 'Plot, story or living man' is obviously of slight importance in this approach.

From this perspective, *October* can be read as a thesis on the class struggle. The spatial stratification of the film, the pronounced use of symmetrical configurations, revolves around two basic symbolic and polar locations, the Winter Palace and the Smolny Institute. Both locations are presented through signature shots of very similar long arcade spaces where organizing activities occur. These activities are antithetical; the Smolny soldiers are well organized and directed, while the cadets and their pompous officers in the Winter Palace feign motivation. Symmetry permeates the imagery and montage of the film. Eisenstein goes as far as 'flipping' shots, even if this means mirror-reversing images to create the symmetric, almost heraldic effect that characterizes *October* from the outset. Thus, when the Savage Battalion is approaching, their train is shown in shots which interact by contrasting diagonal movements created through the mirror imaging of a train that includes one heavy gun and a strange aeroplane contraption that must be the film crew's wind machine (probably used in realizing the storm that greets Lenin at the Finland Station). The text on the side of the railroad car is reversed. Similarly, in the sequence where the Aleksander statue is restored, the emperor is holding the sceptre in his right hand in one shot and in his left hand in the next.

This kind of symmetrical stratification is characteristic of the 'battle theme' in allegorical literature,[30] but also of *October*'s ideological conflict between revolutionary activists and a counter-revolutionary bourgeoisie or arch-reactionary military, where individual skirmishes and attacks anticipate the final battle in and around the Winter Palace.

The Winter Palace and Smolny are inhabited by Kerensky and members of his provisional government on the one hand, and by the Bolsheviks and their Red Guard supporters on the other. Kerensky is ridiculed for his alleged tsarist ambitions, a traditional false pretender theme in the film, which immediately turns him into a class enemy, while the image of the Bolshevik leader Lenin is one of the forceful helmsmen, bracing the banner in the revolutionary hurricane that will sweep all enemies away. When Lenin addresses the crowd at the Finland Station, he looks like the Grim Reaper, Father Time or Saturn, with his banner resembling a scythe and the clock in the background substituting for the hourglass.

However, in the most abstract forms of intellectual montage the difficulty appears to be control: how to limit and direct the associations between these serial images of objects to the intended effect. The more grotesque the juxtaposed images appear, the more fuel and fire are required under the analogy, because 'the grotesque is embodied in an act of transition, of metonymy becoming metaphor, of the margin swapping places with the centre. It is embodied in a transformation of duality into unity, of the meaningless into the meaningful.'[31] If we consider the famous 'For God and Country' sequence, comprised of idols or religious figurines, we notice that the ordering of the images, the non-diegetic nature of some of them and the fact that they do not all belong to the same spatial continuum, amount to a problem of meaning to be solved, a task for a decoder. What then guarantees that the conclusion reached by a Leningrad spectator will not be something like 'Aha! These are exotic objects from Peter the Great's *Kunstkamer*, and Kerensky and his cohorts will soon be joining their lot', rather than a general denunciation of religion? To counter this potential misapprehension, the intellectual montage in *October* time and again puts the cart before the horse by using intertitles to 'assist' in the guiding process, thereby *presenting* the concept rather than *generating* it.

Can we then argue that the elements of intellectual montage and other non-diegetic and symbolic processes in the film represent allegory? Fletcher, for example, suggests that certain 'exotic' and grotesque elements are necessary in some romantic subgenres of the allegorical, such as the Gothic.[32] One of Eisenstein's own references to allegory connects it to myth and mythology. In his speech at the All-Union Film Workers' Conference in 1935, Eisenstein pointed to the fact that certain theories and perspectives that were once considered scientific lose their status as science in the course of time, only to be relegated to the sphere of art and imagery where they are permissible:

> Take mythology. We know that at any one stage mythology is, properly speaking, a complex of science of phenomena set out in a language that is mainly figurative and poetic. All those figures from mythology that we regard as no more than allegory, were at one stage an imagistic summery of our knowledge of the world. Then science moved away from figurative narratives and towards concepts, even though the arsenal of earlier, personified, mythological and symbolic beings continued as a series of stage images, of literary metaphors, lyrical allegories and so on. They cannot endure forever in this role, however, and end up in the archives.[33]

Here Eisenstein's evolutionism is allowing art to sift through the rubble left on the scrapheap of science. The above quotation, of course, was written during the Stalinist times of caution and careful treading in the 1930s, and not during the heroic 1920s when *October* was made. There is no real distinction made between the categories of mythology, allegory and symbolism; they all deal in figurative and poetic language which is doomed either to extinction or to the archives. However, Eisenstein's memoir, *Beyond the Stars*, largely written after his heart attack in 1946, includes a text called 'Dead Souls' containing a more complex and interesting discussion from our perspective. The paradigmatic genre here is the detective novel, with Edgar Allan Poe's *The Murders in Rue Morgue* as a possible progenitor. Eisenstein points to Poe's ubiquitous horror situations of murders or people caught in sealed rooms. He refers to Marie Bonaparte's and Otto Rank's psychoanalytical explanations of memories from prenatal existence, and the universal trauma stemming from being liberated from the womb and released into the cold light of day. Following Rank, he associates this *Geburtstrauma* with the myth of the Minotaur and the labyrinth as an archetypal image of this primary complex. Eisenstein writes:

> In the more contemporary derivatives of that legend [*mif*],
> it is less the situation of the criminal extricating himself from an 'impossible' situation into the outside world, than in the way in which the detective draws the truth out into the open: that is, the situation effectively operates on two levels.
> In a direct sense and metaphorically – transposed from situation into principle. At this point we can see that the latter – the transposing of a situation into a principle – can freely exist parallel to the primary, 'original' situation [...]

> And so the detective story, as a variety of genre fiction – in any of its forms – is historically allied to the Minotaur legend [*mif*] and by extension to those primary complexes which that legend [*mif*] serves to express through imagery.³⁴

While this is a post-*October* discussion, Eisenstein's familiarity with Otto Rank's works goes back to the 1920s, and attention to issues of myth and allegory had been prominent in Russian culture since the neo-Romantics and Wagnerians appeared around the turn of the century. Could *October* then be seen as a myth similar to the Minotaur myth, as a narrative that is allegorically self-revelatory, containing its own decoder's key, its own Ariadne's thread? Eisenstein, however, insists that the Minotaur myth is not an allegory:

> Allegory *consists* [sic] of an abstracted representation intentionally and arbitrarily assuming the form [*odevaetsia*] of a particular image. The figurative form of the expression is then like a myth – the one accessible means of 'making it familiar' [*osvoenie*] and a comprehensible expression for consciousness. Only later does it [consciousness] attain the level at which it is able to put abstract notions into formulated concepts.³⁵

Does Eisenstein then in some sense subscribe to the Romantic and neo-Romantic distinction between allegory and symbol – which the Russian symbolists (Viacheslav Ivanov, for instance) certainly adhered to – that differentiated between an artificial or contrived and a natural and organic use of the symbolic language mode? If we have understood him correctly, there is an appropriate and an inappropriate use of the mythological type of language, a language of images. In ancient times myth served the legitimate purpose of conveying abstract notions and ideas, just as the use of mural paintings or stained glass images in the cathedrals helped to convey lessons from the Bible to illiterate audiences. But to the modern literate mind, the systematic use of a mythic language would be an anachronism, a false disguise ('assuming the form of' in the quotation is *odevaetsia*, 'to dress up', in the Russian original). The appropriation of this kind of language would be admissible and defensible under one condition: that the audience primarily consisted of illiterate individuals who had to be inoculated against the ideological and physical threat of an educationally superior enemy. Enter intellectual montage, the innovative mode used in the construction of Eisenstein's *October*, an imagery form of expression, the one accessible means of 'making it familiar' and a comprehensible expression for consciousness. Only later does it attain the level at which it is able to put abstract notions into formulated concepts.³⁶ *October*, then, can be read at this level as a lesson for the primitive communist mind on how to understand and effectively reach a political and military organization that could defeat a formally superior class enemy. The film as a whole and every other subplot and incident in it serve to teach this lesson, which had previously been delivered by Evreinov's decidedly allegorical mass spectacle of the *Storming of the Winter Palace* in 1920. With *October*, Eisenstein may have wanted to demonstrate by what formal cinematic means this task could be achieved, and thus perhaps prove the evolutionary superiority of film over theatre. Yet, as a monument to the Revolution, *October* seems to confirm the suspicion voiced by Gross: namely, that tearing down the monuments of despots and thus demystifying their hold on the public mind often leads to a re-mystification/mythification of the political powers to come. The process that began with the 'ten days that shook the world' in 1917, symbolically alluded to at the end of *October* in images of swirling clocks from major world's capital cities, ended with the dismantling of the statues depicting leading Bolshevik revolutionaries, including Lenin, Stalin and Dzerzhinsky, and the final collapse of the Soviet Union in 1991, thus bringing another cycle of Russian history to a close.

Notes

1 John Reed, *Ten Days That Shook the World* (New York: Boni & Liveright, 1919).
2 Sergei Eisenstein, *Selected Works, Volume 2: Towards a Theory of Montage*, ed. Richard Taylor (London: BFI Publishing, 1991), 109.
3 In 1935 Eisenstein wrote: 'In fact, in practice there are only a few individual parts of *October* which contain practical suggestions for the *possibilities* of an intellectual construction in cinema, which then manifested themselves as *a certain range of theoretical possibilities*' (Sergei Eisenstein, *Selected Works, Volume 3: Writings, 1935–1947*, ed. Richard Taylor (London: BFI Publishing, 1995), 19, emphases in the original).
4 Angus Fletcher, *Allegory, The Theory of a Symbolic Mode* (Ithaca, NY: Cornell University Press, 1964), 278.
5 Ibid., 322–3.
6 See for instance Viktor Shklovsky, 'Poetry and Prose in Cinema', trans. Richard Taylor, in *Russian Poetics in Translation, Volume 9: The Poetics of Cinema*, ed. B. M. Eikhenbaum (Moscow: Kinopechat, [1927] 1982), 57–9.
7 In his copy of Florence Becker Lennon's *Victoria through the Looking Glass: The Life of Lewis Carroll* (New York: Simon & Schuster, 1945) Eisenstein noted in the margin (dated '11 June 46'), 'Life as a chessboard v Alice. I used it without knowing

Alice as a Hoffmannesque little play in 1920. Repeated it in MMM and constructed "Ivan" on that pattern.'
8 Sergei Eizenshtein, 'Vnutrennyi monolog', in *Metod*, ed. Naum Kleiman (Moscow: Muzei kino/Eizenshtein-tsenter, 2002), vol. 1, 126.
9 See Sergei M. Eisenstein, *Selected Works, Volume 4: Beyond the Stars: The Memoirs of Sergei Eisenstein*, ed. Richard Taylor, trans. William Powell (London: BFI Publishing; Calcutta: Seagull Books,1995), *passim*.
10 Vladimir Tolstoy, Irina Bibikova and Catherine Cooke, eds., *Street Art of the Revolution: Festivals and Celebrations in Russia, 1918–33* (London: Thames & Hudson, 1990), 137–8.
11 See Lars Kleberg, *Theater as Action: Soviet Russian Avant-Garde Aesthetics* (London: Macmillan Press, [1980] 1993), 64–5.
12 Katerina Clark, *Petersburg: Crucible of Cultural Revolution* (Cambridge, MA: Harvard University Press, 1995), 244.
13 Hillel Schwartz, *The Culture of the Copy: Striking Likenesses, Unreasonable Facsimiles* (New York: Zone Books, 1996), 90, emphases in the original.
14 These shots of the statue may seem to foreshadow the shots of the crowning scene in Eisenstein's *Ivan the Terrible*, this time, however, depicting a tsar very much alive and active.
15 This statue was situated not in Petrograd but outside the Cathedral of Christ the Saviour in Moscow, thus giving the impression of revolutionary action in that city preceding the events leading up to the overthrow of the Kerensky government in Petrograd. The opening sequence could thus be seen in part as a reply to scenes in Eisenstein's previous films. Consider the working-class defeats and setbacks in *The Strike* and *Potemkin*. In both films crowds are massacred; in *Potemkin* the Odessa inhabitants sympathetic to the mutinying sailors are fired at and forced down the now-famous steps by soldiers who in one shot are clearly seen against the background of a statue at the top of the steps (the statue is of a French royalist, Richelieu, who served in the Russian Army). In *October* the crowds triumphantly surging up the stairs to depose the 'idol' Aleksander III could be seen as a victorious reversal of the fate of the people on the steps in Odessa. See Clark, *Petersburg*, 263.
16 Kenneth Gross, *The Dream of the Moving Statue* (Ithaca, NY: Cornell University Press, 1992), xiii.
17 Ibid., 50.
18 Vladimir Nilsen, who worked as an assistant cameraman during the filming of *October*, devoted an entire chapter of his book *The Cinema as a Graphic Art* (New York: Hill and Wang, [1936] 1959) (with an appreciation by Eisenstein) to a film adaptation of the animated statue sequence in Pushkin's 'The Bronze Horseman'.

19 Marie-Claude Ropars-Wuilleumier has pointed to the 'reactionary' function of statues in the film. See also Yuri Tsivian, 'Eisenstein and Russian Symbolist Culture', *Eisenstein Rediscovered*, ed. Ian Christie and Richard Taylor (London: Routledge, 1993), 81.
20 See Dmitrii Popov, 'Fotoikongrafiia S. M. Eizenshteina kak material issledovaniia tvorcheskoi individual'nosti rezhissera' (unpublished thesis, Moscow, 1985), 49–58, translated by the author.
21 Eisenstein, *Selected Works*, vol. 3, 30.
22 Ibid.
23 Ibid., 31.
24 According to Katerina Clark, there was a change from temporal to spatial preferences and a consequent change in the way space is perceived and depicted at the end of the 1920s. New cultural and artistic metaphors of a distinctly horizontal character appeared that found expression in the mass spectacles as well as in architectural planning (see Clark, *Petersburg*, 249).
25 Cf. Yuri Tsivian, 'Eisenstein and Russian Symbolist Culture', in *Eisenstein Rediscovered*, 85.
26 Cf. Christopher Read, *From Tsar to the Soviets: The Russian People and Their Revolution, 1917–21* (London: University College London Press, 1996), 174.
27 Eisenstein, *Selected Works*, vol. 1, 157–8, italics in the original.
28 Ibid., 159.
29 Cf. note 4.
30 See Fletcher, *Allegory*, 157–61, 189.
31 Geoffrey Galt Harpham, *On the Grotesque: Strategies of Contradiction in Art and Literature* (Princeton, NJ: Princeton University Press, 1982), 47.
32 See Fletcher, *Allegory*, 261–268.
33 Eisenstein, *Selected Works*, vol. 3, 26.
34 Eisenstein, *Selected Works*, vol. 4, 128–9.
35 Ibid., 129.
36 Ibid. (Cf. Sergei M. Eizenshtein, 'Wie sag' ich's meinem Kinde?!', in *Memuary, Tom pervyi* (Moscow: Redaktsiya gazety 'Trud', Muzei kino, 1997), 99.) ('Edinstvenno dostupnoe sredstvo "osvaeniia" i vyrazheniia dlia soznaniia, kotoroe eshche ne dostiglo stadii abstragirovaniia predstavlenii v formulirovannye poniatiia.')

11

Attraction and Subversion: 'Montage 1938'

Felix Lenz

In his text 'Montage 1938', Eisenstein transformed montage from its programmatic definition as a technique of cinema into a more general principle, which is not medium-specific. This principle can be applied to all other means of expression, in different degrees and at any time.¹ The examples from film, literature, art, acting and personal memories that are given in 'Montage 1938' refer to both external worlds and subjective realms. Eisenstein's focus is on dislocation: if the functional orientation of everyday life destroys the richness of stimuli, then art needs to reactivate and redeploy redundant stimuli. Creativity implies imbuing worlds with life. Such vitality makes a revival of images possible. These are the ideas which define the didactic spirit underlying 'Montage 1938'. What happens, however, when the text not only proclaims such ideas but utilizes the montage principle in its own exposition? It becomes necessary to examine Eisenstein's metaphorical language, the intrinsic nature of the examples he gives, and the cognitive impact resulting from the juxtapositions of his theoretical imagery.

My focus will be first on the subversive forms of montage that make the smuggling of secret communications possible; and second on montage forms which utilize the developmental models of the philosopher Empedocles, where birth and decay, fusion and division, and creation and apocalypse occur as patterns of pictorial metamorphosis. Utilizing the results of this analysis, I then sketch more generally possible perspectives for future Eisensteinian and film studies.

Calls for a supplementary reading of 'Montage 1938'

Eisenstein integrated a number of appeals into 'Montage 1938', urging the differentiated rereading of the text as is proposed here. The most important instance is the definition given of montage itself:

> *Depiction A* and *Depiction B* must be so chosen from all the possible features inherent in the story that the *juxtaposition* of them – specifically the juxtaposition of *them*, not of any other elements – will evoke in the perceptions and emotions of the spectator the most exhaustive, total *image of the film's theme*.[2]

A comprehensive picture that reveals all aspects of a work can only be arrived at by not proceeding from the final synthesis. Rather, we need to first examine all the individual images and their reciprocal interrelationships. Eisenstein also notes that every stimulus creates a picture of the whole in its own way. Accordingly, his first example assumes particular importance, as it not only sketches the basic facts of montage but also the argumentative logic of 'Montage 1938'. Eisenstein already emphasizes here that the same pictorial imagery may well contain a variety of – possibly contradictory – messages:

> A woman in widow's weeds was sobbing upon a tombstone. 'Console yourself, madam', a [...] passer-by said to her. 'The mercy of heaven is infinite. Somewhere in the world there is another man beside your husband with whom you will be able to find happiness.' 'There was', she sobbed in reply. 'Such a man did live, but alas ... this is his grave.' The whole effect of this little story rests on the fact that a grave and a woman in mourning beside it will always, according to conventional deduction, lead to the conclusion that this is a widow mourning her husband whereas in fact the object of her grief was her lover![3]

The mistaken passer-by is an avatar of the reader of the article, who similarly attempts in this moment to understand the relationship between the images. This passer-by's reading is as predictable as it is false. Eisenstein demonstrates forcefully here how the sensory effect of images is inevitably like an open equation. Thus, he appeals for critical vigilance: all the examples provided in 'Montage 1938' could mean something different from what at first they seem to suggest.

These appeals are also reiterated in the final examples of 'Montage 1938', where Eisenstein juxtaposes excerpts from a printed version of a comedy by Griboyedov with the text in the original manuscript. The expressive use of punctuation in the original reveals a kind of montage character which has been subject to censorship and now requires reconstruction.[4] Eisenstein focuses attention on what seem to be only minor incidental features to salvage the original spirit of a work. Here he demonstrates in an almost trivial example the detail-oriented method to be used for a second reading of 'Montage 1938'. His most interesting appeal, however, takes the form of a reconceptualization of the role of the recipient:

In fact, every spectator in his own way – from his past experience, from the depths of his imagination [...] creates an image according to those precisely chosen depictions suggested to him by the author [...] All these conceptions are, as images, individual and different, yet at the same time they are thematically identical. And each [...] spectator's image [...] is simultaneously the author's image and – equally – his own image, which is alive and 'intimate'. The image conceived by the author has become flesh of the flesh of the spectator's image, which was created by me, the spectator.[5]

The spectator becomes a creative partner who actively participates in the communion of the work of art, artist and beholder. A work of art's coming into being is predicated on this three-way encounter, in which all three jointly and actively generate images and participate fully in the Eros of this procreative encounter.[6] Eisenstein appeals to his spectators' reservoir of experiences: they should experience in the jointly produced image the epiphany of a mutually shared reality. One can draw a parallel with the Gospel of St John: the 'word was made flesh' (Jn 1.14). In 'Montage 1938' it is the image that is made flesh, and in so doing it takes on a curative character as communion, liveliness and intimacy are collapsing under totalitarian pressures.

'Montage 1938' is pervaded throughout with the attributes of vitality, of vivacious unfolding and of life-giving strength, which are the root qualities of creativity:

What is remarkable about this method? Above all, its dynamism: the very fact that the desired image is not something *ready-made* but *has to arise or be born*.[7]

This same dynamic principle underlies all the vital images.[8]

A vital performance by an actor is based on the fact that he [...] causes [...] emotions *to arise, to develop, to turn into others – in a word to live in front of the spectator*.[9]

For they are all equally based on the vitalizing characteristics and innate features common to every human being, just as they are common to every human and vital art form.[10]

This 'mechanism' of image formation interests us because the way it functions in *real life* naturally serves as a prototype of the method used in art to create artistic images.[11]

The image of that street came to life in my mind.[12]

Herein lies the peculiar quality of every genuinely vital work of art, which distinguishes it from a lifeless piece of work in which the spectator is presented with a depiction of the *results* ... instead of being drawn into a permanently occurring process.[13]

But in the form that they have been cast by the artists who created them, they are images brought to life by *montage-structuring*.[14]

To arrange images according to the principle of montage and to bestow life appear to be one and the same. Montage is thus posited as a tool of life and the outcome is always the birth of images.[15]

'Montage 1938' and contemporary life in the USSR

At a didactic level, all of Eisenstein's examples in 'Montage 1938' describe the formation of images as a vital living process, reflected in the Russian word 'obraz', which for Eisenstein always refers to the unrepresentable (meaning), to the missing third which needs to be produced from the juxtaposition of representations. However, their subject matter suggests the opposite, with almost all the examples concerning decline and destruction: a 'dance of death'.

In the case of the widow, it is love that has died. All that remains for her is a state of 'death in life' beside the grave. The temporal calamity is desolate finiteness. And this allows Eisenstein to describe a classical clock – surreally precise – as a geometrical play of moveable angles. Astronomical time appears to be the opposite of a fulfilled life.[16] He then gives an example from *Anna Karenina*, where Vronsky, in a state of shock over the news of Anna's pregnancy, is unable to read the time showing on a clock – to understand it as a symbol of time. This lack of understanding heralds a whole series of fatal events: an announcement of life as an embassy of death coupled with a loss of the ability to understand images – all in radical antithesis to the unfolding of images as a living process.[17]

Eisenstein slightly refigures this bleak outlook on time with a montage plan which unfolds the typical atmosphere of five o'clock in the afternoon. He summons up mental pictures of all kinds of events which regularly occur at that hour.[18] But even here the emphasis is placed on termination, the loss of light, the end of the day and the exhaustion of work. Had he wished to illustrate only the didactic idea of montage, Eisenstein might have chosen – as he would in 'Dickens, Griffith and Ourselves' (1942) – a morning hour to picture more harmoniously the idea of the unfolding birth of an image.[19] Instead, he remains in a universe of gloom, which connects atmospherically with *Anna Karenina* and its catastrophes.

To clarify the parallels between personal and artistic imagery processes, Eisenstein describes the attempt which he made during his stay in New York to distinguish between streets by memorizing images. At first, this appears to be emotionally neutral, but the aim of grasping New York through marking the peculiarities of sights seen implies at a deeper level a specific intention: the intention of a man who has come to stay.[20] Eisenstein, however, did not stay. Thus here – as in *Anna Karenina* – we have a case of symbolic promise without the gain of a new life.

Eisenstein next quotes a scene from Maupassant's *Bel Ami*. At midnight, a pair of lovers plan to elope and begin a new life together, but the woman fails to appear. Instead of a fusion, a parting occurs. The sacredness of the hour, which was central to their initiative, collides painfully with the church bells' chiming at 'astronomical' midnight.[21] Associatively, this seemingly different subject matter might again reflect the frustrated narrative of Eisenstein's own emigrant aspirations.

The next example involves another symbolically significant theme. Eisenstein describes how, in his film *October*, he heralded the birth of the Soviet Union through a montage of ecstatically rotating clocks, so as to celebrate the arrival of a new utopian era of conflicts resolved and harmonious well-being.[22] Yet, in doing this, he brought a number of ambiguous overtones into play. The *Bel Ami* example just referred to points out the ambiguity of astronomical time. If taken seriously, the dance of the clocks in *October* could equally be read as implying a state of desperation. Ostensibly, the birth of the USSR appears – after the preceding scenes of death and decay – to represent a triumphal achievement, in which finally and indisputably the film's subject matter and the idea of the birth of imagery are united. But, it must be remembered, all preceding births have been stillbirths; accordingly, a shadow of doubt is inevitably cast over the birth of the new state. Both interpretations are not only possible but can be deliberately activated to promote two different general models: one of subversion and one of birth. If we understand *October* as a counterpoint to the previous series of examples, this opens the way to understanding that montages intentionally mobilize both processes of decay and of birth according to choice.[23] Eisenstein has therefore established here two equal models of expressive development with seemingly contradictory aims. If we understand *October* as a prolongation of the series of gloomy examples then it can be inferred that Eisenstein has used montage in this instance in a subversive way: the birth of the Bolshevik state is contextualized as the onset of fatal catastrophes.[24] He is thus able to establish here a new kind of montage which allows him to secretly communicate a warning about a life-threatening development and also to challenge – at least in gesture – an ideological taboo.[25] Here *subversion* may assert itself in place of the *attraction* of processes of birth and decay, producing a transformed relationship with the spectator; that of the shared intimacy of conspirators possessing a dangerous secret. Eisenstein's statement quoted above, that 'the image conceived by the author has become flesh of the flesh of the spectator's image', may be understood here not as lyrical musing but as a case where metaphors of communion acquire their full force and become performative. Accordingly, it could be argued that 'Montage 1938' is concerned with the promotion and establishment of a non-hierarchical community of readers all caught up in the same historical predicament.

Support for such an interpretation is ample. In 'Montage and Architecture' (written in 1937), Eisenstein showed how Bernini secretly accused Pope Urban VIII of sexual abuse in a series of reliefs at the centre of St Peter's Basilica in Rome.[26] In 'Laocoön' (also written in 1937), Eisenstein explained the subversive rhetoric underlying the anti-tsarist posters of Dobuzhinsky.[27] And in *Ivan the Terrible* – as has been shown by Joan Neuberger[28] – we find him working with similar means.

The smouldering threat of danger provoked by the *October* example is subsequently confirmed by Eisenstein citing the archetypal catastrophe: he quotes Leonardo da Vinci's working notes for a representation of the Deluge, the great biblical flood, as a prototype 'montage script'.[29] If the clocks sequence in *October* is to be understood as a negative sign, then the great flood would be an avatar for the political forces of destruction, providing a virtual realm for the representation of pain and scenes of mass death. By contrast, if *October* is to be understood as the birth of man's self-determination, then Leonardo's great flood can be seen as an illustration of victory of the forces of death and decay in nature. However viewed, the image of death dominates these examples. The biblical flood implies the reversal of a prior universal process of birth, now replaced by a total annihilation of all forms of life. This brings the inner contradiction of 'Montage 1938', the contrast between multifarious images of life and scenarios of destruction, even more sharply into focus. It demonstrates how Eisenstein, by drawing on Leonardo, manages to mobilize the highest unresolved and irresolvable forms of tension.

In Leonardo's 'scenario', countless humans perish in a natural disaster. By contrast, the next illustration deals with the fate of a single person, a man who, under the pressure of a court case, is about to commit suicide. In terms of the imagery involved, a mass scenario is exchanged for that of a single individual, and the hostile nature of a society. Eisenstein's theoretical articulation – as in some of his previous examples – follows closely his aesthetic paradigm of ecstasy, which is defined as a leap into the opposite.[30]

Eisenstein proceeds now to explain how he himself would convincingly stage a suicide attempt.[31] His approach does not focus on the guilt of a person who has misappropriated public money; instead, he emphasizes the personal shame which is involved, and the pain of embarrassing isolation and loss of friendships. This gives rise to a fatal loss of trust, which poisons a whole life's world. After the diversion of the legendary great flood, Eisenstein evokes directly the consequences of the October Revolution, as these are evident in the pressures of 1938.

In addition to his dominant pattern of a leap to the opposite, Eisenstein also creates a second model of ecstasy, in which a cell grows into its final shape.[32] The example of the court case with the suicide is preceded by the October Revolution and followed by a reference to an execution. The imagery of this is taken from Pushkin's *Poltava*:

> In this scene, the theme of 'the end of Kochubei' is expressed with particular intensity through the image of 'the end of Kochubei's execution'. The image of the end of the execution itself arises and grows out of a juxtaposition of the 'documentary' depiction of three details which conclude the execution:

> 'Too late', a witness said to them
> And pointed to the field. For there
> The men were taking down the fateful scaffold,
> A priest in somber vestments was at prayer,
> Into a cart two burly Cossacks
> Were lifting up the oaken box.[33]

Eisenstein balances this deathly climax with another scene from *Poltava*, in which a woman prisoner is able to begin a new life after escaping under the cover of darkness.[34] As before, he makes use of the principle of ecstatic dramaturgy in the 'cut' between two examples so as to turn a specific stimulant into its opposite: the resurrection of a woman issues out of the execution of a man. Already, the outbreak of the October Revolution veered into a deathly flood, then this genocidal event is transformed into the death of an individual. The flood simultaneously functions as a countermovement to the social-critical line produced by the October Revolution that precedes it and the suicide which follows.[35] Eisenstein not only strings these fatal scenarios together in 'Montage 1938' but also uses the methods of ecstatic dramaturgy. Since these methods do not relate to the theoretical questions underlying 'Montage 1938', they are not explicitly addressed here. Instead they become in an unprecedented way a technique for Eisenstein's theoretical articulation. In 'Organic Unity and Pathos' it is the other way around. Here the theoretical theme is the question of ecstasy, while the form of articulation is rooted in the definition of montage in 'Montage 1938'. This correlation between manifest and latent articulated pattern in Eisenstein's approach will be addressed in the conclusion as a direction for further research.

Fittingly, another turnabout follows the execution and flight scenes. Eisenstein's strategy here is arguably motivated by the reading habits of censors, as, after the court case, the execution and the flight scenes, he uses only uncontentious examples in the closing sections of his text. The main example is a fourteen-line appearance of Peter the Great, taken from Pushkin's *Poltava*, which is analysed over the course of several pages as a didactic climax.[36] If we accept the programme of 'Montage 1938' as equally comprised of two elements, 'Montage' and '1938' as an epoch, then the appearance of Peter the Great must be seen as the centre of the first didactic level of text, and the suicide as the centre of the second. Eisenstein's didactic and subversive *élan* accordingly shapes essentially different examples as climaxes. And, further, he effectively conceals his subversive centre behind the didactic crescendo at the end of the essay.

In *Poltava* Pushkin allowed Peter to step out of a tent into the open after uttering a loud unarticulated cry.[37] The form-shaping impulse here is obviously the figuration of a birth.[38] As in the case of the *October* example, the conception of the birth of images and a specific subject matter are again directly and expressively united. This technique of doubling the expression at decisive points is taken from Japanese Kabuki theatre, which Eisenstein was familiar with, and described as early as 1928, based on scenes of hara-kiri.[39] But why, one must ask, does he mark just these two moments in 'Montage 1938' with this technique of doubled-layered consonance? From a political perspective Peter the Great represented a starting point of dynastic or even despotic power, while the revolution marked the end of tsarism. But Eisenstein's sequence of examples reverses this chronological order. In a way the promises of the revolution are reversed by a return of a monarch. From this point of view the only two emphatically harmonizing moments in 'Montage 1938' – the October Revolution and the emergence of a despotic monarch, Peter – together mirror the historical path that led to Stalinism.[40]

In 'Montage 1938', Eisenstein was able to hold up a critical mirror to his contemporary world, setting up a montage of subversions by means of paradigmatic transformation. His central illustration of this kind of montage is not to be found in any single quotation or example, but in 'Montage 1938' itself, taken as a whole.

Image metamorphosis: Eisenstein and Empedocles

The subversive stratum is supplemented by two patterns, which enhance and complement each other. These are images either of birth, development and the differentiation of life, or of processes of decay, where stable elements dissolve into fragments. Birth and death thus determine opposite goals for image construction and effect a restructuring of montage through their rhythmic patterns. 'Montage 1938' utilizes examples in ecstatic dramaturgy, a montage of subversions and an underlying polar developmental model. The latter can also be understood in terms of gesture. In 'Vertical Montage' (written in 1940) Eisenstein proposed that every vital scheme of composition is based on a gesture as the starting point for further development.[41] Here we find the same quality: birth implies patterns of growing and rising, decay patterns of disintegration and falling. This consideration allows the polar developmental model of 'Montage 1938' to be related to Eisenstein's aesthetics of revolution, which is also founded on pattern structures. In fact, revolution understood in these terms turns out to be a highly dramatic and complementary combination of birth and decay. Revolution is an upheaval in which an old world dies and a new one is born. Then, other than in the case of the revolutionary model, where decay is only relegated a negative evaluation that is subsequently overcome in glory, birth and decay now appear as equals. An historical back-coupling of montage to the dynamics of the revolution as occurs in *The Battleship Potemkin* is transformed in 'Montage 1938' into a cosmic form of back-coupling, in which birth and decay are aesthetically perpetuated as laws of nature.[42]

Leonardo's biblical flood alludes to that aspect of fall and decay which turn a differentiated world into an undifferentiated one, engulfed by water. The opposite is provided in 'The Little Humpbacked Horse', written in 1947. Eisenstein explicitly states here that the separation of heaven and earth, and land and water, in Genesis prefigure the processes of montage:

> How could it be that I had never detected in the old biblical legends [...] the notion of that separation which forms the basis for the striving of the 'isolated' for a fusion at a higher level, there, where previously amorphous formless [...] non-differentiation had reigned in place of the promised, creatively integrated, unity? I blush at the thought that, since the time of my very first steps, I [...] only ever [...] began with one and the same – with separation.[43]

The genesis of the world and the great flood function for Eisenstein as ultimate models for montage, anchoring the evolving patterns of image metamorphosis in cosmic forms of imagination. Eisenstein's reasoning here comes close to the work of the Greek pre-Socratic philosopher Empedocles, who, in his ancient text, similarly envisaged simultaneous opposite directions of development. Although Eisenstein himself never made this connection, the structural affinity of both authors will help to clarify some important points.[44] Empedocles' *Physika* (*On Nature*) characterizes the cosmos as a cyclical process. Its elements of fire, water, earth and air are understood as gods, while also being designated in a biological metaphor as roots.[45] Two divine principles propel the elements into endless states of becoming. The principle of conflict forces elements which have melted together to part again, and resume their original states as independent elements. At this point the principle of love intervenes.[46] The elements then strive towards each other and combine until a new state is reached. In *sphairos*, all of the elements are united in a perfect undifferentiated totality.[47] Oliver Primavesi, editor of the Empedocles papyrus discovered by Alain Martin in 1990, characterizes this as follows:

> According to Empedocles the universe is made up of constant elements. The history of the universe however is the product of the regular and repeated backward and forward movement between two extreme states of the elements. These two extreme states operate in opposition to each other but are in their own way always equally perfect. The consummated 'many' alternate with the consummated 'singles'. In the case of the 'many' we are dealing in their state of consummation with a quadruplication. The 'many' have then attained consummation when the four elements of fire, water, earth and air as four chemically pure masses take possession of the strictly confined domains of power to which each is entitled ... Pure and unmixed, the four masses are beyond the obligations of growth and decay for the period of this state of aggregation. The opposite state of consummation, that of unity and singularity, is reached then when these elements are harmonically bound together in their totality to become a single living organism of spherical form, the *sphairos*.[48]

For Empedocles, complete disintegration and the perfect synthesis correspond to two complementary and equally important models of development, which together – and only together – determine the ongoing existence of the world.

As early as 1929 we find Eisenstein arguing along similar lines. Firstly, his well-known idea of a spherical book corresponds to Empedocles' idea of the *sphairos*: the spherical book was intended to mediate between the opposing ideas underlying montage.[49] Secondly, in 'The Fourth Dimension in Cinema' (1929), Eisenstein offered two incompatible definitions of 'overtonal' montage.

The first emphasizes the full synthetic sonority of stimuli and is comparable with Empedocles' idea of the *sphairos*:

> This montage is not constructed on the *individual dominant* but takes the sum of *stimuli* of all the stimulants as the dominant [...] In this way the physiological sum total of the resonance of the shot as a whole, as a complex unity of all its component stimulants, is taken to be the general sign of the shot. This is the particular 'feeling' of the shot that the shot as a whole produces [...] The basic sign of the shot can be taken to be the final sum total of its effect on the cortex of the brain as a whole, irrespective of the ways in which the accumulating stimulants have come together.[50]

While Empedocles is discussing the cosmos, Eisenstein is addressing the brain, so Empedocles' ideas about physics are comparable to Eisenstein's ideas relating to perception.

Eisenstein's second definition of 'overtonal' montage emphasizes the articulation of separate stimuli and can be seen to parallel Empedocles' state of complete division:

> [The] most moving type of structure [...] will be that, where the conflict of pieces of montage are not only presented as the conflict of physiological complexes [...] but where beyond that it is possible to recognize how each single, individually formed stimulus is juxtaposed with the comparable stimuli of neighbouring pieces of montage in an independent state of conflict. In this way we arrive at a [...] form of polyphony in which [...] the independent parts of the various instruments combine organically to build their own lines in the [...] full body of orchestral sound.[51]

Eisenstein's cosmological examples and his theoretical concepts echo the Empedoclean pattern. But it is not only in Eisenstein's theory that we find the separation or melding together of stimuli and their ability to figure birth or decay. This is also a feature that characterizes all possible dimensions in his creative work: single images and cuts, sequences and whole films. Joan Neuberger, for example, finds in *Ivan the Terrible* 'cycles of birth, death and resurrection'.[52] Such patterns have their roots in both processes of perception and cosmic processes. What was conceived by Empedocles as a cosmological model is transformed by Eisenstein into a means of aesthetic articulation. Empedocles was concerned with existence, transformation and terrestrial animation; Eisenstein is concerned with the same, but in the context of the image. The result is a perfect example of Eisenstein's idea that the arts inherit structures which were once scientific concepts.[53]

Common to both Empedocles and Eisenstein is the evocation of vitality. Empedocles employed biological metaphors: his most important substantive designation of the elements is ῥιζώματα (*rizómata*: roots).[54] He frequently uses biological verbs such as γίγνεσθαι (*gignesthai*: to be born, to come to be),[55] φύεσθαι (*phyesthai*: to grow, to spring up),[56] διαφύεσθαι (*diaphyesthai*: to grow apart),[57] συμφύεσθαι (*symphyesthai*: to grow together),[58] τίκτειν (*tíktein*: to beget),[59] τεκνοῦν (*teknoun*: to engender)[60] and αὐξάνειν/αὔξειν (*auxanein/auxein*: to grow, to increase).[61] Empedocles understood the primal elements as forces creating vegetable or botanical life, and also as physical and mineral processes of separation and amalgamation.[62] In 'Organic Unity and Pathos' (1939), Eisenstein combined vegetable and metallurgic patterns to characterize ecstatic processes. His vegetable model leads to the idea of temporal proportions along the lines of the proportions of the Golden Section.[63] The metallurgic model, on the other hand – as with Empedocles – leads to an image of cosmic ecstasy:

> The *moment* of culmination is understood here in the sense of those points in a process through which water passes at the *moment* of becoming steam, ice – water, cast iron – steel [...] And if water, steam, ice and steel could psychologically register their own feelings at the critical *moments* – moments of achieving the leap, they would say they are speaking with *pathos*, that they are in ecstasy. [...] Born out of the pathos of the theme, the compositional structure repeats that single basic principle by which organic, social and all other processes of the formation of the universe are achieved.[64]

Conclusion

Considering its theoretical significance and complex relations with other parts of Eisenstein's theoretical endeavour, 'Montage 1938' has considerable relevance to twenty-first-century concerns. It deals with the transformation of anthropological qualities of life and perception into aesthetic design, with the transformation of physical states into emotionally charged ideas, and with the transformation of events into procedural patterns involving Eisenstein's ecstatic dramaturgy: revolutionary upheaval, birth and growth, death and decay.[65]

A central question must be how Eisenstein combines not only different media but also very different dimensions and layers of pictorial articulation. To explore this, we must consider existing explanations of the key Einsteinian notions of montage and ecstasy. In 'Montage 1938', montage is transformed from a specific aesthetic device into a generally more flexible principle, while

Eisenstein's ecstatic dramaturgy becomes crucial to his articulation of theory. At the same time, he makes increasing use of the term 'process', which provides a 'third' dimension against which both montage and ecstatic articulation can be measured. Eisenstein's language associated with the term 'process', mostly associated with living phenomena, represents the essential aura in which images are conceived – to arise, to be born, to drown, to develop, to turn into others, to be drawn into a permanently occurring process, to become 'flesh of the flesh' of the image. The term 'process' is more general than 'montage' and does not allude to specific means – such as cuts or long takes – by which images are to be created. It is equally applicable to montage cinema, continuity editing and the modern idea of 'slow cinema'. The claim of montage to be a tool of unlimited possibilities has led to difficulty in dealing with highly heterogeneous forms, leaving only the possibility of case-by-case analysis. 'Process', on the other hand, encompasses ordered events within clearly defined environments, thus allowing differentiation: the creation of the world, the end of the world, revolution, being torn apart, being born, stepping out, fleeing, nightfall, daybreak, awakening, smuggling messages, partings, dying. It is the 'processual' perspective in 'Montage 1938' that makes its complexity possible. And this complexity is the result of the overlapping of montage as an abstract means and the world of processes as a concrete and structured pictorial realm. Eisenstein does not thematize this, but it seems to me that it is just this collision between montage and processual shape which provides the real appeal of 'Montage 1938'. Eisenstein did not specifically write a theory of processes.[66] Rather, he used the diversity of processual shapes of his examples, in preference to thematizing the interdependence of montage and patterns of process. It would be a rewarding task to examine closely the relation between montage and patterns of process. The present chapter demonstrates that it is possible, for example, to explain the logic of 'overtonal' montage from such a perspective. Empedocles' valorization of regular oppositional patterns of process makes it possible to address contradictions inherent in the 'overtonal' montage: the different conceptions of 'overtonal' montage effectively merge together with patterns of process to then become a whole.

To uncover more of Eisenstein's processual patterns, it would be necessary not only to focus on his main concepts but also on related secondary concepts. I have highlighted the term 'process' in 'Montage 1938' and its several applications, considering their relations to montage and ecstasy. However, a broader rereading from this point of view could offer systematic insights into how many structures and processual patterns are overlaid in films and texts and what can be achieved through their specific mixtures. This would allow Eisenstein's heterogeneous examples to be considered not only as evidence of recurrent concepts such as montage and ecstasy but also as a way of systematically differentiating between the various qualitative features of these concepts. Subsequently every type of example – bodily, choreographic, dialectical, spiritual, cosmic, metallurgical, botanical, social, historical, religious, ritual, erotic, animal, form-bound, colourful or musical – could be related to a specific sediment of artistic articulation. If Eisenstein's examples are grouped together into classes or types of process, as suggested here, the result would be a new analytical instrument which – analogous to the medieval 'four senses' of scriptural interpretation[67] – would be able to unveil multiply articulated 'senses' of image interpretation.

A second programmatic perspective follows. The shift of significance from questions of montage to questions of process implies a continuation of Eisenstein's project of combining anthropological patterns of experience and artistic means of articulation.[68] In this area, we could consider such varied concepts as Van Gennep's and Turner's rites of passage, Campbell's hero's journey, Eliade's concepts of religious pattern, Jung's ideas about individuation, Edinger's taxonomy of alchemical patterns or the more recent efforts of Bischof to relate systematically mythological structures to patterns of child development.[69] Such a point of view allows us to connect the expertise of new researchers with those whom Eisenstein actually knew and valued, in the areas as diverse as narratology, anthropology and psychology. Such a programme, with a focus on anthropologically based procedural patterns, would make Eisenstein also a decisive contributor to contemporary research questions and give his idea 'of cinema as a copy of man's psychological apparatus'[70] new recognition and relevance.

Acknowledgment

I am deeply grateful for the collaboration of Dr Lewis Wickes in developing this chapter in English.

Notes

1 See Antonio Somaini, 'Cinema as "Dynamic Mummification", History as Montage: Eisenstein's Media Archaeology', in Sergei M. Eisenstein, *Notes for a General History of Cinema*, ed. Naum Kleiman and Antonio Somaini (Amsterdam: Amsterdam

University Press, 2016), 25–6: 'Eisenstein never theorized cinema's medium specificity, but rather always considered cinema in an intermedial perspective, as a medium remediating previous media and relocating previous forms of spectatorial experience.'
2. Sergei Eisenstein, 'Montage 1938', in *Selected Works, Volume 2: Towards a Theory of Montage*, ed. Michael Glenny and Richard Taylor (London: BFI Publishing, 1991), 299, italics in the original.
3. Ibid., 297.
4. See ibid., 322.
5. Ibid., 309–10.
6. See Somaini, 'Cinema as "Dynamic Mummification"', 70: 'What Eisenstein imagines, in other words, is an ecstatic "flow" that circulates between the artist, the work, and the spectator: a flow which becomes possible if all three of them "participate" in the stream of dialectic, ecstatic energy which runs across all natural phenomena.'
7. Eisenstein, 'Montage 1938', 309, italics in the original.
8. Ibid., 302.
9. Ibid., italics in the original.
10. Ibid., 326.
11. Ibid., 300, italics in the original.
12. Ibid., 301.
13. Ibid., 302, italics in the original.
14. Ibid., 310–11, italics in the original.
15. See Felix Lenz, 'Organizing Pictures – *The Master's House* (1997) and *Cinema: A Public Affair* (2015): Movies by and about Naum Kleiman', in *The Flying Carpet. Studies on Eisenstein and Russian Cinema in Honor of Naum Kleiman*, ed. Antonio Somaini and Joan Neuberger (Zurich: Éditions Mimésis, 2017), 203–4.
16. Eisenstein, 'Montage 1938', 299.
17. Ibid., 300: 'From the example with Vronsky we saw how under the influence of a powerful affect, that connection can be broken, and how depiction and image then become detached from each other.'
18. Ibid.
19. I am referring here to passages from Charles Dickens's *Oliver Twist*. See Sergei M. Eisenstein, 'Dickens, Griffith and Ourselves', in *Selected Works, Volume 3: Writings, 1934-1947*, ed. Richard Taylor (London: BFI Publishing, 1996), 208: 'How often have we encountered this construction in Griffith's work! […] With the same play of light, from the burning street-lamps to those that are extinguished; from night to dawn and from dawn to the brightness of full daylight.'
20. Eisenstein, 'Montage 1938', 300–1.
21. Ibid., 303–4.
22. Ibid., 304.

23 We are concerned here, on account of such a contrasting turn of fate, with an application of Eisenstein's ecstatic dramaturgy. See Sergei M. Eisenstein, 'Organic Unity and Pathos', in *Nonindifferent Nature* (Cambridge: Cambridge University Press, 1987), 27: '"To be beside oneself" is not "to go into nothing". To be beside oneself is unavoidably also a transition to something else, to something different in quality, to something opposite to what preceded it.'

24 Regarding the serialization of comparable attributes in associated images, see Sergei M. Eisenstein, 'The Fourth Dimension in Cinema', in *The Eisenstein Reader*, ed. Richard Taylor (London: BFI Publishing, 1998), 111-12: 'In fact, even if we have a series of montage shots: (1) A grey haired old man, (2) a grey haired old woman, (3) a white horse, (4) a snow converted roof, it is far from clear whether this series works on "old age" or "whiteness". This series might continue for a very long time before we finally come upon the signpost shot that immediately "christens" the whole series with a particular "sign." That is why it is better to place this kind of indicator as near as possible to the beginning.'

25 Herbert Eagle argues that the late Eisenstein provides tools subsequently used by dissident east European filmmakers. See Herbert Eagle, 'Visual Patterning, Vertical Montage, and Ideological Protest: Eisenstein's Stylistic Legacy in East European Filmmakers', in *Eisenstein at 100 – A Reconsideration*, ed. Al LaValley and Barry P. Scherr (New Brunswick, NJ: Rutgers University Press, 2001), 169-90.

26 See Sergei Eisenstein, 'Montage and Architecture', in *Selected Works*, vol. 2, 68-80.

27 See ibid., 124-31.

28 See among others Joan Neuberger, 'The Politics of Bewilderment: Eisenstein's *Ivan the Terrible* in 1945', in *Eisenstein at 100: A Reconsideration*, 227-52.

29 See Eisenstein, 'Montage 1938', 305-8.

30 See Eisenstein, 'Organic Unity and Pathos', 27.

31 See Eisenstein, 'Montage 1938', 311-316. Anne Nesbet interprets this description as Eisenstein's own response to the experience of totalitarian pressures. Anne Nesbet, *Savage Junctures: Sergei Eisenstein and the Shape of Thinking* (London: I.B.Tauris, 2003), 182-3: 'The shadow side of pathos, in the Soviet Union of the 1930s, was terror. A taste of this terror comes in the essay "Montage 1938", when Eisenstein discusses [...] how an actor identifies with the character he plays.'

32 See Eisenstein, 'Organic Unity and Pathos', 13-15.

33 See Eisenstein, 'Montage 1938', 316-17.

34 Ibid.

35 See Sergei M. Eisenstein, 'On Recoil Movement', in *Meyerhold, Eisenstein and Biomechanics – Actor Training in Revolutionary Russia*, ed. Alma Law and Mel Gordon (Jefferson, NC: McFarland, 1996), 192-204.

36 Eisenstein, 'Montage 1938', 317-21.

37 Ibid., 318-20.

38 Comparable image figurations are common in *The Battleship Potemkin*. See Felix Lenz, *Sergej Eisenstein: Montagezeit. Rhythmus, Formdramaturgie Pathos* (Munich: Fink, 2008), 103–5, 118–20, 126, 148, 162–3.
39 See Sergei Eisenstein, 'The Unexpected', in *Film Form. Essays in Film Theory*, ed. Jay Leyda (New York: Harcourt, 1949), 23: 'Occasionally (and usually at the moment when the nerves seem about to burst from tension) the Japanese double their effects. With their mastery of the equivalents of visual and aural images, they suddenly give *both*, "squaring" them, and brilliantly calculating the blow of their sensual billiard-cue on the spectator's cerebral target. I know no better way to describe that combination, of the moving hand of Ichikawa Ennosuke as he commits hara-kiri – *with* the sobbing sound off-stage, *graphically* corresponding with the movement of the knife' (italics in the original).
40 Eisenstein shows the same method at work in Pushkin's writing. See Eisenstein, 'Montage 1938', 321: 'Depiction and verse coincide precisely in extent and sequence only, once […] This is not by chance. This concordance in the articulation of both depiction and verse marks the most significant "shot" within the montage composition.'
41 See Sergei Eisenstein, 'Vertical Montage', in *Selected Works*, vol. 2, 332–7, 371–6; Lenz, *Sergej Eisenstein: Montagezeit*, 23–46, 275–88; Francesco Pittassio, 'Serguei Eisenstein: l'acteur manquant', in *Eisenstein dans le texte* (= *Cinémas*, vol. 11, nos. 2–3), ed. François Albera (Montreal: Cinémas, 2001), 199–224.
42 See among others Lenz, *Sergej Eisenstein: Montagezeit*, 101–8, 117–25.
43 Sergei M. Eisenstein, 'Das Wjatkaer Pferdchen', in *Zur Farbe im Film* (Potsdam: Hochschule für Film und Fernsehen der DDR, 1975), 37–40. Translated from German by Lewis Wickes. (The poem 'The Little Horse of Vyatka', which was the basis of an animated film by I. Ivanov-Vano in 1947 that Eisenstein wrote about, is usually known in English as 'The Little Humpbacked Horse'.)
44 In general, relating Eisenstein to philosophical concepts is a promising undertaking, and more recent philosophical thinkers should also be included. For this endeavour Julia Vassilieva provides an inspiring panorama of ideas. In her 'Montage Eisenstein: Mind the Gap', in *Film as Philosophy*, ed. Bernd Herzogenrath (Minneapolis: University of Minnesota Press, 2017).
45 See Empedokles, *Physika*, in *Die Vorsokratiker*, ed. Jaap Mansfeld and Oliver Primavesi (Stuttgart: Reclam, 2011), 440–563, 446, 448 (Fr. 49 and 51). For advice on Empedocles and questions of classical philology, I am grateful to my father Dr Lutz Lenz.
46 Regarding the powers of love and conflict, see ibid., 462 (Fr. 66b, 240–55).
47 Ibid., 478 (Fr. 75 and 76).
48 Oliver Primavesi, 'Empedokles', in *Grundriss der Geschichte der Philosophie: Die Philosophie der Antike, Volume 1: Frühgriechische Philosophie*, ed. Hellmut Flashar, Dieter Bremer and Georg Rechenauer (Basel: Schwabe Verlag, 2013), 696. Translated from German by Lewis Wickes.

49 See Somaini, 'Cinema as "Dynamic Mummification"', 91: 'Eisenstein wrote, on August 5, 1929, a note in which he formulated the idea of organizing the various essays on the theory of montage that he had written during the 1920s in a book having the shape of a "rotating sphere".'
50 Eisenstein, 'The Fourth Dimension in Cinema', 113, italics in the original.
51 Sergej M. Eisenstein, 'Die vierte Dimension im Film' (1929), in *Jenseits der Einstellung: Schriften zur Filmtheorie*, ed. Felix Lenz and Helmut H. Diederichs (Frankfurt am Main: Suhrkamp, 2006), 126. Eisenstein crossed out the quoted passage in the manuscript, thus it is missing in many versions of the text. Translated from German by Lewis Wickes.
52 See Joan Neuberger, *Ivan the Terrible* (London: I.B.Tauris, 2003), 86–7.
53 Sergei Eisenstein, 'Speeches to the All-Union Creative Conference of Soviet Filmworkers' (1935), in *Selected Works*, vol. 3, 26: 'It is very curious that certain theories and viewpoints, the expression of scientific and theoretical knowledge in one historical period, lose their scientific value in the next; but they persist, possible and admissible not as science but as art and imagery.'
54 See Empedocles, *Physika*, 446 (Fr. 49b, 1).
55 Ibid., 462, 464, 466, 468 (Fr. 66b, 240, 266, 289, 322).
56 Ibid., 462, 472, 474, 540 (Fr. 66b, 240; 68b, 8; 69b, 14; 157a, 1).
57 Ibid., 462, 472 (Fr. 66b, 233, 236, 241, 248; 68b, 9).
58 Ibid., 472, 510 (Fr. 68b, 7; 110).
59 Ibid., 462 (Fr. 66b, 235).
60 Ibid., 484 (Fr. 87, 13).
61 Ibid., 462, 482, 524 (Fr. 66b, 232, 245; 84; 125, 4), emphases in the original.
62 Ibid., 462 (Fr. 66b, 235–40).
63 Goethe's work offers a useful midpoint between Empedocles and Eisenstein. Goethe's writing on the metamorphosis of plants offers a fully compatible model to Eisenstein's ecstatic dramaturgy. See Johann Wolfgang Goethe, 'Versuch die Metamorphose der Pflanzen zu erklären', in *Johann Wolfgang Goethe: Sämtliche Werke. Briefe Tagebücher und Gespräche* (Frankfurt am Main: Deutscher Klassiker Verlag, 1987), vol. 24, 109–51. See also Elena Vogman, *Sinnliches Denken: Eisensteins exzentrische Methode* (Zurich: Diaphanes, 2018), 119–36. See Eisenstein, 'Organic Unity and Pathos', 13–27; Lenz, *Sergej Eisenstein: Montagezeit*, 108–17.
64 Eisenstein, 'Organic Unity and Pathos', 35–6.
65 Eisenstein uses another constellation of the same processual elements in *Ivan the Terrible*. Here we have a heartbreaking simultaneity of vital, life-confirming and deathly tendencies. See Lenz, *Sergej Eisenstein: Montagezeit*, 322–3, 351–2.
66 Naturally there are attempts at this, for instance when Eisenstein sets himself in a pre-cinematic epoch and on account of this searches for basic concepts which are not dependent on cinema. See Eisenstein, 'Laocoön', 192: 'What can that cinematic *Urphanomen* be […] outside cinema? For an author who is not a

film-maker, what can its attraction be when he is working within his own, non-cinematic art form? The main attraction will, of course, be the essential content of that phenomenon: *movement*. And more precisely: not so much movement as such but the *image of movement*.'

67 An imitation of the four senses of interpretation is to be found in the layers of Eisenstein's conception of apparent, secret and pre-logical subject matter. See Anna Bohn, *Film und Macht: Zur Kunsttheorie Sergej M. Eisensteins 1930–1948* (Munich: diskurs film Verlag, 2003), 114–15; and Russian State Archive of Literature and Arts (RGALI) 1923-2-1148, lines 63–7.

68 See Somaini, 'Cinema as "Dynamic Mummification"', 51: 'Cinema is presented as a medium whose nature can be fully understood not so much by emphasizing its *medium specificity*, the properties that distinguish it from other media, but rather by revealing all its intermedial connections with a wide variety of other media, techniques, art forms, public spectacles, and religious rituals.' Also, ibid., 61: 'Since the beginning of the 1920s, since his very first texts on the nature of the "expressive movement" and on the "montage of attractions" in theatre and cinema, Eisenstein had always tried to find the *psychological* and the *anthropological foundations* of the aesthetic principles he was elaborating […] In books like *Method*, *Montage*, and *Nonindifferent Nature* Eisenstein had tried to untangle the web of conscious and unconscious associations which lies behind every creative intuition, and to find some solid, psychological foundations for […] aesthetic principles.'

69 See Norbert Bischof, *Das Kraftfeld der Mythen: Signale aus der Zeit, in der wir die Welt erschaffen haben* (Munich: Piper, 1998); Joseph Campbell, *The Hero with a Thousand Faces* (New York: Meridian Books, [1948] 1956); Keith Cunningham, *The Soul of Screenwriting* (New York: Continuum, 2008); Edward F. Edinger, *Anatomy of the Psyche: Alchemical Symbolism in Psychotherapy* (Chicago: Open Court, 1991); Mircea Eliade, *The Sacred and the Profane: The Nature of Religion* (New York: Harvest, [1959] 1961); Mircea Eliade, *Cosmos and History: The Myth of the Eternal Return* (Princeton, NJ: Princeton University Press, [1949] 1974); Leo Frobenius, *Das Zeitalter des Sonnengottes* (Berlin: Reimer, 1904); Arnold van Gennep, *The Rites of Passage* (London: Routledge, [1909] 1977); Carl Gustav Jung, *Symbole der Wandlung* (Olten: Walter-Verlag, [1912] 1971); Georges Kubler, *The Shape of Time* (New Haven, CT: Yale University Press, [1962] 2008); Margaret S. Mahler, Fred Pine and Anni Bergman, *The Psychological Birth of the Human Infant: Symbiosis and Individuation* (London: Karnac Books, [1975] 1985); Richard Slotkin, *Gunfighter Nation: The Myth of the Frontier in Twentieth-Century America* (New York: Atheneum, 1992); Richard Slotkin, *Regeneration through Violence: The Mythology of the American Frontier, 1600–1860* (Norman: University of Oklahoma Press, 2000); Victor Turner, *The Ritual Process: Structure and Anti-structure* (New York: Aldine de Gruyter, 1995).

70 Sergei Eisenstein, 'The Place of Cinema in the General System of the History of the Arts', in *Notes for a General History of Cinema*, 241.

The Two-Headed Ecstasy: The Philosophical Roots of Late Eisenstein

Massimo Olivero

Eisenstein's research and theorizing of ecstasy culminated in the planned book *Nondifferent Nature*, on which he worked in the 1940s but left unfinished. His concept of the ecstasy of representation aimed to elaborate on the possibility of formalizing the excess of pathos and widening the limits of representation to capture what is not figurable. For Eisenstein, the filmic forms used to achieve ecstasy must work alongside each other in the creation of a work of art that is both 'organic' and 'pathetic', where all the elements participate with maximum intensity in the production of the general theme.

The principle described by Eisenstein is an ecstasy produced by visual solutions, like superimpositions or extreme close-ups; by editing rhythm; by using depth of field and the optical distortion of perspective; and, in his later audiovisual cinema, through the combination of editing and sound. What he wanted to achieve was reaching the highest levels of consciousness after plumbing the primitive layers of pre-logical thought, with a method that mobilizes simultaneously and in dialectical tension both regress and progress. He aimed to transfigure matter, in a universe that he understood as inherently interconnected, into a new qualitatively higher stage, where every element is shaped by a process of mediation with all the parts involved. However, very often this shaping will not be perfectly mastered, since the invisible forces of pathos exceed the author's deliberate will; thus, the pathos of the image goes beyond the limits established by the idea, the rational meaning of the work.

It is therefore important to distinguish two polarities at work in Eisenstein's theory and practice of ecstasy, which can be traced to his favourite bipolar model embodied in the Greek myth of Dionysus. In this, the dismembered body of Dionysus, reconstituted into a new transfigured entity, permitted the coexistence of two opposing and irreconcilable instances, both vital and destructive, which might represent the two contradictory philosophical positions that seem to appear simultaneously in Eisenstein's art. On the one hand, there is Dionysus as a fragmented body capable of resurrecting, a metaphor for the negative that is determined positively. On the other hand, there is Dionysus who does not deny the negation and enjoys this laceration. On one side, therefore, the Dionysian resurrection resembles the Christian resurrection as the victorious result of the work of the negative, while on the other hand, it ostensibly manifests its radical opposition to the cross of Christ, and Dionysus thus incarnates 'something higher than all developed, resolved and suppressed contradiction – transvaluation'.[1] The first reading proposes a Hegelian Dionysus, which can be placed in a dialectical relationship with his other, Apollo, as an expression of rational and harmonic form. The second reading brings Dionysus closer to the mythical figure of Zarathustra, conceived as a nihilistic vision of reality and as such opposing all forms of dialectics.

The myth of Dionysus, or Bacchus in Roman tradition, is cited by Eisenstein as both a political and an artistic model. It represents the unity of a community that is divided and reconfigured into a new, qualitatively superior unity. As in the ecstatic form, 'the primitive and terrestrial Bacchus decomposed and was reborn, after having united its various parts, in a more precious, superior, "divine" form'.[2] Eisenstein's reading is very close, if not equivalent, to Hegel's dialectical conception of Dionysus as the metaphor of a community or a work of art which negates negation. Yet, at the same time, Eisenstein interprets the dithyrambs as 'a moment of profound, synthetic unity not only between expressive forms (singing and dancing, music and movement) but also between actors and spectators, scene and audience'.[3] Thus, he recovers the idea of the synthetic unity of the work of art as immediacy, an indistinct fusion of the elements that compose it, following Lévy-Bruhl's law of participation in primitive societies. Relating the law of participation to the principle of *pars pro toto*, Eisenstein explained:

> At that stage we were still without the unity of the whole and the part as we now understand it. At that stage of non-differentiated thinking the part is at one and the same time also the whole. There is no unity of part and whole, but instead obtains an objective identity in representation of whole and part. It is immaterial whether it be part or whole–it plays invariably the role of aggregate and whole.[4]

Thus, the regressive dimension of the discourse on ecstasy does not enter completely into the dialectical process, and requires an independent and parallel interpretation with respect to the reading which sees Dionysus as a body that constantly resurfaces from its destruction.

Ecstasy as a dialectical movement

For Eisenstein, to speak of the non-indifference of nature means to construct a dialectical aesthetics, where the work of art first goes through a negation, before returning to itself, with a second negation denying the previous one in a veritable alienation of alienation. Thus, the work becomes, to use Hegel's terminology, a 'second nature' – a dimension created by the action and the creative spirit of the artist, a non-indifferent nature: not poor like the non-human one, but one that is qualitatively superior to the previous condition. It does so by first producing figures of pathos that alter and distort its formal structures and representative elements, and then recovering a higher meaning from within itself that gives shape and unity to its alienated parts. This second nature involves the conquest of ecstasy, which can be compared to the self-consciousness of Hegel's spirit in its artistic form, expressing both the truth of nature and the road to self-awareness taken by the subject as it becomes *in and for itself*. Eisenstein uses this Hegelian expression 'an und für sich' (in and for itself) when he speaks of fire as a metaphor for ecstasy in his essay *On Disney*: 'Fire as an aesthetic [...] spectacle is based on the dialectical "writing model" (like ecstatic compositions!).'[5]

In the same text Eisenstein also evokes Heraclitus' dialectic and its metaphorical manifestation in fire as a figure of *pathos* producing ever-changing images, while simultaneously embodying *logos*, the measure and the limit, as the founding principles of communal unity. For Eisenstein, the destructive drive of *pathos* is always associated with the constructive force of *logos* which, thanks to the 'golden rule' of the razor magnate King S. Gillette – 'to maintain a half-turn from the maximum point' – prevents his works from tumbling into the void of formlessness or from solidifying into an immutable synthesis. For, as Eisenstein notes, 'In the practical application of the principles of polyphonic montage, one must stick to that same "golden rule" of King S. Gillette – to maintain a half-turn from the maximum point.'[6] The solution, then, is to step back, because the tension must not be lost by exploding, the screen must not be lacerated and the image must not fade away. With this 'golden rule', Eisenstein avoids reverting to the sphere of '"pure" effect, feeling, sensation, "state"', using the aesthetic and ethical principle of proportionality that goes back to Greek tragedy, the *katechon* (brake), which is the prohibition that condemns all bad infinity, all excess leading inevitably to self-destruction or hubris.[7] It is a gesture that helps prevent any dissolution of the artistic form, while also assuring effectiveness on the political level, respecting the *logos* as a calculation of the limits and the equilibrium of society. This means that the two contradictory forces at work in Eisenstein's cinema must continue to join forces on screen, without one of them ever destroying the other. The ecstatic image, a result of the process through which representation is saturated with different meanings and contradictory sensations, is like a balloon which is about to explode, but is still able to resist this impulse by expanding (the ecstatic figure of excess). Alternatively, it can explode but will immediately reconstitute, with the figure becoming another figure, richer and more powerful than the previous one.

Eisenstein's ecstatic form is similar to Hegel's description of 'the Bacchanalian revel in which no member is not drunk'; that is to say, this is the form in which every expressive solution (image, colour, sound) is permeated with pathos, manifesting itself lyrically, excessively, disturbingly, while still using 'words' (mimetic forms) that are explicit, 'transparent and simple', effective.[8] An example of this first definition of ecstasy can be found in the scene in Disney's *Snow White and the Seven Dwarfs* where the Queen transforms herself into a witch. This transformation mobilizes negative pathos for the creation of a new productive configuration which is similar to the operation that Eisenstein performs on filmic form. The sequence perfectly displays the dialectical process in which elements are qualitatively transformed: the Queen is transformed into a new more effective figure, to deceive and kill Snow White. Facing her faithful raven, the Queen explains her 'dialectical' project, finds the magic formula to revert to her opposite (the witch) and turns a simple apple into a deadly weapon. After the Queen drinks the potion, everything begins to rotate, to blend with what surrounds it, to dissolve into a formless, magma-like matter. The Queen's body then begins its metamorphosis, entering into an ecstatic condition. In full organic communion with its pathetic transformation, the objects in the room also become distorted and transformed from their usual state: a whirlwind of coloured abstract lines invades the screen and carries everything along in its movement. The transformation of the Queen is accompanied by images of storms, with clouds and lightning, and superimpositions of green liquid evoking the action of the magic potion, rising to permeate the entire screen and thereby producing images bordering on abstraction. The completion of her mutation into a witch signals the end of the moment of pathos when the representation is reconfigured. This regression on the formal level thus constitutes the achievement of actuality for the Queen on the narrative level. She is therefore a figure capable of mastering the rise of the negative, of converting it for her needs and of expressing this idea through plastic forms.

This prime example of eidetic ecstasy matches what Eisenstein described in a letter sent to Anita Brenner in Mexico in 1932, in which he defined its objective, cinematographic and theoretical dimensions, all of which are deeply connected to the viewer. It is the formulation of ecstasy that has 'the closest possible relationship (at least in intentions and objectives) with the principles of dialectics'.[9] I am using the term 'eidetic' to define this type of rational ecstasy, referring to the fact that in philosophical language, eidetic refers to knowledge gained through vision. This term allows me to define ecstasy as an intellectual intuition of essences.

Ecstasy as regress: Fall, expenditure, dream

The other pole of ecstasy is close to the idea of expenditure, the regressive impulse that tends towards indeterminacy, the indistinct fusion of elements and the perceptible immediacy of pathos. It is an anti-dialectical dimension, resonant with the ideas of such thinkers as Nietzsche, Freud and Bataille. This subjective-personal dimension of ecstasy finds its most obvious manifestation in Eisenstein's Mexican drawings, with their extreme cruelty and semantic ambiguity. A particularly striking example can be found in a sketch drawn in a letter addressed to the critic Léon Moussinac that represents a nearly naked man in a horizontal position, his stomach protruding and his hair standing on end. His arms and legs are splayed out and tied to four horses pulling in opposite directions to tear him apart. This drawing carries the title *Eisenstein Quartered by his Occupations*, an ironic self-portrait in which Eisenstein shows himself torn between different demands and cultural interests, by reference to a traditional medieval torture. Eisenstein often cited the anguish provoked by his vast knowledge and an endless curiosity that he could not satisfy and make productive. At the time of making this drawing, he was clearly aware that he had many more projects still in draft form than completed works, as if there were a force of inertia preventing him from finishing them. This unproductive force is the equivalent of the centrifugal tendency, which pulled him in many directions, and which he visualized in an image of pain and death. The figure can also be read as referring to the risk of annihilating the organic structure of the work, and it resonates with other figures of pathos that have a sacrificial dimension:

> My cruelty, which did not find an outlet with flies, dragonflies, and frogs, coloured my choice of theme, method and the credo of my work as director. In fact, people in my films are gunned down in their hundreds; farm labourers have their skulls shattered by hoofs, or they are lassoed and buried in the ground up to their necks (*México*); children are crushed on the Odessa steps (*Potemkin*); thrown from rooftops (*The Strike*); are surrendered to their own parents who murder them (*Bezhin Meadow*); thrown on to flaming pyres (*Alexander Nevsky*); they stream with actual bulls' blood (*The Strike*) or with stage blood (*Potemkin*); in some films bulls are poisoned (*The Old and the New*); in others, tsars (*Ivan the Terrible*); a shot horse hangs from a raised bridge (*October*) and arrows pierce men lying spread-eagled on the ramparts outside a besieged Kazan (*Ivan the Terrible*).[10]

All the figures of pathos described above, if considered out of context and beyond their productive role in the films' staging, are well suited to emphasize a certain partiality for violence, a self-justifying cruelty, the pure pleasure of shocking and fascinating the public with horrific images of wounded flesh. These barbaric acts, if grasped in their symptomatic independence, do not allow for reconstitution after the bodies are destroyed, for any finality to be reached, or for the hope of resurrection. Here, the risk of nothingness emerges, the laceration of the skin that Eisenstein wanted to block with the ruse of the 'half-turn back' in the theory he borrowed from Gillette. Ecstasy thus gives concrete form to the ever-present threat of becoming an end in itself, totally detached from the contents it presents. Its results are then confined to the realm of pure visual effect, the pure 'image event', whose function is neither to represent nor to signify, but to validate itself. This tendency is already evident in the milk-separator sequence in *The Old and the New*, in which the milk separator literally squirts on Marfa's face, producing an explosion of liquid that inexorably recalls the act of ejaculation (considered as pure expenditure/pleasure). Here, the idea of fertility is subverted by the dispersive wasting of sperm, thus referring to orgiastic enjoyment that is not obtained 'through the channels of "normal" genital sexuality' but instead 'in going beyond the point of no return, spills libidinal forces outside the whole, at the expense of the whole';[11] in other words, to the detriment of the work's organicity. This second aesthetic principle allows us to discover 'the "other" Eisenstein, the one who [solves differently] the impasse constituted by the contradiction between sensory and intellectual'.[12]

These figures of ecstasy are therefore both an organic image and an open image, an image of the gash that opens, mortally wounding the body without hope of resurrection. Eisenstein assumes this regressive dimension when he asserts, evoking Freud, that the possibility of attaining harmony, peace and unity with nature is only possible through self-destruction and the death of the body.

Beyond his own work, Eisenstein finds this regressive ecstasy in other artists: for example, in Disney's *Dumbo*, in the visionary delirium sequence when the two protagonists, the elephant and the mouse, dream of plasmatic pachyderms while under the influence of alcohol.[13] The figures are represented in an extreme state of pathos, where the only common denominator is the principle of metamorphosis. The size, consistency and resistance of the bodies changes constantly, as do their colours: everything is subject to the principle of fluidity and plasmatic elasticity. Instability affects every figure, to the point of forming an incoherent, incomprehensible space where everything can be flipped into its opposite. The image itself shatters several times under the impact of too many elephants in the shot: another plastic manifestation of the idea of ecstasy as an explosion following a quantitative increase. The figures are deformed, reaching the intensity needed to produce 'degrees of fusion', where all outlines delineating the shot's features disappear completely.

This ecstatic vision has no logical justification within the diegesis; it is to be interpreted more as a series of attraction-images. The sequence seems then to be created for the pure pleasure of witnessing a chaotic, unconstrained, delirious representation: it testifies to the 'plasma appeal', the immediate attraction of the plasmatic figures in a perpetual condition of instability. As described by Eisenstein: 'One could call this the *protean element*, for the myth of Proteus [...] or more precisely, the appeal of this myth – [is based] upon the omnipotence of plasma, which contains in "liquid" form all possibilities of future species and forms.'[14]

Dialectic or antinomy? The chiasmus as a means for considering ecstasy

Eisenstein declared that there is 'ecstasy in touching (simultaneously) both poles, *logos* and *pathos*'.[15] In a letter to Anita Brenner, he proposed a reunification of these two poles to grasp 'the conception of art in its totality': the union of theory and practice, of the art which is born of ecstasy 'just as, according to Nietzsche, tragedy arises from the spirit of music', and of reason which uses the 'anatomical scalpel of materialism, directed towards the most esoteric areas, so to speak, of human experience and "spirit".[16] Eisenstein therefore speaks of unity, of inclusion of the two contradictory tendencies, which are the same as those described here as regressive ecstasy and eidetic ecstasy. These two positions seem to coexist and oppose each other in his thought and work but, in my opinion, they are not reconciled in a true synthesis: it would be more accurate to speak of a paradoxical 'dual-unity', a union of *logos* and *pathos* in which sensory immediacy is never definitively suppressed.

Alternatively, this dual unity can be described as collaboration/conflict, which must be considered both as an intense form of rational knowledge and a troubling enigmatic vision expressed in the ambiguity of ecstatic figures, such as the mother on the Odessa steps or Marfa's face spattered with milk. This ambiguity cannot be completely resolved or dissipated, just as the Paris arcades described by Benjamin 'are house no less than street' and the prostitute is 'seller and sold in one'.[17] We should consider the collaboration and the struggle between these two positions not as a definitive choice between dialectic or antinomy, but rather as a chiasmus, a figure where 'we keep what we overturn', a figure of speech that gives a good sense of Eisensteinian hesitation.[18] The chiasmus is the figure expressing both the reversal used by dialectical thought and the return inherent to antinomic thought, which 'does not offer resolution through a process of overcoming'.[19] In this sense, Eisenstein posits a dialectical synthesis which reconfigures the contradictory elements in a qualitatively new way, such that they cannot be removed from this process in their original form. This burning synthesis of the highest form consists more of an immediate fusion, where contradictory elements, instead of recognizing each other as in a mirror (a speculative, affirmative and positively rational moment), blend as in a distorted, opaque mirror (a regressive-negative moment).

Eidetic ecstasy, with its development based on the idealist subject-object dialectic of the negation of negation, goes beyond any passive restitution of the reflection of reality and imposes a global, rational vision of the real, because it is transformed by conscious human action. On the contrary, regressive ecstasy expresses a radical indictment of the materialist myth of unlimited progress, of the definitive destruction of any preceding stage of history, and of human culture and productivist utilitarianism.

Eisenstein's theory of ecstasy thus has a double face, and coincides both with the figure of *Fantasia*'s Sorcerer, who possesses the absolute mastery of the forms of *pathos*, and at other times with that of the Apprentice/Mickey, who is dominated by these same forces. Finally, a figure of ecstasy is a formal exercise of the synthesis of openings and the opening of syntheses, the point of maximum intensity of a work in which Dionysus speaks with the voice of Apollo.

Notes

1   Gilles Deleuze, *Nietzsche and Philosophy* (London: Continuum, 1983), 18.
2   Sergei M. Eisenstein, *Dickens et Griffith: Genèse du gros plan* (Paris: Stalker, 2007), 102, translated by the author.
3   Antonio Somaini, 'Cinema as "Dynamic Mummification", History as Montage: Eisenstein's Media Archaeology', in *Sergei M. Eisenstein: Notes for a General History of Cinema*, ed. Naum Kleiman and Antonio Somaini (Amsterdam: Amsterdam University Press, 2016), 46.
4   Sergei Eisenstein, *Film Form: Essays in Film Theory* (New York: Harcourt Brace Jovanovich, 1977), 132.
5   Sergei Eisenstein, *On Disney* (Calcutta: Seagull Books, 1986), 47.
6   Sergei Eisenstein, *Nonindifferent Nature*, trans. Herbert Marshall (Cambridge: Cambridge University Press, 1987), 385.
7   Ibid., 179.
8   Friedrich Hegel, *Phenomenology of Spirit* (Oxford: Oxford University Press, 1977), 27.
9   Sergei M. Eizenshtein, *Metod*, ed. Naum Kleiman, 2 vols (Moscow: Muzei kino/Eizenshtein-tsentr, 2002), vol. 2, 495–6, translated by the author.
10 Sergei M. Eisenstein, *Beyond the Stars: The Memoirs of Sergei Eisenstein* (Calcutta: Seagull Books, 1995), 23–4.
11 Jean-François Lyotard, *Des dispositifs pulsionnels* (Paris: UGE, 1973), 56, translated by the author.
12 Jacques Aumont, 'Rileggere Eisenstein', in Sergei M. Eisenstein, *Il montaggio* (Venice: Marsilio, 1986), xxi, translated by the author.
13 Eisenstein uses the term 'plasmaticity' frequently in his essay on Disney. He explains it as follows: 'The rejection of the constraint of form, fixed once and for all, freedom from ossification, an ability to take on any form dynamically. An ability which I would call "plasmaticity," for here a being, represented in a drawing, a being of a given form, a being that has achieved a particular appearance, behaves itself like primordial protoplasm, not yet having a stable form, but capable of taking on any and all forms of animal life on the ladder of evolution' (Eisenstein, *On Disney*, 47).
14 Eisenstein, *On Disney*, 64, italics in the original.
15 'Eisenstein's Metod', in Naum Kleiman, 'Grundproblem e le peripezie del Metodo', in *Sergej Ejzenštejn: oltre il cinema*, ed. Pietro Montani (Venice: La Biennale di Venezia, 1991), 289.

16 Eizenshtein, *Metod*, vol. 2, 495, translated by the author.
17 Walter Benjamin, *The Arcades Project* (Cambridge, MA: Harvard University Press, 1999), 10.
18 Dominique Chateau, *Dialectique ou antinomie? Comment penser* (Paris: L'Harmattan, 2012), 104, translated by the author.
19 Jean-Louis Leutrat, *Échos d'Ivan le Terrible: L'éclair de l'art, les foudres du pouvoir* (Brussels: De Boeck Université, 2006), 124, translated by the author.

13

Ivan the Terrible in the Context of Shakespearean Tragedy

Nikita Lary

Eisenstein was a selective reader of Shakespeare. In Shakespeare's tragedies and more particularly in the writings of such scholars as Caroline Spurgeon and Ivan Aksenov, at the time of his work on *Ivan the Terrible* in the 1940s, he found ideas, or rather images – the images of the body and movement – that nourished his conception of tragedy and of Ivan as a figure for tragedy.

The world in which Eisenstein's tsar moves and acts has resonant parallels with that of the kings and would-be kings in Shakespeare's histories. There is a background of similar conflictual concerns – the determination to unify a country and, with it, to quell unrest and rebellion, find loyalty and support, and put an end to dynastic intrigues. Obviously, Eisenstein did not need Shakespeare to create his films about the Russian tsar,[1] whose life and rule had long been a topic of discussion and fascination for Russian chroniclers, historians and scholars. Nonetheless, it is very tempting to hear an echo of Shakespeare's lines in *King Henry IV, Part 1*, 'I will from henceforth rather be myself / mighty and to be feared' when Ivan declares in *Ivan the Terrible, Part II*: 'I *will* be terrible.'[2] Consider too the very opening of the same play, 'So shaken as we are, so wan with care / Find we a time for frighted peace to pant / And breathe short-winded accents of new broils / To be commenced in strands far remote.' These lines find graphic embodiment in the increasingly careworn image of Ivan, along with his strategy for overcoming internecine divisions.

The echoes of *Henry IV* are probably no accident. Eisenstein had staged one of the plays (or some version of them combining the two *Henry IV* plays) early in his career. I have argued elsewhere that the *Henry IV* plays were the sources of particular episodes in the *Ivan the Terrible* films and explored tragic motifs in them.[3] In this chapter I want to take Eisenstein's conception of Ivan as a tragic character and look at the ways Eisenstein's investigations of Shakespearean tragedy helped him to realize it.

I begin with two quotations about the hero of *Ivan the Terrible*:

> After my films about collectivities, without heroes and plots, my first attempt to make a film about a man who appeared to me as a super-being was to take for hero a man combining a duality within unity of character.⁴
>
> One can give key moments in the fate of this man, who was moved by the idea of sovereignty; who to attain it was prepared to sacrifice friends and settle scores with his confidants and family members; and who for the sake of his ideals spared neither himself nor others [...] We wanted to raise the figure of Ivan the Terrible above the incidental everyday traits of his character and, first and foremost, to try to capture the marks of tragic majesty in his historical role.⁵

We may, furthermore, apply to Ivan a third, more general quotation about a class of characters in literature and film in which 'the historical representation of a particular person is replaced by an artistically generalized type, and the chronicle of events is raised to the cluster of dramatic collisions of a generalized tragedy'.⁶ Ivan inhabits and moves in a space of tragedy defined by collisions with the external world and by internal division or conflict.

Eisenstein's work on *Ivan* coincided with intensive study of and reflection on Shakespeare's tragedies, including *King Lear, Coriolanus, Macbeth* and, in lesser measure, *Hamlet* and *Othello*. Two critics were of particular importance to him: Ivan Aksenov, a friend and teacher of Eisenstein's and the author of essays and books on Shakespeare and other Elizabethan playwrights as well as the translator of several of their plays;⁷ and Caroline Spurgeon, who wrote *Shakespeare's Imagery and What It Tells Us*.⁸ Eisenstein had a copy of Spurgeon's book in his personal library and filled it with multiple underlinings. His reflections about Shakespeare found their way into his writings and lectures and into a chapter in a major book *Montage*, written in 1937 at a time of crisis for Eisenstein, after his film *Bezhin Lug* had been destroyed, further artistic work was denied to him and he faced the possibility of arrest and deportation to a labour camp. Naum Kleiman, to whom Eisenstein scholars and film students are deeply indebted, retrieved the manuscript fragments of this work from the material preserved by Pera Atasheva, Eisenstein's widow and the custodian of his work. After sorting them out, Kleiman found he had an essentially complete work and published it.⁹ The chapter on Shakespeare in *Montage* is suggestive in itself, but it needs the wider context of the book to be fully understood.

Eisenstein's readings of Aksenov and Spurgeon were of particular help to him in developing Ivan as an ambiguous, inwardly divided and, finally, tragic character. He takes two dominant images from Aksenov and Spurgeon: (1) the body; and (2) movement and change (movement within movement). These images are something like metaphors informing the work: recurrent, iterative metaphors. Much has been written about the importance of the image or the *obraz* for Eisenstein. For him, when a representation is transformed into an image (*obraz*), it is removed from the particular and is generalized.[10] The image is the material of drama and, in some cases, tragedy. The question is, what kinds of image (*obraz*) lead to tragedy? In the two completed parts of the film Ivan develops into a tragic character – in potentiality and in actuality.

Let us take first the image of the body in Aksenov and Spurgeon. Aksenov stresses the centrality of the person in Shakespeare's work and in particular 'the centrality of the harmonically constructed person' and 'the ways of attaining this harmony'.[11] For Eisenstein a person is connected with an image of the body (which, of course, he could use directly in film): 'The fact that the human personality is at the centre of Shakespeare's main theme and the centre of his endeavour directly leads to the conjecture that this theme and idea will "strive" to take form in images connected with the body.'[12] This connection with the body means that Eisenstein's emphasis will not be on the reflectiveness of a Hamlet or a Macbeth, or even of a Richard II or at moments of Henry IV. It is tempting to apply the idea about the centrality of the harmonically constructed body to Eisenstein's film: Ivan deviates more and more from this image in the course of the film.

Eisenstein finds strong support for the importance of the image of the body in Spurgeon. In the chapter on Shakespeare in *Montage* he quotes her: 'The proportion of Shakespeare's body images to the whole is considerably larger than that of any of the other dramatists examined. Ben Jonson comes nearest him as regards number.'[13] The images of the body extend from the whole body to the limbs (arms, legs) and body parts (the head, face, mouth, eyes). The images of the whole body *and* its parts play a central role in Eisenstein's view of tragedy (which it should be noted was not fully developed).[14] Tragedy, he held, had its roots in the ancient ceremonial cults in which the ritual dismemberment (*sparagmos*) of a deity or hero (such as Dionysius, Orpheus or Hippolytus) was followed by theophany: 'The apotheosis in which the torn limbs were reunited and the god or demon was resurrected.'[15] Release was characteristic of tragedy. As a properly pathetic, ecstatic art, tragedy left one with a 'feeling of relief and liberation at the highest point of tension of the drama'.[16] Suffering underwent ecstatic transformation. Elsewhere, Eisenstein spoke of the release of 'prelogical' forms of consciousness (which he also referred to as 'undifferentiated sensuous thought').[17] His ideas on ritual dismemberment and resurrection are taken up and developed in the chapter 'Dionysius and Oziris', which precedes the chapter on Shakespeare in *Montage*.

Eisenstein draws on both Aksenov and Spurgeon in developing his view of tragedy, specifically, he finds support in their writings and their focus on the image of the body for his view of the dismembered and reassembled body in tragedy. With reference to Aksenov, he notes that since the person is at the centre of Shakespeare's creative work, 'we are bound to wonder whether in his methods of work there is a distinctive refraction of the resurrected "Dionysius and Osiris method"'.[18] Additionally, with reference to Spurgeon, Eisenstein asks whether at the heart of the imagistic structure of Shakespeare there is 'that same mark of a human body torn into parts and gathered into one'.[19] Yet, in Spurgeon's analysis of Shakespeare's tragedies the restoration of the whole body does not play a critical role, while Aksenov's notion of the harmonically constructed body is more suggestive. Implicit in the images of the tortured body is an image of the harmonically constructed body, from which they are a deviation. The vision of the whole body restored is integral to the plays, even if we do not see a literal reunification in the plays unless it is in a successor king.

In *Ivan the Terrible*, the restoration of the ruler is literal. We see it in Ivan's rising from his sick bed in Part I. Again, after his wife's death (by poisoning), when it seems everything is lost and his only course lies in submission to the condemnation of the church, Ivan draws himself up from his despairing, helpless position beside Anastasia's bier, casting down two massive candle stands. The rest of Part I of the film is experienced as a resurrection (almost orgasmic in its rhythms) and growing strength, until the culmination of the film, at Ivan's retreat in Alexandrova Sloboda, where the people – in a long meandering throng coming out of the vast Russian land – implore him to return. Here, at this juncture, Ivan finds renewal in his bond with the people in an act of mutual submission. Most fully, and most in accordance with Eisenstein's ideas on the centrality of the restoration of the ruler, we find it at the end of Part II of the film, when Ivan reappears in the cathedral after he has supposedly been murdered, whereas in actual fact Efrosinia's son, Vladimir, pretending to be tsar – on Ivan's insistence – has been killed (and in a tempting reading of the film, offered up in a form of sacrifice, with the murderer fulfilling a priestly office). The effect is not so much one of the reassemblage of Ivan's disempowered, splayed limbs (seen for instance when he is leaning against his wife's bier) but rather of renewal (ecstatic renewal), a re-centring and his rebirth as a new, more powerful ruler.[20]

In a development of the image of the human body, both Aksenov and Spurgeon note that it also serves as an image of the state. Aksenov cites the passage about the state in *Coriolanus*:

> The senators of Rome are this great Belly,
> And you the mutinous members. For examine
> Their counsels and their cares, digest things rightly
> Touching the weal o' th' common, you shall find
> No public benefit which you receive
> But it proceeds or comes from them to you,
> And no way from yourselves.[21]

Implicit in this image is the ideal of the harmoniously constructed state.[22] The dismemberment of the state goes with the desecration of its ruler (and the debasement of his subjects). The need for unification of the state gives meaning and intensity to the ruler's need for wholeness. In 'Ivan the Terrible: A Film about the Russian Renaissance of the 16th Century', Eisenstein wrote: 'At that time the centralization of state power in the hands of an absolute monarch was a requirement for the salvation and survival of the country and the government.'[23] He then connects the need for the unity of the country faced with the selfish interests of the *boyars* (Russian states aristocracies) in the sixteenth century with the urgent, present necessity to fight the military onslaught of Nazi Germany and prevent the destruction of the country. There is a direct parallel here with Shakespeare. In lectures delivered between 18 February and 22 April 1942, at the very height of his work on *Ivan*, Eisenstein talked about images of the dismemberment of the state in *King Lear*:

> Shakespeare turned to this theme at the very moment when the dismemberment of England was a possibility [...] From this point of view, *Lear* is opposed to the division of the state, as is shown by the folly of this division here [...] In *Lear* there is the theme of disastrous partition. The basic situation in Shakespeare is the division of the state and ruin. In no other tragedy is there so much injury to the body parts and destruction of the human organism as in this piece [...] Each tiny detail of the work shows the horror of the various things that are occurring.[24]

Likewise Spurgeon writes of *Lear*: 'The sense of bodily torture continues to the end. Gloucester catches the recurrent theme of the tragedy, and crystallizes it forever in the terrible picture of men being torn limb from limb by the gods in sport, to whom they are but as "flies to wanton boys".'[25]

In a lecture in 1938, Eisenstein said:

> In Shakespeare when the unity of the state is combined with the image of the body as a poetic figure of speech, the tragedy based on the dismemberment of the state is constructed on this image: solid torture, tearing apart the body, the dislocation of the arms, the tearing of breasts, the ripping out of eyes. You remember that the ripping out of eyes and squishing them under foot is even

brought into the action, not even into the speech. Of all Shakespeare's tragedies the most inhuman in its handling of the human body is indeed *King Lear*. Leaf through this thing without paying attention to the story, and look at the line of comparisons which operates.[26]

The second fundamental image Eisenstein derives from his reading of Spurgeon, in particular, is that of movement. He sees a close connection between the imagery of the body and the imagery of movement. In ways I note here, he sees that it is film that gives the image of movement its ultimate realization. He quotes Spurgeon:

> The more we study these main groups of images which constitute the greatest part of Shakespeare's imagery, the clearer it becomes that there is one quality or characteristic in them which overpoweringly attracts him throughout, and that quality is *movement*: nature and natural objects in motion. In other words, it is the life of things which appeals to him, stimulates him and enchants him, rather than beauty of colour or form or even significance.[27]

Eisenstein sees in the first instance movement of a particular body in progression in time and space, as in a biography or in Shakespeare's chronicle plays, and in the second instance movement of any mobile object in general.[28] Movement – through the phases of life and the problems of rule – provides a basis to generalize the experience of the ruler. Ivan's struggles, personal or political, point the way to tragedy.

Movement within movement, namely change, represents the fullest development of this image. Change is related to images of growth, decay and death. The legend of Dionysius – of his dismemberment and death and then his reappearance – is an image of the life of nature. At the heart of this legend there is a fundamental proto-image of the critical turning points of the seasons. Eisenstein refers to the growth and development of cereals, in which the point of maximum development of the plant with the formation of the kernels of seeds is also the point at which the plant dies, until the seeds in turn are destroyed and germinate. The moment of fullest growth is also the moment of the beginning of decay, and the moment of death is also the beginning of new life. Movement contains the seeds of its own undoing and also of new growth. Eisenstein finds the fullest expression of this in Shakespeare's Sonnet 15: 'When I consider everything that grows / Holds in perfection but a little moment.'[29] This verse was also referred to by Spurgeon: 'Shakespeare is particularly interested in the processes of growth and decay, and as he expresses it in the fifteenth sonnet ("When I consider everything that grows") in the likeness between man and plants in coming painfully and with many struggles and checks to perfection, to stay there but for a moment and then begin to decay.'[30]

There is a connection here with the tragic mystery of the body that dies and is reborn. This is one place where Eisenstein could find in Spurgeon a connection with his view of tragedy as a reassemblage of the body, with the seasons providing a proto-image of the Dionysian myth. Movement as a recurrent, iterative metaphor points the way to a more radical disturbance of the work, an inner disturbance, in which the process of disassemblage and reassemblage is built into the structure of the work.

> As regards Shakespeare's imagistic structure it could be said to be a move from the gathering and assemblage of scattered limbs into a different proto-image – to an assemblage of the same limbs under the conditions of sequentially changing positions of a body that is not torn apart – a body that breaks the static assemblage of its parts as it passes from one phase of motion to another. The transposition of this to a series of concrete images is not just one of a number of film methods, it is *our basic phenomenon of film*.[31]

In film – that is, traditional frame-shot film – movement and change, in the form of disintegration and reintegration, become something other than, or apart from, recurrent motifs or determinants of the plot. They are basic to the structure of film. The eye passes from one arrangement of the elements of the shot in one frame to another arrangement of the elements in the following frame.

> In the imagistic structure there is a transition from the assembly and collocation of dispersed limbs into a new proto-image – the assembly or collocation of the same limbs under the conditions of the sequentially changing positions of a body that has not been torn apart, a body that breaks the static collocation of its parts as it passes from phase to phase of its movement.[32]

The change between image A and image B takes place in the space between the two images. Elements in that space that are not seen (because the space is not seen) become significant in the formation of the new image B. Eisenstein imagines a shrinking of the space between the two images till the point where the destruction of the old image is also that where the construction of the new image begins.[33] The death and rebirth characteristic of tragedy are thus built deep into the structure of film.

Eisenstein asserts that Shakespeare, in his own noncinematic way, develops this basic archetypal form (*Urphenomen*) of film through a focus on the image of motion. For an example of the field of application of the image of motion, I will cite here a passage from Spurgeon's book. Speaking about *Henry VIII*, one of Shakespeare's least-known plays and one she acknowledges is not written entirely by him, Spurgeon lists:

> bodily action of almost every kind: walking, stepping, marching, running and leaping; crawling, hobbling, falling, carrying, climbing and perspiring; swimming, diving, flinging and peeping; crushing, strangling, shaking, trembling, sleeping, stirring, and – especially and repeatedly – the picture of the body or back bent and weighed down under a heavy burden.[34]

Other plays in which Spurgeon finds a similar use of this imagery of bodily action include *King Lear*, *Hamlet* and *Coriolanus*. What is interesting in the quoted passage is the list of all the metaphors or images of movement given by her. The image – the image of action or movement – is constructed by a kind of *montage* and, in the process, it becomes a structuring principle.

It might follow that film was uniquely suited to the development of the tragic form. One objection to this is that if viewers are not aware of the psychological or physiological process that enables them to perceive motion in film as the frames succeed one another on the screen, then the basic imagistic structure of film should not play a role in their reception of any particular film as a tragedy. At most, the inherent tragic structure of film might play a role in the filmmaker's work – in this instance, Eisenstein's – in the conception and development of a tragedy. Conceivably, the imagistic structure of film might trigger in the viewer a need to search for images of wholeness and unity in a world 'out of joint'. For the viewer, as for the filmmaker, there might be a particular satisfaction in the tragic construct.

To conclude: through his immersion in Shakespearean tragedy – at the time of German aggression and Stalinist dictatorship – Eisenstein discovered its continued relevance. In spite of the revolution, history had no safe, final destination. At critical moments history found transcendence in tragedy. And moreover – tragedy was not finally defeatist.

Notes

1. *Ivan the Terrible* (1946–8), a projected three-part film, two of which were completed.
2. William Shakespeare, *King Henry IV*, Act 1, Scene 3, 5–6; Sergei M. Eizenshtein, 'Ivan Groznyi', in *Izbrannye proizvedeniia v 6-ti tomach* [Selected works in 6 volumes], ed. Pera Atasheva (Moscow: Iskusstvo, 1964–71), vol. 6, 337.

3   See Nikita Lary, 'Henry IV', in *Reading with Eisenstein*, ed. Ada Ackerman and Luka Arsenjuk (forthcoming); and Nikita Lary, 'Tragic Interconnections and Intersections', in *The Flying Carpet: Studies on Eisenstein and Russian Cinema in Honor of Naum Kleiman*, ed. Antonio Somaini and Joan Neuberger (Paris: Éditions Mimésis, 2017), 197–203.
4   Sergei M. Eizenshtein, *Neravnodushnaia priroda*, in *Izbrannye proizvedeniia*, vol. 3, 138–9.
5   Sergei M. Eizenshtein, 'Gosudarsvennyi chelovek', in *Izbrannye proizvedeniia*, vol. 1, 200.
6   Sergei M. Eizenshtein, *Montazh*, ed. Naum Kleiman (Moscow: Muzei kino, 2000), 242.
7   Lars Kleberg gives a fascinating account of Aksenov's connections with the avant-garde in Russia and abroad in the revolutionary and early post-revolutionary years and his struggles to survive as a scholar and a translator during the struggles to impose a putative Marxist-Leninist orthodoxy throughout the field of cultural production. Lars Kleberg, 'Ivan Aksenov, Shakespeare, and Ben Johnson', in *The Flying Carpet: Studies on Eisenstein and Russian Cinema in Honor of Naum Kleiman*, ed. Antonio Somaini and Joan Neuberger (Paris: Éditions Mimésis, 2017), 179–96.
8   Caroline Spurgeon, *Shakespeare's Imagery and What It Tells Us* (Cambridge: Cambridge University Press, 1935).
9   In an oblique allusion to Lewis Carroll, Kleiman speaks of it as a retrieval 'from beyond the looking-glass wonderland', in part because of the tall standing mirror hiding the manuscript pieces.
10 In his introduction to *Montazh*, Naum Kleiman looks at the way Eisenstein constructs images of repression and revolt in *The Battleship Potemkin* and of massacre in *The Strike* through montage sequences combining intercut shots with deliberately contrasting compositions and textures, metaphors and synecdoche, writing. 'With this kind of montage an image ceases to be a [rhetorical] "figure" and becomes a "structure" that is capable of shifting the perception from the visible to that which is not seen, from the particular to the general – to the "fifth dimension".' Naum Kleiman, 'Introduction', in Sergei M. Eizenshtein, *Montazh* (Moscow: Muzei kino/Eizenshtein-tsenter, 2000), 23.
11 Eizenshtein, *Montazh*, 243.
12 Ibid., 246.
13 Spurgeon, *Shakespeare's Imagery*, 49.
14 See Eisenstein's ideas developed as early as 1933–4 in 'Rezhissura', in *Izbrannye proizvedeniia*, vol. 4.
15 Eizenshtein, 'Rezhissura', 261.
16 Ibid., 259.

17 See, for instance, the transcripts of Eisenstein's lectures to fourth-year film students in the VGIK (Vsesouznyi Gosudarstvenyi Institut Kinematographii) library: 4-i kurs: 13 May 1935.
18 Eizenshtein, *Montazh*, 243.
19 Ibid., 245.
20 These scenes of the renewal and self-discovery of Ivan stand in vivid contrast to the first symbolic assemblage and construction of the figure of the ruler in the coronation scene at the opening of Part I, where we see Ivan adorned with the costume and the assembled accoutrements of power seated on his throne.
21 William Shakespeare, *Coriolanus*, Act 1, Scene 7.
22 Eizenshtein, *Montazh*, 249.
23 Eizenshtein, *Izbrannye proizvedeniia*, vol. 1, 191.
24 Eisenstein, Lecture transcripts, VGIK, 18 February 1942.
25 Spurgeon, *Shakespeare's Imagery*, 243.
26 Eisenstein, Lecture transcripts, VGIK, 27 February 1938.
27 Spurgeon, *Shakespeare's Imagery*, 50, emphasis in the original.
28 Eizenshtein, *Montazh*, 246.
29 Ibid., 48.
30 Spurgeon, *Shakespeare's Imagery*, 87–8.
31 Eizenshtein, *Montazh*, 247, my italics.
32 Ibid.
33 See Eizenshtein, *Montazh*, 249.
34 Spurgeon, *Shakespeare's Imagery*, 253.

Part Five

Space, Place, Legacy

14

From Moscow to Ferghana, or from the Avant-garde to National Form

Nariman Skakov

Remy de Gourmont's Catholicism, Elizabethan ballads and national form

On 23 February 1943, as part of his grand *Method* project, Sergei Eisenstein wrote an essay 'On the issue of the Formula: "National in Form, Socialist in Content"'.[1] Typically multilingual and eclectic, this represented a rather belated reflection on Stalin's famous definition of proletarian culture as 'national in form, socialist in content', a dictum that had dominated artistic discussions in the Soviet Union in the 1930s. Drastic changes in Soviet ethnic policy in the late 1930s, together with patriotic pathos during the war with Germany, had intensified Russo-centric discourses in the USSR, and thus Eisenstein's return to the formula, which at least appeared to celebrate national diversity, is surely significant. This was an overdue theoretical engagement with an already somewhat dormant discourse. However, it was probably the location where he was writing, Alma-Ata – the capital of the Kazakh SSR and the Oriental home front – that prompted the director to return to the topic of national form.

Putting the historical and political context aside, this short essay marks a pinnacle in Eisenstein's own investigation of the issue of content and form, one of the constant concerns of his theoretical inquiry. It is noteworthy that the essay began with an error: in his manuscript, instead of 'national in form' he initially wrote 'national in content'.[2] This slip of the director's pen actually points to a very important aspect of his conceptualization of the form–content dichotomy. For Eisenstein, form and content were always symbiotic. As early as 1925, in 'The Problem of the Materialist Approach to Form', he argued that form produces meaning – making the delivery of content efficient. Moreover, any work of art can be identified as revolutionary as long as its form is defined by the revolutionary material with which it engages.[3]

The presumed unity of form and content is amplified even further in 'Perspectives', one of the key essays that summarized his theoretical views of the 1920s. There, Eisenstein wrote:

> How many bayonets have, for instance, been broken on the question of 'form and content'!
>
> All because the dynamic, active and effective act of 'content' [*soderzhanie*] as 'containing [*sderzhivanie*] within oneself' has been replaced by an amorphous, static and passive understanding of content as contents [*soderzhimoe*].
>
> How much inky blood has been spilled because of the persistent desire to understand *form* only as deriving from the Greek *phormos* or wicker basket – with all the 'organisational conclusions' that flow from that!
>
> A wicker basket where those same unhappy 'contents' bob about on the inky floods of the polemic.[4]

Eisenstein replaces the passivity of form as container and content as filler with a dynamism wherein the two interact with each other. Through a maze of lexicographic and etymological twists and turns, he arrives at the conclusion that the function of form is *disclosure* – it is not a static containment but always an active process of uncovering. He writes:

> 'Disclosure' [*obnaruzhenie*] characterises image from a different, socially active standpoint: it 'discloses', i.e. establishes the social link between a particular phenomenon and its surroundings.
>
> [...] 'content' [*soderzhanie*] – the act of containing [*sderzhivanie*] – is an *organisational principle*.
>
> The principle of the organisation of thinking is in actual fact the 'content' of a work.
>
> A principle that materialises in the sum total of socio-physiological stimulants and for which form serves as a means of *disclosure*.[5]

This stance seemingly challenges Stalin's prescriptive understanding of national form as a passive vessel, replacing it with an active dialectical tension between form and content. Nation as an essence-free form is replaced with a dynamic understanding of formal function – form not only holds content, but discloses it. Content itself is endowed with an active function. Eisenstein's stance challenges the official line that content plays a 'leading role' and discouraging any innovative engagement with form by arguing for the indivisible form–content relationship.

Nevertheless, the 1943 essay brings to light a new set of challenges that were not raised in earlier essays. It makes a remarkable rhetorical turn by evoking

Catholicism and sixteenth-century song writing in the context of arguing that discursive tension between form and content is always characteristic of epochs in which cardinal ideological changes occurred, with the October Revolution being one of the greatest.[6] Eisenstein then proceeds to discuss how Catholicism utilized pagan forms for its own needs and adapted them to deliver new 'ideological' content. His discussion revolves around two essays by the French symbolist poet, novelist and influential critic Remy de Gourmont: 'A Religion of Art' (1898) and 'The Psychology of Paganism' (1900). De Gourmont argued that Catholicism is a paganized form of Christianity, fusing the eternal with the transient and the cerebral with the sensual. It also borrows its aesthetic sensitivity from the pagan tradition.[7] Eisenstein succinctly renders this as: 'The idea in Catholic art comes from Christianity, while its formal rendering comes from paganism.'[8]

Insisting on the inherent adaptability of formal devices, Eisenstein dedicates the second half of his essay to Elizabethan ballads, a genre typified by the transformation of secular, often crude love songs into spiritual hymns.[9] Again, an old form delivers new content and breaks down the hierarchy of genres. He observes a similar tendency in the poetics of Aleksandr Blok, who used Roma songs and other 'kitsch' forms to deliver his own set of (revolutionary) themes. Regardless of epochs and geographical locations, art presents a continual flow of aesthetic evolution where high and low genres interpenetrate each other. Immersion in the vernacular of popular forms becomes a necessity, while historical continuity evolves into a trope that renegotiates differences (high and low, familiar and alien).

This continuity is dialectically balanced by a still-productive concept of rupture in the social domain. A dynamic steadiness in the flow of time is enabled by constant and inevitable social upheavals. Thus, the discursive kernel of the essay lies in Eisenstein's conceptualization of rupture in historical time, be it the emergence of Christianity or the October Revolution, through the prism of continuity. He argues that it is always possible, and sometimes even necessary, to deliver a new message by acknowledging past achievements in the formal domain. This was a truly idiosyncratic take on the socialist realist premise of artistic continuity: the official style disdained the immediately preceding avant-garde tradition as an unproductive leftist deviation, and proclaimed itself the ultimate pinnacle of artistic development. For Eisenstein, however, art finds itself on an infinite developmental spiral with significant historical cataclysms and disruptions providing mere convolutions.

From the tropics of Tehuantepec to the desert of Ferghana

Eisenstein's 1943 vision of national form and socialist content was deeply rooted in several of the director's unrealized projects and his theoretical inquiries that took place in the 1930s. Visiting Mexico in 1931 was clearly a defining moment of his career where exposure to radically alien cultures would profoundly influence his later theoretical outlook. The simultaneous coexistence of different layers of time in one space would have been a key component of *Que viva México!*. Presenting a vision of cultures at different stages of development in one geographical space was to be accomplished by dividing the film into different novellas. As Eisenstein explained: 'The cohesion of the novellas was maintained by a number of traversing lines. Their linkage to each other secured by an historical feature. Not according to historical epochs, but to geographical zones.'[10]

As with the categories of time and space, form and content would be brought together by the creative vision underpinning *Que viva México!*, and they featured prominently in the document titled 'Rough Outline of the Mexican Picture', written in English for potential financial backers of the film in the United States.[11] Eisenstein started this by suggesting that the sarape, a blanket worn as a cloak by people in Latin America, could be a potent symbol of Mexico in his film:

> So striped and violently contrasting are the cultures in Mexico running close to each other and being centuries far away. No plot, no whole story could run through this sarape without being false or artificial. And we took the contrasting independent closeness of its violent colours as the motif for constructing our film: six episodes running one after another – different in character, different in people, different in animals, trees and flowers. And still held together by [the] unity of the weave – the rhythmic and musical construction and the unrolling of the Mexican spirit and character.[12]

While different historical temporalities were not unified though their subject matter at the level of content, the director suggested that *form* – a structure made of the divergent stripes of a sarape – should serve the unifying function. The 'unity of the weave' becomes a core formal device that integrates divergent elements while still preserving their inherent difference.

More importantly, a few pages later Eisenstein alludes to the practice that imperial Spain and the Catholic Church had of appropriating Aztec art and architecture. He writes: 'Statues of saints that arose on the spots of pagan altars [...] Catholicism and paganism. The Virgin of Guadalupe worshipped by wild dances and bloody bull fights.'[13] This artistic continuity, manifest in the conversion to Christianity without abandonment of past pagan deities – an unexpected synthesis – evolves into a more general understanding of the uninterrupted continuity of *form*. Content can be new but forms are everlasting. It is clear that the crux of Eisenstein's 1943 essay, developing the idea of continuity of form, was grounded in his Mexican experience, observing the clash of diverging temporalities in Aztec and Catholic cultures.

The symbiosis of Mexico's mythological past and revolutionary present would have been further developed in *The Ferghana Canal*, Eisenstein's 1939 semi-documentary and semi-fictional project, for which the theme of *progress–regress* was extrapolated from Mexico to Uzbekistan in the Soviet Orient. This film would have tackled, in the director's own words, 'the theme of tomorrow that has become today'.[14] The convergence of divergent temporalities, 'primitive' and 'pre-logical' forms of thinking, would all regain discursive significance in the Uzbek project.

Eisenstein outlined a temporal triptych in *Ferghana Canal* – a fourteenth-century feudal prologue, in which Tamerlane's Mongol forces invade the medieval city of Urgench, would be followed by a pre-revolutionary drama depicting the confrontation between poor peasants and usurers who sell water at high prices, then a heroic contemporary tale of the construction of the 240-kilometre-long Ferghana Canal by 160,000 Soviet Central Asian peasants. Historical flashbacks would culminate in the act of construction in the present. 'Organic' connection is crucial for how the film would establish continuity: 'From here, from the Soviet land, from the peak of social development achieved by humanity, we were preoccupied with something else: not with a picture of disintegration but with one of the connectedness of time. [This comprised] a picture of blood circulation of epochs, their connections, their transition from one to another, a picture of successions and co-existences.'[15] This statement resonates strongly with Eisenstein's concept of national form as an entity that functions as a guarantor of historical continuity. Time serves as an animating force behind social progress and aesthetics.

On 22 July, Eisenstein made a simple drawing depicting 'the structure' for the planned film, showing three towers of different heights.[16] The two taller towers represented the medieval and socialist periods and were connected by the shorter imperial one. The significance of the first and third parts lies in them being united thematically by the redirection of rivers, although this redirection had diametrically opposite intentions. The middle episode, set in the recent colonial past, was supposed to be a limbo in which people fell victim to nature and to evil exploiters who used water as a means of manipulation. Accordingly, the film was intended to open with a scene of mass murder. Tamerlane's army built a dam and deprived the city of its water source. The ensuing drought killed almost all of the inhabitants of Urgench, until a few stonemasons took revenge on the invaders by unleashing the obstructed water onto them and forcing them to retreat. This temporary dam functioned as a deadly force and its lethal essence was supposed to be dialectically balanced by a life-affirming act – the construction of the Ferghana Canal centuries later, a spring of life and prosperity in the Soviet land.

In October 1939, the Ferghana film project was abruptly halted, after Eisenstein was forced to abandon the historical prologue due to political pressure 'from above'. The structure of *Ferghana Canal* could no longer hold. The three-part division of the film, extending back to the region's historical past, was of utmost significance to the filmmaker, whereas depicting the coexistence of different temporalities was apparently problematic to Soviet ideologues.

However, the unfinished project's importance should not be underestimated. It vividly reveals the attempt by a key avant-gardist to push the boundaries of Modernism. The eastern republic becomes a reservoir for defamiliarizing experiences – its inherent difference is enhanced by means of radical transformation. As Eisenstein put it in one of his *Pravda* articles, 'Everything here is unusual. The land has become unrecognizable. For days, for weeks, in even less than a month, the area where the canal is being built has been transformed. It is not melancholy for the past, but pride and rapture that this unusual land evokes: its name is Fergana.'[17] 'Unusual' is a significant modifier in this short text – the Uzbek land becomes a marvel of the socialist project. Orientalist exoticism is replaced with a socially progressive fascination.

The central Oriental aspect of *Ferghana Canal* is certainly the figure of Tokhtasyn, an Uzbek singer who supposedly oversees its narrative progression. He functions as Eisenstein's Virgil, guiding the viewer through a pre-revolutionary feudal and colonized hell towards the classless Paradiso of socialist Uzbekistan being constructed. The epic singer preserves his 'primordial roots', for he is a possessor of the 'authentic' national heritage. As such, Tokhtasyn serves as a medium connected to the stages of the earlier, sensuous ways of operating. His 'primordial roots' endow him with an authority that would allow him to deliver the medieval prologue as an epic song in the film.[18] According to the initial plan,

Tokhtasyn would sing the first song about the siege by Tamerlane's troops, tell his own story in the second song, set in the recent colonial past, while in the third song he would 'directly enter the action and act independently'.[19] This was a movement from contemplation towards modern action, with the first and third parts truly epic in form.

In the second part, Tokhtasyn features as a psychological character, when he must trade his young daughters to a moneylender in exchange for limited access to water for his dried-up field. He challenges the moneylender after his allotted half-hour of irrigation expires, and becomes involved in a spontaneous riot when paupers break the dam and flood the streets of the settlement. Tokhtasyn barely survives the lynching, while his son, referred to in the script as Tokhtasynov – the Russified form of the name Tokhtasyn – escapes to participate in an anti-colonial rebellion in Andizhan, and later, during Soviet times, becomes one of the leading engineers of the Ferghana Canal. The singer, who remembers the conflicts of the past and had himself experienced colonial tsarist oppression, then becomes the witness of a modern heroic tale, the conquest of nature's blind forces.[20] Reunited with his son at the construction site, he is given the privilege of opening the dam in a ceremony that will unleash torrents of water. However, the old man gives this privilege back to his son.

This scene was supposed to be followed by one of the most bizarre sequences in the film – a so-called 'prayer' for Stalin in which Tokhtasyn kneels down, raises his hands and utters the words: 'May the name of the man who has brought us together be blessed, and may his happiness be greater than ours [...] May his heart be with us forever [...] His name is the symbol of happiness!'[21] Stalin is thus posited as the gatherer of the people who perform the feat of labour. The trope of friendship between the peoples, a Stalinist rendering of internationalism, would be the key discursive plane of the film. Uzbek, Tajik, Kazakh, Kirghiz, Turkmen, Russian and Armenian peasants are shown all working together on the construction site. Towards the end, during a collective feast, they enjoy performances by Khalima Nasyrova, an Uzbek soprano, and Tamara Khanum, née Petrosian, a Ferghana-born singer and dancer of Armenian descent. This leads to the final scene, in which Tokhtasyn would be given the privilege of 'hand[ing] the water over' to the Tajiks: he cuts the ceremonial ribbon across the canal marking the border between the Uzbek and Tajik republics, with a single knife blow. In this jubilant ending, water unites nations and also erases borders, as is evident in Eisenstein's drawing *The Uzbek Extends His Hand to the Tajik* (Figure 14.1).

Figure 14.1 Eisenstein, *The Uzbek Extends His Hand to the Tajik*. Courtesy of the Russian State Archive of Literature and Arts (RGALI).

The figure of Tokhtasyn also proves to be essential for the general formal design of *Ferghana Canal*. Eisenstein reflects on Tokhtasyn's craft – the ancient oral tradition of epic singers – and argues that its ability to unite the disparate elements of the past into a cohesive image (*edinyi obraz*) is similar to the general principles of montage, which produce a unified vision out of unrelated fragments of filmic material.[22] He wonders:

> How did this unexpected junction of ancient epic song with the ultra-cinematic device of montage and filming occur? Only because the image of every work of art, since ancient times, is constructed in a 'montage' way [...] And let this foray into the structure of Tokhtasyn's song, which follows the principles of songs composed by the people, serve as a further example of how the principle of montage-like creation of images in art is prevalent and profound.[23]

The figure of Tokhtasyn establishes the centrality of montage, connecting epic tradition with cutting-edge modernist aesthetic practice. For Eisenstein, montage as a formal method is instrumental in producing meaning. At the same time, montage provides a means to support the continuity of culture and serves as an indispensable epistemic tool in which past tradition plays a key role. The *epos* of Tokhtasyn is thus central to the film as a structuring device.

Framing national form

Work on *Ferghana Canal* had a profound effect on Eisenstein the theorist. Shortly before the project was halted, he made an important set of notes in his diary while still in Tashkent. Written on 1 October 1939, they comprise the director's earliest systematic theoretical attempt to engage with the formula 'national in form, socialist in content'. Eisenstein begins with a bold statement that the notion of 'true image' (*istinnyi obraz*), arguably the fundamental operative principle of his aesthetics, is inherently linked with the discourse of national form. He writes:

> Toward a question: *Of representation and generalized image* and their unity in the 'true' image.
>
> It's important to say that this interrelationship, on the highest social–stylistic level of the problem, is completely encompassed in the formula: national in form and socialist in content.[24]

The interplay between 'representation' (*izobrazhenie*, a mere pictorial fact) and 'generalized image' (*obobshchennyi obraz*, an analytic artistic impression) is key. As Eisenstein argued in 'Montage 1938', aesthetic synthesis is a procedure in which a number of separate static and factual *representations*, gathered in the director's mind and vision, evolve into an emotionally arresting *generalized image* – an analytic and logical comprehension of a set of representations that reveals the unchanging quality of a broader phenomenon.[25] That is, the generalized image turns the clichéd aspects of the world into its self-revealing image. Using the figure of Tokhtasyn, the director shows how the singer also produces a generalized image as his epic craft transforms a mere fact into a profound impression of reality:

> Tokhtasyn's song is not a scientific treatise, it is not a historical chronicle with word-for-word commentary that documents every detail. Tokhtasyn's song is almost a legend, it is a popular epos, it is a popular *skaz*. As it is, it carries its strength not in a meticulous documentariness but in that *general image*, which amalgamates the appearance and fate of many cities [...] of the East into a unitary tragedy of sands and water that have been set free by wicked human will and the hatred of different peoples toward one other.[26]

Eisenstein argues that his film will engage fully with the epic genre, with song as a key narrative component, and form as a respectful tribute to it. By recollecting the dramatic past and conflating it with the socialist present, Tokhtasyn elevates the region's natural condition (its lack of water) to the level of the human condition. Centuries of conflict reach their climax in a feat of collective labour that overcomes antagonistic nature and celebrates Soviet friendship among peoples. Epic tradition materializes in the epic construction effort.

However, according to his theoretical notes, the clash of *representations* and *image* culminates in something qualitatively different – the 'true' image. The word 'true' always appears in quotation marks, which indicate that Eisenstein realizes the word is not being used in its commonly accepted sense. One might speculate that the tension between factual *representations* and a fictional *artistic image* results in a *'true' image* that can aspire to transcend this very reality–fiction dichotomy – it enters the realm of ultimate truth, a reconciliation of logical rationality with pre-logical sensuality.

Transcendence is accomplished again by a tension between form and content. According to Eisenstein, national form belongs to the domain of the sensuous (a pre-logical stage), while content dwells on the analytic, cerebral level. The two can provide a higher symbiosis manifest as the 'true' image:

> The same formula 'national in form, socialist in content' encompasses the whole basic scheme of the artistic image's dynamism, that is, the phenomenon of art itself.
>
> The national as a more ancient *stage* of the socialist. Form as an earlier *stage* of cognition – *sensuous* in relation to content – a stage of cognition – of the cerebral.[27]

For Eisenstein, nationalist consciousness, as a reaction to colonial rule, functions as a precondition for a revolution that, in its turn, leads towards a classless socialist society – a more progressive state.[28] Thus the national, as a state or stage, precedes and leads to its socialist counterpart. Form, in its turn, becomes a subsidiary, though essential, entity in relation to content: it represents a sensory-emotional rendering of content. National form, as an engagement with the epic genre in *Ferghana Canal*, together with its socialist content – the construction effort and the workers' true socialist consciousness – will produce the *ultimate truth*, which exists on a post-logical plane. As Eisenstein concluded in his notes: 'The formula, as we may see, is entirely constructed according to the same unity and mutual interpenetration of the pictorial and artistic-abstracted, becoming amalgamated in the truthful-figural, and manifests itself as the highest point on this path: a point of style.'[29] This rather convoluted fragment seems to deliver a simple message: to achieve the final 'point of style', nations and forms have to undergo a process of evolutionary development.

This idea is developed further in the director's grand theoretical treatise *Method*. In one of the earliest iterations of its structure Eisenstein outlined three key parts: 'I. On Montage', 'II. On Composition', 'III. Summation'.³⁰ The final part, a set of ultimate theoretical conclusions, was preceded by a still-unpublished *Einführung* – German for 'introduction', the term Eisenstein preferred to the Russian *vvedenie*. Strikingly, this text, which summarizes the key aesthetic principles of filmmaking, is dedicated *exclusively* to the question of national form.

In this *Einführung*, Eisenstein set out to unpack the theoretical potential of Stalin's 'national in form, socialist in content', which constituted for the director nothing less than 'the most profound of all that has been said concerning the nature of art', because it 'contains the entire dynamics of interrelation within art as a process, [as well as] within the work of art as an organism'.³¹ To be more precise, its importance lays in alluding to a complex interaction between form and content. This is arguably the pinnacle of the director's theoretical exploration of montage – a formal procedure that makes meaning possible. It also evolves into a key point of reorientation, for such operative principles as evolutionary stages, regress and androgyny, the core of Eisenstein's late theoretical lexicon, are directly linked with it.

Eisenstein starts, as if mirroring his 1939 notes, by stating that national consciousness is an earlier stage of human socio-historical development while socialist consciousness is the highest.³² This continuity implies their interdependence, for the two represent end points on the continuum of historical development. He elaborates: 'From the self-concept of the family the self-consciousness of the clan derives; from it emerges national consciousness; from a reconsideration of the nation, from the class point of view, grows the highest self-consciousness, that of international unity, of working people in their struggle with capitalism, a socialist consciousness emerging in national forms.'³³ National form is framed not as a mere aesthetic category but as an enabling component of social development – it is present in its nascent 'form' at every level of the social relational structure.

Moreover, Eisenstein once again relates this progression to the relationship between form and content – the former precedes the latter and the two are placed on the continuum of evolution: 'Thus, socialism is a certain antecedent [entity] in relation to the national, and the formula tells us through this what is most important regarding the interrelation between form and content. ~~Form is also content~~ Form is older than content by one cycle.'³⁴ Yet again, a slip of the writer's hand establishes an equivalence between form and content that is replaced by an evolutionary relationship. Form precedes content. A few sentences later, Eisenstein elaborates further:

> Content, in a formally disorganized state, is a formulation; while form is content that is articulated one step *behind* in relation to a formulation, which is undeniably the most progressive 'form' of the 'organization' of thought, that is, it is evolutionary stage connected [with], but is of a different degree of correspondence to, content.[35]

This dense wordplay creates a maze of reflexive interrelationships and interdependences. Stadial succession facilitates procedures of both correspondence and difference. Form simultaneously both *is* and *is not* content (and vice versa). This is a significant re-evaluation of the form–content pairing, in that it undermines the hierarchical relationship that marked the official Soviet definition, and even Eisenstein's own early attempts at theorization of the form and content interrelationship.

Such theoretical 'vagueness' intensifies even further at the end of the *Einführung*, which Eisenstein concludes with a rhetorical openness:

> According to the Stalinist formula, we know one thing: form is one step behind in relation to a formulation of content.
>
> That is, the same stage, verbalized in a language that is one phase earlier than the logical language that formulates the thesis.
>
> What kind of language is it? Where should it be found? How to discover it?
>
> Here the formula does not provide a further answer. One has to go through a diversity of real practice, so one can practically arrive to the same position in its analysis: in a theoretical summary, in a theoretical generalization [one has to] once again ascend toward and encounter this primary and foundational formula, which was grasped and articulated in the short thesis: national in form, socialist in content.
>
> We invite the reader to join us on this path.[36]

Eisenstein's own practical application of his theoretical elaborations can be seen in his attempt to find a cinematic equivalent to the Persian-style miniature. In a note written in July 1939 at his dacha in Kratovo, near Moscow, before starting to film material for *Ferghana Canal*, he recalled an earlier 'Persian' project. In 1933, after his return from Mexico, he had expressed interest in adapting Ferdowsi's epic poem *Shāhnāmeh*, seeing that as an 'abreaction' to the unfinished *Que viva México!* – a release of the repressed exotic Mexican material. Since it would most likely have required another trip to a foreign country, while the director's talent was desperately needed in his native land, the head of the State Cinema Corporation, Boris Shumiatsky, intervened to veto the project.

In spite of not being allowed to adapt Ferdowsi for Soviet viewers, Eisenstein did not abandon his interest in Persian miniature style and its cinematic equivalence. While teaching at the State Institute of Cinematography in 1934, he delivered a lecture on this subject. In this, he discussed numerous attempts to use, often mechanically and unsuccessfully, old forms to render new content: for example, such traditional Russian crafts as Palekh lacquer painting or embroidery to depict contemporary industrial scenes.[37] He also referred to Spanish Catholicism, Diego Rivera's use of religious composition in his frescos of proletarian life, and his own engagement with Golgotha and St Sebastian iconography.[38] Clearly, the realization that came to him in Mexico – that aesthetic forms endure and new content can be delivered through them – continued to shape the director's vision and theoretical concerns.

What interested Eisenstein in Persian art related primarily to perspective, as traditional miniaturists did not use foreshortening. Classical Persian miniatures present a system of so-called *vertical* (or isometric) perspective that displays figures as overlapping each other, while elements of the setting, such as lakes or carpets, appear flat on the page. As a consequence, 'nearer' figures are shown below larger figures, and the only way to indicate the relative position of elements in the composition is by overlaying them. The Latin word *perspicere* means 'to see through', whereas the Persian miniature presented a multiplicity of kaleidoscopic gazes directed at the world – a different way of looking.

In his 1934 lecture Eisenstein argued that filmmakers can create the same effect as a Persian miniature by introducing two distinct vanishing points within a shot. To do so he adapts mattes, which are used in special effects filmmaking, to combine two image elements (usually foreground and background) into a single integrated final image. So, by filming the background from a radically vertical point of view, Eisenstein could create an illusion of two incongruent perspectives.[39]

The Ferghana project led Eisenstein to return to this earlier attempt to conceptualize a 'Persian-style shot' that would reproduce the basic stylistic features of Persian miniatures on the film screen. In his 1939 diary notes on the question of national form, he considers illustrating his theoretical elaborations: '*How it ought to be* (illustrations: a foray into examples of resolutions [in the sphere of] the plasticity of the "Eastern" composition of the Uzbek material).'[40] This novel way of (re)presenting reality, corresponding to established 'Eastern' visual practices, was a practical demonstration of the inherent adaptability of formal devices with their ability to travel throughout different times and locations. The stylistic form of the Persian miniature, which had historically influenced certain artistic practices found on the territory of contemporary Uzbekistan, finds renewed life in a different medium and with a different content.

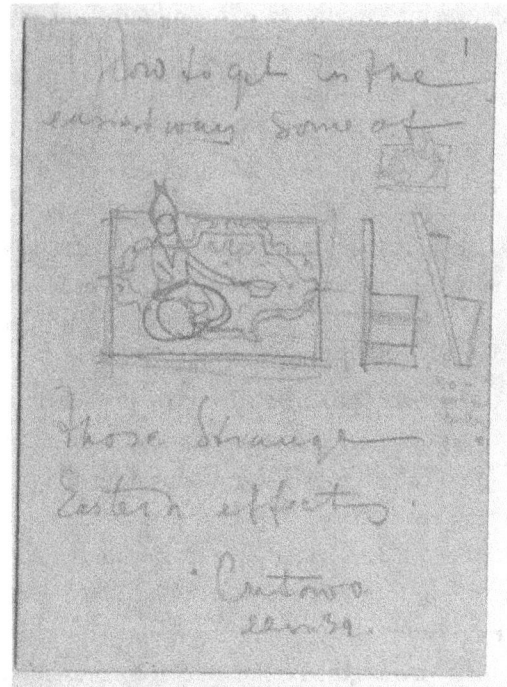

Figure 14.2 'Eastern' effects achieved by placing figures and objects on different 'podiums', either tilted or at various heights. Courtesy of the RGALI.

A set of drawings in the Eisenstein archive presents different visual styles for the three parts of *Ferghana Canal*.[41] 'Eastern'-style images dominate the first part, involving a number of palace interiors which invite this mode of representation. Figures in most of these images are placed at different levels (two, three and even four) and the director proposed a number of solutions for how to achieve the effect of a vertical perspective. An interplay of different visual and spatial scales is another solution Eisenstein discusses extensively and visualizes in his sketches. For some exterior scenes in the first part, he suggests making an intentionally small waterfall, which would create the effect of spatial incongruity; he also suggests setting the camera's field of vision at a wide angle, so the horizon is not visible and the vanishing point cannot be easily located (Figure 14.2).[42]

Eisenstein's engagement with 'Eastern' visual culture was not a mere episode in his rich artistic biography. Rather, it was interconnected with broader aesthetic discourses and remained continuously present throughout the 1930s until his death in 1948. In 1940, for instance, in a speech at the Creative Conference on Problems of Historical and Historical-Revolutionary Film, he argued that historical landscape should be shot as if from a distance, and should include only representative, generalized features.[43] Reality, however, should not be distorted arbitrarily by artists, which amounted to rejecting the avant-garde procedure of 'defamiliarisation' – distorting reality to enhance our perception of it. Generalization, as a mode of abstraction, replaces defamiliarization. To illustrate his point, Eisenstein recollected his visit to Uzbekistan (Figure 14.3), when he realized that the non-naturalistic perspective of Persian-style miniatures actually derives from real experiences of space in which objects are arranged in certain ways:

> If you go to an old, good teashop, and drink tea on the fourth platform up, then you will be able to see all the figures arranged like that sharply defined miniature.
>
> If you ride out to the paddy fields, which are also arranged in terraces, you will get the same impression.
>
> We are all used to the stylised forms of trees in miniatures – circular, oval and so on. But if you go past mulberry trees of a certain period, you will see that they have been pruned in just that way.

Figure 14.3 Eisenstein in an Uzbek teahouse.

[…] In this way, the miniaturists, not having spoiled their eye on other types of painting, were able to look at the special features of points of view which were created around them.[44]

Stylized ways of representing reality, he argues, are deeply rooted in the real experience of space and of the natural environment. Here, the avant-garde finally reconciles itself with 'reality', and the *generalization* of key aspects of the latter replaces its *distortion*.

* * *

On New Year's Eve 1932, soon after his return from Mexico, Eisenstein recorded the following entry in his diary:

> Form as a phase of content – one of the best propositions.
> It encloses a conclusion, made previously: that form is the same idea, expressed by way of atavistic methods and by means of reasoning.
> Let art be … a synthesis.
> A complete triad.
> Thesis – common sense […]
> Antithesis – a step backward in terms of phase of reasoning.
> And synthesis: a marriage of the sharpest consciousness with full-blooded primitiveness.
> This is, of course, the alpha and omega of what can be said and done about art.
> The concept of the idea and of form as stages is astoundingly lucid and complete in its harmony.[45]

Here, Eisenstein brings together some key concepts – evolutionary stages, primitivism, synthesis, and the form and content dichotomy – which would feature prominently in his late theoretical speculations. Later the same day, he resolves to begin working on his 'general method', referred to as 'a system' at this time:

> I have everything. A system in its entirety can be created. It ought [to be created].
> Without fail.
> Mexico?!!
> I challenge myself.
> The challenge has been accepted.[46]

This challenge was indeed taken up, as the section 'Emergence from the Crisis' in *Method* makes clear. Written in a terse asyntactic prose, it posits:

> Form, submerging us with its principles into the very bottomless depths of sensuous thinking.

> An abstractly formulated logically sharpened thesis an idea of content.
>
> And a wondrous alloy of the two in that unity of form and content, which, in a mutual interpenetration, give birth to that which we are accustomed to calling a work of art.
>
> Approaching January 1935, I'm pacified. Cured, confident, convinced.[47]

Interdependence of form and content thus emerges as central to the development of Eisenstein's understanding of art as a system. His Mexican experience, and the series of unrealized projects and intense theoretical work that followed it, proved to be crucial. The historical continuity and the coexistence of archaic and modern ways of life that he witnessed in Central America created an unexpected juncture between the main aesthetic categories of form and content and the new theoretical path of his *Method*. Engagement with the question of national form and socialist content evolved into one of the persistent refrains of his post-Mexico theoretical explorations. The sense of historical continuity, rootedness in the incessant flow of time, something that was absolutely crucial for Eisenstein in the 1930s, culminated in the conviction that new messages could be delivered in archaic forms.

Indeed, one section of *Method*, entitled 'Obsession (Idée fixe)', began with the claim that his discovery of the function of regress contributed to ending the delusion that defamiliarization can help to reveal the 'mystery of form'.[48] Regress becomes a key point of reorientation, moving Eisenstein from his earlier avant-garde convictions, to theorize the practice of montage in modified, yet still unequivocally modernist, terms. The essay then proceeds with a discussion of 'idée fixe', the compulsive, and thus atavistic, appearance of a certain leitmotif as a narrative device. As Eisenstein puts it, 'Such an important element in the construction of things – the principle of the containing of a thing by means of unity of theme – is a direct splinter from the psychological image of a state of "being possessed".'[49] He recalls how different 'obsessive' motifs functioned in his unrealized films: murder in *An American Tragedy*, gold in *Sutter's Gold* and water in *The Ferghana Canal*. The 'failed' projects proved to be productive and the 'failures' led to major discoveries. A few pages later, he analyses the structure of the Ferghana project, emphasizing scenes that would depict Tamerlane's conquest of Urgench by diverting rivers that supplied the city with water. We might conclude that Eisenstein himself diverted the river of his creative talent to irrigate and nourish his theoretical terrain. Although he did not live to see the conclusion of these pursuits, *Method*, though fragmented and unfinished, exists and encourages its readers to continue its author's quest.

Notes

1. Sergei Eizenshtein, 'K voprosy "Natsional'noe po forme, sotsialisticheskoe po soderzhaniiu" (katolitsizm, i iazychestvo, Remy de Gourmont, Elizavetinskie ballady)', in *Metod, tom 2* [*Method*, vol. 2], ed. Naum Kleiman (Moscow: Muzei kino/Eizenshtein-tsentr, 2002), 374–7.
2. Russian State Archive of Literature and Arts (RGALI), 1923-1-1343, l. 19.
3. Sergei Eisenstein, 'The Problem of the Materialist Approach to Form', in *Selected Works, Volume 1: Writings, 1922–1934*, ed. and trans. Richard Taylor (London: BFI Publishing, 1998), 60.
4. Sergei Eisenstein, 'Perspectives', in *Selected Works*, vol. 1, 153–4, italics in the original.
5. Eisenstein, 'Perspectives', 154, emphasis in the original.
6. Eizenshtein, 'K voprosy "Natsional'noe po forme"', 374.
7. Ibid., 375.
8. Ibid., 376.
9. Ibid., 376–7.
10. Sergei Eizenshtein, *Montazh* (Moscow: Muzei Kino, 2000), 92.
11. Museum of Modern Art (MOMA), Eisenstein Collection, folder A ('Que viva México!' Manuscript text with drawings), 1.
12. Ibid., 1–2.
13. Ibid., 8.
14. Sergei Eisenstein, 'The Film about the Fergana Canal', *Studies in Russian and Soviet Cinema* 5, no. 1 (2011): 160.
15. Sergei Eizenshtein, 'Kommentarii k rezhisserskomu stsenariiu fil'ma o Ferganskom kanale', in *Voprosy kinodramaturgii. Vypusk III. Sbornik statei* [Comments on the screen play for the film about Ferghana Canal] (Moscow: Iskusstvo, 1959), 335.
16. RGALI, 1923-1-504, l. 2, and RGALI, 1923-2-199, l. 3.
17. Sergei Eisenstein, 'The Land Has Become Unrecognizable', *Studies in Russian and Soviet Cinema* 5, no. 1 (2011): 160.
18. RGALI, 1923-2-197, l. 2.
19. Eizenshtein, 'Kommentarii k rezhisserskomu stsenariiu fil'ma o Ferganskom kanale', 337.
20. Petr Pavlenko and Sergei Eisenstein, 'The Great Fergana Canal', *Studies in Russian and Soviet Cinema* 5, no. 1 (2011), 131.
21. Ibid., 153.
22. Eizenshtein, 'Kommentarii k rezhisserskomu stsenariiu fil'ma o Ferganskom kanale', 352.
23. Ibid., 352–3.
24. RGALI, 1923-2-1160, line 32, emphasis in the original.

25 Sergei Eizenshtein, 'Montazh 1938', in *Izbrannye proizvedeniia v 6-ti tomach, tom 2* [Selected works in 6 volumes, vol. 2], ed. Pera Atasheva (Moscow: Iskusstvo, 1964), 159.
26 Eizenshtein, 'Kommentarii k rezhisserskomu stsenariiu fil'ma o Ferganskom kanale', 352, my italics.
27 RGALI, 1923-2-1160, l. 35, emphasis in the original.
28 RGALI, 1923-2-1160, l. 33.
29 RGALI, 1923-2-1160, l. 34.
30 Naum Kleiman, 'Problema Eizenshteina', in Sergei Eizenshtein, *Metod, tom 1*, ed. Naum Kleiman (Moscow: Muzei kino/Eizenshtein-tsentr, 2002), 17.
31 RGALI, 1923-2-240, l. 3.
32 RGALI, 1923-2-240, l. 8.
33 RGALI, 1923-2-240, l. 10.
34 RGALI, 1923-2-240, l. 22.
35 RGALI, 1923-2-240, l. 22–3, emphasis in the original.
36 RGALI, 1923-2-240, l. 24–5.
37 RGALI, 1923-2-613, l. 28.
38 RGALI, 1923-2-613, l. 27–30.
39 RGALI, 1923-2-613, l. 33–4.
40 RGALI, 1923-2-1160, l. 34, emphasis in the original.
41 RGALI, 1923-2-198, l. 1–42.
42 RGALI, 1923-2-198, l. 4.
43 Sergei M. Eizenshtein, 'Problemy sovetskogo istoricheskogo fil'ma', in *Izbrannye proizvedeniia v 6-ti tomach, tom 5* [Selected works in 6 volumes, vol. 5], ed. Pera Atasheva (Moscow: Iskusstvo, 1964), 122.
44 Sergei Eisenstein, 'The Problems of the Soviet Historical Film', in *Selected Works, Volume 3: Writings, 1934–1947*, ed. Richard Taylor, trans. William Powell (London: BFI Publishing, 1998), 136.
45 Sergei Eizenshtein, 'Moia sistema' [My system], *Kinovedcheskie zapiski* 36–37 (1997–8): 24.
46 Ibid., 24–5.
47 Sergei M. Eizenshtein, 'Vykhod iz krizisa' [The solution to the crisis], in *Metod*, vol. 1, 138.
48 Sergei M. Eizenshtein, 'Oderzhimost' (Idée fixe)', in *Metod*, vol. 1, 215.
49 Ibid., 223.

March 1949, Melbourne: Eisenstein in Australia

Adrian Danks

Introduction: Screening *Potemkin*

In early March 1949, the Melbourne University Film Society (MUFS) launched its first-ever screening programme with an Orientation Week presentation of Eisenstein's *The Battleship Potemkin* (1925), promoting it as a 'special treat' as well as the 'most powerful and inspired work that the cinema has produced'.[1] Despite the passing of a little over twenty-three years between its initial showings in the Soviet Union and this screening, Eisenstein's landmark film was, nevertheless, a provocative choice at that moment in Melbourne. The MUFS's carefully weighed decision needs to be seen in light of a rising tide of anti-communism, with Australia increasingly taking its lead from the United States in matters of international and even internal politics. It also reflects a cultural climate in which the Minister of Public Information in the state of Victoria (of which Melbourne is the capital) called for the banning of films from communist nations, as well as criticizing the 'use of the [recently formed] State Film Centre for propaganda'.[2] The minister argued that the centre should only import films from countries 'friendly' to the interests of the British Empire, a category to which Eisenstein's film most certainly did not belong.[3]

The burgeoning activities of MUFS and its decision to screen *Battleship Potemkin* also need to be seen in relation to the development of a truly collaborative film society movement in Australia, a movement which had gained momentum from 1946 and developed many of its key components and institutions by 1948 and 1949, as well as the establishment of various leftist and socially progressive organizations, including the highly influential Realist Film Unit (the RFU, formed in late 1945) and the emerging federation of film societies in a number of states. Another key context for this initial screening was the election of the conservative Liberal-Country Party federal government in December of the same year, led by Robert Menzies, which considerably strengthened anti-communist sentiments across the country and unsuccessfully attempted to ban the Communist Party of Australia by various means, including ultimately a divisive federal referendum in September 1951. The rise to power of the Menzies government would also lead to the federal dominance of conservative politics in Australia for the next twenty-three years.[4]

Although the long-delayed Australian release of *Potemkin* should be framed within an emerging leftist film culture and its desire to access key works of the medium for educative, aesthetic and socio-political purposes, organizations such as the RFU and MUFS were also significant for the ways in which they joined these activities to broader community practices to fulfil, as in the manifesto of the Realists, a policy of 'develop[ing] the use of films as a force for social progress, as a weapon in the struggle for peace and socialism'.[5] As a means of achieving this, the RFU screened films in other venues, such as factories and the Brotherhood of St Laurence, as well as in their New Theatre base in Flinders Street in Melbourne's central business district. They also offered special workshops in film appreciation. One symptomatic topic for discussion offered in these workshops was 'Eisenstein's thesis that the principle of montage can be found in the creative process in all arts', demonstrating a focus on contemporary politics, social issues *and* filmmaking.[6] Partly as a result of this, it is possible to see the direct influence of Eisenstein and some of his contemporaries on a small number of filmmaking groups, such as the RFU and the Waterside Workers Federation Film Unit, both of which were producing work partly inspired by classic montage-driven Soviet cinema, as well as Griersonian-style documentary, in the generally moribund local film industry of the 1940s and 1950s.[7]

It also needs to be noted that the Australian censor had only recently passed a 16mm print of *Potemkin* for exhibition at the time of the inaugural MUFS screening. The film's eventual release and screening in 1948, after the print spent a further six weeks in customs, was tied into the campaign in Victoria to defeat the 1948 Cinematograph Films Bill, a draconian piece of legislation that would have severely damaged the emerging film culture ecology of Melbourne and Australia more broadly.[8] This bill was both political and commercial in its motivations – its main supporters were exhibitors and distributors, dominated by powerful US and British interests, which had restricted local production since the 1910s – and it was specifically aimed at the organization that imported *Battleship Potemkin*, the RFU.[9] The bill was introduced into parliament with the following statement: 'It [the bill] may [...] and I hope it will, be a check on the activities of the Realist Film Unit, which up till now has played merry hell with its propaganda exhibitions.'[10]

Eisenstein comes to Australia

Potemkin was finally screened on 22 August 1948. The release of Eisenstein's films in Australia, just six months after the director's death, was reported in the press, particularly in socialist- and communist-affiliated publications.[11] Reflecting broader international patterns of distribution and exhibition, this highlights the specificity of place, the significance of local developments, organizations and transnational connections, and the importance of specific individuals in fighting for the release of particular films.[12] These are patterns that are undoubtedly mirrored in the often-peripatetic release of Eisenstein's films in other countries. For example, although *Potemkin* had famously been shown at the London Film Society in 1929, it was not generally available for screenings in Britain until 1954.[13] Although some reporting around the belated release of *Potemkin* highlighted the supposed creaky antiquity of the film, its reception was more remarkable for the ways in which it noted the still relevant political lessons that the film had to offer, despite being made in 1925 and set during the unsuccessful 1905 Russian revolution. This was partly due to the general paucity of international cinema shown on Australian screens before the early 1950s. For example, in Melbourne in the late 1930s and 1940s only one (and occasionally two) commercial cinemas screened what were commonly called 'continental films', and none provided the formal or political challenges of the work of Eisenstein or even Vsevolod Pudovkin.[14]

At the time of *Potemkin*'s release, the only Eisenstein films to have received limited non-commercial release in Australia were *October* – in a severely cut-down version called *Ten Days That Shook the World*,[15] *Alexander Nevsky*, which was shown at the very end of the Second World War with the support of the United Nations Association, and the first part of *Ivan the Terrible*, with the support of the Australian-Russian Society in 1946.[16] These last two appeared in a period of some optimism for popular leftist or socialist culture in Australia, for which the release of *Potemkin* provides a kind of epitaph. The screenings of each of these films were relatively widely reported in the press, particularly by such communist newspapers as *Tribune* and the *Guardian*, but also received generally positive critical responses across the political spectrum, often to the detriment of mainstream Hollywood cinema, and were seen by large audiences at various makeshift venues such as town halls and at some suburban cinemas. But these occasional screenings also reflect the lack of consistent outlets for such films in Australia, coupled with a recognition of Eisenstein's name and reputation beyond the actual screenings and viewings of his films – as indicated by a bizarre Brisbane *Sunday Mail* profile from April 1945 that identified Eisenstein and Pudovkin as 'millionaires in Moscow'[17] – as well as the widespread desire for a cosmopolitan film culture in Australia. In the process, they provide a clear illustration of the long almost twenty-year 'tail' of Eisenstein's arrival in Australia.[18]

Becoming Eisenstein

One of the most fascinating aspects of the Australian reception of Eisenstein's films before the early 1950s is the way in which particular ideas about the director, his movements in the Soviet Union, Europe, Hollywood and Mexico, and reports on particular projects he was working on – including several which never came to fruition – circulated long before the films did. This was partly due to the highly restrictive censorship in place in Australia, which led to the general banning of most feature films from the Soviet Union: the first reported screening of a Soviet film was something called *In Lenin's Country* in late 1929 and only a handful more were screened throughout the next decade.[19] However, as in many other parts of the world, Viktor Turin's *Turksib* (1929) had a successful release in Australia in the early 1930s, and the compilation film *Modern Russia* was distributed and exhibited by the Friends of the Soviet Union in 1935, preceding their much more contentious attempts to import *Ten Days That Shook the World* the following year. But most knowledge of Soviet cinema in this period, and of Eisenstein in particular, was gleaned from reports of overseas screenings, wire services, influential international publications such as *Close Up*, and from the gradual translation and publication of Eisenstein's writing. Deane Williams has convincingly argued that this 'reception' was generally characteristic of the reiterative or adaptive nature of leftist film culture in Australia during this period.[20] As in New Zealand, few, if any, local commentators or critics had travelled outside their own country, and all were severely hamstrung in their viewing habits and film knowledge by the 'tyranny of distance' and the cartel-like local film exhibition practices.[21] There were several mainstream press references to Eisenstein making *The General Line* in 1929 (a film not shown in Australia until 1949/50), and the difficulties he suffered in aligning the politics of the film with a shifting Stalinist agenda.²² But the first sustained reporting of Eisenstein's work concerned his sojourn at Paramount in 1930, and the compromised production of the subsequent *Que viva México!* This was plainly due to the overwhelming focus on Hollywood production in the general press, as well as the novelty of a notorious Bolshevik being on contract there. These reports routinely referred to Eisenstein's mistreatment by Paramount and by Upton Sinclair, who was central to the financing of his Mexican odyssey, but are also revealing for the ways in which they highlight Eisenstein's manically driven work ethic, his combative and visionary artistic personality, the more abstract qualities of his filmmaking, and the excesses of his distinctive aesthetic, all in the absence of actual evidence from any of the films themselves. One example is a report from the *Sydney Mail* in February 1933: 'Sergei Eisenstein, the most distinguished of Russian film directors, has challenged all moving-picture conventions by making a film which is 200,000 feet in length and would take more than 24 hours to show [...] Photographs of the scenes from the film indicate that it contains passages of exceptional dramatic force and pictorial beauty.'²³ Meanwhile, a writer for *Smith's Weekly*, an influential independent paper of the time, quizzically opined that 'SERGEI EISENSTEIN has done it again, but I suppose it will make no difference to Australian audiences.'²⁴

Throughout these reports, and in later critical responses to the first actual screenings of Eisenstein's films between 1936 and 1948 – reflecting a chronologically jumbled and delayed release of four key films – the filmmaker is uniformly referred to as the world's greatest or 'most imaginative and able modern director'.²⁵ But he remained a figure who Australians had no way of judging or directly experiencing, except through international reports, the evidence of a few reproduced stills, received opinion and Eisenstein's own writings.²⁶ The latter only became more widely available in the late 1930s through the public library system, although were sufficiently regarded for *The Film Sense* to be reviewed at some length in the *Sydney Morning Herald* in 1943.²⁷ Although *Que viva México!* only later emerged in versions never authorized by Eisenstein, its 'reception' in Australia established the key paradigm for the discussion of all of Eisenstein's subsequent work: as a maverick genius out of step with both capitalist and communist orthodoxy; an unparalleled filmmaker championed by many, including Cecil B. DeMille and Douglas Fairbanks; and a potent symbol of the vast terrain of international cinema not shown in Australia due to commercial and ideological interests. He was none the less considered a visual, composite and distinctively cinematic artist who challenged the restrictive commercial realities of filmmaking, exhibition and distribution. At this time, and increasingly later, his work was placed in the vanguard of the push for 'film appreciation', through non-commercial exhibition, distribution and education. This was certainly central to the championing of Eisenstein by the Realist Film Unit/Association as well as the emerging film society movement.

Releasing Eisenstein

Eisenstein's films did largely, if problematically, enter the category of 'classics' in the 1950s, quickly becoming a repertory cinema staple, to the point where MUFS could look back nostalgically and critically on its earlier enthusiasm, and now position the films as works almost exclusively of textbook film history.[28] But it is important to note the extraordinary duration of the period in which his work remained controversial, politically potent, aesthetically challenging and even seemingly threatening to broader Australian society. This is reflected in the 'release' pattern of the films.

The first Eisenstein film to be screened in Australia was *October*, shown as *Ten Days That Shook the World* in late 1936, eight years after its production. Its release profited from the burgeoning leftist cultural movements and organizations (such as the workers clubs) that emerged in the early 1930s. It also satisfied the growing fascination with film as an art form, and chimed with transnational and international developments in film exhibition and distribution centred around companies such as Kino Films, as well as the economic privations of the Depression. Despite the still prohibitive duty charged on all films imported into Australia, the emergence of the lighter and more portable 16mm projection led to liberalization of what could be classed as an exhibition venue, and so made such screenings more possible. It also galvanized protests against censorship. Although some earlier Soviet films such as *The Five-Year Plan* had been banned outright, the public outcry against the federal censor's refusal to allow the release of *Ten Days That Shook the World* set an important precedent for ways in which public support was roused against the censoring of specific movies. The initial ban on the film by the Commonwealth censor of the time, Creswell O'Reilly, was overturned in face of pressure from a broad coalition of leftist and civil liberties groups (similar groups would protest the continued ban on *Potemkin* eleven years later). As often happened, the film ran into further difficulties when local bans were imposed, forbidding screenings in certain civic venues such as the Sydney Town Hall and more widely in Victoria.[29] Although *Ten Days That Shook the World* was screened to large audiences throughout urban, suburban and country Australia, it did not attain a Victoria-wide release until January 1937. In many ways, Melbourne emerges as the most contested and active space in these debates, screening practices and emerging film cultures, a place it has largely retained in the Australian context over the following eighty years.

A key aspect of any local film culture is the presence of individuals who work tirelessly to ensure its continued health and productivity. Many of these may be under-recognized or even 'lost' in overarching histories of national and international film culture. Probably the central figure in Eisenstein's 'story' in Australia, and one of the key people in the development of Australian film culture in the 1930s and 1940s, was Ken Coldicutt, also one of the central contributors to the RFU. He was integral to the struggle to import *Potemkin* and disseminate writings on film history and theory. Coldicutt wrote significant early pieces on Soviet cinema – such as 'Cinema and Capitalism' in 1935, long before he'd seen almost any of the films in question[30] – and was centrally involved in distributing and widely exhibiting *Ten Days That Shook the World*.[31] Subsequently, he became the key figure in the screening activities of the Spanish Relief Committee in 1937, when almost single-handedly he toured the country with a portable 16mm projector showing imported prints. Coldicutt's various activities – including establishing a library, distribution network, bookshop, and organizing film criticism workshops and filmmaking unit – reflect the central importance of Eisenstein's early work to this broadly leftist film culture. Later, Coldicutt was quite dismissive of *Alexander Nevsky* and *Ivan the Terrible*, although as his colleague at the RFU Bob Mathews commented, 'Ken was a product of Eisenstein.'[32] Although the RFU belonged to a broader film society movement – offering a number of realist documentaries, early avant-garde staples, Chaplin shorts, whatever was available from Eastern Europe and war-horse classics such as *Metropolis* (1926), *The Blue Angel* (1930) and, of course, *Turksib* – it is clear that Eisenstein's work, ideas and name became truly talismanic in this period.

Conclusion: Eisenstein's long tail

This chapter has charted the distribution and exhibition of Eisenstein's work in Australia in the 1930s and 1940s, revealing patterns that are specific to this particular country and time, while broadly connected to international trends. I have also tried to clarify Eisenstein's place in an emergent Melbourne film culture during this period, as well as the uses to which his name and films were put. Although he was important for the formation of this culture, his work is not widely seen or discussed today outside academia, and has not been for some time.[33] The programmes of MUFS, the Melbourne Cinémathèque, the Melbourne Film Society and other local cinemas and film societies show Eisenstein virtually disappearing from their schedules after the mid-1960s. There was a partial resurgence in the exhibition of his work in the 1970s, due to the importation of better prints and the discovery of his first film *The Strike*, as well as engagement with more radical film theory inspired by the rise of film studies in the academy, and poststructuralist approaches to cinema and culture more generally. But the partial sidelining of Eisenstein also signifies a break with the politically charged and often leftist 'social-change' agenda of the early film society movement, and a realignment of the film canon in terms of auteurism and other agendas.

Focusing on the first twenty years of the peripatetic exhibition and reception of Eisenstein's work in Australia sheds light on the broader international pattern of his work's reception, and how this depended on a range of factors, including local political conditions, ties to such influential countries as the United States, Britain and the Soviet Union, and the relative balance between art cinema, government support and funding, and the film society movement in a particular cultural ecology. Central to the circulation of Eisenstein's films in Australia was the emergence of leftist political arts organizations in the 1930s, and the development of the film society movement, film education and state film centres in the 1940s. Understanding the motivations and contexts behind the MUFS screening of *The Battleship Potemkin*, together with the 'long tail' of Eisenstein's Australian emergence and his relative contemporary absence from both repertory cinemas and the curriculum, involves bringing to light a wider and deeper history than merely that of the seminal screening in 1949.

Notes

1 'The Battleship Potemkin', *Farrago*, 3 March 1949, 7.
2 Windsor Fick, 'Melbourne's first new wave', in *There is More to Films than the Goldwyn Girls Know*, ed. Quentin Turnour and Windsor Fick (Melbourne: The Melbourne Cinémathèque and the University of Melbourne Archives, 1999), 3.
3 See the statement from Kent Hughes, State Minister for Education, in Deane Williams, *Australian Post-War Documentary: An Arc of Mirrors* (Bristol: Intellect, 2008), 48.

4   Menzies is Australia's longest serving prime minister and between 1939 and 1941 had previously occupied the role as leader of the United Australia Party.
5   See John Hughes, *The Archive Project: The Realist Film Unit in Cold War Victoria* (Melbourne: John Hughes/Early Works, 2013), 47.
6   See Williams, *Australian Post-War Documentary*, 46.
7   For a discussion of this work and the period in general and its relation to leftist culture, see Williams, *Australian Post-War Documentary*. John Hughes's documentary *Film-Work* (1981), which focuses on the Waterside Workers Federation Film Unit and includes a brief moment where Keith Gow outlines this direct influence on productions such as *The Hungry Miles* (1955). Only a handful of fully locally produced feature films were made during this era.
8   The eventual release of the film from customs was reported by Melbourne's *The Age*, 29 July 1948, 3.
9   At this time, the organization was in the process of changing its name to the Realist Film Association to better reflect its commitment to film exhibition as its core activity.
10 See the quotation from John Cremean in Hughes, *The Archive Project*, 52.
11 See, for example, 'Eisenstein was a Genius of Film', *Tribune*, 20 March 1948, 5.
12 A brochure was produced to accompany these screenings titled *Eisenstein and Potemkin* and included reprinted essays by Léon Moussinac and Ivor Montagu and extended quotations from various writers including C. A. Lejeune and Ernest Lindgren.
13 See Henry K. Miller, 'From *Battleship Potemkin* to *Drifters*', in *The Soviet Influence: Battleship Potemkin and Drifters*, DVD Booklet (London: British Film Institute, 2012), 1.
14 See Albert Moran, 'Alternative Exhibition: Non-mainstream Film Venues in Australia', in *A Century of Australian Cinema*, ed. James Sabine (Port Melbourne: William Heinemann, 1995), 112–29.
15 See, for example, '*Ten Days*: Dramatic Soviet film', *The Argus*, 25 January 1937, 4. Nevertheless, the writer still acclaims the screening of the film at the New Imperial, stating that 'such defects, however, can't detract from the fine qualities of "Ten Days"', and that the film 'represents a standard that Hollywood has sacrificed to "stars and box-office"'.
16 *Ivan the Terrible* was often shown to celebrate particular occasions. It was screened to mark Red Army Day in Perth in 1946, for instance.
17 Ralph Hewins, 'There are Plenty of Millionaires in Moscow', *The Sunday Mail Magazine*, 15 April 1945, 3. This article was syndicated from London's *Daily Mail*.
18 Eisenstein never visited Australia or appeared to offer any comment upon it or the fate of his films there. The one concrete reference to Australia found in his work, in English translation at least, is his discussion of 'the kangaroo'

in *Nonindifferent Nature*, trans. Herbert Marshall (Cambridge: Cambridge University Press, 1987), 184–6.
19 The actual identity and even proper name of this film is difficult to determine.
20 Williams, *Australian Post-War Documentary*, 26. The author writes specifically here about the film criticism of Ken Coldicutt, a figure I will discuss later in this chapter.
21 For a fascinating and detailed account of this film culture environment in New Zealand, see Simon Sigley, *Transnational Film Culture in New Zealand* (Bristol: Intellect, 2013). According to Sigley, the first Soviet film reported to have been screened in New Zealand was *Road to Life* (Nikolai Ekk, 1931) in July 1933. The *Battleship Potemkin* had its first screening on 21 October 1946 at the Wellington Town Hall (Sigley, *Transnational Film Culture in New Zealand*, 43).
22 See '*The General Line*: Eisenstein's new film', *The Daily News*, 9 November 1929, 3. This article was also published in *The Canberra Times*.
23 G. M. L., 'At the Pictures', *Sydney Mail*, 15 February 1933, 15.
24 S. C. W., 'Eisenstein's Latest', *Smith's Weekly*, 28 January 1933, 10.
25 Neville de Lacy, 'Russian Films to Replace Propaganda with Entertainment', *Sunday Mail*, 21 April 1935, 22.
26 Eisenstein's books were later widely advertised in various leftist publications.
27 R. G. H., 'The Film of the Future', *The Sydney Morning Herald*, 20 November 1943, 6.
28 This is characteristic of much of the writing in the publications produced by MUFS in the 1950s and 1960s such as *Annotations on Film*.
29 See, for example, the December 1936 ban placed on screenings of the film at the Sydney Town Hall before being moved the Majestic Theatre in Newtown. 'Censor Bans Notable Soviet Film', *The Daily Telegraph*, 5 October 1936, 1.
30 Ken Coldicutt, 'Cinema and Capitalism', *Proletariat: University Labor Club Magazine* (April–June 1935), 11–15.
31 A detailed account of Coldicutt's activities around the release of this film and others can be found in an unpublished article titled 'The Use of Film by the Left in Australia – A Personal Summary', held by the University of Melbourne Archives.
32 Interview with Mathews in John Hughes's essay film, *The Archive Project* (2006).
33 For example, the Melbourne Cinémathèque, the organization that emerged out of MUFS in 1984, has only screened a single season and couple of one-off sessions dedicated to Eisenstein over the last thirty-five years. This is an organization I have been involved with as co-curator and president since the late 1980s.

16

How to Curate Eisenstein?

Oksana Bulgakowa

Many years ago, I wrote an article, 'Comment éditer Eisenstein' (How to Edit Eisenstein).[1] My intention was not to indicate that I knew how to do it; rather, to understand how the selection of Eisenstein's texts and their composition (and in this sense, their interpretation) was dictated by discursive modes of the time, such as semiotics, intertextuality, Lacanian psychoanalysis, deconstruction, the visual, spatial and anthropological turns. Published collections of Eisenstein's work constantly 're-created' Eisenstein and reflecting a changing understanding of his personality and theoretical legacy. In the early 1960s, these 're-creations' were mainly memoirs that fitted into the wave of the Soviet Thaw, like Ilya Ehrenburg's *People, Years and Life* (1962), which rehabilitated the avant-garde and its artists who had been eradicated from public discourse for three decades, or to the narcissistic self-reflexivity of existentialist autobiographies such as Jean-Paul Sartre's *Les mots* (*The Words*) (1963). In Russia, Eisenstein's memoirs were first published in the literary magazine *Znamia* and then republished in the first volume of his *Selected Works*.[2]

The German edition of *Schriften*, compiled by Hans-Joachim Schlegel, was based on another principle: its four volumes organized Eisenstein's writings around four silent films, giving the impression that Eisenstein's theory arose directly as an appendix to his cinematic, socially active practice.[3] This edition followed the very common idea of presenting Eisenstein's key works, the masterpieces – a very popular conception of exhibition practice ever since. Eisenstein's works were read through the double frame of structuralism and Marxism. At that time, structuralism was seen as saving the humanities by providing the objectivity of an exact discipline, explaining both the structure of society and the structure of the text. Eisenstein was read unambiguously as a leftist structuralist and an early semiotician, and this understanding ensured interest in him at home and in the West.

In 1980s, French, Italian and English Eisenstein editions used a different approach, moving from structuralism to psychoanalysis and cultural studies, discourses that replaced semiotics. Eisenstein's texts on the fine arts fitted a new model: the problematization of the gaze, corporeality and space. Michel Foucault, discovered in Russia in the 1990s, directed the interest of researchers to problems of the body, power and sexuality, and towards Eisenstein's diaries, which could shed light on these subjects. However, a new discursive and editorial mode was on the way. Giorgio Colli's and Mazzino Montinari's critical edition of Friedrich Nietzsche, *Sämtliche Werke*, the publication of Aby Warburg's unfinished atlas *Mnemosyne* and Walter Benjamin's fragmented *Arcades* offered a view of the text as a field of writing and rewriting, with corrections, variations, references, marginalia, drawings and doodles.[4] The editors of these works had to deal with non-linear manuscripts and often presented them as facsimiles, which provoked uncertainty about how to read them – from left to right, like a book, or from the centre to the periphery, like an image? Eisenstein fitted into this new mode with his unfinished work *Method* (1932–48), a gigantic fragment made up of a conglomerate of quotes and notes – a text constantly deformed by the author, which could be understood as his comments on his own outline.

This editorial practice is closely related to how Eisenstein exhibitions have been staged. In this chapter, I look at how Eisenstein has been curated and what the subjects and concepts of these shows, the selection of materials and the principles of display convey about an understanding of Eisenstein, curatorial fashions and *Zeitgeist*.

I begin this discussion by referring to an exhibition that was not dedicated to Eisenstein, but rather reflected the contemporaneous state of film and photography: *Film and Photography* (commonly known as *FiFo*). First shown in Stuttgart in 1929 before travelling to Zurich, Berlin, Danzig and Vienna, *FiFo* was one of the first-ever multimedia shows. El Lissitzky designed the Soviet section and involved Eisenstein in its preparation. A duoskope, an apparatus patented in 1922 that allowed advertising films to be shown on a loop of about 10–15 minutes' length at department stores, occupied a prominent place in the Soviet hall, according to historical photographs. Several reviewers reported that Eisenstein clips were shown continuously on a duoskope.[5]

FiFo was a new form of exhibition that not only offered a sensuous visual experience but also created an abstraction, presenting ideas transmitted via images, connecting objects through a narrative that the museum visitor had to discover by themselves. The strategy was challenging – it forced visitors to combine different activities: walking, perceiving static and moving images, reading and thinking. The flow of images in the exhibition was influenced by a filmic model similar to Eisenstein's intellectual montage, releasing associations, triggering a movement of thought from one shot to another, and producing meaning out of the juxtaposition and collision of images.[6] While Eisenstein was testing the order of images in his montage, the exhibition and book designers tried to structure the world's visual variety as it had been in cross-sectional films such as Walter Ruttmann's *Berlin: Symphony of a Great City* (1927) and August Sander's series *Faces of Our Time* (1929), and in photo montages in new magazines such as the German *Querschnitt*.[7] This principle was also transmitted into the construction of the text which delivered a montage of fragments, quotations and pictures to make the message self-evident. In *Arcades*, Walter Benjamin described this method as: 'I have nothing to say. Only to show.'[8]

The second Eisenstein exhibition was also ahead of its time. In 1932, the Becker Gallery in New York presented only Eisenstein's Mexican drawings; these were put on sale at Sotheby's, London, by his heirs in 1989.

In later exhibitions, Eisenstein's curators have moved away from the presentation of his works in chronological order, documenting the development of the master in a kind of temporal sequence, to the demonstration of causal connections of selected motifs and abstract ideas (a synthesis of arts), and to the creation of different contexts for Eisenstein's oeuvre (from cave paintings to the avant-garde). Curators have looked for new ways to organize the exhibition space and materials within it: they have used video installations, staged space as an intertext or metatext, and concentrated on films, graphic works or the totality of his work. Thus, how Eisenstein has been exhibited has depended on the political situation, changing exhibition practices, technological innovations and the understanding of film's place within the fine arts.

First steps

The first Eisenstein exhibition took place ten years after his death at the Moscow House of Art Workers in 1957/8 in anticipation of the release of the second, previously censored, part of *Ivan the Terrible* (1958). The exhibition presented photographs, stills, film posters, drawings, story boards and manuscripts and can be seen in Vasilii Katanian's documentary *Sergei Eisenstein* (1958). In 1958, during the Brussels World Fair, *The Battleship Potemkin* was listed as one of the twelve best films ever produced. The international rediscovery of Eisenstein continued with an Eisenstein week in East Berlin in April 1959, which included a retrospective, a conference at the Academy of the Arts (with the participation of Maxim Shtraukh, Sergei Yutkevich, Jay Leyda, Rostislav Yurenev and Jerzy Toeplitz) and an exhibition that included three hundred drawings, presented at the House of German-Russian Friendship. The modest exhibition catalogue mentioned the Brussels listing of *The Battleship Potemkin* and celebrated Eisenstein as a great artist of the revolution. The drawings were selected by Pera Atasheva and reviewed in the art magazine *Bildende Kunst* by the art critic Kurt Schifner, who called them 'image-stenogramms' (*Bild-Stenogramme*).[9]

This selection (with small variations) travelled though the European capitals. Three hundred of Eisenstein's drawings were shown together with enlarged stills and posters at the Cinémathèque Française in 1960,[10] in the Cineteca Italiana in Milan in 1961,[11] in London at the V&A in 1963,[12] and then in Leverkusen in 1963–4.[13] A reduced version of 150 drawings was exhibited during the film festivals in Venice in 1972 and Locarno in 1982,[14] and at the Netherlands Film Museum in 1979.[15] In 1972, a full retrospective of Eisenstein's films and a large exhibition were presented by the Amsterdam Film Museum and the Stedelijk Museum (Figure 16.1).

In 1973 Naum Kleiman curated an Eisenstein exhibition in Tokyo, which was staged over two levels in the old department store Matsuzakaya, using drawings, stills, manuscripts, costumes and artefacts from Eisenstein's apartment museum in Moscow (Figure 16.2).

Kleiman also curated the first conceptual exhibition for the Academy of the Arts in East Berlin in 1970, which was later repeated at the Academy of the Arts in West Berlin (Figure 16.3). In this exhibition, a chronological approach was abandoned in favour of focusing on a few motifs. The show celebrated Eisenstein as a visionary artist who was looking for the synthesis of all arts, for correspondences between light, space, colour and music in the audiovisual counterpoint. The East and West Berlin exhibitions also presented a recent reconstruction of the previously forbidden and subsequently lost film *Bezhin Meadow* (1937/68). Sergei Yutkevich and Naum Kleiman made a stills montage out of frames saved from the editing table, along with the stills and sketches for the second part of *Ivan the Terrible* (also censored in 1946) and a storyboard for a colour film about Pushkin titled *The Loves of a Poet*.[16] The unrealized Pushkin project provided not only colour correspondences on the level of the plot development but also touched on the conflict of the poet with power and censorship. Through this exhibition, the image of Eisenstein as a revolutionary artist changed to that of Eisenstein as a censored artist.

Figure 16.1 Exhibition in Amsterdam, 1972.

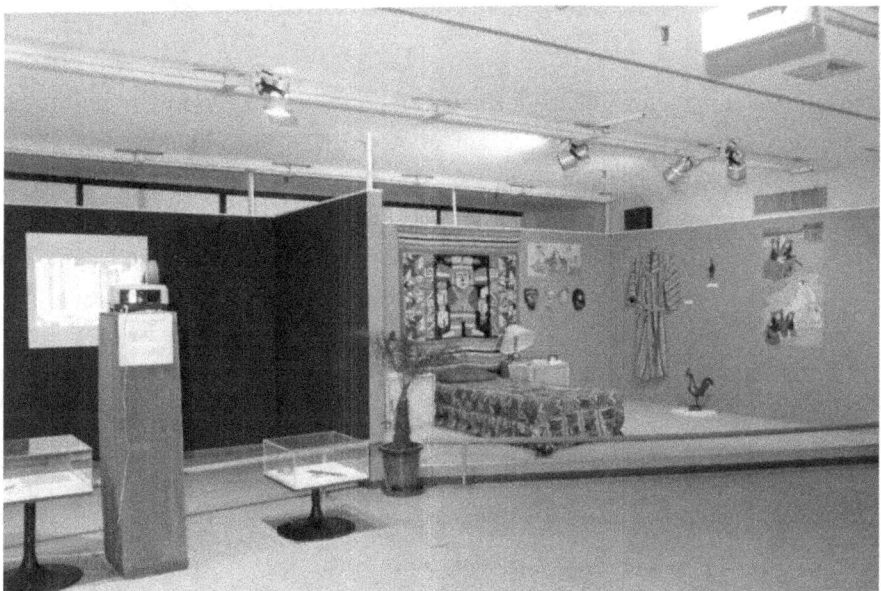

Figure 16.2 Exhibition in Tokyo, 1973.

Figure 16.3 Exhibition in West Berlin, 1971.

All these early shows lasted for between ten days and two weeks, published only small brochures, and were not photographed and documented. On a methodological level, they revealed the problem: how to present film through non-filmic material, such as programmes, stills, posters, costumes, film techniques and memorabilia? Federico Fellini once said to Pier Marco De Santi:[17] 'There is nothing sadder and more sclerotic than banishing film into a museum. The cinema museums look like cemeteries. Nobody goes there. Nobody visits them. They are dusty and terrifying. They are like a retirement home for old people.'[18] For Fellini, film was a spectacular dream which cannot and must not be approached with the tools and methods of traditional museology; he fantasized about something like a theme park. However, unlike Fellini, Eisenstein was not connected to popular culture, at least to the popular culture known in the West. Instead, he was the face of Soviet communist political ideas.

The first of the 1970s Eisenstein exhibitions took place in an art museum, presenting Eisenstein as a visual artist who directed films, rather than as a director who drew. Three institutions followed this principle in 1978. In Mexico City, the Cineteca Nacional exhibited Eisenstein's Mexican drawings from their own collection. In Lyon, the Musée des Beaux-Arts presented the show *Eisenstein 1848–1948, suite de dessins*, curated by Hélène Laroche from the France-URSS Society. This was subsequently shown at the Centre Pompidou in Paris; however, it was not placed in the prestigious space of Musée de l'Art Modern, but at the rather marginal CCI (Centre de Creation Industriel), which no longer exists.[19] The selection of 150–152 drawings was similar to the earlier Eisenstein exhibitions and the drawing cycles were still mixed with costumes and set designs, storyboards and preparatory sketches for the films. However, the space helped to contextualize Eisenstein as an original draughtsman with a distinctive style.

At that time, art museums were starting to use film loops (as photochemical prints or transferred to video tapes) in their displays. In 1972, Harald Szeemann was appointed curator of *documenta* 5. Szeemann radically rethought the possibilities of curatorial practice, urging colleagues not to simply assemble items but to conceive of an exhibition as a total work of art. Szeemann's famous 1983 show *Der Hang zum Gesamtkunstwerk* was centred around a utopian idea of how a broad range of artists – Wagner, Gaudi, Steiner, Appia, D'Annunzio, Kandinsky, Scriabin, Schönberg, Mondrian, Schwitter, Duchamp, Picabia, Cage, Beuys, Broodthaers, Syberberg, Nitsch and Kiefer – combined art and social practice. The exhibition travelled from Zurich to Vienna, Berlin and Düsseldorf, where it was shown between May and June of 1983. Six months later, from 3 September to 2 October, the Düsseldorf Kunsthalle presented Eisenstein in a similar manner – as an artist with a clear attraction to the total work of art that defined the concept of the show itself.

Eisenstein as *Gesamtkunstwerk*

Two exhibitions in art museums tried to embrace the 'whole' Eisenstein; however, they did so with different accents – on the ecstatic and on the eccentric. The Düsseldorf show presented Eisenstein as a political artist of the revolution and as a synthesizing genius; as a Leonardo da Vinci of the twentieth century who made caricatures, theatre and opera productions, worked as a set and costume designer, created film masterpieces, drew storyboards and mise en scène sketches, but was also a gifted draughtsman (without any dealer's contract). In his graphic cycles, he reworked nostalgic impressions from Mexico and Berlin, pursued mythological motifs and transformed iconic biblical images of Golgotha, Salome, John the Baptist and Saint Veronica. Naum Kleiman worked on the exhibition together with Ulrich Krempel, an art historian and curator, then director of the Sprengel Museum in Hanover.

Kunsthalle Düsseldorf was an important institution at this time, whose superintendent Jürgen Harten curated significant exhibitions of contemporary painting as well as the Russian avant-garde (like the first Malevich exhibition in Germany in 1980) and totalitarian art in Europe (in 1987). *Example Eisenstein: Drawing Theatre Film* tried to convey how Eisenstein's biography, arts and politics anticipated the idea of a synthesis of the arts – a Soviet answer to the recent big exhibition staged by Szeemann. The show united film posters, stills, enlarged photograms, costumes for *Ivan the Terrible*, memorabilia, film clips and 260 drawings. The sections were structures within the political paradigm of the time: the struggle against totalitarianism. The curators tried to cover every possible aspect of Eisenstein's work – childhood drawings, projects in Meyerhold's workshop, theatrical productions, masterpieces of the silent period (his revolutionary tetralogy), the Mexican film and Mexican drawings. His drawings *Nothing* and *Despair* – tortured, flowing figures without heads that formed pyramids and circles, produced in the years of the Great Terror (1937–9) – were presented under the label 'Antifascism'; *Alexander Nevsky* was displayed as a prophetic vision of history; and the sketches for *Valkyrie* as anti-fascist interpretation of Wagner. During Eisenstein's career his film style changed considerably, but not the style of his drawings and the curators had to deal with these contrary developments.

The overlap of arts and politics in Eisenstein's practice acquired an unexpected resonance in 1983. Two days before the opening, on 1 September 1983, a plane of the Korean Airlines flew into Russian airspace and crossed over the Kamchatka Peninsula, where secret Soviet military installations were located. The passenger jet did not respond to messages and was shot down. The reception of the Eisenstein show in Germany was overshadowed by this tragic event and the reactions it triggered.

The second exhibition was *Eisenstein 1898–1948: His Life and Work*. Curated by Ian Christie and David Elliott at the Museum of Modern Art in Oxford, before travelling to London and Manchester,[20] this show took place at a much more favourable political moment. In 1988, Perestroika was under way, generating widespread interest in all things Russian. This exhibition moved away from Eisenstein's old politicized image, tied to a Stalinist or anti-Stalinist position. Instead, Christie and Elliott, who had made his name as a curator of contemporary art,[21] tried to trace the roots of Eisenstein's creativity in eccentrism and staged their exhibition with a deliberately eccentric touch. The recently discovered film

Glumov's Diary was shown and the museum reconstructed the theatre design for *The Wise Man* as a 3D model. A life-size photograph of Eisenstein shaking hands with Mickey Mouse was placed at the entrance of the exhibition and a comically suggestive photograph of Eisenstein astride a Mexican cactus that he had sent to Ivor Montagu became a highly recognizable image, afterwards almost a brand (Figure 16.4). The 3D display adopted the eccentric gestures and theatralized space of the British Film Institute's recently opened Museum of the Moving Image, a space which presented film as experience.

These were the first and last exhibitions that tried to encompass the 'whole' Eisenstein. After this, attempts to represent the totality of his work and life were considered passé. After the very successful blockbuster exhibitions of the Russian avant-garde (*Paris–Moscow, 1900–1930* in 1979 and *The Great Utopia: 1915–1932* in 1992), a wave of exhibitions on totalitarian art travelled through Europe. Eisenstein exhibitions also shifted focus with the rediscovery of further unexpected aspects in Eisenstein: his erotic, queer, mystical and mischievous sides. Drawings from the private collection of Svetlana and Rauf Akchurina were presented in Moscow in 1998 and in Budapest and Pecs in 1995 and 2005.[22] In 1999, Jean-Claude Marcadé and Galia Ackerman published *Dessins secret* (Secret Drawings), a part of Alloy's collection. In 2006, the exhibition *A*

Figure 16.4 *Eisenstein: His Life and Work*, Museum of Modern Art, Oxford, 1988.

Figure 16.5 *Unexpected Eisenstein*, GRAD, London, 2016.

Mischievous Eisenstein, which featured a number of Eisenstein's erotic drawings, ran as part of the Cannes International Film Festival, motivated, perhaps, by the lesbian, gay, bisexual and transgender (LGBT) movement's desire to find legitimation through association with many celebrated artists of the twentieth century.

Other specific exhibitions included the 2016 *Unexpected Eisenstein* in the GRAD Gallery, London, curated by Ian Christie and Elena Sudakova (Figure 16.5), exploring Eisenstein's significant yet often overlooked relationship with England. Earlier, the exhibition organized to celebrate Eisenstein's centenary at the Berlin Academy of the Arts in 1998, *Glass House, Valkyrie*, aimed to explore his German connections, and projects such as his collaboration with Edmund Meisel and conception of expressive movement in the context of German schools of thought.[23]

Graphic artist

In the next wave of exhibitions, curators returned to Eisenstein as a graphic artist of pure form, specifically, line. This emancipation first happened in two group exhibitions. In 1990, Eisenstein was presented with other Soviet film directors including Alexandr Dovzhenko, Lev Kuleshov, Sergei Parajanov and Yuri Il'enko in the show *From Eisenstein to Tarkovsky* at the Lenbach House, Munich.[24] In 1993, the New York exhibition *Drawing into Film* placed Eisenstein's storyboards alongside those of such directors as Alfred Hitchcock, Federico Fellini, Rainer Werner Fassbinder and Tim Burton.[25]

In 2000, Eisenstein was finally celebrated in a solo exhibition at the Drawing Center in New York that later travelled to the Ex-Centris, Montreal. *The Body of the Line* was curated by Jean Gagnon and sponsored by the Daniel Langlois Foundation, an institution that supports artists working in new media, which was demonstrated through the decision to publish the catalogue as an interactive CD. The exhibition's focus was placed on a specific style of drawings developed by Eisenstein that was characterized by what he called animated plasmatic linearity.[26] The preparatory sketches for *Ivan the Terrible* were meant to be perceived here as independent graphic works, but the display had a clear cinematic reference, with the walls in the white cube of the gallery painted black, the line of drawings resembled a strip of film.

In 2009, *Sergei Eisenstein: The Mexican Drawings* in Antwerp, curated by Anselm Franke and myself, took a different approach. The selection of drawings and their display highlighted Eisenstein's graphic cycles; for example, *Duncan's Death* was displayed as a development in sequence, allowing viewers to follow the process of drawing. Series of agonizing deaths, violence and obscenity, such as bullfights, images of Macbeth, Werther and Salome were interlaced with depictions of Mexican life and biblical contents. Eisenstein practised in these sketches a kind of *écriture automatique*, a flood stemming from the graphic unconscious, producing a large number of variations (up to 150 sheets with a recurring motif) based on Mexico's hybrid imagery, which he treated like an historical tableau of junctures and simultaneities. In an uninterrupted dynamic line, he explored principles of the transformation of forms. The technique of contour drawing – for Eisenstein a medium to explore states of ecstasy and the relationship between stasis and mutation – was marked in these cycles by the coexistence of geometric forms and amorphous lines.[27]

The decision to hold an Eisenstein exhibition was notable as the Antwerp Gallery Extra City, the former industrial area transformed into an art space, presented only conceptual art, and Anselm Franke was known as a curator of new media. However, the discovery of Eisenstein as an emancipated graphic artist was very soon put into a new perspective, influenced by intertextuality and intermediality.

Intertexts and cross media

The entanglement of arts and politics that influenced Eisenstein exhibitions in the 1970s and 1980s was replaced in the 1990s by a new framework: a focus on the links between film, arts and media, and, later, by film, arts and sciences. In this period, curators tried to uncover Eisenstein's connection to visual culture, starting from cave paintings. Dominique Païni, who was the director of the Cinémathèque Française from 1991 to 2000, put together a series of exhibitions establishing parallels between cinema and other arts, which included *L'Art et le 7 e art* (Monnaie de Paris, Musée des Beaux-Arts de Tourcoing, 1995); *Hitchcock et l'art, coïncidences fatales* (Centre Pompidou, Paris; Musée des Beaux-Arts, Montreal, 2012) and *Antonioni e le arti* (Palazzo dei Diamanti, Ferrara, 2013).[28]

At the beginning of the twenty-first century, this approach began to look at the parallels between film and the arts from different perspectives. On the one hand, film began to be seen as a continuation of the fine arts in a new mass-culture form, which could be evaluated and ennobled by being exhibited side by side with classical painting. On the other hand, film was increasingly perceived as a living archive of visual memory that cannibalized not only the old arts but also advertisements and pop culture and produced powerful iconic images. For younger generations, film – not the museum – became a storehouse of visual culture, before being displaced by graphic novels, manga, digital platforms and social media, where a museum's pictures function as backgrounds for selfies. Eisenstein exhibitions anticipated this trend.

In 1992, the Frankfurt Film Museum presented Eisenstein in the context of the Soviet avant-garde, including his work with Mayakovsky's ROSTA and his set design for the play *Mystery-Bouffe*, Rodchenko's constructions, collages and photographs, El Lissitzky's sketches for *Victory Over the Sun*, Liubov Popova's paintings, the Stenberg brothers' posters and set designs by the Vesnin brothers. The show celebrated Eisenstein's connections with Russian constructivism, Meyerhold's eccentric theatre and the Left Front.[29] The enthusiastic art history students Sebastian Deisen, Britta Grütter, Ursula Haberkorn and Ralf Hutzler curated this elaborate exhibition and included stills and clips from Eisenstein's films and 39 of Eisenstein's drawings amid 139 items coming from different institutions.[30] The exhibition's design was theatralized, including a set design imitating some parts of *The Battleship Potemkin*. However, even at the time of its opening the approach of this exhibition was already outdated, with curators elsewhere starting to look for new structures. Understanding of the relationship between film and fine arts has changed, and become connected to the practice of such filmmakers as Peter Greenaway and Harun Farocki, who have presented their video works in a gallery space. Video and film installations became an obligatory part of museums, and cinema exhibitions found themselves in a new universe: they were now part of contemporary art. Eisenstein was rediscovered once more, not only as an intertextual but also an intermedial artist, and henceforth his exhibitions had to be informed by the development of contemporary art.

In 2016 to 2018, *Proof: Francisco Goya, Sergei Eisenstein, Robert Longo* (Garage, Moscow; Brooklyn Museum, New York; Deichtorhallen, Hamburg), curated by Kate Fowle and Robert Longo, explored the relationship between the artist and power in the time of historical cataclysms (wars, revolutions and violence).[31] But, their display was focused on different medial embodiments of the subject and on relationship between different media, with forty of Eisenstein's drawings and clips from his films in slow motion juxtaposed with Goya's etchings and gigantic abstract works by Longo.[32]

In *Ejzenštejn – La rivoluzione delle immagini*, the Uffizi Gallery, Florence, similarly contrasted Eisenstein's images with Italian art of the late Middle Ages and early Renaissance.[33] The selection of seventy-two drawings, all from the State Archives of Literature and Art in Moscow, was based on two principles: the autonomy of his graphic art and the same style of drawing, characterized by a linearity. The drawings were arranged as photograms and presented through the display in dialogue with film clips. They ran in close rows along the large walls in Sale di Levante, although the big screens with moving images dominated the vitrines with small drawings.

The exhibition *Montage of Attractions* at the Moscow Multimedia Art Museum, curated by Olga Sviblova and Anna Zaitseva, was even more radical, staging space as an intertext or metatext.[34] The curators explored two topics: the affective power of the masses and the charismatic power of leaders. On the first floor, numerous screens of many sizes presented images of crowds from *The Strike*, *Potemkin* and *October*, whose chaotic movement was charged with high energy that threatens to destroy everything, yet was also full of apocalyptic excitement and contagious euphoria. The second floor displayed gigantic close-ups from *Alexander Nevsky* and *Ivan the Terrible* as well as small photographs of the *Die Walküre* rehearsals from the Museum of the Bolshoi Theatre, rare drawings from the Bakhrushin Museum, Eisenstein portraits taken by famous photographers, and private memorabilia such as a reticule and earrings. The earrings (a present from Eisenstein to Marianna Stroeva, the daughter of his friend who worked as his assistant, were inscribed 'Do not cast pearls and make the mistake of your teacher') were shown along the walls of darkened galleries under special lighting. The digital presentation of the film clips was central, with other media displayed on the margins, producing an impression of the remains of private life, of an intimate retreat, where people (and exhibition visitors) could escape from the ever-present crowds and tyrants.

The Eisenstein exhibition at the Centre Pompidou-Metz, *L'Œil extatique: Serguei Eisenstein, cinéaste à la croisée des arts*, curated by Ada Ackerman and Philippe-Alain Michaud, which ran from September 2019 to February 2020, used the same principle of space staged as a metatext but pursued another goal (Figure 16.6). The curators combined two contradictory tendencies: popularizing Eisenstein and uncovering his specific relation to the fine arts. Along with Eisenstein portraits and drawings, they also presented his most impressive and expressive film clips, following a chronological trajectory and encompassing all his films, as well as the unrealized project *The Glass House* (1926–9). But, at the same time, the curators created intertextual and intermedial connections between Eisenstein's imagery and paintings, engravings, etchings, sculptures, posters and collages. Montage was the main principle that organized the juxtapositions. Sometimes the references were

Figure 16.6 *L'Œil extatique: Serguei Eisenstein, cinéaste à la croisée des arts*, Centre Pompidou-Metz, September 2019–February 2020.

suggested by Eisenstein's writing – Piranesi and Japanese prints admired and analysed in his texts, Grandville's animals, Frank Lloyd Wright's and Mies van der Rohe's architectural sketches, Posada's prints, the frescos and painting of the Mexican painters. Sometimes the references were deciphered or drawn by the curators. A stair passage from *The Strike* was presented in the middle of Piranesi's *Prisons*. Michelangelo's sculpture was surrounded by *Potemkin's* sailors. The format illustrated that Eisenstein not only referred to the rich context of visual culture but also created new iconic images, which have been reproduced many times.

These exhibitions worked through all possible media, producing an unprecedented effect, and making the process of perception self-reflexive: film animated sculpture, painting and architectural sketches; moving images could be seen in a new way through 'frozen' moments on engravings, prints, photographs or drawings; music opened another dimension, switching from image to sound; and different media illuminated and sometimes eliminated each other.

Multimedia Eisenstein exhibitions have juxtaposed two types of perception: the contemplation of static images and the hypnotic effect of moving images. They have made Eisenstein part of a new conceptual art; however, visitors have had to deal with the usual problems connected to installations where the apparatus changes and, to paraphrase Deleuze, the time-image is replaced by a space-image. As visitors can move freely, unlike film spectators, the sense of space becomes different according to their choice of perspective. This subjective activity has consequences, since the installation constantly produces an insecurity in the viewer because of its temporal openness. Work becomes in principle fragmentary and incomplete – the number of components that should be considered as meaningful is not defined, and the viewer is confronted with a need to find meaning beyond the Kuleshov effect.

Virtual exhibitions

The uncertainty of viewers' experiences is avoided in virtual exhibitions, which were the first explorations of intertextual and intermedial connections in Eisenstein's oeuvre, before curators made their moves in the real space of the museum. The first exhibition of this kind was on DVD, with Yuri Tsivian's multimedia essay on Eisenstein's visual vocabulary made for the Criterion edition of *Ivan the Terrible* (2001), in which he compared Eisenstein's images with paintings by Holbein and Botticelli as well as alchemical and masonic symbols. Tsivian also traced the developments of some visual motifs in the films (such as coins, swans, shadows, gestures and mise en scène). In 2000, the Daniel Langlois Foundation released the web publication *The Visual Universe of Sergei Eisenstein*, dedicated to one of Eisenstein's early sketchbooks dating from 1914, when he was sixteen years old.[35] On this web page that I developed, I examined the recognizable influences, references and quotes in the sketchbook, and made a discovery: the motifs and forms elaborated by the teenager just graduating from school were recognizable in the subsequent imagery and drawings of the fifty-year-old world-famous film director. His circular men and angular old women, masks from the *commedia dell'arte* and elongated plasmatic levitating figures, his bestiary (bulls, peacocks, lions and ravens) reappeared in his work at different stages and in different media: photographs, moving images, sets and costumes for the eccentric theatre productions and Wagner opera, in the physiognomic types, in the series of his later erotic, nostalgic, parodistic drawings. This web page traced these connections as well as Eisenstein's affinity with both old and contemporary painting. The sources of his first book of 150 drawings – Grandville's man-animals, Daumier's floating forms and Greek parodies, Olaf Gulbransson's Art Nouveau caricature and modernist set designs – are not imitated but lightly stylized; they are 'underneath' his fantastic world. The theatre of modern life is partly reflected in his bestiary. Works of high art – icons, paintings by Academicians or Itinerants – are objects of parody, as well as postcards, comics and illustrated covers of pulp fiction. The lines are dancing, the figures are levitating, their form is plasmatic, the circular and angular shapes are interconnected, and the drawings have no defined centre. Later, Eisenstein would analyse these features in Tintoretto and Caravaggio, El Greco and Disney.

Eisenstein's ideas on montage were inspired by the way in which he dealt with images. In his first project for a spherical book, he conceptualized montage as an archive of visual memory. Montage is not a linear chain where one image is placed after another. It creates instead an imaginative space where one vanishing image is superimposed, covered by an emerging one. To perceive these images, the viewer is forced to forget and remember – for the entire length of the film. To facilitate this process, film uses old techniques from *ars memoria*, rhythmic recurrence, the same techniques that Eisenstein used in his first book of drawings – creating series of forms that model and stage the recollections of distant and proximal shapes and figures.

Dietmar Hochmuth and I employed a simple technique for a virtual exhibition created for Google Art & Culture, an introductory crash course on the most iconic images produced by Eisenstein, entitled *Eisenstein: My Art in Life*.[36] While all links in the virtual exhibition of the Langlois Foundation were programmed and selected by the curator, Google suggested different variations of all possible contexts using the vast variety of its virtual exhibitions. Some links were obvious – like the parallel with Alexander Kluge's project *Nachrichten aus der ideologischen Antike, Marx – Eisenstein – Das Kapital* (DVD, 2008). Others were at the first sight inexplicable, such as links to many Holocaust memorials, or to the life trajectories of victims with the surname 'Eisenstein'. However, they reminded me about many letters in the Moscow archive that Eisenstein received from East European Jews with the surname of Eisenstein, asking him whether they were relatives. Thus, this random contextualization generated by search engines, brought me back to the destiny that Eisenstein had avoided.

Anthropological turn: 'Objectivizing' Eisenstein

Following the turn in art theory towards 'things', and a reciprocal interest in the social history of things, the epistemic status of objects in the history of science, and 'thingness' debates in literary and philosophical studies, a new way of thinking emerged.[37] Ethnographers have begun to understand that while they fill museums with enormous collections of things, the meaning of these things is usually transmitted only by actions and mostly in secret rituals, and therefore remains neither conveyed nor understood. This has led to changed practices of exhibition, evident for example in *Memories of a Nation* (British Museum, 16 October 2014–25 January 2015), which presented five hundred years of German history in two hundred objects, such as Charlemagne's crown, Gutenberg's Bible, Volkswagen Beetles and the gate to Auschwitz; or *Things: Sharing Stories* (Weltmuseum, Vienna, 25 October 2017–28 February 2019).

Vera Rumiantseva-Kleiman's and Naum Kleiman's reconstruction of Eisenstein's apartment at the Film Museum in Moscow (opened in 2018) displays his private things – the furniture, books and artefacts that can tell stories (Figure 16.7). Mundane objects, such as teacups, suitcases and rugs, were transposed into the museum space, which staged a complete universe of them.

Indeed this contemporary trend towards thingness was deeply rooted in Eisenstein's own approach, since he curated his private space like a conceptual artist – Ilya Kabakov *avant la lettre*. In 1935, after moving into a new apartment on Potylikha (the one reconstructed at the Film Museum on 120 square metres), he sent his mother a list of the items that she absolutely had to bring him: a

Figure 16.7 Eisenstein's apartment at the Film Museum in Moscow.

piano, a wardrobe, the round table, her Kuznetsov porcelain tea set, the samovar, tablecloths and silverware. But, unlike the homes of many Moscow artists, Eisenstein's new living space left anything but a bourgeois impression. A wooden angel from a church served as a tie and suspender rack, and was sometimes replaced by a menorah. Immediately next to it hung a boxing glove autographed by Harpo Marx. Everyday things appeared as carnival props. The furniture looked like fragments of theatre sets, or might have come out of film storage: a brocade chair stood next to a Bauhaus piece; the chandelier was made out of the remnants of four old film cameras. The enormous bed bought from a family of American Jewish repatriates was covered by a bright Mexican rug. But most of the space was taken up by books. The library was organized idiosyncratically: Stanislavsky stood next to the Bible; Hegel was upside down, since that was how Lenin thought Marx had dealt with Hegel's dialectic; an album on the Russian painter Ilya Repin was used for studying costume history. However, not all of Eisenstein's books are presented in this reconstruction, as some of the most valuable were taken into the Russian State Library, and not all of his personal items have survived.

The new turn to the study of things exists simultaneously with another change in curatorial fashion – exhibition as an essay, as a construct mirroring conceptual art, with a temporal delay and requiring new display practices which can translate meaning. In this kind of exhibition, it is not important to present original art objects but rather ideas that could be conveyed without auratic material embodiments. For example, the curators of *Parapolitik: Kulturelle Freiheit und Kalter Krieg* (3 November 2017–8 January 2018) at the Haus der Kulturen der Welt in Berlin could not show the original of one of Jackson Pollock's paintings so instead showed a black-and-white copy produced on a Xerox machine.

This practice was evident in the exhibition *Sergei Eisenstein and the Anthropology of Rhythm*, curated by Marie Rebecchi and Elena Vogman in collaboration with Till Gathmann in Rome and Berlin.[38] The exhibition explored the intersection of the aesthetic, political and anthropological dimensions of Eisenstein's unfinished film projects: *Que viva México!* (1931–2), *Bezhin Meadow* (1935–7) and *The Ferghana Canal* (1939), his portrayals of Mexican, Russian and Uzbekistan rural life, respectively. The small cabinets included copies of Eisenstein's drawings and manuscripts, display cases that contained anthropological books he read, photographs and postcards, film clips and an original video consisting of mug shots made for the selections of types for the crowd scenes in *Bezhin Meadow*. The subject of the exhibition was not the art as such, but the reconstruction of an ethnographic gaze in Eisenstein's work.

The new trend of thing-oriented exhibition design helps to overcome heterogeneity in the displays of film museums. In this type of design, things are not treated as nostalgic fetishes but as triggers releasing ideas. The thing should become a text and its materiality is not important. But the problem remains: does it really speak in its materiality, or its immateriality?

Acknowledgements

I would like to thank Naum Kleiman, Anna Geber, Elena Vogman, François Albera and Ian Christie, who helped me in my research.

Notes

1 Oksana Bulgakowa, 'Comment éditer Eisenstein?', *Cinémas: Journal of Film Studies*, 11, nos. 2–3 (2001): 27–67.

2 Sergei Eizenshtein, 'Avtobiograficheskie zapiski', in *Izbrannye proizvedeniia v 6 tomakh* [Selected works in 6 volumes], ed. P. Atasheva, Iu. Krasovskii and V. Mikhailov (Moscow: Iskusstvo, 1964), vol. 1, 210–540.

3 Sergei Eizenshtein, *Schriften* (Munich: Hanser, 1974–84).
4 Walter Benjamin, 'Das Passagen-Werk', in *Gesammelte Schriften*, vol. 5, ed. Rolf Tiedemann and Hermann Schweppenhäuser (Frankfurt am Main: Suhrkamp, 1982); Friedrich Nietzsche, *Sämtliche Werke: Kritische Studienausgabe*, ed. Giorgio Colli and Mazzino Montinari (Berlin: De Gruyter, 1999); Aby Warburg, 'Bilderatlas Mnemosyne', in *Gesammelte Schriften: Studienausgabe*, ed. Martin Warnke and Claudia Brink (Berlin: De Gruyter, 2012).
5 Karel Teige wrote that the duoskope showed 'fragments from *Potemkin*, *Strike* and Vertov's *Kino-Glaz* and *Lenin Kino-Pravda*' (Karel Teige, '"Fifo" ve Stuttgartu', *Red* 2, no. 10 [1929]: 321). *Film-Kurier* indicated also that there were two duoscopes in the 'Russian Hall' presenting clips from Eisenstein's, Vertov's and Shub's films. Cf. 'Die Avantgarde im Stuttgarter Programm', *Der Film-Kurier* 11, no. 139 (13 June 1929): 4. I am indebted to Michael Cowan and Thomas Tode for pointing to these sources.
6 Cf. Olivier Lugon, 'Dynamic Path of Thought: Exhibition Design, Photography and Circulation in the Work of Herbert Bayer', in *Cinema beyond Film: Media Epistemology in the Modern Era*, ed. François Albera and Maria Tortajada (Amsterdam: Amsterdam University Press, 2010), 117–41.
7 Cf. Michael Cowan, *Walter Ruttmann and the Cinema of Multiplicity: Avant-Garde – Advertising – Modernity* (Amsterdam: Amsterdam University Press, 2014), 55–108.
8 Quoted after the editors' preface in Benjamin, 'Das Passagen-Werk', 574.
9 Reprinted in *Zur Eisenstein-Woche vom 10–18, April 1959* (Berlin: Gesellschaft für Deutsch-Sowjetische Freundschaft, 1959), 19–22.
10 Cf. Léon Moussinac, 'Eisenstein dessinateur', *Les Lettres française*, no. 820 (14 April 1960): 1.
11 The exhibition *300 Disegni di Serghei M. Eisenstein* was organized by Gianni Comencini and Walter Alberti, Cineteca italiana and the Union of Soviet Filmmakers, and presented at the Palazzo Reale di Milano from 16 March to 4 June 1961. The drawings were on loan from Pera Atasheva.
12 *Drawings: Eisenstein*, presented by the Friends of the National Film Archive at the Victoria and Albert Museum, London, from 26 September to 10 November 1963.
13 Sergei Eisenstein, *300 Zeichnungen: 6. Dezember 1963 bis 19. Januar 1964 at the Städtische Museum Leverkusen, Schloß Morsbroich* (Leverkusen: Lenz-Druck, 1964). The small catalogue presented the list of the exhibited drawings along with the texts by Ivor Montagu and David Robinson.
14 *L'Officina Eisenstein: Dai disegni ai film*, 35th International Film Festival, Locarno, 31 July–20 August 1982; 150 drawings were selected by Pier Marco de Santi and Naum Kleiman.
15 *S. M. Eisenstein: Schetsen Tekeningen* (Amsterdam: Nederlands Filmmuseum, 1979). The exhibition was first presented in Arnhem (3–18 October) and then in Amsterdam (23 October–2 November).

16 The exhibition in East Berlin presented 150 items and was shown in the foyer of the Academy of the Arts in January 1970. The exhibition in West Berlin took place from 3 to 18 June of the same year. It should have presented four hundred items (photos, manuscripts, posters, diagrams and a number of unpublished original drawings), as was stated at the letter explaining the concept of the show but the number of items was reduced. Some memos discussing this project are at the Archive of the Academy of the Arts Berlin (AdK-W 174, AdK Dok-AdK-W 3729, Foto-AdK-O 473, AdK-O 0804, AdK-W-Archivdirektion 070, AdK-W 95–09). The East Berlin Academy published a 32-page booklet: Ruth Herlinghaus, ed., *Synthese der Künste und Kunst der Synthese in der Theorie und Praxis Sergei Eisensteins* (Berlin: Deutsche Akademie der Künste zu Berlin; Leipzig: Günther, Kirstein & Wendler, 1970). Both shows were compiled by the Association of Soviet Filmmakers, curated by Naum Kleiman.

17 Pier Marco De Santi curated a Fellini show and organized four of Eisenstein exhibitions in Italy – in Pisa, Turin, Pesaro and Locarno. See *Mostra Eisenstein: dei bozetti teatrali ei disegni per il cinema*, ed. Pier Marco De Santi (Pisa: Gabinetto disegni e stampe dell'Università di Pisa, 1980); *Officina Di Eisenstein: Dai Disegni Ai Film: Mole Antonelliana, from 7 February to 5 April 1981*, ed. Pier Marco De Santi (Turin: Museo del Cinema, 1981); *I disegni di Eisenstein: Salla della Repubblica del Teatro Rossini, 19 December 1981–14 January 1982* (Pesaro: Teatro Rossini, 1982); *L'Officina Eisenstein: Dai disegni ai film*, ed. Pier Marco De Santi (35th International Film Festival, Locarno, 31 July–20 August 1982). De Santi also published a catalogue of Eisenstein's drawings that reproduced a Soviet edition: *I Disegni di Eisenstein*, ed. Pier Marco DeSanti (Rome: Laterza, 1981); and a book with the drawings for *Die Valküre*, the subject of his exhibition at the Teatro Rossini in Pesaro (Pier Marco De Santi, *La messinscena della Valchiria* [Florence: Nuova Italia editrice, 1984]). He also exhibited some of Eisenstein's materials from the Museum of Modern Art (MOMA). The exhibition at the Film Museum Torin was a multimedia show, also showing film clips in a separate space.

18 Pier Marco De Santi, 'Per la costituzione di un Centro Multimediale del Cinema', Predella, available online: http://www.predella.it/predella/predella16/DESANTI.htm (accessed 15 October 2019).

19 The exhibitions published two different catalogues: *Eisenstein 1848–1948, suite de dessins*, ed. Hélène Laroche (Lyon, Palais Saint-Pierre, Musée des Beaux-Arts, 1978); *S. M. Eisenstein, Esquisses et Dessins*, ed. Jacques Aumont and Bernard Eisenschitz (Paris: Ed. Cahiers du Cinéma, Ed. de l'étoile, 1979).

20 Museum of Modern Art, Oxford, 17 July–29 August 1988; Hayward Gallery, London, 29 September–11 December 1988; Cornerhouse, Manchester; 29 December 1988–5 February 1989. The catalogue was titled *Eisenstein at Ninety*, ed. Ian Christie and David Elliott (Oxford: Oxford Museum of the Modern Art, 1988).

21 David Elliott was Director of the Museum of Modern Art, Oxford, 1976–96, after which he served as director of the Moderna Museet, Stockholm, and the Mori Art Museum, Tokyo. In 1995, he co-curated a large traveling exhibition 'Art and Power' exploring the relationship of art with the totalitarian regimes in Europe.
22 3–27 April 1995; Gallery Mucsarnok, Budapest; 28–31 September 2005, Pecs; 11 April–13 May 2007, Budapest. All shows were curated by Anne Gereb, who also published a catalogue of Akchurina's collection, reproducing a Russian album edited by Mark Kushnirov: *Risunki Sergeia Eizenshteina, 1942–1944*, Kollektsiia Lidii Naumovoi (Moscow: Iskusstvo, 2004); *A Mischievous Eisenstein* (Saint Petersburg: Slavia, 2006).
23 Due to financial problems the exhibition was cancelled and only its catalogue was produced: *Eisenstein und Deutschland*, ed. Oksana Bulgakowa (Berlin: Henschel, 1998).
24 Igor Jassenjawski curated the show and edited the catalogue *Von Eisenstein bis Tarkowsky: Die Malerei der Filmregisseure in der UdSSR. Katalog zur Ausstellung in der Städtischen Galerie im Lenbachhaus, München, Bilder, Zeichnungen, Filme von Dowschenko, Eisenstein, Essadse, Gabriadse, Iljenko, Kuleschow, Minajew, Mitta, Naumow, Paradschanow, Tarkowsky*, 8 March–6 May 1990 (Munich: Prestel 1990).
25 Eisenstein's storyboards came from Jay Leyda's collection at MOMA. Annette Michelson wrote a foreword to the exhibition brochure: *Drawing into Film: Directors' Drawings: Sergei Eisenstein, Alfred Hitchcock, John Huston, Fred Zinnemann, Akira Kurosawa, Orson Welles, Federico Fellini, Robert Benton, Terry Gilliam, Martin Scorsese, David Lynch, Rainer Werner Fassbinder, Tim Burton* (The Pace Gallery, 32 East 57th Street, New York, 26 March–24 April 1993).
26 Oksana Bulgakowa and Dietmar Hochmuth, eds., *Sergei Eisenstein: Disney* (Berlin: PotemkinPress, 2015), 25, 33, 40, 56, etc.
27 We wanted to collect all of Eisenstein Mexican drawings preserved in private and state collections, but the financial limitations meant we were not able to fulfil this aim.
28 For example, Antonioni reproduced in *Zabriski Point* (1970) the compositions of contemporary painters and photographers such as Jackson Pollock or Walker Evans; Alfred Hitchcock collaborated with Salvador Dali (*Spellbound*, 1945). At this time, Païni was also suggested as the curator for the exhibition about Eisenstein at the Centre Pompidou but he later resigned from this task.
29 *Sergei Eisenstein im Kontext der russischen Avantgarde, 1920–1925* (Filmmuseum Frankfurt, 17 December 1992–18 February 1993).
30 Seventeen Russian and German institutions including the Tretyakov Gallery, Shchusev Architecture Museum and Bakhrushin Theater Museum in Moscow, Sprengel Museum in Hannover, Folkwang Museum in Essen, Museum fur Angewandte Kunst in Zurich provided materials for the exhibition.

31 'Exhibition "Testimonies": Francisco Goya, Sergei Eisenstein, Robert Longo', Garage Museum of Contemporary Art, available online: https://garagemca.org/ru/exhibition/francisco-goya-sergei-eisenstein-robert-longo-proof (accessed 8 November 2019). The show in Garage ran from 30 September 2016 to 5 February 2017; at the Brooklyn Museum from 8 September 2017 to 7 January 2018; and in Deichtorhallen from 17 February to 27 May 2018.

32 'Review Proof: Francisco Goya, Sergei Eisenstein, Robert Longo', Deichtorhallen Hamburg, available online: https://www.deichtorhallen.de/ausstellung/proof (accessed 8 November 2019).

33 *Ejzenštejn – La rivoluzione delle immagini* curated by Marzia Faietti, Pierluca Nardoni and Eike D. Schmidt, Sale di Levante degli Uffizi, 7 November 2017–7 January 2018.

34 *Sergei Eisenstein: Montage of Attractions*, Multimedia Art Museum (MAAM), Moscow, 24 November 2016–16 March 2017.

35 'Oksana Bulgakowa: Sergei Eisenstein, A Visual Universe', The Daniel Langlois Foundation, available online: http://www.fondation-langlois.org/html/e/page.php?NumPage=749 (accessed 8 November 2019).

36 'Sergei Eisenstein: My Art in Life', Google Arts & Culture, available online: https://artsandculture.google.com/exhibit/sergei-eisenstein-my-art-in-life/YgKC3Cneu0iiKg (accessed 8 November 2019).

37 Arjun Appadurai, ed., *The Social Life of Things* (Cambridge: Cambridge University Press, 2011); Bill Brown, *A Sense of Things: The Object Matter of American Literature* (Chicago: University of Chicago Press, 2003); Bruno Latour, *Reassembling the Social: An Introduction to Actor-Network-Theory* (Oxford: Oxford University Press, 2005); Bernard Stiegler *Technics and Time*, vol. 2 (Stanford, CA: Stanford University Press, 1998); Frank Trentmann, *Empire of Things: How We Became a World of Consumers From the Fifteenth Century to the Twenty-first* (London: Allen Lane, 2015).

38 The exhibition was shown from 20 September 2017 to 19 January 2018 at the Nomas Foundation, Rome, and from 20 April to 25 May 2018 in the Diaphanes Gallery, Berlin.

Index

Academy of the Arts, East Berlin and West Berlin 264
Ackerman, Ada 274
Adami, Valerio 164–7
Aksenov, Ivan 220–3, 226
Alexander Nevsky (Eisenstein, film) 18, 28, 253, 257, 268, 273
Alexandra (Sokurov) 94, 101–3
allegory 6–7, 173–87
All-Union Creative Conference of Soviet Filmworkers 1935
  Eisenstein speech 9–10, 21, 64–5, 80, 185
American literature 78, 79
Amsterdam Film Museum (formerly in Vondelpark, now EYE Filmmuseum) 264
androgyny, notion of 96, 103, *see also* bisexuality concepts
animal imagery 77–9, 82, 84
anthropological perspectives 80, 112
Antwerp Extra City Gallery 271
Ape. Primitive. Child (Vygotsky and Luria, book) 80
archaic thinking *see* primitive thinking
art
  dialectic of works of art 64–9
  experience of 117–21, 132–3
  magic of 145–6
  monumental theatre 175–7
  'narrative figuration' trend 164, 165–6
  parallels between film and the arts 272–5
  and politics 29, 35–7
  screams in 152–67
  see also drawings (Eisenstein); montage; painting; prints
Atasheva, Pera 220, 264
atomic age 43–4, 53
Australia, distribution of Eisenstein's works in 251–8
Averbuch, Roza 139

Axel's Castle: A Study in the Imaginative Literature of 1870–1930 (Wilson), Eisenstein's notes on 61–9

Bacon, Francis 156–64
Balzac, Honoré de 47–8, 62
Bambi (Disney), design sketches 49
Barbaro, Umberto 153
Bataille, Georges 67, 153–4, 213
The Battleship Potemkin (Eisenstein, film) 6, 8, 15, 26, 53, 68, 94, 272
  'best film' listing 263–4
  hypnotic effects 144–5
  motifs and landscape 30–1, 32–3, 50
  pathos in 116
  screams 6, 152–3, 155, 156–67
  screening in Australia 251–4, 257
  Solzhenitsyn on 92
  Tarkovsky on 92–3
Bekhterev, Vladimir 6, 133, 138, 140, 144
Bellour, Raymond 145
Bely, Andrei 31
Berdyaev, Nikolai 100
Beyond the Stars: The Memoirs of Sergei Eisenstein see *Memoirs* (Eisenstein)
Bezhin Meadow (Eisenstein, film) 2, 264, 279
bisexuality concepts 5, 75, 96–100, 103
Blok, Aleksandr 233
body, image of 220–6, *see also* resurrection; screaming
The Body of the Line exhibition, New York and Montreal, 2000 271
Bonaparte, Marie 185
Botticelli, Sandro 113, 122, 123
Bourgois, Christian 164
Brenner, Anita 62, 80, 213, 215
Breton, André 67
Bruner, Jerome 133
Bulgakowa, Oksana 271, 276
Burrow, Trigant 84
Burton, Tim 271

Caravaggio, Michelangelo Merisi da 153–4
censorship in Australia 251, 252–3, 256
Chelpanov, Georgy 133
chiasmus 215–17
Chinese landscapes (art) 44, 45–6, 49, 120
Christianity 22–3, 98–9, 139, 210, 233, 243
    Catholicism 112, 135, 142, 233, 234–5, 243
Christie, Ian 268, 270
Christophe, Henri 18
chuvstvennoe myshlenie see sensory-emotional processes/sensuous thought
cinema, political impact of 27–8, 41–2
Cinémathèque Française 8, 264, 272
Cineteca Italiana, Milan 8, 264
Cineteca Nacional, Mexico City 266
Čiurlionis, Mikolajos 45
classical themes in art 113–16, 123
Coldicutt, Ken 257
Colli, Giorgio 262
Collins, Joseph, *The Doctor Looks at Literature* 75
constructivism 96, 272
content and form 8, 231–48
Cosgrove, Denis 29
Cowley, Malcolm 61
Cowley, Peggy (née Baird) 61
Crane, Harold Hart 61–2
cross media and intertexts 272–5
cruelty 94–6, 214
cultural-historical theory 11, 133–6, 141

Daney, Serge 2
Daniel Langlois Foundation 8, 271, 276, 277
Daumier, Honoré 62, 68, 276
De Gourmont, Remy 233
Deleuze, Gilles 162–3, 275
Deren, Maya 6, 140–4
Derenkowsky, Solomon 140
Didi-Huberman, Georges 113–14, 139
diffuseness 45–8, 50–4, 119–20
Dionysian legend 7, 115, 209–211, 221–2, 224–5
disarticulation 46–7, 50, 52, 53
Disney, Walt 48–9
    Bambi 49
    Dumbo 215

    Method section on 76–7
    Nonindifferent Nature critique of 49
Disney section of *Method* (Eisenstein, writing) 2, 76–7, 80, 84
Doctor Mabuse, The Gambler (Lang, film) 130–2
documenta 5, 267
Documents (journal) 67, 153–4
Dovzhenko, Aleksandr 21, 96, 271
Drawing into Film exhibition, New York, 1993 271
Dürer, Albrecht 110, 113, 114, 116

ecstasy 5, 6, 7, 11, 37, 46–7, 48, 97
    cinematic examples 50–1, 118, 119
    control 53–4
    as dialectical movement 211–13
    eidetic 213, 216
    emotional response to film and art 117–21
    formula of *see* pathos, formula of
    polarities 209–217
    principles 46–7, 50
    as regress 213–15
    religious 116, 135, 139
    see also hypnosis
Ehrenburg, Ilya 261
eidetism 137
Eisenstein, Sergei
    apartment 277–8
    biographies of 73–4
    bond with Leonardo 20, 73 *see also* Leonardo da Vinci
    distribution of works in Australia 251–8
    drawings by 1, 2, 19, 68, 74, 82–3, 98–100
    exhibitions 263–79
    Gospel subjects 98–9
    montage 112
    self-portraits 97–8, 100, 213–14
    engagement with *psy* disciplines 133–46
    exhibitions 8–9, 261–79 *see also titles of individual exhibitions*
    film projects, unrealised
        An American Tragedy 18, 19, 248
        Black Majesty 19
        Capital 15–17

Dzhungo 2, 15
The Great Ferghana Canal 8, 42, 51, 112, 235–40, 243–5, 248, 279
The Glass House 15–17, 19, 274
Sutter's Gold 19, 248
formula pafosa 109–11, 116–23
Lawrence and 73–87
masculinity 5, 95–6
reputation 1–2, 103–4, 255–6
sexuality 96–7, 100
status in Soviet Union 91–3, 220
theatrical projects, unrealised
Garland's Inheritance 2, 15
King Hunger 2, 15, 23
Patatras 2, 15
Triapitsyn 15
Warburg and *see* pathos, formula of
writings 1–2, 5, 17–21, 26–37, 123, 145–6, 164, 176, 185–6, 190–203, 231–3, 239, 261–2, *see also* titles of individual works
Eisenstein 1898–1948: His Life and Work exhibition, Oxford, London and Manchester, 1988 8, 268–9
Eisenstein: My Art in Life (virtual exhibition) 276–7
Ejzenštejn – La rivoluzione delle immagini exhibition, Florence, 2017–18 273
ek-stasis see ecstasy
Elizabethan ballads 233
Elliott, David 268
empathy 117, 122
Empedocles 7, 190, 198–201
Engels, Friedrich 34–5, 65, 117
English literature 73, 86, *see also* Lawrence, D. H.
'engrams' 115, 122
ethnographic practice in exhibitions 277–9
'Even and Odd: Bifurcation of the Singular' (Eisenstein, essay) 17–18
Evreinov, Nikolai 175–6
Example Eisenstein: Drawing Theatre Film exhibition, Düsseldorf, 1987 8, 268
exhibitions 8–9, 261–79
intertexts and cross media 272–5
objects 277–9
virtual 275–7

Fassbinder, Rainer Werner 271
Fellini, Federico 266, 271
femininity 100–3, *see also* bisexuality concepts
Ferenczi, Sándor 97
Film and Photography exhibition (FiFo), Stuttgart, 1929 8, 262–3
fission (disarticulated seriality) 53
form
and content 8, 231–48
dissolution into landscape 31–5
formula pafosa see pathos, formula of
Foucault, Michel 262
Fowle, Kate 273
Franke, Anselm 271
Frankfurt Film Museum 272
Frazer, James 11, 141
The Golden Bough 73, 79, 80, 85
Freudian psychoanalysis 84–5, 86, 97
From Eisenstein to Tarkovsky exhibition, Munich, 1990 271

Gagnon, Jean 271
Galperina, Elena 63, 66
Gastev, Alexei 140
Gathmann, Till 279
Gavarni, Paul 62, 68
The General Line or *The Old and The New* (Eisenstein, film) 6, 15, 18, 51, 53, 67, 68, 123, 254–5
gestures 110, 113–15, 123
Gillette razors 53–4, 211, 214
Gogol, Nikolai 31, 48, 53
The Golden Bough (Frazer, book) 11, 73, 79, 80, 85
Granet, Marcel
La pensée Chinoise (1934) 17, 45
El Greco 34, 44, 110, 118, 120
Grillparzer, Franz 18, 19
Gross, Kenneth 178, 187
Grundproblem 4, 5, 9–10, 64, 79, 81

'Hands: Thoughts on Professional Growth' (Sokurov, essay) 94–6
Der Hang zum Gesamtkunstwerk, 1983 267
Harten, Jürgen 268
Hawthorne, Nathaniel 79, 80
Hegel, Georg Wilhelm Friedrich 7, 10, 210, 211, 212, 214

Henry IV (Shakespeare, play) 219
Hirschfeld, Magnus 97
history and allegory 6–7, 173–87
Hitchcock, Alfred 271
Hochmuth, Dietmar 276–7
hypnosis 6, 130–46

Il'enko, Yuri 271
intellectual montage 5, 7, 173–87
intertexts and cross media 272–5
Ivan the Terrible (Eisenstein, film) 1, 7, 27, 51, 53, 219–26, 253–4, 257
   hypnotic effects 144–5
   landscape and mutability of form 32–3
   motifs 275–6
   rejection by Stalin 91
   Solzhenitsyn on 92
   Tarkovsky on 92–3

Joyce, James 4, 22, 62–3, 66–9, 74, 75, 76
Jung, Carl 84, 97, 203

Kabuki theatre 109, 197
Kannabich, Yuri 6, 136
Katanian, Vasilii 263
Katsushika Hokusai 68
Kehrer, Hugo 34, 120
Killen, Andreas 130
King Lear (Shakespeare, play) 119, 220, 223–4, 226
Kleiman, Naum
   curating Eisenstein 264, 267–8, 277
   on Eisenstein drawings 68
   publishing Eisenstein works 18, 37, 41, 220
Kluge, Alexander 277
Konovalov, Dmitry 6, 138–9
Krafft-Ebing, Richard 97
Krempel, Ulrich 268
Kukulin, Ilya 92
Kuleshov, Lev 271
Kunsthalle Düsseldorf 267–8

Lady Chatterley's Lover (Lawrence, book) 73, 74–5, 82
landscape 26–7, 29–37
   diffuseness and disarticulation in film 50–4, 119–20
   in motion 47–50
   musicality 45
   seriality 45–7

landscapes (art) 44–7
Lang, Fritz
   Doctor Mabuse, The Gambler 130–2
Lawrence, D. H. 62, 73–87
   hostility to cinema 76
   Lady Chatterley's Lover 73, 74–5, 82
   Leavis on 86
   notoriety 74–5
   The Plumed Serpent 75, 77, 82, 86
   'The Prussian Officer' 82–3
   reputation 86
   St Mawr 76–9
   Studies in Classic American Literature 78, 79, 80–1, 85
Le Bot, Marc 166
Leavis, F. R., on Lawrence 86
Leonardo da Vinci 20, 21, 74, 119, 195, 198, 267
Lévy-Bruhl, Lucien 11, 141, 210
   La mentalité primitive 79–80, 85
Lissitzky, El 262, 272
literary realism
   theory of 51–2
Longo, Robert 273
Lotman, Yuri 93
Loyola, Ignatius 116, 135, 140
Lukács, Georg 48, 51–2
Luria, Alexander 6, 10, 11, 74, 80, 133–4, 136–7, 139, 141, 143, 146

Macpherson, Kenneth 73, 74, 75
'The Magic of Art' (Eisenstein, essay) 145–6
Malraux, André 73
Marin, Louis 158–9
masculinity and aggression 95–6, 103, *see also* bisexuality concepts
Maupassant, Guy de 33, 34, 194
The Mechanics of the Human Brain (Pudovkin, film) 133
Melbourne, Victoria, film culture 251–8
Melville, Herman 79, 80–1
Memoirs (Eisenstein, book) 1, 22–3, 73–4, 75, 84, 111, 164
memory, theories of 63, 115, 122
La mentalité primitive (Lévy-Bruhl, book) 79–80, 85
Method (Eisenstein, book) 1, 2, 4, 8, 22, 30, 47–8, 80–1, 121, 145–6, 262
   Disney section 2, 76–7, 80, 84

impetus for 79–80
purposes 64, 141–2
second volume planned 17
sections 2, 21, 231, 240–2, 248
see also *Regress–Progress*
Mexico 62, 80, 86, 111–12, 234–5
drawings 263, 268, 271
indigenismo policy 36
transformative immersion in nature 35–7
see also *Que viva México!* (Eisenstein, film)
Michaud, Philippe-Alain 274
Michelangelo 22, 275
Michelson, Annette 1, 3, 27–8, 61
A Mischievous Eisenstein exhibition, Cannes 2006, 269–70
Mitchell, W. J. T. 29
Mnemosyne atlas (Warburg) 110, 112, 114–15, 262
montage 6–7, 112, 114, 123, 238, 263, 274–5, 276
definition 190–1
intellectual montage 5, 7, 173–87
'Montage 1938' 190–203, 239
Montage (Eisenstein, book) 1, 67, 220
Montage of Attractions exhibition, Moscow, 2016–17 273–4
Montagu, Ivor 10, 75, 269
Montinari, Mazzino 262
Moscow House of Art Workers 263
Moussinac, Léon 152, 213
multimedia exhibitions 272–5
Munch, Edvard 156
Musée des Beaux-Arts, Lyon 267
Museum of Modern Art, Oxford 268–9
music 26, 33, 47–8
eye music 45, 47
landscape musicality 45
'The Music of Landscape and the Fate of Montage Counterpoint at a New Stage' (Eisenstein, essay) 26, 28, 30–1, 35–7
myth and mythology 7–8, 80, 113, 174, 180–7
see also pagan traditions in Christianity; rituals and ceremonies

narrative figuration (*nouvelle figuration*) trend 164, 165–6
Nesbet, Anne 30, 31, 62

Netherlands Film Museum 264
New Mexico 111–12
Nietzsche, Friedrich 262
Nonindifferent Nature (Eisenstein, book) 2, 26, 30, 31–7, 41–54, 209
definition of concept 41
Disney critique 49
pathos and 110, 116–21, 122
Notes for a General History of Cinema (Eisenstein, book) 2

occasionalism 44
October (Eisenstein, film) 1, 6–7, 15, 93, 102, 144–5, 173–87, 194–7, 253–4, 256–7
L'OEil extatique: Sergueï Eisenstein, cinéaste à la croisée des arts exhibition, Centre Pompidou-Metz, 2019–20 9, 274–5
Olwig, Kenneth 29–30
'On the Play of Objects' (Eisenstein, essay) 26
One Day in the Life of Ivan Denisovich (Solzhenitsyn, novel) 1, 91–2

pagan traditions in Christianity 112, 233, 234–5, *see also* myth and mythology
Païni, Dominique 272
painting 34, 44–7, 118–19, 156–67
Parajanov, Sergei 271
pars pro toto (artistic device) 4, 152, 181–2, 210
pathos 5, 37, 97, 209
and *logos* 209–217
pathos, formula of 5
common source 111–13
Eisenstein's *formula pafosa* 109–11, 116–23
Warburg's *Pathosformel* 109, 110–11, 113–16, 121–3
Pavlov, Ivan 133, 134, 138
La pensée Chinoise (Granet, book) 17, 45
People, Years and Life (Ehrenburg, book) 261
'Persian' project 242–3
Piranesi, Giovanni Battista 44, 46–7, 119, 275
The Plumed Serpent (Lawrence, book) 75, 77, 82, 86

Poe, Edgar Allan 185
Poussin, Nicolas 158–9
pre-logical thinking 10–11, 64–5, 80, 209, 235, 240
The Primal Phenomenon: Art (Eisenstein, book) 2, 10
primitive thinking 4, 10–11, 64, 80, 235
prints 44, 46, 275
progress and regress *see* regress
Proof: Francisco Goya, Sergei Eisenstein, Robert Longo exhibition, 2016–18 273
Proust, Marcel 4, 62–9
'The Prussian Officer' (Lawrence, story and Eisenstein, drawing) 72–4
psychoanalysis 5, 133
    Freudian 84–5, 86, 97
psychology 6, 11, 137, 140–4
    cultural-historical theory 11, 133–6, 141
    Russian schools 133
psychotechnics 6, 133, 134–6, 139, 143–4
Pudovkin, Vsevolod 134, 152, 253, 254
Pushkin, Aleksander 178, 196, 197, 264

Que viva México! (Eisenstein, film) 2, 19, 36, 80, 86, 111, 234, 255, 279

Rank, Otto 97, 185–6
realism, Lukács on 48, 51–2
Realist Film Unit (RFU) 251, 252–3, 257
Rebecchi, Marie 279
Red Cavalry (Eisenstein, unfinished project) 2, 15
The Red Wheel (Solzhenitsyn) 92
regress 5, 95, 97, 110, 132, 145, 248
    ecstasy as regress 213–15
    paths of 121
    regress and progress 4, 64–6, 209, 235
Regress–Progress (Eisenstein, writing) 63, 64, 67, 68–9, see also *Method* (Eisenstein, book)
Renaissance art 113–16, 118–19, 123
Renoir, Jean 48
restraint 53–4
resurrection 7, 118–19, 200, 210, 214, 221–2, *see also* Dionysian legend
Riabchikova, Natalia 61–2
ritualized behaviour 140–4

rituals and ceremonies 80, 111–12, *see also* myth and mythology
Rodin, Auguste 22
romanticism, political 44
Rose, Shirley 82
Rozanov, Vasilii 5, 100, 103
Rumiantseva-Kleiman, Vera 277
Russia
    Stalinist period 27–8, 42–4, 91–3, 220, 231–2, 237
    Thaw era 1, 91, 94, 261
    status of Eisenstein 91–3, 220

Sadoul, Georges 153
Salazkina, Masha 36, 80
Sand, George 33, 34
Sartre, Jean-Paul 261
Schama, Simon 29–30
Schlegel, Hans-Joachim 261
Schmitt, Carl 44
Schwartz, Hillel 177, 179–80
screaming 6, 152–67
self-portraits (Eisenstein) 97–8, 100, 213–14
self-portraiture 31, 32–5
sensory-emotional processes/sensuous thought 4, 10–11, 26, 31, 34–5, 64–5, 76, 80–1, 142, 146, 181, 221, 240
Sergei Eisenstein and the Anthropology of Rhythm exhibition, Rome and Berlin, 2017–18 279
Sergei Eisenstein: The Mexican Drawings exhibition, Antwerp, 2009 271
seriality 45–7, 52, 53
Seton, Marie 73
Shakespeare, William 73
    tragedies 7, 119, 219–26
Shaw, George Bernard 73
Shklovsky, Viktor 1
Shub, Esfir 130, 132
Siqueiros, David Alfaro 62
Sokurov, Alexander 5, 93–104
    Alexandra 94, 101–3
    critique of Eisenstein 94–6
    reputation 93, 103–4
Solzhenitsyn, Alexander 93
    One Day in the Life of Ivan Denisovich 1, 2, 91–2
    The Red Wheel 92

Soviet films in Australia 251–8
Spurgeon, Caroline 219, 220–6
St Mawr (Lawrence, novella) 76–9
Stanislavsky, Konstantin 135
The Storming of the Winter Palace (performance) 175–6
The Strike (Eisenstein, film) 1, 15, 94–5, 116, 117, 131, 132, 137, 159, 162–3
structuralism 261
Studies in Classic American Literature (Lawrence, book) 78, 79, 80–1, 85
subversion 190–203
Sudakova, Elena 270
Surikov, Vasily 156–7
surrealist writers 4, 62–3, 65–8
Sutter, John 18
Sviblova, Olga 273
synecdoche 181, *see also pars pro toto* (artistic device)
Szeemann, Harald 267, 268

Tarkovsky, Andrei 92–3, 96
Ten Days That Shook the World (Eisenstein, film) 253–4, 256–7, *see also October* (Eisenstein, film)
Ten Days That Shook the World (Reed, book) 256–7
theatre, mass spectacle 175–7
theatre projects, unrealized *see* unfinished projects
Theremin, Leon 137
Tisse, Eduard 30, 33
Tokhtasyn (fictional character) 236–9
Tolstoy, Leo 35, 48, 51–2
Toshūsai Sharaku 68
'Toward a Preface for the Unfinished Pieces' (Eisenstein, writing) 18–20
Tsivian, Yuri 30, 275–6

'Twenty Years Later' (Eisenstein, writing) 21
Tygai, Alexander 133–4

Unexpected Eisenstein exhibition, London, 2016 270
unfinished projects 2, 8, 15–23, 234, 248, 264, 274, 279

Vassiliev, Sergei 21
Victoria & Albert Museum, London 264
violence 94–6, 214
virtual exhibitions 275–7
The Visual Universe of Sergei Eisenstein (web publication) 9, 276
Vogman, Elena 279
Vöhringer, Margarete 134
Vygotsky, Lev 6, 11, 80, 133, 134–5, 137, 141, 143, 146

Warburg, Aby
    Botticelli essay 113, 122, 123
    Dürer essay 110, 113, 114
    Mnemosyne atlas 110, 112, 114–15, 262
    Pathosformel 5, 109, 110–11, 113–16, 121–3
Weininger, Otto 96–7, 100
Williams, Deane 254
Williams, Raymond 29
Wilson, Edmund
    Axel's Castle: A Study in the Imaginative Literature of 1870–1930 (1931) 61–9
Wollen, Peter 1

Yutkevich, Sergei 264

Zaitseva, Anna 273
Zakharov, Basil 18, 19
Zola, Émile 47–8, 50, 51–2, 55n18, 95, 119